FAMILY, SELF, AND SOCIETY

EMERGING ISSUES, ALTERNATIVES, AND INTERVENTIONS

Edited by

Douglas B. Gutknecht, Ph.D.,
  Coordinating Editor
Edgar W. Butler, Ph.D.
Larry Criswell, Ph.D.
Jerry Meints, Ph.D.

UNIVERSITY
PRESS OF
AMERICA

Copyright © 1983 by

University Press of America,™ Inc.

4720 Boston Way
Lanham, MD 20706

3 Henrietta Street
London WC2E 8 LU ENGLAND

Printed in the United States of America

ISBN (Perfect): 0-8191-3078-8
ISBN (Cloth): 0-8191-3077-X

Dedicated to our students, families, and
a peaceful world for future generations
of students and families.

ACKNOWLEDGEMENTS

We are indebted to many selfless people who have assisted us in the preparation of this book: our colleagues who shared their time, perspective and research with us; our Deans, Cameron Sinclair, Chapman College, Orange, California, and David Warren, University of California, Riverside, who shared their encouragement and material support with the processing and preparation of our manuscript; our students in courses such as Marriage and the Family, Sociology of the Family, Alternative Lifestyles, Human Sexuality, Family Dynamics and Crisis Counseling, Family and Marital Counseling, who served as our inspiration and critics; all who assisted in typing and manuscript preparation, Elizabeth Sharon Zimmer and Mary Schaleger, Chapman College, Orange; Marge Souder, Wanda Clark, Marilyn Dick, and Nancy Rettig, University of California, Riverside. We would like to underscore our appreciation to two excellent journals which deserve our support: Society and Family Coordinator (now Family Relations). Finally, a special thanks to our families and loved ones for their constant encouragement and love.

TABLE OF CONTENTS

ix

PREFACE

Seldom can any work serve all the needs, interests, and intellectual predilections of its intended and eventual readers. Our coverage is weighted in the direction of non-traditional topics, social policy, alternative family patterns, family interventions, and therapy. One of our goals has been to go beyond the many fine readers that ritually cover all the agreed upon traditional topics in the field. Hopefully, we have provided a sense of the complexity, diversity, controversy, and vitality of the field of marital and family studies. We believe our book can be used as either a core or supplemental reader in a number of courses including marriage and the family, alternative life styles, and family therapy. Many of the articles were written to offer both students and practitioners insight into therapeutic and intervention strategies of use to counselors, community workers, clinicial sociologists, social workers, and human resource and relations specialists. Although the majority of articles are written by sociologists and social workers, the topics covered and conceptual focus is interdisciplinary.

Traditional introductory summaries which merely repeat textual materials have been ignored in favor of an integrated essay format. We believe that the former introductions often save the student the rigorous effort and reward of providing their own summaries, synthesis, and criticisms. Each of our four introductory sections offers us the opportunity to make known our own value biases and evaluation of the current family and where it is headed. However, we hope that the range of selections reflect both the strengths and weaknesses of modern marital and family life.

FAMILY, SELF, AND SOCIETY IN TRANSITION: INTRODUCTORY ISSUES AND THE EMERGENCE OF PRIVATE AND PUBLIC STRUGGLES

Edgar W. Butler, Ph.D.*
and
Douglas B. Gutknecht, Ph.D.*

I. INTRODUCTORY ISSUES

Profound changes are occurring in the way Americans view the institutions of marriage and family. One of the most crucial areas of concern for the viability of American Society and Democracy concerns how we interpret and adapt to the increasingly difficult social changes that are buffeting our basic social institutions, both public and private. Interpretations of how the family is changing, altering, coping with public made changes, problems, social trends, and impacts is the focus of this book. Only by unraveling the threads of both public and private relationships and their impacts upon the changing family, can we offer significant social support systems. No one can deny that today both the family and the economic system are under extreme pressure to perform and both require more comprehensive understanding about their interrelationships and functioning.

Two current, partially accurate portraits, emerge from the vast number of articles and books on marital and family life. The first view considers the family as in a state of crisis, decline, or collapse. The second view paints the family as merely going through a natural, inevitable, and historically recurrent set of changes and transitions. The former view often ignores the strengths of families and highlights features that indicate breakdown, whether divorce statistics, family violence, or alternative lifestyles. The latter view sometimes mythifies the past and romanticizes the present, while ignoring the tremendous pressures that families labor under. However distraught we may become over the plight of the family, we should not become blind to the reality of the numerous problems these families and society have in contemporary society. The inevitability of change and more positive view of the role of social conflict in social life, mixed with both patience and a sense of activism regarding the relationships of private, and public life, may still allow a more flexible, humanistic, and fulfilling family life in the long run. Although not tied to a mythic nostalgia or a selective historical view of old fashioned family virtues, we also are not wedded to a simplistic view of domestic crises. Our view of the need for a resilient family and marital life requires us to enlarge our understanding of how the larger structure of the public world, our class society, ethnic and racial conficts, political and ideological disputes over the welfare state, impact the family.

Public and Private World

The essential dilemmas of modern life alternate between the horns of a private - public dichotomy:

It goes without saying that this character of marriage has its roots in much broader structural configuration of our society. The most important of these, for our purposes, is the crystallization of a so called private sphere of existence, more and more segregated . . . yet defined and utilized as the main social area for the individual's self realization . . . public institutions now confront the individual as an immensely powerful and alien world . . . . (Berger, 1977:9).

The private world includes numerous social relations which include family, friends, neighbors, religion, and voluntary associations. Close ties that the family once had with the public world in neighborhood, street, community, and local life has been eroded by the forces of urbanization, industrialization, and bureaucratization. Such a situation has created marital and family institutions dependently embedded in a matrix of social forces and conditions it cannot influence.

In these terms one can see the broader mix of family functions which confuse both private and public involvements. Families have lost much public clout; the family has turned inward and its functions limited to the tasks of emotional nurturance and psychological support. However, the very emphasis on the family as limited to these domains, actually in-

2

tensifies the pressures for family supports because the ideology of equality assumes all familes possess some resources to build self-esteem and provide adequate sponsorship in the contest for social mobility. In fact the great inequalities in our society demand that we reject a simplistic view of the private family and its truncated functions. The lack of public support actually intensifies the vulnerability of families to emotional and psychological shocks and pressures. We believe the family must become more activistic and involved with the public world. This means pressuring those making public, employment, or governmental policy decisions to recognize the impact of these decisions on marital and family life, both traditional and alternative.

The picture of changing family functions and the recognition of tremendous burdens on family life should not, however, lead us to assume either the need for or the possibility of a mythic, self-sufficient family. There are two basic assumptions of this myth: (1) that parents alone are responsible for what becomes of their children; (2) that families are free standing, independent and autonomous units, relatively from social pressures. Adequately functioning families, in the mythic view, are those that can somehow cut themselves off or insulate themselves from public demands, social forces, and outside pressures. The myth of self-sufficiency like the myth of the "haven in a heartless world" must be put to rest because the modern world is so interdependent. Individuals are blamed and considered inadequate because the realm of the private is severed from the social public or political:

> What has changed is the content and nature of family life. Families were never self-sufficient or as self-contained as the myth made them out to be . . . they are extraordinarily dependent on 'outside forces' and influences, ranging from the nature of parents' work to the content of television programming, from the structure of local schools to the organization of health care. All families today need and use support in raising children; to define the 'needy' family as the exception is to deny the simplest facts of contemporary life. (Kenniston, 1977:22)

3

The Family As A Public and Political Issue

Here we raise the issue of the importance of the public dimension in viewing family life. The family can no longer sustain the myths of privacy, isolation, self-sufficiency, haven from a heartless world, and emotional sanctuary. In fact, conservatives, liberals, and radical groups all now march behind the banner of protecting and nurturing families.

Skolnick (1981:42), in an symposium issue of Transaction on future families, discussed what she calls the 'new domesticity':

> In part, the new mood reflects the movement
> of the 1960's generation into the next stage
> of the life cycle - marriage, or at least
> cohabitation, and childbearing. In part,
> it reflects the realization by feminists of
> what men have always known (but not always
> said) - that work without love and intimacy
> is not enough. But the new domesticity
> seems also a response to the social and eco-
> nomic landscape of the 1970's. Faced with
> job scarcity, a declining standard of living,
> and uncertain ties about the future, many
> people are turning inward to home, family,
> and private life.

For those long committed to public understanding and involvement, the new emphasis on the element of private seems to confound old stereotypes regarding conservative - liberal domains of interest.

For example, the Oakland based friends of families was begun by Michael Lerner with Oakland City Councilman Wilson Riles, Jr., to address the fact that the right has made political points with its emphasis on perserving traditional family values. Lerner emphasizes the frustrations of a public world, particularly the stress and frustrations of the work place, as the source of domestic strife. Lerner's group opposes the Family Protection Act introduced by U.S. Senator Paul Laxalt (R. Nev.) in 1969 which op- poses abortions for minors, free legal services for homosexuals, sexually integrated school sports pro- grams, etc. Lerner's group hopes to provide a pro- family organization for liberals and progressives, the trade union movement, the liberal wing of the church,

4

community service organizations, and minorities. The
program centers around the connection of personal
stress and the work world, while emphasizing justice,
fairness, love, and mutual caring. The family has now
come out of the left-wing closet and is no longer just
a public issue for conservatives.

Novak has written praises of the bourgeois or
middle class family with its emphasis on the importance of private property, merit, child rearing, individuality, freedom from state control, and the belief
that one's family position is not guaranteed by birth
but must be earned through effort and excellence:

> The bourgeois family is no affinity for the
> values of an urban rather than rural civili-
> zation, with its consequent emphasis upon
> those habits of mind and society suited to a
> pluralistic, rapidly changing environment. .
> through its emphasis upon the nuclear family
> and the individual rather than upon the en-
> tire family network, the clan, and the ethnic
> group . . . The Bourgeois family does make
> judgments. It does so not only in codes of
> ethical conduct and in schemes of self-
> improvement, but also in terms of practical
> achievement. The code of the bourgeois family
> is to measure - to measure in order to compete
> against oneself, to inspire self-improvement,
> to better oneself (1981:66-67).

In this book we examine the reality of modern family
life, its limitations and need for repair as a public
and social process. Realism is defined as "a more
down to earth view of the American household. Even
'normal' families, it must be recognized, are less
than ideal, that intimate relations of any sort inevitably involve antagonism as well as love" (Skolnick,
1980:115).

We now turn to definitions and issues that provide a context for some of the debates and discussion that this book examines regarding the current
and future state of the family.

II. THE FAMILY AND MARRIAGE IN CROSS-CULTURAL PER-
     SPECTIVE

From cross-cultural surveys, at least three dis-

5

tinctive family types generally emerge (Stephens, 1963). The most basic, the nuclear family, consists of a married man and woman and their offspring and, in some instances additional persons who reside with them. The nuclear family is, of course, the modal family in our society; in the majority of other societies nuclear families are generally combined to form larger units. A second type are polygamous families, two or more nuclear families affiliated by plural marriages. A third type is the extended family, two or more nuclear families affiliated through an extension of the parent-child relationship rather than of the husband-wife relationship. On the surface, there is an apparent universality of family and kinship networks in all known cultures.

Cross-cultural studies show that family patrilineal institutions in which descent, inheritance, and so on, follow the male are associated with "higher" cultural levels, whereas matrilineal families generally are associated with "lower" cultural levels (Murdock, 1949). Levels here are measured by domestication of animals, riding, metalworking, and general occupational specialization, including agriculture, pottery, weaving, and so forth. Our contemporary marriage and family types are descendants of an early Judaic-Christian background which evolved over 2000 years. Before Christianity, in early Rome, marriage was highly variable (Summer, 1906). Later, with the expansion of the Roman Empire and power throughout Europe, a Christian "church" marriage, which included the notion of monogamy became dominant at the upper levels of society.

At the lower levels was "free marriage," which was based on consensus, delivery of the bride to the groom, and the conscience of the man, whose duty it was to observe and keep the marriage. The wealthier classes utilized a variety of documents to regulate property rights for the bride in marriage. Marriage in Roman law was such that it involved a conjunction of male and female and required a correlation of their entire lives. In practicality, however, there was no common property and the union was dissolvable almost at the man's pleasure. A woman in adultery was severely punished, whereas a man was not. When Christianity took over the Roman free marriage, couples of the lower classes uttered their consensus in a church before three or four clergymen, and a certificate was prepared. Even though the ceremony took place in a church and involved clergy, it was primarily a civil ceremony.

Ancient German marriage consisted primarily of oral agreements and up until the ninth century included a great number of concubines. However, there were class differences, the upper classes being involved in a solemn ceremony which the lower classes did not have.

Man's property remained his until the Middle Ages. Property then became common property so that "when the coverlet is drawn over their heads, the spouses are equally rich." Thus, the custom of witnesses accompanying the newlyweds to their bedchamber arose to make sure the marriage was consummated, and in several societies, all the males participated - just to be certain.

Around the thirteenth century, the church remodeled ideas and institutions, and marriage came under its influence and control. Subsequent consummation by religious rights only constituted "irrevocable marriage." There was no question that men held the power and responsibility and that women had less esteem, authority, and so on. During the medieval era, men could have multiple wives, and for them adultery was not against the law. Subsequently, after males were open to church censure for adultery, it was entered into the legal process (but not enforced). The Decrees of Trent (1563) established the place of marriage in the common law of the church. Marriage was to be celebrated in church and before witnesses. The church required permission, thus preventing mixed marriages between a religious and non-religious person.

Puritans went in a reverse direction, requiring only a civil ceremony until the eighteenth century and eventually accepting the Catholic position and requiring a religious ceremony. Up until very recently, this format of marriage within the church, requiring permission of the clergy, has been followed. Emerging alternatives that are becoming prevalent in our society may ignore or alter these religiously sanctioned views.

III. MARRIAGE AND FAMILY DEFINED

Marriage is a socially legitimate sexual union, begun with a public announcement, undertaken with some idea of permanence, and assuming a more or less explicit contract that spells out reciprocal rights and obligations between spouses and between spouses and any children they may have (Stephens, 1963:5). From this perspective, a socially legitimiate sexual union means that the married couple will not come into conflict with some social or legal norms or be punished for having sexual intercourse. Thus, a married couple does not have to be discrete about the fact that they are having sexual intercourse. Another condition is a public announcement ranging from a simple announcement to an elaborate ceremony that includes feasting, fancy dress, processionals, religious observances, and so forth. This also implies some idea of permanence; that is, it is not a one-night or short-term contract and it will last "til death or divorce do us part." With the marriage contract, there is an assumption of obligations, which may or may not be specific and formalized. The marriage contract, whether very formal or only an assumed understanding between couples, varies among societies. It spells out reciprocal obligations between spouses and between spouses and children.

The areas associated with this definition are as follows:

1. Socially Legitimate Sexual Union. Appropriate times of socially approved sexual intercourse within marriage vary. In almost every society there are certain taboo periods during which marital sexual intercourse is not permitted, such as during the menstrual cycle and the postpartum period. Of course, in our society the overtly stated values and norms are that sexual intercourse is only permissible when it occurs within marriage. In many other societies, this is not necessarily true and extramarital sex in some form or another is permitted (Ford and Beach, 1951:113-118).

2. Public Announcement. Virtually all societies have elaborate marriage ceremonials which qualify as a public announcement that marriage is about to commence or has commenced.

3. <u>Some Idea of Permanence</u>. The idea of permanence is, of course, a relative one. Stephens
cites the Navaho Indians, where only about
one woman out of three and one man out of
four reach old age with the same spouse; some
men had six or seven different wives in
succession. Such serial marriage occurs
throughout the United States.

4. <u>The Marriage Contract</u>. This is, perhaps, the
vaguest of the measures although generally
applicable in our society, overtly or covertly
such contracts exist in every society.

The family, then, is defined as follows:

I will define the family as a social arrangement based on marriage and the marriage contract, including recognition of the rights
and duties of parenthood, common residence
for husband, wife, and children, and reciprocal economic obligations between husband and
wife (Stephens, 1963:8).

There are problems with this definition of the family:

1. <u>Economic Obligations</u>. One of the attributes
defining the family is marriage, which we discussed above. A second is reciprocal economic
obligations between husband and wife. This is
a substantial problem because reciprocal economic obligations are difficult to measure.
There are many societies in which husband and
wife belong to different economic units. Also
there are some societies in which husband and
wife do not own property in common. Similarly, at times the nuclear family is often not a
separate economic unit but, instead, a subsi-
diary of a larger economic unit, most commonly
an extended family - multiple generations.
Also, the nuclear family may be "split" by
having unilineal kin groups; that is, allegiance to parents on each side of the nuclear
family. Because of this or other customs, the
husband and wife may have little or no property in common. Finally, in many societies
wives must also do subsistence work and are
partially or wholly self-supporting. Thus,
reciprocal economic obligations in a universal

9

definition of the family appears to be a questionable criterion.

2. Common Residence. A third defining attribute of the family is common residence for husband, wife, and children. This also poses problems since an earlier study by Murdock (1949) of 125 societies showed that about one-fourth of them were characterized by mother-child households, with the father, for at least a good part of the time, living in another residence.

3. Rights and Duties of Parenthood. This definitional element has the same problems as reciprocal economic obligations since in many instances children live with the father separately or with the father in a unilineal fashion; also there are substantial numbers of matrilineal societies in which father and children belong to different kin groups.

There is no known society that clearly and unequivically does not have a family by his definition. However, he says that while some come very close to qualifying as such, there are others that are doubtful, for example, the Nayars, a Hindu cast group living in southern India. According to his survey of ethnographic materials in relationship to the Nayar, they do have a socially legitimate sexual union, although there is some doubt whether the marriage begins with a public announcement. Similarly, the union is not undertaken with the idea of permanence and it is doubtful that there is a marriage contract. Apparently there is no reciprocal economic obligation between husband and wife and, similarly, no comon residence for husband, wife, and children. The rights and duties of parenthood evidently do not apply to the father.

Similarly, the kibbutzim of Israel also are doubtful insofar as the definition of family is concerned. In the kibbutzim, marriage is a socially legitimate sexual union, begins with a public announcement, and is undertaken with some idea of permanence. However, there is some question of whether or not there is a definite marriage contract and there is some question of whether or not there are economic obligations between the husband and wife. A common residence for husband and wife exists but not for children. Similarly, there are few rights and duties of parenthood. Thus, there is some question of whether parents and children actually form a family according to the definition outlined by Stephens.

Another doubtful case is Jamaica, where common-law marriage exists as a variant form of mateship. Since it is extremely expensive for a person to get married - a "proper" marriage involves church, wedding fees, special clothes, and other expenses - there are a substantial number of illegal, common-law unions. Some of these are relatively permanent or at least undertaken with the intention of being permanent. Another type of common-law marriage, temporary concubinage, is a result of the itinerant sugar-cane workers and others that move from town to town striking up sexual liaisons. A third common-law pattern is the fatherless family. A woman lives with her children and has a succession of lovers. Sometimes they stay with her for a while in her home, and sometimes they don't even do that. Thus, it appears that there are some exceptions to the criteria that Stephens uses to define marriage and the family. These exceptions are few, although undoubtedly as more ethnographic evidence becomes available, other societies will fall into the doubtful category.

One contemporary approach to the definition of marriage and the family is related to perceptions of the participants (Constantine and Constantine, 1973: 17). From this point of view, marriage is a relationship in which one person sees himself or herself as committed or bonded to another or others in significant ways involving intimacy and assumptions of continuance. Thus, two or more people are married if they perceive themselves to be married; that is, to be committed to the relationship. This, of course, is a phenomenological approach to marriage. From this point of view, a marriage license, in a legal sense, codifies in some instances what several people already perceive as being a marriage. In other instances, this allows the notion of a family and/or marriage to exist even though according to our current legal code no such family exists. That is, it may exist perceptually, in the minds of the individuals who consider themselves involved in a "marriage" or "family." This, according to the Constantines, might enable one to discern whether a son and his girlfriend are "married" or "just living together."

There are a number of cross-cultural regularities regarding marriage and the family; among them are the following (Stephens, 1963):

1. Mothers in the same house with young children.

2. There is an almost universal menstrual cycle sex taboo.

3. Societies with a fairly high percentage of mother-child households require a change of residence for all adolescents or prepubertal boys - that is, the boy does not sleep under the same roof with his mother.

4. Mothers are expected to be married.

5. Marriage is not undertaken for a specified short-term period.

6. There is recognition of kin ties beyond the nuclear family.

It also appears that women are very rarely more privileged or more powerful than men. Almost universally, tasks such as hunting are done by men, while tasks such as grain grinding and housekeeping are done by women. Men rarely given deference to women unless it is a common man and a noble woman.

IV. FAMILY POSITIONS AND ROLES

Within the types of structures of families and households, there are always a variety of positions, or statuses. Positions or statuses in the nuclear family consist of wife, husband, and offspring. Of course, in other cultures and societies, both past and present, there are different designations, but in each instance positions and statuses within a kinship or family network existed. Each position or status has a role or roles assigned to it. In the position of wife there are a variety of roles such as maid, cook, mother, housekeeper, sex partner, and so on. "Expectations" and "behavior" are two separate facets involved in roles, and it is important to make the distinction between role expectations and role behavior because they may be substantially different in families, even though the positions are the same. This difference is between structural form and behavior associated with the structural positions.

Positions and roles require interaction with other persons, and this is called inter-role penetration. Inter-role penetration may result in cooperation or it may result in conflict or other types of behavior depending on the differing "expectations" with regard to behavior in inter-role penetration. That is, persons interacting with each other, perhaps a wife and her husband, may have different kinds of expectations for each other, but the behavior may or may not match the expectations. Thus . . .

After a review of family literature, eight roles in the position of spouse, parent, or both were identified. These are: provider, housekeeper, child care, child socialization, sexual, recreational, therapeutic, and kinship. Traditionally, housekeeper, child care, and sexual roles have been assigned. . .to the wife, . . .and kinship and child socialization roles to both . . . part of the research task is to determine to what extent spouses feel that roles should be shared and to what extent they are, in practice shared. . .(Nye and Gecas, 1976:13).

Role analysis allows a reflection about numerous dimensions of family life:

Along with the normative dimension (what should be done or who should do it) and the behavioral dimension,. . .we will also consider the degree to which individuals are committed to the roles (role commitment) the evaluation of their own and their spouse's role performances (role competence), the extent to which they worry about their role performance (role strain), the amount of conflict which occurs over these roles (role conflict) and the outcome of role conflict (role power). (Nye and Gecas, 1976:14)

There may be a conflict between the norms of society, family, and individuals regarding expectations if there is a deviation from one or the other. Thus, there is a need to distinguish between generalized norms of society and individualized expectations by members within a family. All of the above, that is, positions, roles, role expectations, and role behav-

13

ior, are influenced by values. Values are orientations toward life, the specific aspects of which are
related to family, children, consumerism, career,
security, lifestyle. Values are those ends or moral
purposes worth working towards.

The latest reports on current state of our society and institutions indicate both a profound malise
and a lingering sense of optimism that "new rules" are
emerging regarding issues of the quality of our lives,
in lieu of purely quantitative and materialistic concerns (Yankelovich, 1981). Individuals in all walks
of life, but particularly the middle class, appear to
have come to some understanding of the psychic costs
associated with useless competition and status striv-
ing, as well as the social costs of isolating their
private lves from public involvements and support
structures. The private search for self-fulfillment
is eroding, according to some, and being replaced by
a new "ethic of commitment" and at least the first
transitional signs that social and public connections
to our private lives through mediating institutions
such as community, church, neighborhood, family must
be renewed and supported (Berger, 1977).

This analysis highlights the importance of the
relationship between private and public lives and how
marriage and family life mediates these two worlds.
Likewise our idea of values points to the extreme importance of private intentions and public actions and
behavior: even if we don't always live up to our intended standards and values in action, we must assume
some responsibility for the failure of institutions
like the family. Although we may act with the best
intentions in choosing to marry or remain single, divorce or remain married, the key question is if we
abdicate responsibility for the negative consequences
of whatever decisions we choose. We often rationalize
our actions or choose those values that fit our behavior without reflection. Muddled intentions and moral
drift often result.

Such excuses no longer work in a world of diminishing resources and complex interdependencies: although we may intend no harm by our individual actions
the consequences we build into options as a result of
our choices offer our children a concrete world they
must cope with. Hiding behind bureaucratic rules or
blaming larger social forces doesn't absolve each of

us of the need for critical moral thinking about the public world we are creating and how it may destroy our private lives. Affirmation of the time, space, and opportunity for private reflections and living doesn't free us from the need to know and act as publicly responsible and committed individuals. The link between private and public world is more pertinent now than ever: the forces tearing at the fabric of family life are public, social and structural and intimately effect the very grounding of our social future and commitment to a sane and better world (C. W. Mills, 1959).

BIBLIOGRAPHY

Berger, Peter

1977   "Marriage and the Construction of
Reality" in <u>Facing Up to Modernity:
Excursions in Society, Politics and
Religion</u>, New York: Basic Books.

Constantine, Larry
 and Joan Constantine

1973   <u>Group Marriage: A Study of Contempory
Multilateral Marriages</u>, New York:
Macmillan.

Ford, Clellan S.
 and Frank A. Beach

1951   <u>Patterns of Sexual Behavior</u>, New York:
Harper & Row.

Kenniston, Kenneth

1977   <u>All Our Children: The American Family
Under Pressure</u>. New York: Harcourt,
Brace Jovanovich.

Mills, C. W.

1959   <u>The Sociological Imagination</u>, New York:
Oxford University Press.

Murdock, George P.

1949.   <u>Social Structure</u>, New York: Macmillan.

Novak, Michael

1981   "The Bourgeois Family in Decline"
<u>Society</u>, Vol. 18, No. 2, Jan., Feb.

Nye, F. Ivan &
V. Gecas

1976   "The Role Concept: Review and Delinea-
tion. In F. Ivan Nye (ed.), <u>Role
Structure and Analysis of the Family</u>.
Beverly Hills, California: Sage.

Skolnick, Arlene

   1981   "The Family and Its Discontents"
              Society, Vol. 18, No. 2, Jan., Feb.

   1981   "The Paradox of Perfection" Annual Editions, 1981. Dushkin Publishing Co.

Stephens, William N.

   1963   The Family in Cross-Cultural Perspective, New York: Holt, Rinehart and Winston.

Sumner, William Graham

   1959   Folkways, New York: Dover (first published in 1906).

*Dr. Edgar W. Butler is Chair of the Sociology Department, University of California, Riverside.

*Dr. Douglas B. Gutknecht is a member of the Sociology Department and Coordinator of the M.S. Degree in Human Resource Managment and Development, Chapman College, Orange, California.

CHAPTER 1

THE EMERGENCE AND RESOLUTION OF RELATIONSHIP, SEX ROLE AND GROWTH INTERRUPTION RUTS IN MODERN SOCIETY

Douglas Gutknecht*
Jerry Meints*

I. INTRODUCTION

This article examines the nature of relationship ruts which produce intra-psychic (or personal) conflict or stress. Stress here emphasizes the subjective consciousness of the individual who is juggling competing social demands, expectations, roles, or relationships. Conflict refers to role relationships with others and it refers to socially generated or public dimensions of personal problems and psychic pain or stress.

Intra-psychic stress results from psychic fragmentation or war within the self. Such a war is subjectively experienced as "part of me wants out of our relationship, while another part of me wants to stay in the relationship." Personal and intra-psychic stress is related to being in an interpersonal bind or a rut. Such relationship ruts have psychic consequences.

Relationship ruts develop when one becomes "stuck" in a conflict relationship. Hence one is ultimately stuck socially in a role position and psychically in one's consciousness and unable to find a resolution to the war within the self (the self torture game). Although self torture is decidedly social in origin, we need not solve all of societies' games in order to deal with many aspects of psychic pain in the short run. A long run solution requires systematic changes in the conditions causing personal pain. In fact psychic pain may prevent the raising of consciousness which is one element of ongoing social change. The arbitrary distinction between the importance of either intra- and inter-psychic conflict and stress mirrors the wasteful debate regarding whether institutional change is more important than personal or vice versa. For the remainder of our analysis we will speak of intra-psychic conflict in order to suggest the often social basis of personal stress.

19

Individual intra-psychic conflict does not occur in a vacuum. Social and cultural features pervade the individual psyche and add fuel to the fire of personal turmoil. Given the interaction between society and the individual, it is necessary to provide a brief sketch of the societal context giving rise to intra-psychic conflict. We take seriously the humanistic premise that many emotional difficulties are curable given: (1) awareness of the social context of intra-psychic conflict; (2) awareness of relationship ruts; (3) a Gestalt approach to intra-psychic conflict; and (4) techniques for relieving relationship ruts. Perls (1977) condemned the proliferation of "techniques" (since people tend to get lost in them at the expense of experiencing the here-and-now). However, some existential or phenomenological grounded techniques potentially enhance the awareness of experience rather than lose one within the technique itself.

II. AWARENESS OF THE SOCIAL CONTEXT OF INTRA-PSYCHIC CONFLICT

Sociologists define culture as a set of symbols and ideas such as language, values, beliefs, standards, and expectations that are both created and transmitted by societal members. Culture and society would not be possible without an ability to use symbols that allow a sharing of common meanings. The sharing of meaning through language also allows us to reflect on and change culture and its standards and normative expectations. Individuals do create new cultural values and standards that allow us to reshape the ongoing direction of society, social interaction, and the self.

In a society itself a victim of tremendous complexity, fragmentation, segregation, and excessive size, individuals encounter less awareness and concern for their private difficulties and problems of adjustment and living (Szasz, 1961; Lasch, 1979; Sennet; 1977; Klapp, 1978; Dreitzel, 1977). Lost boundaries of self are a result of being caught between public and private roles, between our needs as individuals and demands placed upon us by society and state (Bensman and Lilienfeld, 1979). The dilemma of retaining individuality in a world that creates excessive public contradictions and conflicts is great.

Such lack of concern over individuals' private lives and troubles, even though publicly generated, leaves the problem of individuals facing difficult life transitions and problems in relative isolation. Another dilemma that modern men and women consistently face is the plurality of world views or life worlds (Berger and Luckman, 1966). Such plurality results from modernity in which the expansion of the area of human choice, options or decision is accompanied by the propensity to become vulnerable to change. It often appears easier to leave social relationships than deal with structural conditions and contradictions that strain relationships. The social and economic conditions of modernity and capitalism are of less interest here than relevance of such situations for the sociological-psychological and interpretive meanings derived.

In modern societies, identity becomes more fragile as modern consciousness moves from a situation of fate to choice or the multiplication of options (Berger, 1971, 1974, 1980). The modern world easily confers identity but also provides many opportunities to change it. The existence of numerous personal and life style options suggests that choosing to transform oneself and one's situations is not only readily available but a possibility throughout the life cycle. We often ignore the existence of a relatively wide range of contradictory values in American culture and how they often provide support for structures that fragment us and cause personal pain. The priority and balance of these cultural values at the societal level tells us much about the potential social contradictions and ultimately personal problems. Our very social diversity often robs us of psychic energy because we fail to view social change and humanistic individual change together.

The nature of integrated consciousness requires an expansion of energy unleashed by social involvements and creative use of conflict. Enlarged role responsibilities actually allow the expansion of psychic and physical energy not its contraction (Marks, 1977; Spretzer et al., 1979). Social involvement in numerous meaningful activities, where one is not caught in rigid role expectations, ruts, and binds, actually allows creative energy to expand. The nature of meaning is socially constructed as is alienation, pain, stress, and meaninglessness (Berger and Luckman,

1966; Bensman and Lilienfeld, 1978; Sennet, 1980).

Failure to recognize such a creative tension and pluralism in social structures and value patterns results from a fear of conflict and tension within ourselves and in our relationships, communities, and institutions. We thus reject or repress those certain aspects of ourselves often due to our failure to trust ourselves, our choices, and our ability to accept responsibility. Thus the rejection of diversity within and around us is sustained by devices which limit the development of a more tolerant, growing, or humanistic self.

We often exaggerate our fears of growth by blocking out, withdrawing, turning off, selectively perceiving, stereotyping, and projecting. We often invest energy in false assumptions, illusions, and expectations that deny our real perceptions, complexity, and wholeness. We somehow feel guilty when conflict inevitably arises within ourselves, or we feel betrayed when conflict arises in our relationships. In the first instance we learn to block, repress, or constrict our feelings. When we can no longer contain our feelings they often burst out in those periodic and destructive fits of accusation, bitterness, or feelings of betrayal and hurt. Instead of a constant and controlled stream of dialogue we often receive and give a onesided out-pouring of indignation and blame. Such a denial of diversity and conflict leads to a splitting of self and a subsequent psychic dependency upon intimate others. To understand how social structure constrains our psychic lives let's turn to the institutional relationships at the intersect of self and society.

III. AWARENESS OF RELATIONSHIP RUTS

Ruts Defined

We experience many structural and cultural binds and ruts in American society that are basically value dilemmas, supported by certain institutions. Such dilemmas often prevent us from understanding conflict and problems in our social and intimate relationships. In this paper we define a rut as a habitual pattern of response that is culturally learned and sanctioned; and which prevents us from acknowledging a wider range of possibilities in ourselves and our relationships.

22

One can thus speak of both cultural ruts and personal ruts. A rut involves a categorical mode of thinking and perceiving that leads us into win-lose games and double bind situations. These ruts exist at the interaction between culture, social structure, and the self.

A rut often distorts our approaches to new situations, predetermining our response, as we repeat the same self destructive and undesirable behaviors. We often become so dependent on habitual responses we fail to integrate a broader perspective that might allow us to learn new ways of thinking, perceiving, or communicating. We feel frustrated and disappointed because a rut precludes enjoyment, feeling, growth, etc.

Environmental Vs. Self Support

We habitually rely on external sources of support for our feeling of well being. We despise or fear any sense of insecurity or unpredictability. Sometimes we must suspend the external world in order to act on our own intuitive arrangement of reality. We must understand our growth and happiness often depend on self-support and our own awareness of meaningful alternatives and possibilities.

Specific Ruts

Many problems in our personal and interpersonal lives accumulate because we fail to understand the contradictory nature of assumptions and expectations which our culture fosters. We fail to see how problems accumulate and compound because we don't label or identify them in a more strategic, and integrated manner. Relationship ruts derive from the following contradictory values, beliefs, and expectations:

A) Sex roles rut
B) Growth Interruption Rut
C) Romantic love
D) Losing oneself in family roles
E) People as property

A. The Sex Role Rut: Sex roles are defined as a
    pattern of behavioral expectations imposed upon a
    specific sex type. Sex role expectations have the
    tremendous power to both constrain behavior and

define personal identities. All of us have, at
one time or another, been forced to respond in
culturally determined patterns simply because
of our particular sex type.

Sex roles seem to range in intensity from
highly rigid to fluid or androgynous sex roles.
Sex roles are, to a certain degree, unavoidable.
Sex roles become relationship ruts however when
they are interpreted and responded to as rigid
mandates for living. While sex roles are becoming
more fluid, the strong, silent, inexpressive American macho male John Wayne stereotype continues to
dominate the cultural media. Similarly, woman are
socialized into objectified, passive, and orna-
mental roles which deny their intellectual and
creative abilities.

When couples respond to rigid role expectations that trap her in the kitchen and him in an
aggressive career, the consequences are usually
rut producing. Like all roles, sex roles demand
us to behave in ways which lack natural or spon-
taneous self creation. To that extent, it can be
said that rigid sex roles force us to perform unnatural acts. For example, there is a tremendous
difference between cooking a meal for sheer joy
it brings, and cooking a meal that is, has, and
will continue to be expected as part of your role.

Sex roles serve certain positive social functions that tend to maintain their continued existence. Sex roles lead to a division of labor in
the relationship which serves practical needs such
as meals, income, housing, clothing, maintenance,
etc. Relationship ruts arise when sex role differentiation extends beyond practical needs into
personal identities.

For example, a woman who is identified as
"suzy homemaker" has little room to develop her
potential in other areas. A couple that rarely
reverses roles are living in a sex role rut. Sex
role reversal offers an opportunity to develop
both empathy for one's partner and broader personal talents. Women can feel a tremendous sense
of accomplishment and power over their lives after
having mastered the simple act of tuning up their
own car. Men also feel exhilerated as a result

24

of successfully creating a gourmet meal.

Sex role ruts extend into the bedroom where it is the responsibility and duty of a macho male to satisfy his partner. She too, being the seductive feline temptress, must passively moan a writhing chorus of "of you brute" attesting to both his masculine prowess and her feminine dependence upon him, sometimes even to the extent of "faking an orgasm."

This scenario is the epitome of sex role relationship ruts and belies the general consensus among sex therapists and researchers, who suggest that performance expectations often lead to sexual dysfunctions. Each cannot assume responsibility for the other's orgasm. Rather, each assumes responsibility for their own orgasm as well as the responsibility to communicate one's sexual needs, frustrations, desires, fantasies, and feelings. Only then can one transcend sex role ruts and rise to the level of authenticity.

Growth Interruption Rut: Interruptions in the process of growth usually result in confusion about the boundaries between the self, others, and the environment. The "well integrated" person is one "who can live in concernful contact with his society, neither being swallowed up by it nor withdrawing from it completely" (Perls, 1973).

The inability to maintain this balance leads to "growth interruptions" and "neurotic disturbances." Unlike the classic definition of neuroses as a "functional nervous disorder," Perls (1973) explains neuroses as "a state of imbalance in the individual that arises when simultaneously he and the group of which he is a member experience different needs and the individual cannot tell which is dominant." Neuroses results in an "inadequate sense of identity" due to "inadequate self support." Perls delineates four "neurotic mechanisms" which lead to growth interruptions:

1) INTROJECTION: Introjections are facts, standards of behavior, feelings, evaluations, or ways of acting that an individual has added to their behavioral repertoire without assimilation. The process of assimilation occurs when

one properly examines or de-structures novel or foreign knowledge (introjects) that is forced or imposed on them and <u>selectively</u> integrate all, part, or none of the knowledge, depending on their own needs at that time.

"There should not be conflict in a good relationship," or "marriages should last forever," are two examples of introjects. The individual operates according to these standards, even though they may directly contradict their experience, without ever stopping to evaluate them. When the introjector says, "I think," he usually means, "they think."

2) <u>PROJECTION</u>: A projection is the opposite of an introjection. Projections are feelings, beliefs, or desires that originate in the individual but are attributed to other individuals or objects in the environment. Since the individual fails to recognize his/her beliefs or feelings, they are perceived as originating in others. The other is then perceived as directing the content of the projection toward the projector him/herself. Essentially what the projecter is doing is making others responsible for that which resides in him/herself.

A man unaware of his desire to relate to many women sexually will believe that a lot of women wish to relate to him sexually. An individual unaware of acting negatively towards others complains of others behaving negatively towards him/her. "When the projector says "it" or "they" he usually means "I."

3) <u>RETROFLECTION</u>: Retroflection means "turning back sharply against." The retroflector will do to him/herself what he/she did or tried to do to others. The retroflector will become the target of behavior by substituting him/herself in place of the environment. Energy originally extended outward to the environment, for purposes of manipulation in order to satisfy one's own needs, will now be redirected (or retroflected) inward. For example, a conflict which once existed between the individual and the environment has now become an

"inner conflict," either between two opposing
behaviors or between two parts of the personality. "I can't let myself do that" or "I
feel so angry at myself" are two examples of
retroflection. The retroflector tends to see
"I" and "myself" as two different people.
Retroflection is apparent when the individual
uses the reflective "myself."

4) CONFLUENCE: When there is not a distinction
between the self and others or between the
self and the environment, the individual is
said to be in confluence with it. If the individual is in confluence with others too
much, s/he will lose all sense of him/herself.
Consequently, the individual will not be able
to experience themselves.

Very often in relationships, the two
partners become very much a "part" of each
other. They share the same beliefs, likes and
dislikes until they are no longer individuals,
but instead, they are just an extension of
each other. If the confluence between the
partners is carried to extremes, the individuals will not tolerate any differences and
will demand likeness. When an individual
says "we" it is difficult to determine who
s/he is referring to, themselves or the rest
of the world. The use of "we" makes it obvious that that individual is in a state of
confluence.

IV. A GESTALT VIEW OF INTRA-PSYCHIC CONFLICT
RESOLUTION

Gestalt theory (i.e., a psychological subset of
existential theory) presupposes an organismic basis to
the process of intra-psychic regulation. The holistic
doctrine stands in direct contrast to "Cartesian dualism" which asserts an ontologial split (i.e, mind---
body); as well as a whole host of assorted cosmologi-
cal dualities (e.g., natural---supernatural, worldly
---other worldly, man---god, subject---object, etc.)
(Speigleberg, 1969).

Holism postulates that man is a unified organism
(Perls, 1973). Research into Eastern Mysticism and
Yoga practices (e.g., fire walking, the control of the

heartbeat and blood pressure, etc.) have lent further empirical plausibility to the notion that the mind and body may function in concert (Pearce, 1971). The "higher conscious" control of the autonomic nervous system suggests that the "pathways" between consciousness and the body have always been available, yet have seldom been exercised (Weil, 1971).

Consensus Theory

Gestalt's organismic emphasis suggests many parallels to consensus theories. Consensus theories include the more traditional psychology, balance theory, cognitive dissonance, and functionalism.

Structures and Functions

Consensus theories loosely suggest that the organism is composed of interrelated <u>structures</u> (or parts) which <u>function</u> towards the maintenance, balance, equilibrium, or adjustment of the whole (Dushkin, 1973). Changes in one part necessarily affect other parts of the integrated system or organism.

Gestalt theory suggests a similar organismic adjustment is operative. Consensus theories postulate practical or survival <u>functions</u> as the basic organizing principle. Gestalt theory asserts the necessity of maintaining homeostasis via the process of integrating the conflicting aspects (or characters) of the self, into awareness (Perls, 1969).

Gestalt Model of Conflict Resolution

Perls (1973) interprets Freud as saying that intra-psychic reality is a "constant conflict" between the id and the superego. He characterizes this conflict as "endless and unbreakable;" "man struggles until death," (Pearls, 1973:42).

In contrast, the gestalt image of conflict resolution is much more melioristic. Perls (1973) describes a process similar to the following model presented in figure 1-a.

		ground		
NEED	ORIENTATION	FIGURE	MANIPULATION	CLOSING
		ground		GESTALT
		CATHEXIS		

FIGURE 1-A: Conflict Resolution, adapted from Perls
              (1973).

IV. TECHNIQUES FOR RELIEVING RELATIONSHIP RUTS

     The following is a list of methods for dealing
with intra-psychic conflict. These methods are far
from complete and should be seen as small steps in
the long walk towards conflict resolution.

Method A.   The Un-Method: Self Regulation/Self
Creation

     Perls et al. (1977) distinguish between intra-
psychic conflicts which are "petty battles" based upon
"semantic mistakes" (i.e., misinterpretations of meanings), and conflicts which are "deeply concernful."
More often than not, concernful conflicts arise when
the "self-regulating," "sponstaneous inner system" is
upset by external introjected stereotyped social
norms. Conflict of this type usually necessitates
either ejection of the unowned prescriptions or al-
ternatively the integration and digestion of the
here-to-fore unowned "should" (Perls, 1977).

     The attendant "pain" and "suffering" of intra-
psychic emotional conflict is not to be avoided since
such discomfort is the means of coming to a "self-
creative solution" (Perls et al., 1977). The suggestion is made that once all the contestants (i.e,
parts) engaged in the conflict are in awareness and
contact, then what follows is not therapy--but a subjective "hard decision" which must be made by the
individual (Perls, 1977).

Method B.   The Tao

     In a further exposition of the conflict resolu-
tion, Perls et al. (1977) draw upon teachings of the
Tao to suggest a methodology for lessening the pain
of unnecessary freak-outs---during the process of
renegotiating equilibrium. This method entails a form
of detachment, i.e., to disengage oneself from pre-
conceived notions of how things "ought" to turn out;
and further a detachment from allegiance to any specific warring contestant or part of oneself---this dis-

29

engagement from the internal dialogue is described as a "creative impartiality" (Perls, 1977). Again, conflict is not seen as a destructive fragmenting of the self, but rather a situation where each part of the self can exercise "reckless savagery" while actively engaged in the creative process of finding (and strengthening) the self.

Method C. Beyond Self Conquest--Therapeutic Laissez Faire

Perls et al. (1977) warns of the dangers of premature pacification, i.e., a stopping of growth via "self conquest" which is defined as neurotic. Premature pacification entails a "truce" or "numbness" to avoid further conflicts which are deeply concernful. Usually what follows is a need to be one-up in subsequent minor "petty battles;" as if to neutralize the "humiliation" of neurotic self conquest (Perl et al., 1977).

Self conquest becomes even more debilitating when the conflict was made unbearable by another person; that is, when premature resignation was chosen out of fear of losing approval from that other person (Perls et al., 1977). Resignation creates a void in the conflict, which "self assertion" once occupied. That void is then filled by identifying with that other person:

> That is, instead of pressing on to the new self one would become in the unknown solution of the conflict, one introjects the other self. Identifying with it, one lends it to the force of one's own aggressions now disengaged from the advancement of one's own needs. These aggressions are now retroflectively turned against those needs... (Perls et al., 1977, 421-422, emphasis added).

The solution to such neurotic premature pacification lies in contacting the "coming solution." One must:

> Free the aggression from its fixed target, the organism; make the introjects aware in order that they may be destroyed; bring the compartmented interests (the sexual, the social, etc.) back into contact and

conflict; and rely on the integrative power
of the self (Perls et al., 1977:428).

Such a solution sounds like "therapeutic
laissez faire," yet Perls (1969) argues that to attempt solving a persistent problem, or to seek the
closure of unfinished business is useless; this notion
has been referred to as the "paradoxical theory of
change" and lends credence to maintaining an attitude
of "therapeutic laissez faire."

> ...deliberate change never, never, never
> functions. As soon as you say, "I want
> to change"---make a program---a counter
> force is created that prevents you from
> change. Changes are taking place by
> themselves. If you go deeper into what
> you are, if you accept what is there, then
> a change automatically occurs by itself.
> This is the paradox of change (Perls, 1969:
> 178).

Method D. Shuttle Technique

The individual shuttles between dialectically
opposed parts of the self. S/he shuttles between
verbalizations and body language or between thoughts
(or fantasy) and action. This technique attempts to
facilitate an awareness in the individual of self as a
unified organism. That two seemingly independent
parts of the self are actually different expressions
stemming from the same conflict.

We are all familiar with the separation of ourselves from physical illness during time of conflict
(i.e., psychosomatic manifestations). "This damn
headache, I wish it would go away," as if the headache were a foreign body invading the individual.
This technique is grounded in holism which denies the
mind/body dualism. Utilization of this technique will
help the individual become aware of the inseparable
relationship between the symptom and the cause of the
conflict.

Method E. Psychodrama

In psychodrama, the individual switches from one
role to another role. For instance, the oppressed
wife and the oppressive husband. The psychodrama

31

technique facilitates an awareness of a split in the personality as a result of introjections. The wife becomes aware that in reality her superego is her oppressive husband. She becomes aware that she is doing the oppressing and is being oppressed at the same time.

Method F. Contacting Breathing

When an individual experiences an emotion whether it be excitement, anger, sadness, etc., the normal breathing process is usually interrupted. For example, when one is excited, the individual takes short, quick breaths, or when one is upset and on the verge of crying, the breath is usually held back for long periods of time. Staying in contact with and maintaining the breath during emotional experiences, especially during negative experiences, may serve to ease the discomfort.

Many eastern disciplines emphasize control of breathing. They believe that inherent in the air we breathe is a quality known as "prana" which is defined as "absolute energy," or "life force." Prana in the air we breathe is analogus to vitamins in the food we eat. Proper contact with and control of the breath at all times allows one to obtain prana. The cultivation of prana over time may result in one having better control over intra-psychic conflict.

V. CONCLUSION

Admittedly, we have not exhausted the list of possible relationship ruts nor the techniques for relieving them. We have merely developed the notion that couples often live much of their lives in socially generated ruts which produce intra-psychic conflict, stress, and pain. We have briefly explored some structural and social-psychological features which give rise to relationship ruts. We have offered both a list of ruts and an example of two such ruts. We then discussed intra-psychic conflict from a Gestalt perspective. Finally, we explicated several Gestalt and existential techniques for relieving relationship ruts.

BIBLIOGRAPHY

Bensman, Joseph and
Robert Lilienfeld

  1979   Between Public and Private: Cost
              Boundaries of the Self. New York:
              The Free Press.

Berger, P.

  1980   Theoretical Imperative. New York:
              Anchor Books.

  1974   The Homeless Mind. London: Penguin
              Books.

  1971   A Rumour of Angeles. London: Penguin
              Books.

Berger, P. and
T. Luckman

  1966   The Social Construction of Reality.
              New York: Anchor Books.

Dreitzel, Hans Peter

  1977   "On the Political Meaning of Culture"
              in Norman Birnbaum (ed.) Beyond The
              Crisis. New York: Oxford University
              Press.

Dunshkin, Group

  1971   The Study of Society, The Dushkin Pub-
              lishing Group: Guilford, Connecticut.

Husserl, Edmund

  1960   Phenomenology and the Crisis of Philo-
              sophy (trans.) Quentin Lauer.

Kaplan, Abraham

  1964   The Conduct of Inquiry. Chandler Pub-
              lishing Co.

Klapp, Orrin E.

1978   Opening and Closing: Strategies of
                Information Adaptation in Society.
                New York: Cambridge University Press.

Lasch, Christopher

1979   The Culture of Narcissism: American
                Life in An Age of Diminishing Expecta-
                tions. New York: W. W. Norton.

Marks, S.

1977   Multiple Roles and Role Strain: Some
                Notes on Human Energy, Time, and Com-
                mitment. American Sociological Review,
                Vol. 42 (December): 921-936.

Pearce, C.

1971   Crack in the Cosmic Egg. Pocket Books:
                New York.

Perls, F.S.

1969   Gestalt Therapy Verbatim. Real People
                Press: Moab Utah.

1976   The Gestalt Approach: An Eye Witness
                to Therapy. Real People Press: Moab
                Utah.

Perls, F.S., R. Hefferline,
and Paul Goodman

1977   Gestalt Therapy. Bantam Books: New
                York.

Sartre, Jean-Paul

1963   Search for a Method. Random House:
                Toronto, Canada.

Scheff, Thomas

1979   Catharsis in Healing, Ritual and Drama.
                Berkeley: University of California
                Press.

Sennet, Richard

    1977   The Fall of Public Man. New York:
                 Vintage Press.

Spiegelberg, Herbert

    1960   The Phenomenological Movement.
                 Martinus Hijhoff, The Hague.

Spreitzer, C.

    1979   "Multiple Roles and Psychological
                 Well-Being." Sociological Focus, Vol.
                 12, No. 2 (April).

Szasz, Thomas

    1961   The Myth of Mental Illness. Founda-
                 tions of a Theory of Personal Conduct.
                 New York: Delta.

Weil, Andrew

    1972   The Natural Mind. Houghton Mifflin
                 Co.: Boston, Mass.

*Department of Sociology, Chapman College, Orange,
California.

CHAPTER 2

THE LONG, LONG TRAIL FROM INFORMATION-GIVING TO BEHAVIORAL CHANGE

David Mace*

The nature of education is explored,
with particular reference to the contrast
between didactic and dynamic objectives.
In this context, questions are raised about
the effectiveness of the classroom as a
vehicle for bringing about the behavioral
and relational changes which appear to be
necessary for the significant improvement
of family life. As a basis for comparison,
the environment provided by a marriage and
family enrichment group is cited as a more
promising setting for initiating relational
readjustment.

As I write this, I can look back over fifty years
of continuous professional service. During those
years a major part of my time has been spent as an
educator, and particularly as a family life educator.
I was giving lectures on family living in 1938. Since
then, in a total of more than 60 different countries,
through the written and spoken word, I have tried to
teach people how to live happily and harmoniously in
the families to which they belonged.

My recollections of these varied experiences are
in themselves very pleasant ones. I have found that,
if there is anything resembling an international pass-
port, it is to be able to introduce oneself as an advocate of good family living. In all of the five
continents, and on both sides of the Iron Curtain,
this identity has unfailingly brought me an open-
handed welcome and a host of kind friends.

So far, so good. But as I now look back and reflect on my efforts to bring enlightenment, the picture is dimmed by a persistent shadow. In the last
few years, through my involvement with the marriage
and family enrichment movement, I have gained some new
insights which inevitably raise questions about the
effectiveness of what I had hitherto been trying to

37

do. These questions refuse to go away, and in this paper I have decided to share them with my colleagues. I do so not in order to spread discouragement, but rather to reexamine what we are doing and perhaps discover some ways of doing it better.

THE MEANING AND PURPOSE OF EDUCATION

Let me begin with the word "education." It derives from the latin verb <u>duco</u>, which means <u>to lead, conduct, draw,</u> or <u>bring</u>; together with the prefix <u>ex</u>, which means <u>out of</u>, or <u>from</u>. The concept is clearly to draw or bring out from the student what is already within him,[1] in terms of capability or potential--to create a climate or environment in which he can develop and utilize his inherent capacity for relational growth and development.

This is not, however, the sense in which we customarily use the word "education" in academic circles. We place the emphasis less on drawing out what is already there, and more on pumping in what is definitely <u>not</u> already there. What we pump in is <u>information</u>, so that the student may process it as <u>knowledge</u>, which is simply information systematically <u>filed</u> in the brain's computer system in such a way that it is later available for instant recall. An educated person is, first and foremost, a person who knows the answers to questions that are likely to be asked, at least in the field in which he has specialized.

I have no quarrel with this so far as it goes. The systematic accumulation of an increasing body of knowledge about ourselves, the world in which we live, and the universe beyond explains the remarkable progress human society has made during the era which we call civilization, and particularly during the last century. Given the massive amount of information that has now been collected, it is obvious that we must have people whose minds are filled with what is known in their particular field of specialization. How this will be changed as computers take over is a question that will be better answered ten years from now.

---

[1]Wherever the masculine pronoun is used hereafter, as in this case, I intend the reference to apply equally to either gender.

Storing knowledge in the brain is not, of course, the only task of our academic institutions. Students must also be trained to use knowledge they have received, by the acquisition of skills. That is the essential difference between the classroom and the laboratory. A clear distinction must be made between learning for knowing and learning for doing. In our particular field the distinction is better expressed as learning for knowing and learning for living.

As family life educators, therefore, we have to ask ourselves how our students make the transition from the classroom, where they learn to know, to the more private environment in which they learn to live. I am afraid that many of us have been content to focus heavily on the first, and leave students to make the transition to the second as best they can. And I am now coming to believe that the process we are expecting of them is far too complex to enable most students to make much significant progress in that direction.

Some years ago I read a statement written by Sidney Jourard (1970) which has haunted me ever since. Here it is:

> I have been struck by the incredible lack of artistry and creativity in marriage partners. Either person may be imaginative in making money or decorating a house, but when it comes to altering the design for their relationship, it is as if both imaginations had burnt out. For years, spouses go to sleep night after night, with their relationship patterned one way, a way that perhaps satisfies neither--too close, too distant, boring or suffocating--and on awakening the next morning, they reinvent their relationship in the same way. There is nothing sacred to the wife about the last way she decorated her house; as soon as it begins to pall, she shuffles things around until the new decor pleases her. But the way she and her husband interact will persist for years unchallenged and unchanged, long after it has ceased to engender delight, zest, or growth.

I could immediately identify with this situation. I saw in it myself, my wife, my relatives, my friends, my neighbors--all caught in a kind of paralysis in

which we seem unable to change our behavior. And I
asked myself whether I really believed that the people
who heard me speak, or who read my books, were somehow
released from their paralysis, and set free to change
their relationships for the better. As I recalled
occasional laudatory remarks, I entertained vague
hopes that one or two here and there might have
achieved this breakthrough; but I could not persuade
myself that what I put into the heads of the rest made
any significant difference in the way they behaved at
home--the tight bonds of long-established habits are
just too powerful.

HOW DOES KNOWING BECOMING LIVING?

I then asked myself how the transition between
knowing and living occurs, and I found that it is,
indeed, complex. To make it more intelligible, I drew
a diagram, which I will use here to continue our discussion. See Figure 1. The best analogy I could find
was rain pouring down from the sky and collecting in
a series of open troughs.

The rain represents information. In our highly
developed culture, this pours down upon our minds all
day and every day. Communication experts have made
fantastic estimates of the amount of information that
continually assails us. The human brain, I understand, can store between three and ten trillion pieces
of information; only a fraction of what we experience.
The rest, masses of it, simply flows out of the open
end of the top trough and is lost forever.

The little that is retained is selected because
we judge it to be important and useful. It is, therefore, processed as knowledge--filed in a manner that
will make it readily accessible for later use. Knowledge could be defined as systematically stored information. Our hope is that our students will organize
for themselves a mental file on family living, and
that this will come in handy when an exam has to be
taken or a term paper written.

That, however, is for us only one objective.
Our real hope is that we have planted a store of knowledge that the student will draw upon, now or later,
to enable him to manage his family relationship better
than he would have done if he had not taken the
course. That is a fair and reasonable expectation.

But how exactly will it happen? What is the process?

We have to begin by facing the fact that, at
best, only a small part of the knowledge will ever be
used. It is generalized information, not applicable
to the life situations of all students. The hope is,
however, that each student will find something applicable to his particular life situation. In the diagram, this is illustrated by a few drops filtering
through a narrow pipe, out of the accumulated store of
knowledge, and reaching a lower trough which represents insight.

Insight can be defined as a selected piece of
knowledge which I apply to my own personal life because it looks as if it could have special value for
me. If I put this piece of knowledge into use, it
could prevent me from getting into trouble, or it
could enhance my life in some worthwhile way. It
could pay off, by giving me clearer understanding of
myself and of my needs.

An objective of certain schools of psychotherapy
is to produce insight. And this has led some people
to believe that gaining insight is a guarantee of
change. Alas, not so. There are plenty of people
going around who are positively loaded with insight,
but it makes not a bit of difference to the way they
behave. I know this very well, because I have been
there.

What then happens to insight? A product of the
imagination, it is closely related to fantasy. The
knowledge I have acquired enables me to produce pleasant mental pictures. I see myself as a different
person, changed to be more effective, more attractive,
more successful. I see myself reorganizing my family
relationships in ways that are more fulfilling. I am
uplifted by this beautiful dream, and I feel better,
stronger, happier.

Fantasy is a way of escaping from reality. That
isn't bad in itself. Reality is at times so ominous
that escape may be necessary. Like going to a good
movie, our fantasies give us a break and we are re-
freshed and renewed. But it doesn't change reality.
We come back to the same old situation in the end.

41

In all sorts of ways we dissipate new knowledge in fantasies. We are deeply moved by a powerful sermon, see ourselves as kind and concerned about others, living a nobler life. We read self-help books, and imagine that we have done all that the book prescribed, and are now healthy, or reduced in weight, or self-assured. But in the end the dream slowly fades, and we are back where we started, unless, of course, we act on the insight we have received. Again there is a little pipe at the bottom of the trough. A few drops percolate through and get down to the next level. It is the level of <u>experimental</u> <u>action</u>.

Now things are really happening. I have learned something new, I have seen how it could make my life better and happier, and I have summoned the courage to make a decision. I will act! Now we are really in the business of living. At least, I am willing to make the experiment.

Why only experimental? Because I don't yet know whether this is going to be effective. It might not. This is a step in a new direction--toward growth, toward change. I could be wrong--this might not work for me. I'm willing to give it a try, that's all. But that's a lot.

So, I <u>act</u>. And what happens? It may turn out just I as fantasized it would. Or it may not. It may be effective for a time only. I may not have enough motivation to keep it up. Things might take an unexpected turn.

Making a change is always a risk. It is a step into the unknown. I may get hurt. Someone else may disapprove and block my action. I may be thought a fool, and be laughed at.

Unfortunately there is evidence to suggest that the other people in my life may try to stop me from changing. They are part of my system, and change on my part breaks the habit patterns, upsets the balance. This is threatening, and they may, therefore, try to prevent it. I still recall my sense of shock when some of my psychiatric colleagues at the University of Pennsylvania Medical School, investigating the marriages of alcoholics, discovered that when some husbands managed at last to get off the bottle, their wives subtly enticed them back into drinking--uncon-

scious responses, if you like, based on fear of losing
power and having to cope with a firm, assertive husband. But the fact remains that the "significant
others" in our lives tend to resist our attempt to
change our behavior.

So again, much of the water in the trough is
lost. It overflows and is wasted. A great many experimental actions come to nothing in the end.

But all is not lost. Again there is a tiny pipe,
and some drops get through to the next trough below.
This one is commitment to change. It happens when
experimental action is successful, and is repeated
often enough to produce encouragement and the stiffen-
ing of resolve. Behavior modification experts can
tell you how often you may have to repeat the experimental action until the old habit is finally broken
and the new behavior has become firmly established.

Not always does this happen, though. There is
still the possibility that resolve will falter, and
this trough also can leak. However, in the area of
family relationships, I would hazard a guess that
keeping up the change for about a year would mean that
the new knowledge had really been applied to your life
situation. Learning for knowing would then have gone
all the way into being transformed into learning for
living.

THE RELATIONAL FACTOR

But wait a minute. We are talking about family
life. That means relationships. And that must involve
at least two people, and quite possibly more. Now you
will understand why the diagram has a double series of
troughs. In this process we don't walk alone, or
change alone. Learning for living, if it is to be
fully effective, must involve at least two people acting together in each stage of the process. So we will
imagine that we have a married couple. In a relational sense, one can't change without the other. So they
must both move through the whole process together,
step by step. One may take the initiative, but if the
other doesn't go along, the process grinds to a halt.
Every move by the one must be congruent with a similar
move by the other. They must receive the information
and process it together, agreeing that it is relevant
to their shared life. They must gain insight togeth-

er, then they must agree together to make the necessary experimental action. If one draws back or quits,
the game is up. Therefore, if the change is to become
a vital one they must keep it up together long enough
for the mutual motivation to be sustained. What this
means in practice is that both must be sufficiently re-
warded to keep going until the goal has been reached.

All this obviously calls for a complex process
requiring mutual and sustained effort. That is not
easy to achieve. Obstacles will get in the way, disappointment will cut the nerve of effort. But if this
all sounds discouraging, remember that it is balanced
by a very positive advantage. Two people working
together to achieve growth and change can help and
support each other in the task. This is much easier
than doing it alone.

SOME IMPLICATIONS FOR FAMILY LIFE EDUCATION

Where is all this taking us? We started out
talking about family life education, and what does it
suggest? Isn't all this making something relatively
simple into something absurdly complicated?

I don't think so. Afer all, what is family life
education? What is our goal? Is it simply to pour
out information like a shower of rain, letting the
drops fall where they may? Or to fill the student's
brain, or a tiny corner of it, with some scraps of
knowledge about how families function. If that is
all, the task is comparatively simple.

But isn't our goal based on the assumption that
the students either are now, or are likely to be in
the future, members of families? A few of them may be
preparing to be family specialists--teachers, counselors, researchers. But for the rest, isn't our real
hope that they will put into practice the things we
are teaching them?

People need to be informed about the state of
family life in our contemporary culture. They need to
have a clear and balanced grasp of how families function, of the impact of social change and of clashing
value systems. They need to understand the dynamics
of interpersonal interaction between husband and wife,
parent and child. There is no doubt in my mind that

this is a subject that should be included in our educational curriculum.

However, the classroom and the lecture hall are associated strongly with didactic teaching which primarily emphasizes information-giving and knowledge-processing. Occasionally, an atmosphere may be generated that develops personal insights. Unless other members of the family are also participating in the course, even shared insight may not occur. So the further implementation of knowledge-processing must be delayed and carried on elsewhere. Yet those next stages in the process are the ones that present the real difficulties. So what our traditional forms of family life education do is begin a process which is very necessary and very promising, then breaks off and leaves it in the air while the most difficult and the most vital stages remain unaccomplished.

If this seems a harsh judgment, it gains some support from a few recent studies which have tried to measure the effectiveness of marriage preparation programs for engaged couples. Three such investigations have been made respective by Guldner (1971), Microys and Bader (Note 1), and Olson and Morem (1979). I lack the space here to describe these studies in detail, but they separately investigated programs for couples approaching marriage which covered either a weekend, a series of weekly sessions, or a succession of personal interviews. The content of these programs was confined to information-giving and knowledge-processing, in the form of talks, lectures, films, and group discussions. Applying pre-test and post-test procedures to these couples, the investigators found little or no significant change following the educational experience. The learning for knowing did not appear to carry over into learning for living.

Of course groups of engaged couples are not directly comparable with family life educational classes. However, one would imagine that the couples about to marry would be, if anything, more strongly motivated to put what they had learned to practical use in the near future. If they did not seem able to do so, is it likely that students in a course would carry over what they had learned and apply it when they did eventually marry, perhaps years later?

It might be argued that engaged couples are in a highly existential state of mind and, therefore, not easily teachable. Indeed, Guldner did find this to be the case. But the other two studies discovered that for these couples non-didactic premarital approaches were in fact effective--in one case, experiential group sessions, and in the other the use of an instrument that brought the couples into direct communication interchange with each other. It is, therefore, hard to avoid the conclusion that the general effectiveness of family life education in the classroom or lecture hall setting, in contributing to the successful management of later family relationships, remains to be proved.

I am, of course, well aware that this conclusion has been arrived at by other family life educators, and that a number of experiments have been made, with evaluative studies, to try to break out of the limitations set by purely didactic approaches. Available space will allow for only a few references.

Examples are the works of Blood (1972), Carkhuff, (1971), Duvall (1965), Hill (as cited by Kerckhoff, 1961), Kerckhoff (1960, 1961), and Luckey (1963, 1978). Specific experiments are described by Avery, Ridley, Leslie, and Handis (1979), Berger (1968), Cromwell and Thomas (1976), Daly and Reeves (1973), Dyer (1959), Jensen, Brady and Burr (1979), and Olson (1979).

CREATING ENVIRONMENTS FOR GROWTH AND CHANGE

If I may now go back to my diagram, the question here asked is: if the successive stages illustrated by the series of leaking troughs suggests a reasonable representation of the process of learning for living, what kind of environment would be needed to provide the most effective implementation of that process?

My use of the word "environment" is deliberate and important. Every developed human community tends to become a complex assortment of environments, each designed for a specific purpose. A home has different rooms, intended for the performance of particular functions. We eat in the dining room, relax in the living room, sleep in the bedroom. We do things in the bathroom that would be inappropriate in the hall.

46

It becomes natural to us to change our behavior patterns as we move about the house, in accordance with the changes of environment.

Likewise we structure towns and cities to provide a variety of environments, and adapt our behavior accordingly. We buy goods in a shopping center, read or borrow books in a library, worship in a church, learn in a school, receive medical treatment in a hospital. Each of these experiences requires different kinds of behavior on our part, and we become highly skilled in switching from one to the other.

Now suppose we were invited to create an environment in which we could most effectively learn the skills necessary for effective family living, what would it be like? As I asked myself this question, I found that I already had at least a partial answer.

For some years now my wife, Vera, and I have been experimenting with programs for marriage enrichment, and to some extent family enrichment. By this time, although enrichment programs are well known, I still regard the whole movement as being in an early experimental stage. Some research has been done to determine outcomes, but we still have many unanswered questions.

Even so, it seems that the perlexing questions about family life education could be, in part, answered by looking closely at what happens at a marriage enrichment retreat. Let us examine the main components:

1. A group of married couples come together for a weekend, or in a growth group for a series of weekly sessions. Experience suggests that the group must spend at least 15 to 18 hours together, in order to build a sense of community and of mutual trust. This roughly matches the time frame in a one-hour one-semester college course.

2. The leadership of the group is provided by a married couple--the same social unit as the group membership--who should be trained and qualified for their task, which is both to teach and to model what they teach.

47

3. The setting is relaxed and informal. The group of couples, including the facilitator couple, sit in a circle--departing as far as possible from the didactic pattern which has people sitting in rows, looking toward the teacher who is at a higher level, symbolizing authority and detachment.

4. The facilitator couple (or couples) begin with a teaching role, to impart a message. Make no mistake about this, marriage enrichment is based on a well-developed theoretical frame of reference. The knowledge communicated, however, is not presented as didactic material. It is shared as relational experience which the facilitators are offering to the other couples in the group.

5. After each idea of concept is presented and modeled by the facilitators, the other couples are given an opportunity to apply it directly to their own relationship in private interchange with each other; or in some models, in open group sharing. Exercises carefully designed for this purpose are offered--an effective method is for the partners to write down their relevant thoughts and feelings, separately fist, then share them with each other. The purpose is to encourage application of knowledge received directly to the relationship so insight may be generated and shared between husband and wife.

6. Further exercises are offered which allow couples, if they wish, to move straight into experimental activity--trying out new ways of communicating and interacting with each other, and finding out what is effective and comfortable for them.

7. Toward the end of the event, the couples are given an opportunity, in the light of their new insights and experiences, to plan future goals which may open the way for desired growth and change. They may, if they wish, register with the group a shared commitment made to each other.

USING KNOWLEDGE FOR BETTER FAMILY LIVING

What we see here is the deliberate creation of a special environment in which all the components of the transition from knowing to doing can be compassed in a limited period of time. When this is done in the right setting, it appears that these growth processes can follow each other in quite rapid succession.

In this deliberately structured environment, the action part of the learning is not separated from the knowledge intake. They both take place in immediate sequence. In the classroom, by contrast, the students are normally not open to each other experientially, but only intellectually. The experiential follow-up may or may not occur afterwards.

I wish to assert, however, that even in the enrichment group the process of growth and change is not completed. It is only begun. This is the present weakness of the marriage enrichment movement. Nothing more is done in the first weekend experience than to initiate the ongoing growth process. It is, in my opinion, a serious mistake to suggest that some kind of miracle occurs, that couples' lives are changed by the intensity of the experience they undergo. Actually, what happens is only attitudinal change, and any ensuing behavioral change is a process that occurs only over time--as already suggested, one year would be a reasonable period to allow for the necessary alteration of established patterns. What is now being seen more and more clearly, is that what has occurred in the special environment, provided by the group of couples mutually supporting each other, needs to be continued in a similar environment--a "support group" of couples--meeting at monthly intervals for a period of a year with commitment of all couples to behavioral change. I have personally observed dramatic and lasting change, in a number of couples who have followed this process.

While these experiments in enrichment go on, I believe we need to continue our efforts to measure the longitudinal results of the more traditional patterns of family life education. I repeat that I believe didactic courses in family life education have a valid place within our educational system. We have come to where we are today as a result of increased knowledge. Our social and personal services to families are based

49

on knowledge. Part of the reason why family life is
in such serious trouble in our nation is because widespread ignorance about the family maintains a fertile
soil for the dissemination of all kinds of distorted
ideas propagated by ill-informed opportunists. So
knowledge-processing courses on the family must be
continued and increased.

But, the so-called "functional" family living
course needs reexamination. It is embarrassing for
well-informed, trained, and dedicated teachers to
present students information, on the assumption that
they are being trained for more effective family living later, without having empirical assurance that
anything significant really happens to them beyond the
knowledge stored in their heads. Longitudinal studies
are difficult and costly to make. But we really need
to know, with greater degree of precision than we do
at present, to what extent our students are really
learning for living.

It will be readily observed that in ventilating
this concern I am better supplied with questions than
with answers. Yet I reaffirm my belief that there is
unexplored potential both in family life education and
in marriage and family enrichment which awaits our
discovery, and which our culture sorely needs.

Figure 1.

INFORMATION

KNOWLEDGE

INSIGHT

EXPERIMENTAL
ACTION

COMMITMENT
IN GROWTH

SHARED GROWTH

REFERENCE NOTES

1. Microys, G., Baker, E. <u>Do Pre-marital programs really help</u>? Unpublished manuscript, 1978 (Available from the Department of Family and Community Medicine, University of Toronto, Ontario, Canada.)

2. Olson, D., & Morem, R. Evaluation of five pre-marital programs. Unpublished manuscript, 1977. (Available from the Department of Family Social Science, University of Minnesota, St. Paul, MN.)

*David Mace is Professor Emeritus of Family Sociology, Bowman Gray School of Medicine, Winston-Salem, North Carolina 27103.

BIBLIOGRAPHY

Avery, A.W., Ridley, C.A.,
Leslie, L.A., & Handis, M.

  1979   "Teaching Family Relations to Dating
             Couples Versus Noncouples: Who Learns
             Better?" The Family Coordinator, 1,
             41-45.

Berger, M.

  1968   "The Continuous Parent Education Group."
             The Family Coordinator, 2, 105-109.

Blood, R.O.

  1972   The Family. New York: Free Press.

Carkhuff, R.R.

  1971   Developing Human Resources. New York:
             Holt, Rinehart & Winston.

Cromwell, R.E.
and Thomas, V.L.

  1976   "Developing Resources for Family Poten-
             tial." The Family Coordinator, 1, 13-20.

Daly, R.T. and
Reeves, J.P.

  1973   "The Use of Human Interaction Laborator-
             ies in Family Life Courses." The Family
             Coordinator, 4, 413-417.

Duvall, E.M.

  1965   "How Effective are Marriage Courses?"
             Journal of Marriage and the Family, 27,
             176-184.

Dyer, D.

  1959   "A Comparative Study Relating Marital
             Happiness to University Courses Helpful
             in Marital Adjustment." Marriage and

Family Living, 21, 230-232.

Guldner, C.A.

1971   "The Post-marital: An Alternative to
               Premarital Counseling." The Family
               Coordinator, 2, 115-116.

Jensen, M.R.,
Brady, L.G., &
Burr, W.R.

1979   "The Effects of Student Practice on
               Several Types of Learning in a Func-
               tional Marriage Course." The Family
               Coordinator, 28, 217-227.

Jourard, S.

1970   "Reinventing Marriage: The Perspective
               of a Psychologist." In H.A. Otto (Ed.),
               The Family in Search of a Future. New
               York: Appleton-Century-Crofts.

Kerckhoff, R.E.

1960   "Evaluating Family Life Education."
               Merrill-Palmer Quarterly, 6, 187-191.

1961   "Family Life Education in America." In
               H.R. Christensen (Ed.), Handbook of
               Marriage and the Family. Chicago:
               Rand McNally.

Luckey, E.B.

1978   "Relationship of Marriage Counseling and
               Family Life Education." Personnel and
               Guidance Journal, 420-424.

1978   "Family Life Education Revisited." The
               Family Coordinator, 27, 69-73.

Olson, T.D.

1979   "Marriage Education: An Illustration of the Process." Family Perspective, 1, 27-32.

CHAPTER 3

INDIVIDUAL AND FAMILY WELL-BEING OVER THE LIFE COURSE:
PRIVATE AND PUBLIC DIMENSIONS

Douglas B. Gutknecht*

I. INTRODUCTION

Studying the individual within numerous life
paths and stages, including marital, familial, work,
and leisure is becoming a topic of interdisciplinary
interest in the social and human sciences (Brim and
Baltes, 1980; Kenniston, 1977). Sociologists, psychologists, health scientists, anthropologists, his-
torians, educational and policy researchers, each
reveal partial snapshots of a holistic picture, the
implications of which will promote a better understanding of the life-long process of optimum development and well-being, both personal and familial.
This chapter draws inspiration from the work of numerous pioneers in the field of life course research,
family studies, socialization and developmental
psychology (Brofenbrenner, 1970, 1979; Elder, 1974;
Riley, et al., 1972; Clausen, 1972; Brim, 1966;
Riegal, 1975; Neugarten, 1969). The life course is
defined as including numerous paths and dimensions including family, career, educational, leisure, public
service, which provides opportunities, influences, and
obstacles in the unending search for personal development and humanistic social change. The family provides one of the major life paths and contexts for
personal development as well as a challenge for humanistic affirmation of a viable future for unborn generations to come. Numerous issues and problems of life
long development find expression at those points in a
life course where one begins to seriously consider
living together permanently, taking a life-long partner in marriage, deciding to have children, matching
families and career paths, divorcing, starting second
families, or watching grown children leave the nest.

After briefly defining the concept of well-being
in part two, a discussion of the underlying assumptions of this analysis follows in part three. Then
part four introduces the relationship of generational
cohorts, economic and family life course well-being.
Part five probes the dimensions of self and well-
being; while part six discusses the importance of

57

social support systems for general life course well-being, obviously impacting the family.

II. WELL-BEING DEFINED

Well-being is defined as the opportunity to maximize one's potential and enlarge one's possibilities for meaningful transactions with self, family, and society. It requires self-knowledge, including the desire and opportunity for life long learning and meaningful involvement in personal goals, family life, meaningful work, and public activities. Well-being is rooted in a basic biological level of fitness, not just absence of disease, and assures flexibility of self, the ability to deal with ambiguous situations and stressful daily encounters. Individuals derive it from actively defining, interpreting, and constructing meaningful bridges to other humans beings through social involvement whether in family, work, or community. Well-being is more than coping, although this is one tool or skill essential over the long haul, it includes involvement in active and challenging activities. Well-being is rooted in the awareness that aging by itself does not produce inevitable decline of one's human potential for active involvement and meaning. Role obligations at different stages of life provide both opportunity and obstacles for "being" that is well, optimal, actualized, world affirming. This holistic definition is offered only as a starting point for your reflection and expansion.

III. ASSUMPTIONS REGARDING WELL-BEING OVER THE LIFE COURSE

This analysis builds upon fundamental assumptions regarding the humanistic pursuit of well-being over the life course. First, individual change, growth, and development is much more than chronological aging (growing old). The inevitability of change requires a look at self development in an experimental manner, rejecting a rigid view of externally imposed stages and an imposed set of stereotyped expectations.

Second, structured social processes, transitions, patterns, and structures systematically influence and set the stage for personal development and well-being over the life course. Intrinsic dimensions of life course transitions include the timing, continuity, extent, and number of role relationships at different stages of life (Foner and Kertzer 1978). For example, a movement from the role of single to married may create demands, expectations, and disruptions for individuals trying to adapt to other life changes, particularly when also in school or employed. Recognition of possible discontinuities permits a more flexible attitude towards family role experimentation, via dating or living together, in order to prepare oneself for new responsibilities of living in an intimate setting with another human being. Flexible practices that allow individuals to learn about future role obligations help individuals better adapt to changing social demands, ultimately reducing possibilities of excessive role strain and family violence or withdrawal to drugs. Adolescent and young adults need more flexibility and support from society in order to reduce the strains of role transitions and possible discontinuities. Learning how to anticipate and deal with role conflicts and strain is essential for individuals desiring to maximize their human potential. For example, divorce rates are highest for those within the 15-19 year old category, who often lack both material resources and role skills needed to handle life's inevitable conflicts and stresses.

IV. DEMOGRAPHY, ECONOMICS, FAMILY, AND LIFE COURSE WELL-BEING

The idea of generation or cohort is heretaken as a starting point and for comparisons. Social and demographic studies of generational cohorts provide one perspective of how well-being is impeded, or sustained over the life course. Individuals are part of generations or population cohorts when they are born at the same time. Picture society as a large python that swallows a huge pig (i.e., cohort) that moves the entire length of its body as a big bulge. This baby boom bulge is now moving through our American society python creating many consequences because of its large size. Likewise the well-being of individuals in this large post-war baby boom generation is affected by the numerous social and historical events existing at the time of entry and movement.

For example, those born between 1946-1964, called the post-war baby boom generation, experienced an element of communality, as a result of entering society during a time of economic growth, suburbanization, increasing use of automobiles and T.V., expansion of public education, including variations like junior high school and public community college. World War II led to a reduction and delay in childbirth which then spurred a post-war baby boom. Large numbers of baby boom children moving through occupational and family roles at later stages in the life course created both opportunities and obstacles. For example, women of this baby boom generation experienced a marriage squeeze and delayed married for several years longer than previously (Glick, 1979). The principal causes resulted from both large numbers in this cohort entering the marriage market and the fact that the large increase of women in their most marriageable ages (18-24 years) who normally marry men two to three years their senior could not find spouses. This occurred because there are fewer men available from the previous generation. The imbalance of available men to women because of lower birth rates for men in the early fifties began an imbalanced situation which continued every year because the pool of men 2 to 3 years older were born when birth rates were lower.

Today many post World War II baby boomers occupy social roles like college student for longer periods of time because we have stretched the transition period of college as a result of graduate and professional training. Longer periods of schooling provides an escape valve for society because the occupational world can't absorb such large numbers of potential workers, in addition to the larger training requirements of a highly technological society. The consequences for individuals ready to experiment with adult roles, love, sex, marriage, or living together is often negative. The inability to enter the work world and assume adult occupational responsibilities creates transitional problems for those desiring to marry and begin a family after graduation. More graduate school marriages with excessive strains leads to high divorce rates among this cohort. Those who do enter the work world experience increasing competition from a large number of individuals, competing for the same jobs and careers.

Our society must itself learn how to better educate and prepare young adults for the joint responsibilities of being workers, lovers, friends, helpers, communicators, and stress reducers at earlier ages. Part of the task involves learning about the life long developmental tasks of fully functioning human beings

including work and sexuality before major problems
arise. Younger adults need to be challenged and given
meaningful responsibilities for their own futures, including work, love, and society. Young adults themselves need to recognize that autonomy and informed
choice involves responsibility for the rights of
others. We must ask how prepared we are to assume the
responsibility for guiding the growth of others and
sharing intimacy.

This generation influenced the emergence of new
arrangements between family and work paths. Traditionally women's lives revolved around the family, although the pattern began to change after World War II.
First older married women in their 40's and 50's began
to enter the labor force as they completed their
childbirth responsibilities at earlier ages and had
more years to live after their children's departure.
During the late 1960's increases in consumer expectations along with post Vietnam War stagflation contributed to the necessity of more women working. The
economy itself began to depend on women working in the
service sector. Career families began to plan family
and work paths together, in order to insure the quality of life, consumption and future options that middle
class families came to expect as the Post World War II
American dream. More women began to work while raising young children and the percentage of married working women exceeded 50% in the early 1980's, up from
30% in 1960.

The changing nature of economic realities created
altered patterns of life course paths for both men and
women, but particularly for women. Women began to enter the labor force in the 1960's particularly in the
service sector supported by a growing welfare state
mentality. During the late 19th and early 20th century women often staggered their work lives as alter-
nated cycles in which they worked until the childbirth
cycle began. World Wars I and II provided the emergence of development paths where women started work,
stopped for families, and started again in later life
after children left the nest. The newly emerging pattern of planning career or work cycles in conjunction
with family responsibilities began after World War II
but developed most rapidly in the 1960's. Traditionally men plan their involvement in family and career
as simultaneous developments because women assumed the
primary responsibility for child rearing: men's

career lives took precedence over family life. Today
the need for women to contribute to the economic well-
being of the family unit has created potential conflicts over how to integrate career and family responsibilities for both spouses. Likewise the very fact
that a woman contributes to family resources in the
era of excessive inflation enlarges her power and
decision making authority in the family unit. Women,
because they now more often possess independent access to wages, can leave an undesirable marriage because they no longer fear starvation. Likewise men
seemed more concerned with the emerging role of
fatherhood, recognizing the importance of quality time
spent with their children, not mere quantity. The
idea of the quality of time, life planning, and priorities seems to be on the upsurge throughout numerous
social institutions including family, education, leisure, work, and even retirement.

The changing patterns of career and family life
paths creates potential for discontinuities and conflicts because so many married women entered the labor
force at the same time in jobs that might be characterized as low paid, low level, and dead-end. Most of
these jobs were in information processing areas as
clerks, receptionists, and secretaries, or service industries such as health care, education, insurance,
banking, sales, etc. Many of these new-low-level
white and pink collar jobs were temporary, part time,
with few fringes, and no future. However, because
families often needed a working woman to combat the
ravages of inflation, the old escape clause used by
previous generations of women no longer proved available. Women were asked to accommodate their schedules
to both families and employers. Unlike men whose life
patterns altered little upon the decision to marry or
have children, women often must sychronize their family and career paths, with possible conflicts and role
overload the result.

Role overload results in fatigue and other symptoms of stress which both spouses need to recognize.
Fatigue is the physical wear and tear on our bodies.
In addition, time pressure occurs because many individuals don't know how to manage their time in order
to ensure high quality interaction. Such overload
resulting in competing loyalties to home and career
may also intensify emotional conflict unless spouses
are willing to clearly communicate and negotiate the

changing financial, social, and emotional reasons for
working or not working which might reduce guilt and
allow the positive aspects of the situation to stand
out. Higher educated women appear more likely to
force changes in both public and private worlds because working provides both financial and social -
psychological gratifications.

Short term discontinuities may create needed
changes in the long run as women demand changes in
career and family life and men must renegotiate old
sex role, decision making, and authority patterns.
The implications of the increased work force participation, income, and ultimate power in family decision making may upset functional thinking that suggests the necessity in marriage and family life of
rigid and distinct spheres of activity or division of
labor between husband and wife. The husband can no
longer be seen as the sole link to the world of work
(i.e., the instrumental role), the breadwinner, and
the wife the emotional helpmate (i.e., the expressive
role), and nurturer. Well-being may require both
spouses to utilize their undeveloped skills and attributes in order to resolve the many conflicts that lie
ahead. The idea that every marriage is really two,
his and hers, or includes many marriages at different
stages (i.e., childless, childfilled, empty nest) in
the marital cycle, may finally gain acceptance as the
conflictual underside of marital life is brought out
in the open in a more sustained and negotiated manner.
Hopefully such new honesty will reduce hostility and
bouts of brutal violence, which once repressed constantly reappear. Such conflicts may increase the
divorce rate and create marital strains, in the short
run, particularly for working couples wedded in traditional sex roles. However, in the long run all society will benefit by this search for well-being in family life which requires us to humanistically change the
devalued roles associated with the private aspects of
domestic life. Such is best accomplished not by rhetoric but by changes in both public and private dimensions of sexual inequality in domestic role responsibilities, wages, career opportunities, public support
systems for child care, flexible work hours, etc. In
a class society the public realm must be utilized to
lighten the burden of private troubles for families,
particularly for wives and children. This occurs because a class based society pushes those at the bottom
of the economic ladder, particularly single parent

families headed by females, to work in order to survive. Yet the ideology of democratic equality assumes that somehow all families are equal and can prepare their children through private means to compete for a better future. However, without public support, any private energy or initiative families may muster will soon be drained away and the rhetoric of a private sanctuary will become instead a living nightmare.

In this view both the private and public external realms need to become integrated. Personal and public change must both occur; the reordering of relationships between family and work provides one example of how these two dimensions can become integrated in a way that overcomes a traditional emphasis on the super-mom, super-career-women. The changing materialistic pressures of the modern world may force a cultural and ideological reevaluation of inequality, beginning in one of the most important and pivotal institutions, the family, that has merely responded to external pressures during the past 30 years. At this point let's examine the relationship of private and public well-being using a slightly different focus.

V. SELF, FAMILY, AND THE LIFE COURSE: INTRINSIC SOURCES OF WELL-BEING

Well-being over a lifetime is closely related to how we sustain our growing, active sense of self within challenging, opportunity filled environments. Internal dimensions of well-being include a sense of meaningfulness, authentic feelings and emotions, caring attitudes, a high level of cognitive functioning and education, multiple role involvements, biological health, and high level of energy and vigor.

A sober yet hopeful assessment of our situation in the modern world suggests that:

Increasingly today, the members of our society know that we are not set, certain, irrevocable substantial selves. They increasingly recognize that who we are, what we are, is continually in the process of becoming through our continual struggles, are notable to dictate the outcomes of this flux . . . the flux is crucial in our everyday lives (Douglas and Johnson, 1977:66).

Well-being is thus rooted in our view of ourselves as both situation and emergent. Our "brute being" is "that core of feeling and perception that is our innermost selves, our being" (Douglas and Johnson, 1977: 3). Framing this discussion within existential sociology, our intellectual focus must be toward the importance of direct, personal experience, the passion for living, making sense of the world, and responsibly accepting the consequences of our attitudes, values, social decisions, and actions. We construct ourselves as feeling beings in a social world. A belief in indestructability of our deepest being and the importance of our feelings and emotions (i.e., situated being or self), allows us to emerge as selves in process. This view of self rejects rigid reductionism and the belief that people can be reduced to labels. Such labels, leading to tacit approval of predetermined personal, ultimately social changes, channel our attention away from our humanistic possibilities for growth and well-being, particularly within family life. This sense of possibility and purpose is intimately tied to holistic view of consciousness and meaning.

The consequence of blocking our sense of purpose, our vital system, results in the loss of objective meaning; by blocking our larger purposes and outside meanings, we elevate our own petty problems, to unreal and fantastic proportions and become neurotic, anxious, and self preoccupied (Wilson, 1972:225).

We lose well-being as we lose consciousness of our social and human connections; a sense of the larger purposes and values in life. Losing meaning often results in turning inward to guilt, inactivity, and passivity. For example, those who begin to experience family problems often seem destructively prone to turn their gaze on themselves, or project their hostilities on other family members who function as merely mirror images of their own weaknesses. The alcoholic spouse has lost a sense of meaning or purpose. In this view consciousness loses its power to focus, to engage, to take the role of the other, to confront, to connect, to analyze with compassion, to join forces. In fact, "we let the robot take over," we become passive, bored, frustrated, spiteful, amplifying the bad messages and ignoring the good:

Man is a many-layered creature, whose highly

complex structure is largely 'robitic.' The
unconscious mind is an enormous computer,
its circuits need to be 'triggered' by certain definite signals. The vital reserves
by a feeling of suffocation . . . the mind,
health, the whole needs to be exercised. The
mentally healthy individual habitually calls
upon fairly deep levels of vital reserves. An
individual whose mind is allowed to become
dormant - so that only the surface is disturbed begins to suffer from circulation problems (Wilson, 1972:222).

The mind needs to amplify, to contact deep levels of
vital reserves and energy - otherwise the trivial, the
mundane hassles, raise their heads, leading to fragmentation, passivity, breakdown in dialog and communication, stress, burnout, and ultimately dread of
death. Humanistic attitudes toward a sense of possibility and a meaningful future, provide a vision for
caring about others and not giving up after things
don't work out. Affirmation of possibilities, goals
and visions of the future provide a link for our
consciousness.

Humanistic attitude toward self, family and society highlights the possibility of meaning, purpose,
and value priorities by focusing on the concepts of
energy, time, and commitment (Marks, 1977:921-926).
Discounting the scarcity approach to these concepts
we can assume that an expansionary view of self and
consciousness does not drain away vital time and energy by making social commitments. In this view we expand energy and time by enlarging our commitments and
social involvements, if we learn how to prioritize
time. Priority time, time we choose to share with
significant others, or in the pursuit of meaningful
careers, can actually increase our energy, both physical and psychological. The drain view or scarcity
view of time assumes that energy is severely limited.
Believing this can actually become a self-fulfilling
prophecy for us. Again the adage in personal and
family life becomes the quality of time spent with
others, not just quantity. In this view activity becomes a boring routine that tires us, not something
that rejuvenates us. Such rejuvenation can hardly
appear, however, if individuals feel responsibilities
are dumped on them. In contrast, activity can actually produce energy: because it is rooted in our cells

and is triggered by adenosine triphosphate (ATP):

> The body stimulates the production of A.T.P.
> from glucose only through the consumption of
> A.T.P. in activity; hence the process of pro-
> duction of human energy is inseparably a part
> of the consumption of energy. Activity is
> thus necessary to stabilize the production of
> human energy. And even while we are spending
> it we are also converting more of it for later
> use (Marks, 1977:925-926).

Although healthy and nourishing foods and exercise are
obviously an important component of this holistic view
of mind-body integration, one can see that meaningful
projects, goals, values, attitudes, also call forth
vital energy reserves, and expand the vigor for life:

> Abundant energy is 'found' for anything to which
> we are highly committed, and we often feel more
> energetic after having chosen it; also, we tend
> to 'find' little energy for anything to which
> we are uncommitted, and choosing these things
> leaves us feeling spent, drained and exhausted
> (Marks, 1977:927).

Time itself is not scarce but varies with meaningful commitments, valued activities, attitudes towards tasks, cultural scripts and institutionalized
roles:

> Like energy it is flexible, waxing, abundant,
> or scarce, slow or fast, expanded or contracted,
> depending upon very particular sociocultural and
> personal circumstances (Marks, 1977:929).

Such a view is not entirely incompatible with notions
of time as a scarce commodity. We do often feel
stressed and overloaded. Thinking about the quality
and priority of time requires us to plan flexible life
patterns. We must think about ways to better bargain
with ourselves, our families, employers, and government to support trade offs between clock measured,
quantified, obligated, work time, leading to extrinsic
rewards and quality leisure time; that time we truly
cherish which leads to intrinsic rewards, values,
pleasures, and ultimately human betterment.

Lack of commitment often functions as an excuse for noninvolvement, lack of energy, or rushed pace. By constantly misplacing our social priorities we end up being manipulated while failing to communicate to our spouse, friends, and children our needs for disengaging and creatively "closing" (Klapp, 1979: 12-22). Commitment is not a scarce commodity but requires some thought regarding its priorities. The principal point here is the need to reconceptualize the drain - scarcity metaphors, applied to energy, time, commitment, and consciousness. Energy is expanded by meaningful life events, social connections, family, love, friendship, challenging relationships which somehow work to fill us with enthusiasm and motivation. Thus, well-being over the life course increases, as we risk private moments for intimacy, love, friendship, and reach for public, social, and community involvements. The key is that we reflect upon and prioritize those meaningful commitments which will make a difference in our lives.

Human energy is neither infinite nor biologically constant, but instead circumscribed by socio-cultural variables:

> The findings reported here lead empirical support to the proposition the involvement in multiple roles does not necessarily result in role strain . . . additionally, the flow of commitment across roles will shift depending on the stages of the life cycle. These and other factors tend to diffuse the flow of commitments across several activity clusters. While individuals may find general well-being in whatever roles they enact, the findings reported here lend oblique empirical support for Siber's (1974) role accumulation theory in the sense of predicting incremental benefits as a function of multiple roles (Spretzer, et al., 1979:147).

VI. WELL-BEING AND SUPPORT SYSTEMS: EDUCATION, WORK AND FAMILY LIFE

Well-being, both personal and familial, involves innumerable transitions and decisions, regarding comingling paths and time tables for education, family, career, leisure, consumption, and life style. Often transitions, involving new intensive obligations and enlarged tasks, create personal stress, reducing well-being, and the quality of family life. Sheer numbers of individuals, in large cohorts or autonomous and creative individuals, may break out of their rigid patterns, pointing the way to alternative tasks, time tables, transitions, and life paths. Such ground-breaking responses sometimes require larger social and structural changes, in order to institutionalize support systems. Other times individuals break the bonds of rigid expectations by sheer will and self determination. Today we must recognize that family and personal well-being are intimately tied to the available structural and social support systems which either limit or enhance options and potentials.

It is important to have flexible life scheduling in order to break down the arbitrary patterns, time tables, and normative expectations associated with what he calls the "education-work retirement lock-step" (Best, 1980:3-11). This lockstep is made up of old predetermined, institutionalized patterns, that once served a purpose, and are now difficult to change because traditions die slowly, long after the original reasons for existing disappear. The lockstep is a sequence of age and time graded activities - youth for education, adulthood for work, and older age for retirement. This stereotyped sequence is built upon a one-dimensional life plan (e.g., linear life plan), that wastes precious human resources, squanders human energy, and reduces flexible life options. The lockstep is built upon the metaphors of energy scarcity and drain. The option and joy of planning alternate life paths, time tables, and careers over the life course is ignored. Flexible life scheduling remains an undernourished alternative.

There are creative ways to reconceptualize the choices between education and work, work and retirement, education and retirement, which impact individual and family well-being (Best, 1980:35-95). For example, evolving technological skill and knowledge requirements, and rapidly changing, increasingly sophisticated work environments, require new thinking about how education prepares one for work over a lifetime. Meaningful work, one of the most important components of individual well-being, can be promoted by such techniques as lifelong study, retraining, sabbaticals, better career planning, educational credits for work experience, and work credit for time spent in school, pursuing the enrichment of adult learning.

In addition, the idea of cramming all education into narrow arbitrary stages, like youth or early adulthood, prolongs boredom, irrelevance, inactivity, poverty, and practical knowledge of the world. Such lockstep beliefs about education requires a reevaluation of our beliefs that we are through learning once we complete college. Well-being is actually promoted by allowing students to work while in school, join cooperative education programs, and alternate periods of work and education throughout their lives.

Flexible life scheduling should be joined with public recognition of how social support systems encourage or discourage individual, family, and social well-being. We must learn to diversify our options by promoting assessment of individual and family needs, goals, plans by experimental social and policy support programs:

> For educational and economic reasons, work is likely to be increasingly interspaced with education during youth, with the result that youth may no longer be primarily reserved for schooling, and formal education will be extended into the center of the life cycle . . . Finally, increasing levels of educational attainment may further encourage flexible life patterns by fostering work scheduling reforms in response to the needs of better educated workers, new values toward leisure, and pressure for the notation and sharing of limited quality jobs" (Best, 1978:45).

Learning how to cope with lifelong stress, strain, and burnout also indicates the importance of providing support systems to assist families and workers on the job (Warr and Wall, 1975; Cobb, 1976; Seyle and Brecht, 1980; Payne and Cooper, 1980; Girdano and Everly, 1980; Chernis, 1980). Although scarcity metaphors and theories may not govern the use of human energy, the facts of work stress, overload, and role strain remain. Excessive amounts of alienating and meaningless work distract from a human feeling of competence and mastery, which decreases a sense of quality involvement with personal goals, family, friends, and community activities (French, Rosenthal, and Cobb, 1974). Options open to the individual as

70

part of flexible life scheduling allow an individual to arrange a better fit between changing personal needs, family, and work responsibilities and social supports, particularly when the fit creates stress and strain. Let's explore the relationship between family and work.

The emerging emphasis in recent organization literature on human resources and the importances of human relations for productivity has focused attention of the issue of the mutual interaction of family life and work environments (Mouton and Blake, 1981). The family needs to be supported not merely because it promotes productivity and economic growth, but because the foundation of economic and ultimately personal well-being lies in social and ultimately family well-being. One finds, however, compelling arguments that the bottom line of human resources is return or investment (Killian, 1976). What is invested in families dramatically affects how individuals perform on the job. Likewise, what happens at work certainly impacts how individuals respond to each other at home, which in turn carries over into the next work day. Difficulties, conflicts, lack of assistance or resources, stress and strain, in either family or work life, creates an increasing deteriorating situation in both spheres. Our sense of satisfaction and the health of our society is intimately linked to the productive use of our societal and human resources. Our private and public lives do intertwine even if we act as though they are worlds apart.

There are three links which respond to internal family and external work demands. The wife's work link, the husband's work link, and the family link:

> Work links include stamina, one's orientation to the content of what one is doing, one's reaction to the organization where one is employed, and one's relations with the people with whom one works: peers, supervisors, subordinates. The family link, similarly, encompasses many different relations, including those with one's spouse, one's children, and parents, and with the community . . (Bailyn, 1978:121).

The traditional pattern has until recently emphasized the accommodation of family links to work links. Frequency of residential movement, type and number of schools attended, child care options, even family life styles are often influenced by work related pressures and standards. However, the era of the organizational man and the homogeneous suburban family, with one spouse commuting to work and one spouse remaining home, appears over. The forces of inflation and high economic expectations, along with the demands of dual career families for public supports, along with the resurgence of interest in leisure life and personal enjoyment, caused a reevaluation of the value of career advancement, and the need for geographic mobility.

New standards regarding work and family links support the change in couples' values and life goals, emphasizing the importance of intrinsic issues in addition to extrinsic issues. Two wage earners can be more picky about trade offs between more money versus less family life. Longer term involvement in the labor force by women has increased their sophistication in bargaining for equal pay for equal work, and lessens the demand for the male to make bread winner sacrifices for just "any old job." Issues of housing costs and living standards and potential sources of support services by companies and in the community, now become real issues for dual career families. When faced with the decision of moving or staying with the same company, or in the same geographical area, families often choose to stay put.

The growing involvement of women in the world of high finance banking, insurance, and other service and white or pink collar sectors of a post-industrial service society, enlarge demands on both private and public organizations and corporations to respond to this relatively new situation. Increasing numbers of women, now over 50%, work in order to achieve economic and social goals promised by our leaders throughout the post World War II decades. Support systems are emerging more frequently in the corporate world - corporate day care, job sharing (Arkin and Dobrofsky, 1978:122-137), employee assistance, like financial, legal, health, family, and drug counseling, flexible "cafeteria" type benefit packages that allow trade offs between benefits such as child care versus pensions, and relocation job opportunities for one's spouse, in addition to moving assistance expenses and cost of living bonus and adjustments.

Personal and social well-being over the life
course is best facilitated by such progress which
allows more meaningful involvement in personal work,
community, and family life. The key is participation
and learning to forge new relationships, open avenues
of growth, and challenging institutions like the work
place to offer needed support programs and systems.
We must understand the forces that narrow our lives
and place us in rigid work, family, and community
roles and timetables. We can break out of the lockstep mentality. Stereotype and lockstep-thinking,
about education, careers, health, family, retirement,
and institutional change limit our ability to learn
and change. Developing skills, resources, and support
systems require lifelong commitment and participation
in personally meaningful social change projects. Increasing rapid social changes, a fact of life in
America for several decades, also requires the individual to assume more responsibility for personal and
familial well-being. We must become more involved
with those decisions that impact our personal, family
and community life. This task calls for numerous
assessment, decision making, organizational, and
political skills. The problem of supporting family
life in its various dimensions is essentially one of
promoting holistic development of our human potentials
in numerous social dimensions, career, and life paths.
Public well-being should positively impact our sense
of purpose, meaning, commitment and hope for control
over private well-being in an increasingly turbulent
world.

BIBLIOGRAPHY

Arkin, W. and Lynne Dobrofsky

19 78   "Job Sharing" in Robert and Rhona
             Rapoport (eds), Working Couples. New
             York: Harper & Row.

Bailyn, Lotte

19 78   "Accommodation of Work to Family" in
             Robert and Rhona Rapoport (eds),
             Working Couples. New York: Harper &
             Row.

Best, Fred

19 80   Flexible Life Scheduling: Breaking the
             Education - Work - Retirement Lockstep.
             New York: Praeger.

Brim, O.

1966   "Socialization Through the Life Cycle"
             in Orville Brim and Stanton Wheeler,
             Socialization After Childhood: Two
             Essays. New York: Wiley.

Brim, O.G. and
D.B. Baltes (eds.)

19 80   Life-span Development and Behavior
             (vol. 3), New York: Academic Press.

Bronfenbrenner, V.

19 79   The Ecology of Human Development, Ex-
             periments by Nature and Design. Cam-
             bridge, Mass.: Harvard University
             Press.

1970   Two Worlds of Childhood. New York:
             Russel Sage.

Chernis, Albert

1980   Burnout in Human Service Organizations.
             New York: Praeger.

74

Clausen, J.

1972   "The Life Course of Individuals" in
            M. Ruby, M. Johnson, and A. Foner,
            Aging and Society III: A Sociology of
            Age Stratification. New York: Russel
            Sage.

Cobb, S.

1976   "Social Support as a Moderator of Life
            Stress." Psychosomatic Medicine, vol.
            3, no. 5:300-304.

Douglas, T. and
J. Johnson (eds.)

1977   Existential Sociology. New York:
            Oxford.

Elder, Glen

1974   Children of the Great Depression.
            Chicago: University of Chicago Press.

Foner, A. and
D. Kertzer

1978   "Transitions Over the Life Course:
            Lessons from Age Set Societies."
            American Journal of Sociology, vol. 83,
            March: 1031-1104.

French, J.R.P.,
W.L. Rosenthal,
and S. Cobb

1974   "Adjustment as Person--Environment
            Fit." In G. Coello and D. Hamburg and
            J. Adams (eds.), Coping and Adaptation.
            New York: Wiley.

Girdano, D. and
G. Everly

1980   Controlling Stress and Tension. New
            York: Prentice Hall.

Glick, Paul

    1979   "Future American Families" The Wash-
                     ington COFO Memo. 2 (3):2-5.

Highet, Gilbert

    1976   The Immortal Profession. New York:
                     Weybright and Talley.

Kenniston, K.

    1977   All Our Children: The American Family
                     Under Pressure. New York: Harcourt
                     Brace Jovanovich.

Killian, R. A.

    1976   Human Resource Management: A Return On
                     Investment Approach. New York:
                     A.M.A.C.O.M.

Klapp, O.

    1979   Opening and Closing: Strategies of
                     Information Adaptation in Society.
                     New York: Cambridge University Press.

Marks, S.

    1977   "Multiple Roles and Role Strain: Some
                     Notes on Human Energy, Time, and Com-
                     mitment." In American Sociological
                     Review, vol. 42 (Dec.): 921-936.

Mouton, J.S.
and R.R. Blake

    1981   Productivty: The Human Side. New
                     York: A.M.A.C.O.M.

Neugarten, B.L.

    1969   "Continuities and Discontinuities of
                     Psychological Issues Into Adult Life,"
                     Human Development, 12:121-130.

Payne, R. and
C.L. Cooper

    1980   Stress at Work. New York: John
                Wiley & Sons.

Pearing, A.

    1982   "New Claremont College MBA/Ph.D., Pro-
                gram Mixes Business and The Humanities
                to Produce Well-Rounded Leaders." The
                Executive, February, p. 100-102.

Reigel, K.F.

    1975   "Toward a Dialectical Theory of Devel-
                opment," Human Development, 18:50-64.

Riley, Matilda White
M. Johnson and A. Foner

    1972   Aging and Society III: A Sociology of
                Age Stratification. New York: Russel
                Sage.

Seyle, H., and
R.A. Brecht

    1980   Stress and the Manager: Making it Work
                For You. New York: Spectrum Books.

Spretzer, E.,
E. Snyder and
D. Larson

    1979   "Multiple Roles and Psychological Well-
                Being" Sociological Focus, Vol. 12,
                No. 2.

Warr, D. and T. Wall

    1975   Work and Well-Being. Baltimore: Pen-
                guin Books.

Wilson, C.

    1972   New Pathways in Psychology, Maslow and
                the Post Freudian Revolution. New
                York: Taplinger Publishing Co.

*Department of Sociology, Chapman College, Orange, California.

CHAPTER 4

THE DUAL-CAREER COUPLE: CONSTRAINTS AND SUPPORTS

Jane Hopkins*
and
Priscilla White**

INTRODUCTION

There is much evidence to indicate that more and
more highly educated American women will want to pursue a career while maintaining a viable family life.
Although it is difficult to assess the percentage of
professional married women in our society today, it is
reasonable to assume that the percentage has significantly increased along with the general labor force
participation rates of women.   Statistics concerning
the percentage of working married women have been
periodically compiled by the Department of Labor
(Schiffler, 1975).   This data has indicated a remarkable increase in married working women - from 30 percent of the female workers being married in 1940, to
58.5 percent of the workers being married women in
1973 (Schiffler, p. 12).

With this influx of potential career-oriented
women, new and complex family interrelationships will
be developing.   The purpose of this paper is to
delineate some of the stresses and strains which seem
to be concomitant with the adoption of this life
style.   Hopefully, by understanding the conflicts and
overload dilemmas experienced by dual-career families,
professionals such as marriage counselors and other
family practitioners, will be better able to facilitate positive methods of coping with the problematic
aspects of this life style.   To better understand the
source of these strains, it will be necessary to review the pertinent literature which deals with those
factors which influence the maintenance of the dual-
career life style, particularly the level of marital
happiness and adjustment.   With a clearer insight into
the socio-psychological as well as purely physical
factors influencing dual-career women, professionals
serving the community will be better able to influence
smoother role transition for families adopting this
life style.

CURRENT RESEARCH FINDINGS

Fogarty, Rapoport and Rapoport (1971) have distinguished dual-career couples from other couples by describing them as having a high commitment to work on an egalitarian basis and a life plan which involves a relatively full participation and advancement in work. Furthermore, the dyads' careers would be characterized as being highly salient personally, and of a continuous developmental nature.

Rhona and Robert Rapoport, from the Tavistock Institute in London, have become synonomous with dual-career family research. Most of their descriptive research has been based on a sample of 371 highly qualified married career women who graduated in 1960 from the British University. The foci for their study were the dimensions of stress experienced by each of the families. The five major dimensions of stress included: Dilemmas which arise from discrepancies between personal norms and social norms, identity dilemmas, social network dilemmas, role cycling dilemmas, and overload dilemmas.

If we look more closely at the overload dilemmas it becomes obvious that the sheer workload of caring for a family and pursuing a meaningful career would be physically and emotionally taxing. It has been theorized that dual-career family roles are a reversal of the traditional family roles in that the male becomes more involved in the domestic activities of the home as the female becomes more career-oriented. Egalitarian division of labor has been often discussed as a "truth" or basic premise of the dual-career life style. Early studies of the working married mother (usually not a dual-career spouse) indicated that the wife's power tended to increase with employment, particularly in "external" areas relating to financial decisions (Blood, 1963). A basic finding in this early research was that the husband's household labor increases while that of the wife decreases (Blood, 1963; Blood and Hamblin, 1968, Blood and Wolfe, 1960). Thus, these early studies on dual-work families indicated a redistribution of power in an egalitarian direction, a greater equalization of the amount of domestic work done, and an alteration of traditional sex roles.

However, more recent studies with dual-career

80

families indicate that egalitarianism in division of domestic responsibilities and in importance of career advancement are unrealistic expectations for most dual-career dyads (Bryson and Bryson, 1975; Epstein, 1971; Wallston et al., 1975). Basically, these studies have shown that although attitudes may be egalitarian behaviorally, the actual division of home care responsibilities regulates the majority of these responsibilities to the female. These findings are not unusual in light of the fact that a number of researchers have established that the secondary status of the wife's career is, generally, a shared point of view for both dual-career spouses (Holmstrom, 1972; Poloma, 1972; Rapoport and Rapoport, 1971).

Bryson et al. (1975) in their study of professional pairs found that not only were these couples not egalitarian in their division of labor, but that they were no more equal in the division of responsibility than other married couples. They stated: "The major difference between the professional pairs and the married controls (where 38 percent of the wives were employed) is that the professional pair is more likely to employ outside help for these activities" (p. 4). Rapoport and Rapoport's (1972) research data also indicated considerable reliance on outside help for both household duties and child care. However, they indicated that most women in their sample, although responsible for a greater amount of the domestic activities than their husbands, felt fortunate that their husbands allowed them to pursue their dual-role activities (p. 366).

Certainly the level of mutual satisfaction in the dual-career partnership will be influenced by the attitudes and behavior of each spouse concerning egalitarianism. Furthermore, these attitudes will be greatly affected by the availability of quality domestic help and the level of aspiration for a high standard of living held by each partner.

MARITAL HAPPINESS AND DUAL-CAREER LIFE STYLE

Current interest in factors affecting the maintenance patterns of dual-career families is reflected in the research concerned with marital happiness, satisfaction or adjustment of dual-career dyads. Safilios-Rothschild (1970) looked at the relationship between a married women'a degree of work commitment and her de-

gree of marital satisfaction. She found that women
with high work commitment reported a significantly
higher marital satisfaction than women not working
outside of the home.

A women's freedom to choose the dual-career life
style has been hypothesized as an important predictor
of happiness in marriage. Orden and Bradburn (1969)
found that both partners are less happy if the wife
works because of economic necessity than if she participated by choice. The authors also found evidence
that a woman's decision to work strains the marriage
only when there are preschool children in the family.
However, the authors concede that the decision to work
is generally associated with a high balance between
satifactions and tensions for both husbands and wives.

Looking further at the relationship between marriage happiness and career commitment, Bailyn (1970)
found a drop in the level of very happy marriages as
women become work- and career-oriented. However,
these drops in marital happiness did not significantly affect the level of marital satisfaction unless
they were accompanied by the presence of a husband who
emphasized "career" in his own orientation. She found
that marriages tended to be happier when the husband
found satisfaction in both career and family than when
the husband was either just career- or family-
oriented.

Although some of this literature concerning the
career-oriented wife implies that a dual-career partnership will undermine the marital relationship,
Rapoport and Rapoport (1972) postulate another viewpoint which is supported to some extent by their data.
They believe that the marital relationship is more
likely to be strengthened if each partner is economically viable and feels that he/she is achieving a
great deal out of career and family possibilities.
The authors acknowledge the possibilities of overload
and strain but suggest that the wife experiences less
resentment at being exploited and the husband feels
less guilt at having his own freedom to develop than
do more traditional partnerships.

Dual-career marital adjustment seems also to be
contingent upon discriminatory practice from the work
world itself. Rosen, Jerdee, and Prestivich (1975)
found that many managers and executives have stereo-

typic sex-role expectations for career wives and their husbands. The authors speculate that discriminatory managerial practices frustrate the formation of positive attitudes and career commitment of dual-career women. As such, a dual-career women's attempts at role redefinition may lead to increased frustration at home and at work. The end result for both partners of a dual-career unit may well be heightened conflict and stress in the marriage.

Epstein (1971) has pointed out that one of the subsequent problems of the dual-career life style seems to be the guilt women feel who are not conforming to the work-family structures of the greater society. However, several authors have suggested that even if there is greater strain on the relationship, it is this marital-work partnership which creates a potential for greater communication and sense of purpose within the marital relationship (Epstein, 1971; Rapoport and Rapoport, 1972).

The above review of the literature touches on only some of the findings from the major studies. To facilitate conceptualization of the strains and subsequent maintenance of the dual-career life style for females, the authors constructed a model (p. 11). This model should provide an understanding of the factors which influence a women'a choice and maintenance of the life style in relation to the many factors which are potentially stress-provoking. Obviously, societal norms have greatly influenced our attitudes about appropriate behavior for families and specific role expectations for men and women. Dual-career families have few established normative role behaviors so that helpful guidelines for smooth maintenance of this alternative life style are not available. However, what normative expectations do exist for families influence the perceptions and subsequent behavior of family members. The factors influencing strain delineated in the model interact in a complex, forever-changing manner to effect such dyad member's ability to cope with the life style.

We have chosen a number of factors which have shown some indication of being influential in determining the maintenance of the dual-career family pattern. At this time there is a scarcity of empirical evidence that all of these factors do indeed affect the viability of the dual-career family. However, attempts to construct a theoretical model conceptualizing factors that appear empirically or deductively to be of import seems to be a worthwhile undertaking. Such a model is important for family practitioners in providing an understanding of the factors and the integration of environmental/familial factors which contribute in total to the ease of maintenance of the life style.

IMPLICATIONS FOR PRACTITIONERS

All married couples have areas of conflict and would benefit from skilled help in conflict management. However, the dual-career pattern appears to add on a number of new dimensions to the already burdened expectations for the marital relationship. Traditional husband-wife role behavior with the husband providing for the instrumental needs and the wife providing for expressive needs no longer is applicable for marital relationships. Whenever there is role ambiguity for either or both spouses, resolution of conflict and problem-solving becomes more difficult.

Practitioners who work in family and marital counseling have a unique opportunity to provide input for couples who are experiencing the many strains associated with the dual-career life style. As we become more knowledgeable concerning the stresses that are unique to these families a therapeutic "preventive" model should evolve. One strategy available to family practitioners is to provide group experiences for dual-career couples. By sharing common problems, couples would come to feel a sense of community with other dual-career families thus lessening their feelings of guilt and alienation. Dual-career women, especially, have been cited as being anxious about the social consequences of their differing role behavior (Fogarty et al., 1971; Epstein, 1971). Common problem groups would also be helpful as a way to pool knowledge and systemize information on available resources (babysitters, domestic helpers, etc.).

Groups made up of couples at differing stages in the life cycle could provide anticipatory socialization experiences for the younger couples who have not yet faced some of the dilemmas. Mutual sharing of ideas concerning their frustrations and anxieties can increase the coping skills for all group members. Practitioners might also consider having separate male and female groups, especially in the beginning of the group experience when couples may be experiencing high levels of stress. In order to help couples become sensitized to each other's needs, role-playing exercises would be a helpful tool. Re-enacting common household dramas would facilitate the learning of specific conflict resolution skills and provide couples with a sense of mutual support and commonality from other groups members.

Rapoport and Rapoport (1975) have introduced the concept of equity rather than equality as being the basis for a dual-career life style that is flexible enough to accommodate variations across individuals as well as across time. They defined equity as "...a fair allocation both of opportunity and of constraints..." (p. 421). Many dual-career couples become preoccupied with the idea that opportunities and constraints must always be equally divided between husband and wife. The concept of equity emphasizes fairness of division rather than equality of division. Time is a very significant factor in this process. Pressures and demands vary and may bear more on one person or the other at a particular point in time. Therefore, constraints may also vary in the degree to which they impinge on one of the individuals. Given the opportunities and constraints present within a specific situational context what are equitable allocations may not always be equalitarian allocations. It is important for family practitioners to help dual-career couples make the distinction between the concepts of equity and equality. Couples need to acquire problem-solving skills that are oriented toward the creation of equitable alternatives. Couples also must realize that as conditions change, alternatives change. Many solutions may be relatively short-term rather than long-term in the context of a changing relationship.

Teaching couples the process of negotiating and implementing time-limited behavior contracts may provide a structure and framework for resolving family developmental crises in an equitable way. Specific strategies for learning these skills are clearly delineated in a practical manner by Patterson (1971) and Knox (1973). These specific delineations of the allocations of opportunities and constraints for time-limited periods will enhance the feeling of equal participation in the structuring of equitable solutions.

The feeling of "fairness" should be facilitated by this type of problem solving.

Family practitioners should also help dual-career couples learn to be expressive about the constraints of their life style as well as the opportunities. Because the dual-career life style is often based on strong personal values and convictions of the individuals involved, defensiveness and denial concerning the problematic aspects of the life style may occur. Couples should be encouraged to share their experiences related to overload and constraints with one another in a nonjudgmental and nonblaming way. This expressive sharing of problematic aspects as well as positive aspects will, in all likelihood, reduce the level of anxiety and threat experienced in relationship to constraints. Problems can therefore be more easily viewed as opportunities for growth and change rather than assaults against the viability of a variant family form. Rapoport and Rapoport (1975) pointed out the need for dual-career couples to develop a tolerance for "suboptimal" arrangements for one or the other person at specific times. Tolerance of less than ideal circumstances and allocations of responsibilities would certainly be enhanced by the freedom to share openly one's thoughts and feelings in relationship to problems and constraints.

Creating an equitable husband-wife relationship provides the foundation for creating equitable family systems. Parent-child relationships, as well as the marital relationship, must be oriented toward the goal of equity. Satir (1972) suggested that open family systems are characterized by the equal opportunity of all family members to contribute to the rules that govern family living. She suggested a process revolving around "family meetings" where equitable rules and decisions are arrived at by a process of group consensus. Helping dual-career couples learn the skills for implementing family meetings in their homes would probably provide the opportunity for families to change and grow over time as the needs of the family group and of the individuals change. This approach would strengthen the flexibility of the family system so that dilemmas could be more easily and productively resolved.

Because of heavy investments in both familial and professional spheres many dual-career couples may find that leisure time activities become constricted. Input from family practitioners in terms of management skills can help couples organize and plan activities in an efficient and effective way so leisure time can be created. Williams and Long (1975) have suggested strategies for accomplishing what they term as "the self-managed" life style. Planning and effective resource utilization can enhance the possibility of rewarding and relaxing leisure patterns.

These are only a few suggestions for the family practitioners who wish to provide support services for dual-career families. Many other strategies and approaches could and should be developed. Certainly Rapoport and Rapoport (1975) accurately assessed the status of the dual-career family in our society when they stated:

"Laissez-faire is not good enough, what is needed is a broad spectrum approach to research and action programs of all kinds. The challenge is, therefore, squarely before us all" (p. 432).

REFERENCE NOTES

1. Bryson, J., Bryson, R., & Licht, B. <u>Professional</u>
<u>Pairs: Relative Career Values of Wives and Husbands</u>.
Paper presented at American Psychological Association Annual Meeting, 1975.

2. Wallston, B., Foster, M., & Berger, M. <u>I Will</u>
<u>Follow Him: Myth, Reality, Forced Choice</u>. Paper
presented at American Psychological Association
Annual Meeting, 1975.

B I B L I O G R A P H Y

Bailyn, L.

1970   "Careers and Family Orientations of Hus-
                  bands and Wives in Relation to Marital
                  Happiness." <u>Human Relations</u>, 23, 97-113.

Blood, R.O. &
Hamblin, R.L.

1958   "The Effect of the Wife's Employment on
                  The Family Power Structure." <u>Social</u>
                  <u>Forces</u>, 36, 347-352.

Blood, R.O. &
Wolfe, D.M.

1960   <u>Husbands and Wives: The Dynamics of</u>
                  <u>Married Living</u>. Glencoe, Illinois:
                  Free Press.

Bryson, R., Bryson, J.,
Licht, M., & Licht, B.

1976   "The Professional Pair. Husband and
                  Wife Psychologists." <u>American Psycholo-</u>
                  <u>gist</u>, 31, 10-16.

Epstein, C.

1971   "Law Partners and Marital Partners."
                  <u>Human Relations</u>, 24, 549-564.

Fogarty, M.,
Rapoport R., & Rapoport, R.

1971   _Sex, Career and Family_. Beverly
        Hills, Calif.: Sage,

Holmstrom, L.

1972   _The Two Career Family_. Cambridge,
        Mass.: Schenkman, 1972.

Knox, D.

1973   "Behavior Contracts in Marriage Coun-
        seling." _Journal of Family Counseling_,
        2, 22-28.

Orden, S., &
Bradburn, N.

1969   "Working Wives and Marriage Happiness."
        American Journal of Sociology, 74,
        392-407.

Patterson, G.

1971   _Families_. Champaign, Illinois:
        Research Associates.

Poloma, M.

1972   "Role Conflict and the Married Profes-
        sional Woman." In C. Safilios-Roths-
        child (Ed.), _Toward a Sociology of_
        Women, Lexington, Mass.: Xerox.

Rapoport, R., &
Rapoport, R.N.

1971   "Further Considerations of the Dual-
        Career Family." _Human Relations_, 24,
        519-533.

1972   _Dual-Career Families_. New York:
        Pelican.

1975   "Men, Women, and Equity." _The Family_
        Coordinator, 24, 421-432.

Rosen, B., Jerdee, T.H. &
Prestwick, T.L.

1975   "Dual-career Marital Adjustment:
                Potential Effects of Discriminatory
                Managerial Attitudes." Journal of
                Marriage and the Family, 37, 565-572.

Satir, V.

1972   Peoplemaking, Palo Alto, Calif.:
                Science and Behavior.

Safilios-Rothschild, C.

1970   "The Influence of the Wife's Degree of
                Work Commitment Upon Some Aspects of
                Family Organization and Dynamics."
                Journal of Marriage and the Family,
                32, 681-691.

Schiffler, R.J.

1975   "Demographic and Social Factors in
                Women's Work Lives." In S.H. Osipow
                (Ed.), Emerging Woman. Columbus, Ohio:
                Merrill.

Williams, R. L., &
Long, J.

1975   Towards a Self-Managed Life Style.
                Boston, Mass.: Houghton-Mifflin.

* Jane Hopkins is the Director of the Women's Resource
Center, University of Richmond, Richmond, Virginia.

**Priscilla White is an Associate Professor in Child
and Family Studies, College of Home Economics, University of Tennessee, Knoxville, Tennessee.

Reprinted from The Family Coordinator, Vol. 27 (July,
1978): 253-259. Copyrighted 1978 by the National
Council on Family Relations. Reprinted by permission.

CHAPTER 5

MARRIAGE: THE DREAM AND THE REALITY

Luciano L'Abate*
and
Bess L. L'Abate*

One of the major polarizations in marriages of
workaholic husbands is their pursuing of "The
Great American Dream," while their wives are
left to pursue the "Petty Realities of Life."
This polarization is related to other polarities in these marriages with husbands presenting
nice, reasonable, pleasant facades, while their
wives present bitchy, angry and/or depressed
pictures. Diagnosis and therapeutic issues of
this polarization are discussed.

The purpose of this paper is to review one of the
major areas of polarization in marriage that does not
seem to have received the attention it deserves. This
polarization, more often than not, takes place along a
continuum in which the husband pursues his "Dream(s)"
of success, i.e., money, achievement, power, while the
wife is left home to deal with the "Realities" of
life, i.e., children, house, chores, etc. The result
of this polarization is an inability to be or become
intimate (L'Abate & L'Abate, 1979). Trollope put it
well a long time ago:

> A burden that will crush a single pair
> of shoulders will, when equally divid-
> ed-when shared by two, each of whom is
> willing to take the heavier part--become
> light as a feather. Is not that sharing
> of the mind's burdens one of the chief
> purposes for which a man wants a wife?
> For there is no folly so great as keep-
> ing one's sorrow hidden.

Levinson, Darrow, Dean, Levinson, and McKee
(1978) have addressed themselves to the topic of the
function of "The Dream" in the formative development
of man's evolution in personality. Originally this
Dream has a "vague sense of self-adult-world...At the
start it is poorly articulated and only tenuously con-

nected to reality" (p. 35). Eventually, this Dream becomes articulated within the channel of maximal exposure taken by the man, i.e., his occupational choice. He dreams of winning the Nobel prize if he is a physicist or biologist, becoming a renowned writer, winning the Pulitzer prize, becoming a great athlete, artist, businessman, etc. Levinson et al. poignantly described the functions of "The Dream" in the lives of the forty men they studied.

Part of the marital contract for such men, explicit or implicit, is that the wife will help the husband achieve his Dream, whatever it may be. Thus, in this arrangement the marital relationship is initially one-sided. The agreement is for the wife to "help" the husband, as in the cases of nurse-doctor marriages, but there is no clear or explicit agreement that there will be reciprocity in this relationship. The woman initially may agree to help in exchange for material goods or vicarious rewards that may derive from the husband's success. But Levinson et al. (1978, p. 109) note:

> If in supporting his dream she loses her own, then her development will suffer and both will later pay the price. Dynamics of this kind often surface in transitional periods such as the Age Thirty Transition or the Mid-life Transition.

The foregoing quote speaks to the very point of this paper. There are many marriages of hard-driving, competitive, and ambitious executives, managers, achievement- and success-oriented professionals who, through their workaholic investment in their jobs, hope, attempt, want, and oftentimes succeed in fulfilling their Dream. But, this fulfillment may be achieved at a great cost and sacrifice to the marriage and to the family. Failure to actualize the Dream may lead to feelings of inadequacy and failure that may be externalized in the marriage in the form of affairs, blaming wife for lack of support, among others.

Components of this Dream are enacted by the decision that to achieve this goal he will need courage, strength, and determination, as shown through the following characteristics: (a) reason and logic as the means through which the Dream is achieved; (b) strength, courage, determination are demonstrated by keeping his feelings to himself, and repressing, denying, and avoiding any expression of feelings that may possibly suggest vulnerability, weakness, or even worse, inadequacy!

A previous paper (L'Abate, 1975) explained part of family dysfunctionality in terms of the man's rigid inability to switch from a managerial role at work to a nurturant role at home. Further elaboration is needed about the roles of both men and women in coming to grips with issues of intimacy in marriage (L'Abate & L'Abate, 1979). The major dysfunction-producing aspects of this Dream seem to be: (a) drive and intensity of purpose, as shown by excessive and exclusive absorption in the occupational role; (b) inability to shift, differentiate, and integrate demands from work and from home; and (c) inability to experience feelings, to improve dialogue, and achieve intimacy in marriage.

THE POLARITIES OF MARRIAGE

Considerable effort is made by the husband to promote proper appearances. A good first impression is sought through clothing, car, and house. Thus, a great deal of his functioning is directed at presenting the self in as good a light as possible. The wife, on the other hand, is involved with more practical issues; those issues that exist below, or underneath, the flow of self-presentation and go beyond the first blush facade of appearance (L'Abate, 1976). The husband either neglects chores and responsibilities, or is apparently unaware of the trivia that occupy his wife's attention. The more she brings these "Realities" to his attention, the more he resists dealing with them.

One way wives demonstrate their initial involvement and collusion with The Dream is that most of them have no careers of their own. All of their selves have been given to the pursuit and sharing of The Dream without demands of reciprocity. Eventually, when the futility or irrelevance of the collusion hits them, the emotional toll and cost that this Dream has extracted from them usually provokes a depression. If the wives are not depressed at the beginning of therapy, usually they are still angry and frustrated. Eventually they will be able to become depressed, a sign that therapy is working. The husbands, of course, find it much more difficult to get in touch with their underlying feelings of depression. But if therapy is effective, they may be able to get in touch with the emptiness that determined part of the pursuit in the first place. The husbands' selves were given up for professional roles or titles to the extent that little self remains. In fact, many of these men and some of their wives have a hard time understanding the concepts of being, which will be discussed later on in this paper. Some of these existential issues have been considered by Crosby (1976).

Further polarities of the "Dream" role are a nice-nasty quality that covers the man's attempt to achieve success on the outside by being a "nice guy," and putting forth a self-presentational facade (L'Abate, 1976) of a "hail-fellow-well-met" glad-hander, with all of the qualities that accompany such a role. This stance, of course, polarizes the wife toward the opposite extreme of nastiness. Her increasing frustration and loneliness are expressed in "bitchy," angry outbursts and blaming statements that are surprising and incomprehensible to the husband. How could a "nice guy" like him be considered such a lowdown creature? Why does she continue bugging him about small, irrelevant details like plumbing, yard-work, and the infinite little occurrences that take place in the household every day? Why should he be concerned with diapers and diaper rash? He is in pursuit of the far greater Dream that cannot in any way be detoured, sidestepped, or interfered with by such petty irrelevancies. One husband, a worldwide traveler tycoon, became enraged when his wife asked him to deal with the gardening contractor, who for $350.00 a month was not getting the job done. Imagine him having to bother with such trifles! He was involved in multimillion dollar projects all over the USA and in foreign countries! How could she dare bother him with a chore which clearly belonged with the realm of her responsibilities and not his?

The wife's reactions oftentimes are so alien to the picture that the man has of himself and of his role that the discrepancy between the Dream picture and the Reality presented by the wife becomes unacceptable. He becomes unwilling to come to terms with it and begins acting out by becoming even more immersed in his job, picking up a mistress on the side, drinking more, etc. If and when the wife is successful in bringing him into the therapy office, he feels ganged up on by the therapist, if the therapist in any way, subtle or otherwise, sides with the wife's Reality.

These couples may display other polarities:

1. Intimacy and isolation - it is clear that many of these couples never dealt in their marriages with the issues of intimacy. Consequently, they are destined to be isolated from each other in what could seem an "arrangement" rather than a marriage.

2. Enmeshment with families of origin - many of these couples, even after more than ten years of marriage and thousands of miles from their families of origin, remain enmeshed to the point of still spending vacation time with them and fighting with each other over them.

3. Delegation from parents and loyalty binding - Very often these couples present some of the aspects of delegation discussed by Stierlin (1974), to the point that their success is bound to the "failures" of their parents. Their parents' failures (either economic or interpersonal or both) need to be remedied by them.

4. Anniversary reaction or separation phase - oftentimes the major precipitating reason for therapy is ostensibly fear of loss (i.e., finding husband has had an affair) or the children's reaching grade school age and leaving the wife.

5. Another dimension of the dream-reality continuum is the expressive-inexpressive (rational-irrational) distinction (L'Abate, 1980) emphasized for many years by Balswick (1980).

The wife's increasing worry about realistic details of everyday, routine household life (chores) points to another polarization between mates, i.e., pessimism-optimism whereby the wife begins to look at the dark side of family happenings, including the behavior of the identified patient (IP), usually one of their children, while the husband is bound to deny

95

it, by belittling its severity or seriousness, thereby
delaying, until the breaking point, any possible intervention (L'Abate, 1975). The IP, whether the wife
or child, will need to escalate to the maximum level
of noise (attempted suicide, being kicked out of
school, flunking, etc.) to obtain the husband's attention and acknowledgement that something may need to be
done. At this point professional help may be sought.

DISCUSSION

     Some of these conclusions about the woman's role
in a "workaholic" husband's life are supported by the
research of Macke, Bohrnstedt and Bernstein (1979),
who examined the cornerstone of traditional views of
marriage that housewives experience their husbands'
successes vicariously. Macke et al. maintained that
the specific role requirements of traditional marriage
may reduce a woman's self-esteem and render her more
vulnerable to stress. To obtain more verification of
this hypothesis, Macke et al. obtained relevant information from 121 mostly upper middle class women, who
are roughly similar to the couples we see in our clinical practice. They found that a husband's success
affects a housewife's self-esteem positively, but only
indirectly, through its effect on perceived marital
success. Only the husband's income by itself had a
positive effect on self-esteem. Apparently a housewife, according to Macke et al., can translate money
into consumer products or other material means of
increasing her status among peers, and thus indirectly
her self-esteem. Macke et al. also found that other
successes of the husband seem to work against the
self-esteem of those wives who were not working. This
finding, which parallels our findings with clinical
couples, is enhanced by the finding that none of the
above outcomes were present in working wives.

     Boss, McCubbin, and Lester (1979) reviewed how
the wives of corporate executives cope with their
husbands' frequent absences and long work hours.
Their major coping strategies, which we find absent in
the wives we have observed in our clinical practice
and on which we base our generalizations are: (a)
fitting into the corporate life style (frequent entertaining and social group activities; (b) developing
self (as independent from the husband); and (c) establishing independence (emotionally as well as
socially).

DIAGNOSTIC IMPLICATIONS

Diagnostically, one important way of checking on the couple's overinvolvement with work, for the husband, or with children, for the wife (L'Abate, 1975), is to ask them about their priorities. What is more important to each of them in order of preference? Most men will reply: "My family and my work." Most women will say: "My husband and my children." Neither one of them usually mentions the self as an important aspect of priorities (L'Abate, 1976). If and when the concept of self is mentioned, the notion seems to be strange and questionable. However, when the problem is rephrased: "How can a bridge stand on weak pillars?", the point is driven home that the establishment of a functional self is just as important for the marriage as any other priority. When the question is raised: "How can parenthood be achieved without a partnership?", or "How can a partnership be achieved without personhood?", it becomes even clearer that all of these issues have not been considered by the couple. In both mates the self is ill-defined, unclear, and essentially weak.

The woman may show signs of inadequacy, if not hatred, whereas the husband attempts to hold on to the occupational self to achieve a certain degree of selfhood. When the woman who defined herself as "housewife" is asked to find any definition of self that precedes "housewife," developmentally and in importance, she may have a great deal of trouble in coming up with a definition of self that includes concepts of womanhood, personhood, or individuality. The weaker she is in individuation, the more she relies on her husband and her children to define herself. Her self-concept is essentially reactive and external to both sources of satisfaction. The husband will show just as much trouble in understanding the concept of manhood separate from occupational, marital, or tertiarily, familial functions (manager, lawyer, husband, father). It is crucial at this point to assert the importance of a self-concept on which to base the marriage (Crosby, 1976). This assertion is sometimes met by questioning glances. Oftentimes, it is then best to congratulate the couple for losing their selves for the love of the other: "You must have had a self if you lost it!"

The best empirical framework within which some of
the above conclusions can be evaluated, and eventually
tested, is that of Foá and Foá (1974). They not
only have developed an exchange theory that can encompass some of the above, but have also developed
tools to assess it. Briefly, this theory assumes six
classes of resources: Love, Status, Money, Goods,
Services, and Information. A revision of this theory
(L'Abate, Sloan, Wagner, & Malone, in press) groups
Love and Status as components of being, Information
and Services as components of doing, and Money and
Goods as components of having. Within this framework
we can see that many of these couples function very
effectively in the doing and having areas, but are
quite defective or ineffective in the being area.
They do not know how to be, as experienced by: (a)
expression of deep or soft feelings, (b) relaxation
and letting go in leisure time, whereas for them
business and pleasure many times are mixed, (c) inadequate definition of self as separate from an
occupational (manager, lawyer, etc., rather than
"woman" or "person"). As noted previously (L'Abate,
1976), these priorities in resource exchange are
mixed up, diffused, fused, or confused. Their whole
orientation to doing and having is so uncritically
ingrained that understanding the implications of a
being orientation is as difficult as experiencing
feelings or assuming an "I" position.

THERAPEUTIC IMPLICATIONS

What is the goal of therapy under these conditions? Obviously one goal is for the couple to learn
to negotiate realistic and functional objectives for
themselves, and for the husband to learn to give reciprocally while the wife learns to expect, request,
and demand this reciprocity from her husband. Ultimately, the goal will be for them to learn to share
their pain and depression. Previously the marriage
has been on a reactive see-saw or rollercoaster. When
on partner is up, the other is down. Eventually, in
the course of therapeutic intervention, the couple is
able to avoid such examples of affective polarization
and learn to share more emphatically their hurts and
pains (L'Abate, 1977; Frey, Holloy, & L'Abate, 1979).
At this point, the marriage may become a real marriage
and not an arrangement. To reach this point usually
both partners have to learn to negotiate important
issues without incongruent affect or avoidance of the

issues involved. Berkowitz (1977) has essentially developed a position that is very similar to the present one. He stated that:

A central developmental task of the family
is to help its members develop the capacity
to cope with the grief attendant on separation and loss...to work through such feelings,
each member must be able to acknowledge the
affect as present, internal, and belonging
to the self...family members may avoid awareness of such feelings within themselves. The
disclaimed emotions remain powerful unconscious motivators of behavior exerting their
influence despite their denial.

The wife in many ways, at least in the beginning of married life, has colluded with the husband by agreeing with him that, explicitly or implicitly, she would share "The Dream" with him and do whatever would be necessary to help achieve it. How could she now betray him? The sheer force of the Reality brought about by household and childrearing responsi-bility that can only increase with married life even-tually forces the wife to take a second look at her-self and the nature of the marriage. If she does not become aware of her collusion, she does become aware of her giving up of her own self to allow the hus-band's self to prevail unilaterally. Depression, and all of its concomitants (feelings of low self-worth, rejection, fear of abandonment, etc.) come to the forefront, forcing the husband to become involved whether he likes it or not.

Oftentimes, the wife will see individual thera-pists who unwittingly would enter into a collusion with the husband by accepting the wife as a "sick," dependent woman, the IP (L'Abate, Weeks, & Weeks, 1979). Under these conditions, the husband is now free, and treatment becomes a long-drawn affair be-tween the woman and her therapist, where eventually she may get over her depression, but may be unwilling to accept her husband as he is and as he has remained, since no intervention has taken place to change his involvement and love affair with The Dream!

The hard-driving, success-pursuing, reasonable and logic-oriented husband is not only preoccupied by his Dream at the expense of performing his husbandly and fatherly chores, but he also cannot speak about it even though, as therapy unfolds, he comes to realize that his Dream serves to cover up a great deal of hurt and emptiness.

In treatment, the foregoing patterns persist and become, in fact, highlighted. The husband typically smiles a great deal and presents most of the aspects mentioned above. When the wife cries, he becomes embarrassed and either takes it as a personal affront or becomes angry, or avoids dealing with it, because he is unable to emphasize with her tears. He sees the wife's increased dependency and helplessness as a yoke around his neck that is slowing down the process of attainment of his Dream and interferes with his work and his ever-present job commitments. Some of these men (Supermen) are so convinced of their inherent power and attributes that it may take very extreme behavior on the IP's part to convince the husband to join and share the realities of everyday life.

The most difficult part in therapy of these couples is not to side with the wife, but to see her behavior as equally contributing to the overall trouble as the husband's. She needs to be supported without injury to the husband's feelings of inadequacy, or he may feel that both therapist and wife had colluded and "ganged up" on him.

CONCLUSION

We have presented a major polarization of marriage that allows us to put together into one conceptual framework diverse strands of clinical experience and empirical evidence about marriage, its successes and its failures.

B I B L I O G R A P H Y

Balswick, J.

   1980   "Explaining Inexpressive Males: A Reply to L'Abate." <u>Family Relations</u>, 29, 233-234.

Berkowitz, D.A.

   1977   "On the Reclaiming of Denied Affects in Family Therapy." <u>Family Process</u>, 16, 495-502.

Boss, P.G., McCubbin, H.I. &
Lester, G.

   1979   "The Corporate Executive's Wife's Coping Patterns in Response to Routine Husband-Father Absence." <u>Family Process</u>, 18, 79-86.

Crosby, J.E.

   1976   <u>Illusion and Disillusion: The Self in Love and Marriage</u>. Belmont, CA: Wadsworth.

Foä, V., &
Foä, E.

   1974   <u>Societal Structures of the Mind</u>. Springfield, IL: C.C. Thomas.

Frey, J., Holley, J. &
L'Abate, L.

   1979   "Intimacy is Sharing Hurt: A Comparison of Three Conflict Resolution Methods." <u>Journal of Marriage and Family Therapy</u>, 5, 35-41.

L'Abate, L.

   1980   "Inexpressive Males or Overexpressive Females? A Reply to Balswick." <u>Family Relations</u>, 29, 231-232.

L'Abate, L.

    1977   "Intimacy is Sharing Hurt Feelings: A
                      Reply to David Mace." Journal of
                      Marriage and Family Counseling, 3,
                      13-16.

    1976   Understanding and Helping the Indivi-
                      dual in the Family. New York: Grune
                      & Stratton.

    1975   "Pathogenic Role Rigidity in Fathers:
                      Some Observations." Journal of Marriage
                      and Family Counseling, 1, 69-79.

L'Abate, L., &
L'Abate, B.L.

    1979   "The Paradoxes of Intimacy." Family
                      Therapy, 6, 175-184.

L'Abate, L., Sloan, S.Z.,
Wagner, V., & Malone, K.

    In Press   "The Differentiation of Resources."
                      Family Therapy.

L'Abate, L., Weeks, G., &
Weeks, K.

    1979   "Of Scapegoats, Strawmen, and Scare-
                      crows." International Journal of
                      Family Therapy, 1, 86-96.

Levinson, D.J., Darrow, C.N.,
Dean, E.B., Levinson, M.H.,
& McKee, B.

    1978   The Seasons of a Man's Life. New York:
                      Alfred Knopt.

Macke, A.S., Bohrnstedt, G.W.,
& Bernstein, I.N.

    1979   "Housewive's Self-esteem and Their Hus-
                      bands' Success: The Myth of Vicarious

Involvement." <u>Journal of Marriage and the Family</u>, 41, 51-57.

Stierlin, H.

1974   <u>Separating Parents and Adolescents: A Perspective on Running Away, Schizophrenia, and Waywardness.</u> New York: Quadrangle/The New York Times Book Co.

A P P E N D I X
Instructions for Workshop Format

In conjunction with this paper, which in various formats has been given to a variety of organizations, we have found it useful to translate the above abstractions into a direct workshop format. Here are the instructions used with couples (real or simulated). We hope they will help any reader who may want to apply them in a workshop or enrichment format.

How many are here with their spouses?

Those who are not will have to role play with one another.

Now I (We) hope everyone is more or less partnered.

1. For the next 5-10 minutes we want each couple to talk to each other about your dreams or life goals. This should be your personal, individual dreams--not goals as a couple. Possible and impossible.

2. Now talk about where you want to be 5 years from now, 10 years, 20 years. (5-10 minutes)

3. Now talk about the similarities or discrepancies of your dreams. (5-10 minutes)

4. Now discuss the realities that are interfering with your dreams. (5-10 minutes)

5. How much of your past or present life are you giving up or sacrificing for dreams to be realized in the future? Has your marriage paid a

price for the dream? Have your children? Discuss whether it is or has been worth it. (5-
10 minutes)

6. Discuss ways you can integrate your dreams and
   realities so that you both win in the present
   and the future. How many of you will continue
   these dreams at home?

7. Now it is feedback time. Would any one couple
   like to share with us anything they have
   learned about themselves or their marriage in
   these discussions? (Take as much time as it
   seems feasible.)

*Luciano L'Abate is Professor of Psychology and Direc-
tor, Family Study Center, Georgia State University,
University Plaza, Atlanta, Georgia 30303. Bess L.
L'Abate is in part-time private practice.

Reprinted from Family Relations, Vol. 30 (January,
1981: 131-136). Copyrighted 1981 by the National
Council on Family Relations. Reprinted by permission.

CHAPTER 6

FROM GENERATION TO GENERATION:
FATHERS-TO-BE IN TRANSITION

Laurence Barnhill, Gerald Rubenstein,
and Neil Rocklin*

Recent literature presents parenthood as a
crisis and/or growth experience (Russell,
1974). This paper refocuses this issue from
an orientation toward outcome to one on process. It examines the transition into fatherhood in terms of six tasks which must be completed or mastered if this process is to be
gratifying and rewarding. These tasks include
decision-making, mourning, empathic responding,
integrating, differentiating from the extended
family and establishing family boundaries, and
synergizing. These tasks were derived from the
authors' work with groups of fathers-to-be in
a prepared childbirth program. Group work with
these fathers is also described in terms of
appropriate clinical interventions. The role
of self-disclosing, providing information,
eliciting affect, recruiting interpersonal
resources, normalizing, and personalizing are
examined as intervention strategies which can
be utilized in such groups.

Bolman (1968) and Rapaport (1963) have suggested
that the family is the most strategic social unit
toward which preventive psychiatric services should
be oriented. Rapaport's position is that the most
desirable preventive family interventions occur at
key points in the family life cycle. This view is

*Revision of a paper presented to the 1977 American
Orthopsychiatric Association Annual Meeting in New
York, New York. The authors would like to express
their appreciation to the faculty and staff of the
Obstetrics Department of the Genesee Hospital, Rochester, New York. In particular special appreciation is
expressed to the nursing staff for their support and
encouragement.

based on the crisis work of Lindemann (1944), the
developmental epigenetic view of Erikson (1950), and
on constructs which emerge from the family therapy
literature (Ackerman, 1958). Some of the key stages
in the life cycle of families are: getting married
(Rapaport, 1963), bearing the first child (Kaplan &
Maston, 1960; Russell, 1974), going to school (Klein
& Ross, 1958; Signell, 1972), leaving home (Murphy,
1963; Stierlin, 1971), and dying (Lindemann, 1944;
Eliot, 1955; Bowlby, 1960).

We have chosen to focus on "the birth of the
child," including the experience of pregnancy, the
process of childbirth, and the incorporation of the
neonate into the family system as a normal family
developmental crisis. LeMasters (1957) and Dyer
(1963) have presented evidence that from 53% to 83%
of normal couples subjectively experience new parenthood as an extensive or severe crisis. Recent data
presented by Hadley, Milliones, Caplan, and Spritz
(1974), demonstrated objective evidence that 37% of
their clinic patient families reported symptom onset
within nine months of the addition of a new family
member. Work with families during this stage would,
therefore, meet the criteria for both the major types
of direct preventive interventions outlined by Bolman
(1968): milestone or high-risk. It is a milestone
intervention in that the population can be available
during a time of demonstrable change. It is also a
high-risk intervention in that the population both
subjectively and objectively demonstrates increased
risk of developing psychosocial disorders.

A variety of programs have been developed for
preventive intervention at this stage of the family
life cycle (Bolman, 1968; Kessler & Albee, 1975).
It is striking to note, however, that none of these
programs are aimed at new fathers; they focus either
on the mother or on the mother-child relationship.
This is disconcerting because as the importance of the
father in the family becomes increasingly recognized
in the family therapy literature (English, 1954;
Bowen, Dysinger, & Basamania, 1959), he continues to
be ignored in preventive work. This is not the place
to speculate on the reasons for this gap, but it is
often a stereotype of family oriented intervention
programs that fathers "aren't interested."

The stage of childbirth, however, is a time when fathers are interested as well as stressed. It is a critical period for the father because of the dynamic issues confronting him and his family (i.e., his own displacement--becoming the "peripheral person" in the family). Hence, it is during this time that fathers are most available and preventive programs regarding their role can have the most impact. In addition, providing mental health services focused on mothers and the mother-child relationship, while often desirable, may compound the problem for the "father-to-be" as it can reaffirm the father's sense of being the "peripheral person."

PROGRAM GOALS: TOWARD PREPARED FATHERHOOD

In order to examine with fathers-to-be (FTB) some of their issues and concerns, we developed a program for the FTB who were attending childbirth preparation classes. We had three major goals. First, we wanted to sensitize the new father to a variety of issues that he would encounter during this transition. This would encourage him to consciously "work on" issues in order to combat the feelings of helplessness which are described as major characteristics of the state of crisis. Our second goal was to emphasize the father's continuing involvement with and importance to the family. The third goal was to help the FTP combat his subjective sense of isolation by facilitating peer support.

The primary task of these groups was to heighten the awareness of the fathers-to-be as to their attitudes, behavior, and thoughts during their transition to fatherhood. These groups, at times, appeared akin to consciousness-raising groups, fraternity bull-sessions, and/or primitive tribal groups effecting a "rite of passage."

These meetings occurred within the context of a larger prepared childbrith training program. Over the course of five other meetings conducted by nurses, couples examined a variety of relevant issues, including the course of pregnancy, natural childbirth exercises, labor, delivery, possible physical complications, breast-feeding, etc. During the sixth lesson the wives and husbands were separated into two groups. The wives discussed with nurses specific medical issues relating to post-operative procedures and reac-

tions (e.g., unresponsive bladders), while the husbands were informed that they would have an opportunity to discuss issues related to their experiences of
their wives' pregnancies as well as their own entrance
into fatherhood. These groups occurred during the
last half of the last trimester of the wife's pregnancy. It was believed that this period is a potentially stressful one not only for the wife but for
the husband as well as he is typically dealing with
issues of adequacy, normalcy, preparation, "peripher-
alness," etc.

Physicians actively encourage their patients to
attend these classes and expectant parents from a
wide range of socio-economic levels become members of
these classes. Participants in these classes also cut
across ethnic and religious groups. Most couples are
having their first child and the majority are under
30. The groups consisted of from 15-40 expectant
fathers with one or two male leaders. Optimal group
size was 20 or under and one male group leader appeared sufficient. Groups "for men only" created a
quick cohesive bond among the participants which was
lost if curious females were allowed to remain. Typically these groups were 1-1/2 to 2 hours in length.
For most of these fathers, this is their first contact with a mental health professional and for the
professional, it is an opportunity to meet and talk
with a group of men who are at a significant juncture
in their lives.

The expectant fathers met as a group separate
from their wives in order to facilitate an open and
direct discussion of their feelings toward their
pregnant wives, infants-to-be, and new and changing
roles. Their worries, feelings, and past trials and
tribulations associated with the pregnancy and eventual birth of their child were more openly discussed
when the fathers met separately from their wives.
They usually began by relating experiences during
their wife's pregnancy that were stressful. For example, an expectant father might begin to talk about how
he experienced his wife's morning sickness and/or
about her crying episodes. The discussion would move
from this beginning eventually to cover a large number
of issues. The discussion was usually direct and
open, and it was not unusual for a father to exclaim,
"Sometimes she really drives me up the wall. Sometimes I felt like smacking her one. But instead, I

put my arm around her and told her it's okay."

LEADER INTERVENTIONS

The groups were at first unstructured in order to uncover what issues were important to fathers. We opened the groups with "What do you want to talk about?" or "I'm wondering what you guys are going through now," allowing the groups to proceed according to their own dynamic. If groups got stuck at this point, a quick overview of the possible topics would typically free up the participants. This format has continued essentially unchanged as we found the groups covering the same basic issues on their own momentum. Leader interventions were primarily facilitative in order to amplify, clarify, and focus issues.

We found the following six types of interventions helpful to the group task of sharing common concerns.

1. Modeling Self-disclosure. In a one-session group it was important to get into the issues quickly. Modeling self-disclosure served to help the group move quickly to a more personal level and away from the passive-receptive style which was more appropriate in other parts of the childbirth education program. It was, of course, helpful for the leader to have had his initiation into fatherhood and fathering.

2. Providing Information. Covering a variety of cognitive issues rapidly expanded the information base of the expectant fathers. Issues of how to handle the delivery, wife's moodiness, nesting behavior, the sexual relationship, the mother and mother-in-law, the newborn, role negotiations, etc., and questions about breast-feeding, post-partum depression, and possible birth defects were almost always covered and could be easily elicited to clarify misconceptions. Gathering new information with the possibility of sharing it with his wife also helped the expectant father feel he was doing something active rather than having to remain passive and relatively helpless.

3. Eliciting Affect. While cognitive issues were being addressed, it was possible to begin to

focus on the fathers' affective experiences.
It is a rare man who will deny having feelings during this time in his life. Gentle
elicitation of affect enhanced the cohesiveness of the group, thus decreasing the expectant father's sense of isolation.

4. Recruiting Interpersonal Resources. Another
way to decrease the father's sense of isolation was by facilitating the use of resources
within the group. Often, rather than answering questions as "the expert," the leader referred questions to other group members. This
encouraged group interaction, decreased the
dependency on the expert, provided legitimacy
to the father's desire to ask for help, and
enhanced those who could provide support,
direction, or information in this context.

5. Normalizing of Experiences. A major intervention strategy was to provide a context for
normalizing the experiences of these fathers.
Our background in family and crisis theory
provided us a wider range of expectations for
"normal" behavior than most of these fathers
had. We took nearly every opportunity to
attempt to expand the range of behaviors defined as "normal." The average father-to-be
who had no had extensive contact with other
"expecting" couples often experienced his
wife's, as well as his own, responses as
unique and idiosyncratic and rarely as typical (Greenberg & Morris, 1974). While there
were obvious limits to what should be included here, we attempted to expand tolerances
whenever reasonable.

6. Personalizing Interactions. When the group
moved ahead with its tasks and it appeared
that the relevant cognitive, affective, interpersonal, and social issues were being dealt
with, we added a further dimension of dealing
with personal, here-and-now issues. It was
not difficult for most men to talk about the
last childbirth or how their wives were feeling. It was more difficult for the fathers to
talk about their own feelings in the current
situation. When such immediate reality entered the group, however, it enhanced the

110

sharing significantly. It did not appear
necessary in our one-session groups, however, to reach this level of group development to do considerable constructive work.
Indeed, if a group was slow getting started
or larger than optimal in size, this stage
was not desirable. When feasible we worked
with the participants to have them "own" their
otherwise projected fears, concerns, and fantasies.

DEVELOPMENTAL TASKS

From our discussion, with "expectant" and "experienced" fathers, it appears that the process of
becoming a father can be divided into six developmental tasks. These tasks are generally sequential
though they are not necessarily epigenetic in that
there is much overlap and variation in their order of
appearance across individuals. The extent to which
these tasks are completed, resolved and/or mastered
might suggest the outcome during this transition:
crisis or growth. The tasks include the following:

1. Decision-making. Initially the father must
   decide to have a child, or ex post facto,
   accept the reality that he is going to have
   one. With the current availability of con-
   traceptives and legalized procedures for
   terminating pregnancy, this choice is a real
   one in most cases. The decision, of course,
   has both personal implications for the expectant father as well as ramifications in
   his relationship with his spouse. Although
   this issue has unconscious derivatives, only
   the more superficial aspects of this decision-
   making process are discussed.

2. Mourning. While the new father gains the role
   of father he also undergoes substantial loss.
   If he is to be active as a father, he loses
   some personal freedom. His wife's time and
   attention becomes increasingly limited, thus
   decreasing the freedom and flexibility they
   have within that relationship. Much of the
   father/husband's response to this depends upon
   the meaning he attributes to his new role.
   From conception to delivery and through early
   infancy, fathers often report feeling "dis-

counted" (i.e., a sense of being in the background). With the initial excitement of the
newborn (Greenberg & Morris, 1974; Russell,
1974), these losses are often not noticed or
mourned until much later.

3. Empathic Responding. One of the most potentially satisfying tasks of the expectant
father is being able to be supportive and nurturant toward his wife during her pregnancy
and labor. This responsiveness is apparently
due to two factors unique to this task.
First, such responses can be tangible and concrete in that they involve actual tasks rather
than symbolic, relational or emotional ones.
Such tasks allow the father to experience
successful coping which is important in
combating the sense of helplessness that is
characteristic of the state of crisis (Caplin,
1964). Second, it is also unique in that such
"special treatment" is time-limited. While at
times the pregnancy may feel interminable to
both spouses, it has clearly defined temporal
boundaries. Often a difficult part of the
pregnancy occurs (especially in those recently married) when the expectant father (and
new husband) begins to fear his relationship
is permanently changed and that his wife will
demand such special treatment forever.

4. Integrating. At the end of pregnancy comes
the concrete reality of the child who now must
be integrated into the spatial, temporal, and
social life space of the developing family.
While fantasy phantoms and fears disappear
in the warm physical reality of an infant,
so also appear noises and smells at some of
the most inconvenient moments. Integrating
these realities into the family culture is
often complicated by the infant's body rhythms
and his need for space which compete with
those of other family members. Similarly, as
mentioned above, the father needs to maintain
his acceptance of the child while taking a
frequent second, or at least a different,
place in his wife's priorities. The question,
"How much times does the husband spend with
his wife and how much times does he spend with

112

the mother of his child?" is answered by the
ways in which the father integrates these
"fathering" and "husbanding" rsponsibilities.

5. Establishing Family Boundaries and Differentiating from the Extended Family. After the
wife and newborn arrive home, the father participates in redefining the family boundaries
with regard to the nuclear and extended family
and larger social network. These boundary
issues include such concrete matters as how
long visitors can stay with the convalescing
mother, negotiating with family members who
wish to "help out," deciding if and when to
have "private time" for husband, wife and
child in spite of the presence of extended
family members, and issues involving interpersonal influence and power (i.e., both grand-
mother and mother often refer to the infant as
"my child"). The new father must now also alter his role as an individual in his extended
family. He has moved between generations,
becoming primarily a parent rather than a son.
In addition, he becomes connected in a whole
new series of family relationships transforming (or further establishing) his siblings to
(as) aunts and uncles, his parents to (as)
grandparents, etc.

6. Synergizing. The father's last task is developing a sense of trust or faith in the
adequacy of the child, the marriage, the
family, and himself. This includes an
integration of the previous five tasks into a
coherent life style, along with an acceptance
of the father's own imperfections and those of
his family. Establishing a new equilibrium
following the completion of the previous tasks
is the state we call "synergy." Synergy in
this context refers to "a state of...enhance-
ment" (Hampden-Turner, 1970), which is
achieved when there is an affective and
intellectual synthesis of all of these tasks.
Caplan's (1964) suggestion that a psychosocial
crisis often is resolved in six weeks or less
is consistent with our experience, though the
range of normalcy here appears to be quite
broad. Depending on the individual character-

istics of the father, the attainment of this state can be experienced as a relief, a clearing of confusion, a sense of solidity, a "high," etc. It is also this state that marks the end of the three stages of childbirth we have observed in these fathers: preparation, the birth process, and after-shock. The successful resolution of this task prepares the family for their next developmental stage: infancy.

COMING OF AGE AS A FATHER

For a broader understanding, these basic tasks can be organized at two levels: concerns about competency or adequacy in individual family members and concerns about changes in role behaviors.

With regard to adequacy, the expectant father is concerned about his ability as a husband and a father. His most acute and overt anxiety is about his performance as a competent husband during labor and childbirth. Though there is little for him to do, he has a high sense of risk and many questions about how to do things right. There is some concern about after the birth, that is, how to be a father, but this lacks immediacy compared to the birth process. There is occasional concern for his wife's competence as a mother, though it is generally assumed that this spouse will somehow know better than he how to be a parent. One increasingly frequent concern is whether a working woman will be able to adjust to being around the house all day.

The most acute anxiety for the expectant father focuses on the process of childbirth itself, the primary issue being danger to his wife's life and/or that of the neonate. Clearly the star of the show with regard to adequacy concerns is the unborn child. Fears of deformity, miscarriage, and inherited family problems provide one of the major sources of the high level of anxiety characterizing this transition period. All expectant fathers must come to terms with this issue, though the means vary. Other concerns regarding the newborn are gender preference and naming. For some these are small issues, for others with strong extended family or cultural roots, they are significant adequacy concerns.

114

Changes in interactions brought about by the new-born child necessitate role transitions for the expectant father in three major transactional areas: his relation to his new child, his wife, and the outside world. The most obvious role transition is developing a role in relation to the new child. While the development of this role begins before the birth of the child, the father does not get sufficient tangible feedback for clarifying this role until after the child is born. In developing new role behaviors, the father is concerned about how he will relate to the child and how the child will relate to him. As noted above, a common question relates to how one learns "how to father." The most popular answers to this question are that such skills come from one's own father, peers, and books.

Another obvious role transiton is with the expectant father's spouse. Developing the role of co-parent can result in role strains and stresses in the previously established husband-wife role structure. It is, thus, a realistic concern for the new father whether he will continue to have a satisfying marriage and if so, on what basis. Most specifically, the major change is related to sharing and receiving less of his wife's attention. This tangible change often results in a sensation of loss, of being left out, or of being deprived though the subjective meaning of this change varies for each individual.

With regard to the social environment outside the family, the father has two major tasks. First, he has a role in determining the time-space dimensions as well as the permeability of the family's boundary. The second major task of the father is integrating himself and his new child into the extended family. With a first child, the father is now both a parent and a son. In addition, he transforms his siblings into aunts and uncles, his parents into grandparents, etc., so that he cannot help but increase his experiencing of his family's link to the past and the future.

CONCLUSIONS

The prepared childbirth classes frequently found in hospitals throughout the country offer unique opportunities for the mental health professional. They provide the professional with a forum to explore significant events in the life of most fathers. In the past, most of the focus has been on the expectant mother, but there is a recent and growing interest in the expectant father's role. Prepared childbirth reaffirms the role of the father in the birth of the infant. He no longer needs to be a worried, hand-wringing, frightened father pacing back and forth in the waiting room who passively awaits the proclamation from the physician, "You are the proud father of a bouncing baby." The father's role has moved from the waiting room to the delivery room. He has become an active, important, and integral part of his child's birth. Accompanying this new and different role is an interest in the impact a new family addition has on the expectant father and his relationship to his wife and those around him.

B I B L I O G R A P H Y

Ackerman, N.

  1958   The Psychodynamics of Family Life.
                   New York: Basic.

Bolman, W.

  1968   "Preventive Psychiatry for the Family:
                   Theory, Approaches, and Programs."
                   American Journal of Psychiatry, 125,
                   458-472.

Bowen, M., Dysinger, R.,
& Basamania, B.

  1959   "The Role of the Father in Families with
                   a Schizophrenic Patient." American
                   Journal of Psychiatry, 115, 1017-1020.

Bowlby, J.

  1960   "Grief and Mourning in Infancy and Early
                   Childhood." Psychoanalytic Study of the
                   Child, 15, 11-12.

Caplan, G.

  1964   Principles of Preventive Psychiatry.
                   New York: Basic.

Dyer, E.

  1963   "Parenthood as Crisis: A Re-study."
                   Marriage and Family Living, 25, 196-201.

Eliot, T.

  1955   "Handling Family Strains and Shocks."
                   In H. Becker & R. Hill (Eds.), Family
                   Marriage and Parenthood. Boston:
                   Heath.

English, O.S.

  1954   "Psychological Role of the Father in
                   the Family." Social Casework, 35,
                   323-329.

Erikson, E.

1950   Childhood and Society. New York:
Norton.

Greenberg, M., &
Morris, N.

1974   "Engrossment: The Newborn's Impact
Upon the Father." American Journal
of Orthopsychiatry, 44, 520-531.

Hadley, T., Jacob, T.,
Milliones, J. Caplan, J.,
& Spritz, D.

1974   "The Relationship Between Family Devel-
opment Crisis and the Appearance of
Symptoms in a Family Member." Family
Process, 13, 207-214.

Hampden-Turner, C.

1970   Radical Man: The Process of Psychosocial Development. Cambridge:
Schenkman.

Kaplan, D., &
Maston, E.

1960   "Maternal Reactions to Premature Birth
Viewed as an Acute Emotional Disorder."
American Journal of Orthopsychiatry,
30, 118-128.

Kessler, M., &
Albee, G.

1975   "Primary Prevention." Annual Review of
Psychology, 26, 557-591.

Klein, D., &
Ross, A.

1958   "Kindergarten Entry: A Study of Role
Transition." In M. Krugman (Ed.),
Orthopsychiatry and the School. New
York: American Orthopsychiatric Asso-
ciation.

LeMasters, E.E.

1957   "Parenthood as Crisis." Marriage and
                Family Living, 19, 352-355.

Lindemann, E.

1944   "Symptomatology and Management of Acute
                Grief." American Journal of Psychiatry,
                101, 141-148.

Murphy, E.

1963   "Development of Autonomy and Parent-
                Child Interaction in Late Adolescence."
                American Journal of Orthopsychiatry,
                33, 643-652.

Rapaport, R.

1963   "Normal Crisis, Family Structure and
                Mental Health." Family Process, 2,
                68-80.

Russell, C.S.

1974   "Transition to Parenthood: Problems
                and Gratifications." Journal of Mar-
                riage and the Family, 36, 294-301.

Signell, K.

1972   "Kindergarten Entry: A Preventive
                Approach to Community Mental Health."
                Community Mental Health Journal, 8,
                60-70.

Stierlin, H.

1971   "Parental Perceptions of Separating
                Children." Family Process, 10, 411-428.

**Laurence Barnhill is Coordinator of Outpatient and
Emergency Services, South Central Mental Health Center, Bloomington, Indiana 47401. Gerald Rubenstein
is Director of Consultation and Education, University
of Rochester Medical Center, Department of Psychiatry,
Rochester, New York 14642. Neil Rocklin is Assistant
Professor of Pediatrics, University of Virginia Medical Center, Child Rehabilitation Center, Commonwealth
Court, Charlottesville, Virginia 22901.

Reprinted from The Family Coodinator, Vol. 28 (April,
1979): 229-235. Copyrighted 1979 by the National
Council on Family Relations. Reprinted by permission.

CHAPTER 7

LIMITATIONS OF THE FAMILY AS A SUPPORTIVE INSTITUTION IN THE LIVES OF THE AGED

Russell A. Ward*

Considerable evidence exists that the extended family continues to be a significant source of support for older people. There are limitations to its effectiveness in meeting certain needs, however. While the family is particularly effective in acute, emergency situations, it is poorly suited to the provision of long-term assistance. Family interaction may offer only minimal social integration, and few meaningful roles for old age, concerns which are likely to rise among the aged in the future. More thought might be given to age peers as an alternative to the family.

Modern societies are encountering increasing numbers and proportions of older people. In the United States, the number of people 65 and over has risen from 3 million in 1900 to over 22 million currently, and is expected to reach 30 million by the year 2000. Their proportion of the population has grown to more than 10%, and may eventually be as high as 15%. Growth has been particularly great among the "old-old" (75 and over). Recognition of these trends has raised concern about society's continuing ability and willingness, to address the needs of its older members adequately. This is exemplified in debate over the presumed future financial crisis in Social Security. Thus, there is a need to analyze the future needs and possible sources of support of older persons in modern societies.

The nature of the aging experience for any individual is shaped by the social and cultural context within which aging occurs. An important part of this context are the systems of support--material, social, and psychological--affecting the ability of older people to live independent, satisfying lives of their own choosing. The supportive context within which the aged live may be particularly critical, since it has been suggested that they display greater "environmental docility," whereby their behavior is shaped more completely by the environment than is true for younger persons (Lawton & Nahemow, 1973).

The family constitutes an important supportive institution in the environment of older people. It is the intention of this paper to explore both the potential and limitations of the family as a source of support for the aged in modern societies.

THE CHANGING FAMILY CONTEXT OF AGING MEMBERS

The family has always played an important role in determining the status and security of older people. One reason given for the higher status of the aged in at least some preindustrial societies is the respect, authority, and economic and social security accorded to them within the extended family (Simmons, 1960; Rosow, 1974). When an extended family system exists, older people become the beneficiaries of reciprocity within a network of mutual dependence. "Social security" meant involvement in a large network of family relationships.

During the 1950's and 1960's, a number of observers suggested that this extended family system was breaking up into autonomous nuclear family units (Parsons, 1959; Burgess, 1960; Goode, 1963). This was presumably the consequence of industrialization and urbanization, which resulted in new institutions taking over family functions (e.g., education, protection), a new occupational system stressing universalism and personal mobility, and an urban milieu of secondary relationships to replace family contacts. Cowgill (1974) has suggested that modernization, and particularly urbanization and mass education, creates residential, social, and intellectual separation of the generations through residential mobility and status inversion (children acquire higher status than their parents). If these analyses are correct, the aged would increasingly be cut off from family-based assistance, and would have to rely more heavily upon formal helping institutions.

More recent work has suggested, however, that this epitaph for the modern extended family was premature and exaggerated (Sussman & Burchinal, 1962; Shanas et al., 1968; Adams, 1970; Troll, 1971). It appears that the aged are more integrated into industrial society than was previously thought, and that the family plays an important role in this integration. The evidence shows substantial residential proximity and regular interaction, even in the absence of close proximity, between elderly persons and their families. Though older people generally prefer to live independently of their families, and increasingly have done so, a substantial minority live with children or other relatives. Considerable aid and services--money, shopping, child care, illness assistance, etc.--flow back and forth across generations, and the family continues to be an operating social network to compensate for and replace social losses associated with aging. Indeed, the potential of the extended family network is greater than ever, since the widespread four-generation family is a distinctly modern phenomenon. Studies indicate that family assistance during emergencies is often preferred, and sought first, over formal community helping agencies (Quarantelli, 1960; Hill, 1970). In terms of social contacts, older persons interact more frequently with family than with friends or neighbors (Riley & Foner, 1968).

It is clear, then, that the extended family has remained a viable social institution offering assistance and support in a variety of ways to its older members. The modern family has been referred to as a "modified extended family," or sometimes as "intimacy at a distance," to reflect the fact that although families are less likely to live together, they do maintain regular contact. This contact is fostered by what Adams (1967) terms "positive concern"--a long-standing, durable interest in the welfare of other family members.

Variation exists in extended family involvement, of course, as well as in the need for family assistance. For example, older women are more likely than older men to be widowed and living alone, but they are also more likely to have cultivated extended family ties (Adams, 1970). The extended family is likely to be less available for migrants to retirement communities and rural older people left behind by out-migration of the young. Wylie (1971) has suggested that black families are more receptive to the aged than white families, and there is evidence of considerable interaction and mutual aid within black extended families (Hays & Mindel, 1973; Sussman, 1976). Societies themselves appear to differ in the strength of

123

the extended family. For example, the family in
Denmark appears to be less close-knit than in the
United States or Great Britain (Shanas, et al., 1968),
while Japan may have the greatest integration of older
people into the family of any modern, industrial
society (Palmore, 1975).

While granting these variations in the extended
family, it is evident that social policy directed at
the aged must take into account the continuing role of
the extended family as a source of social contacts,
social and emotional support, and financial and personal assistance. To do so effectively, however, requires not only an appreciation of the usefulness of
family ties, but also a recognition of their limitations. This is true whether we wish to formulate
social policy, or we are trying to advise those helping professionals who work with the family. To illustrate, let us look at some selected issues.

WIDOWHOOD AND BEREAVEMENT

As couples age together, it is quite likely that
many needs which had been met elsewhere will be increasingly focused on the marriage relationship, as
children leave the home, retirement occurs, and contacts with other persons are limited by poor health or
death. Thus, widowhood for an older person may create
a severe crisis in the ability to fulfill interpersonal needs. More generally, the aged may encounter
what Kastenbaum and Aisenberg (1976) refer to as "bereavement overload." As one ages, the deaths of con-
temporaries occur more frequently, with less time to
adjust to each new loss. The extended family is a
particularly useful institution in assisting older
people facing widowhood and bereavement. It offers a
variety of social relationships as potential replace-
ments, and can render many services to the recently
bereaved.

Studies indicate that the extended family does
function quite effectively at such times, providing
emotional, social, and financial support. In her
study of widows in Chicago, Lopata (1973a) found that
children, particularly unmarried children, were effective as objects of care and attention to replace the
deceased husband. They provided close interpersonal
ties when they were most needed, and performed many
helpful tasks, such as taking care of funeral arrange-

ments, cooking, and cleaning. Another study (Glick, Weiss, & Parkes, 1974) of both widows and widowers showed similar patterns of assistance. For example, female kin often assumed responsibility for household tasks, and brothers-in-law were often particularly supportive of widows.

But these studies also illustrate the limitations of the family as a supportive institution. Glick, et al. (1974) found that bereavement processes continued at least throughout the first year of widowhood. Most family members returned to their own lives following the funeral, however, so that reactions of the widowed to their loss were often intensified after the funeral. Lopata found that widows were frequently unwilling to undertake too many family obligations, partly because of a sense of vulnerability to exploitation. The proportion of widowed persons living alone has increased from 20% in 1940 to 50% in 1970 (Chevan & Korson, 1972). This reflects the competition, role reversal, and status inversion involved in sharing a household with children, as well as a growing ethic of allowing children to live their own lives. There is little evidence of any major new involvement in family affairs by those who are widowed (Lopata, 1973a; Pihlblad & Adams, 1972), and this appears to be as true for blacks as for whites (Lopata, 1973b; Arling, 1976). Contact with one segment of the extended family--in-laws--is quite likely to be broken by widowhood (Lopata, 1973a; Rosenberg & Anspack, 1973).

THE FAMILY AND INSTITUTIONALIZATION

The rising population of nursing homes over the past 25 years has sometimes been taken as evidence of rejection of the aged by their families. In fact, there is little evidence that older people are forced into institutions because of family abandonment (Shanas & Maddox, 1976). This is not meant to deny that some older people are neglected by their families, but institutional populations are disproportionately drawn from those who are childless, widowed, and living alone. Those who enter nursing homes typically do so after a variety of alternatives, including living with family, have been tried, so that institutionalization signals a growing imbalance between service needs and the capacity of community supports to meet those needs (Townsend, 1965).

There is no question that community-based services should be a high policy priority, partly to
provide more alternatives to institutionalization.
The extended family can continue to play an important role in providing support in the community, but
again we must recognize the limitations of the family.
Caring for an aged person carries the potential for
family burdens and friction. Any system of community
services must consider both benefits and costs relative to institutionalization, and a point will be
reached at which costs of caring for someone in the
community outweigh institutional costs. Costs to the
family are not only material, but social and emotional
as well. This is illustrated by a study comparing
hospital and home care of schizophrenics (Pasamanick,
Scarpitti, & Dinitz, 1967). The study found that
patients did equally well when kept in the community,
with substantial financial savings, but there were
important costs to the family during the first six
months of home care, including: trouble at night,
worry and concern, upsetting deviant behavior; disruption of household routines, physical strain, and
losing time at work. Such studies, as well as the
earlier material on widowhood and bereavement, suggest
that the family continues to be an important source
of emergency assistance, but that family members may
be unwilling to continue this assistance for long
periods of time, or the costs to the family of such
assistance may prove prohibitive without substantial
support from the larger community.

THE NATURE OF FAMILY INTERACTION

To this point we have focused largely on the
family as a source of material and emotional assistance during times of acute need. Another function
of the family which has been stressed, however, is its
role as a network of relationships which can provide
social integration. Because of the loss of roles,
particularly through retirement and widowhood, and
other barriers to social interaction--poor health,
lack of transportation, etc.--the aged may become isolated and marginal to the ongoing social worlds around
them. Rosow (1974) has stressed the normlessness and
rolelessness of old age, and the failure of socialization processes at the end of the life cycle. This
marginality and anomie may well create confusion,
alienation, and disengagement. Atchley (1977) has
pointed out, however, that the lack of an "old age

role" may be counteracted through particularistic roles performed by each individual older person. It is here that the family may play an important role in social integration, and the evidence of proximity and frequency of interaction suggests that this may be the case.

But there is room for skepticism about the socializing functions of the extended family. While proximity and contact appear relatively high, we know surprisingly little about the quality and meaning of interactions between older people and their families. Existing patterns of interaction do not necessarily imply emotional closeness of warmth, and contacts may be largely ritualistic. Blau (1973), for example, suggests that "intimacy at a distance" may only be a euphemism for pseudo-intimacy and marginal status in the family. Certainly a few contacts each week hardly constitute a meaningful social world.

The grandparent role offers a case in point. Studies of grandparenthood suggest that it carries limited significance and is primarily symbolic and ritualistic, with little meaningful involvement in the lives of grandchildren (Neugarten & Weinstein, 1964; Kahana & Kahana, 1971; Wood & Robertson, 1976). This seems to be equally true for blacks (Jackson, 1971). Studies of grandchildren indicate that they have favorable attitudes, but distant relationships with grandparents--they are not chosen as companions, advisors, or role models (Kahana, 1970; Robertson, 1976). Grandparents seem to be "nice people" who have little impact on the lives of grandchildren. If other family roles are similar, there is little basis for true social integration or the development of meaning-ful role activities.

AGE PEERS AS A SUPPLEMENT TO THE FAMILY

If the extended family's role in social integra-tion is limited, perhaps age peers would be an effec-tive supplement or substitute. From childhood on, friends play important roles in socialization, provid-ing emotional support, information, and opportunities for role rehearsal (Hess, 1972; Rosow, 1974). Though financial assistance is rare, older people's friends often help during emergencies and check up on well-being (Riley & Foner, 1968). Even one intimate friend seems to serve as a buffer against age-linked social losses (Lowenthal & Haven, 1968).

Studies of a variety of age-segregated living arrangements suggest that they enhance social integration by providing age and cohort peers for interaction, and such settings may become a social community, with its own statuses, roles, and networks of mutual assistance (Messer, 1967; Rosow, 1967; Bultena & Wood, 1969; Hochschild, 1973; Sherman, 1975a, b; Wax, 1976). Thus, the aged are embedded in an ongoing system of social relationships, instead of possibly sporadic and ritualistic family contacts, and are socialized into new roles and norms. Evidence suggests that older people are freer in certain ways around age peers than with family members. For example, they can engage in leisure "careers" and activities which might be derogated as "silly" by the larger society. Of particular importance is the fact that involvement with age peers seems to facilitate discussion and legitimation of death, through role models of how to react to the death of others and how to face up to one's own death (Hochschild, 1973; Marshall, 1975). The family rarely provides this, since older people tend to view death as a taboo topic for family discussions.

The effectiveness of age peers opens up the possibility of using older people as service providers, not just service recipients. The use of peers for providing support and assistance has long been recognized in such diverse programs as Alcoholics Anonymous, Synanon, and Weight Watchers. Older people are already playing effective roles in retirement counseling, widow-to-widow programs, and telephone reassurance programs, but the potential for their involvement has only begun to be tapped. Older volunteers can perhaps yield benefits that family and other service providers cannot--reassurance and support from a peer--as well as providing opportunities for meaningful activities for the volunteers themselves. We have seen with widowhood that the family's involvement is relatively short-lived. This is one area where peers (other widows) can make unique contributions. To some extent this may occur informally, through involvement in a "society of widows" (Cumming & Henry, 1961).

As with family ties, however, there are limitations to the utility of age peers. Mutual assistance and a sense of community are by no means inevitable results of age-segregated living (Jacobs, 1975; Sherman, 1975a, b). In addition, Lopata (1973a) noted that many of the widows she studied seemed to have lost the capacity to use neighbors as a source of social contacts. This may be a particular problem for men, whose friendships are typically less involved and intense than those of women. Finallly, emotional ties to family often remain more salient than friends or neighbors, even when family interaction is minimal. Age peers do not really substitute for family ties; rather, the two types of relationships provide different things, as noted by Hochschild (1973, p.96) in her study of an old-age apartment complex:

> In a deep sense and over the long run, the two kinds of relationships did not really compete; one could not replace the other even in the "time filling" sense. To the widows, children are a socio-emotional insurance policy that peers can never be. Kin ties run deeper and have a longer history than peer ties. When a grandmother is in deep trouble, she turns to blood ties first. When a widow needs a lot of money, she turns to kin; when she needs "something to tide her over till payday," she turns to a neighbor. When there was an accident or death in the building, peers were the first to find out, but kin were the first to be called.

CONCLUSIONS AND IMPLICATIONS

When we speak of aging and the family, we are referring to a type of community-based supportive institution. Many types of community-based services need to be available to the aged (Beattie, 1976; Ward, 1977a). The task for policy-makers and those who work more directly with the family is to determine where the family best fits within a system of formal and informal approaches to meeting the needs of older people. The extended family has clearly played a continuing supportive role, and this role will certainly continue in the future. Nevertheless, we must recognize that the family is effective in some arenas, but not in others. Our policies should aim to support family functioning where it is effective, and support alternatives where it is not. Additionally, as the nature of society and of aging within that society change, we must recognize that the role of family will also change.

Litwak and Szelenyi (1969) have pointed out some of the differences among the social relationships in which older people are embedded. Neighbors, because of their close proximity, are best-suited to provide immediate assistance, as well as a regular check-up on well-being. Friends, on the other hand, provide a reference group and sociability based upon consensus and homophily. The key functions of the family relate to its unique involvement in long-term commitments and reciprocal assistance. This partly explains why older people will turn to the family during emergencies, whether illness, bereavement, or natural disaster, instead of to neighbors, friends, or formal agencies. While neighbors or friends may provide "favors," such relationships lack the history of reciprocity and emotional dependence which make help-seeking seem appropriate. Similarly, assistance from family lacks implications of welfare or dependency often attached to formal agencies, since the long history of reciprocal interactions portrays assistance as one's "earned right." And one can perhaps eventually repay kin, but not a service bureaucracy.

The key role of the extended family lies in dealing with acute problems faced by the aged. The mobility characteristic of modern societies has made a neighborhood-based family network of ongoing social relationships increasingly rare, except perhaps in urban working-class areas, but this mobility has also spread the family out geographically so that at least some kin can respond with relative quickness to the needs of other kin. Whatever the emergency--financial, health, housing, bereavement--the family is still the most effective and efficient responder to the needs of the aged, and is still the most welcome helping institution. Assistance is not without its costs to those family members who provide it, however, and programs should aim to support the role of the family by providing assistance in the form of money, manpower (e.g., visiting nurses), and counseling. To simply rely on the family to fill the gap without supporting its role can only weaken its ability and willingness to do so.

The limitations of the extended family are also important in assessing the future needs of the aged.

It seems clear that the extended family is no longer appropriate to meeting the long-term, chronic needs of older people--money, nursing care, housing, transportation. In this sense, the classical extended family of preindustrial times has passed on. This is due, in part, to the development of other social institutions to meet these needs (however inadequately they may do so) and the separation of the family through residential mobility, which makes lengthy assistance to the aged very disruptive of normal family functioning. But it is also true that the tremendous value placed on freedom and independence in modern societies limits the willingness of kin to sacrifice their own lives to help the aged, and also limits the willingness of the aged to request such assistance and thereby become dependent.

In addition, the extended family is not universally available. It appears to be more important in the working-class than in the middle-class. The rural and suburban elderly are likely to be more isolated from family assistance, since rural dwellers are likely to be faced with out-migration by younger family members and suburban residents may, themselves, have moved away from kin. Some recent immigrant groups may still be embedded in an ongoing extended family structure. Women are generally more involved in extended family affairs than men, so that men may benefit less from family assistance. Policies directed at the aged must take into account this variability in the availability of the extended family.

In some ways, the relative importance of the extended family may decline in the future, as the nature of aging cohorts and their needs change. Future cohorts of older people can be expected to be better off financially, better educated, and in better health. Palmore (1976) cites evidence that the relative status of older people in the United States is already rising. Uhlenberg (1977) points out that succeeding cohorts of the aged will be increasingly similar to each other, as immigration has declined and mass education has reached more recent groups of older people. Such trends suggest that many of the problems of cultural dislocation and severe hardship will be less prominent in the future, so that all helping institutions, including the family, will be less burdened. Remaining service needs are likely to be focused on the longterm, chronic problems of the "old-old" (75+), who constitute an increasing proportion of the older population. These are the needs which seem least amenable to family intervention.

Treas (1977) has also suggested that the effectiveness of the family as a helping institution may decline in the future. Declining fertility implies fewer descendants for aging parents to call upon, and there will be increasing numbers of "old-old" persons whose offspring are themselves elderly. Treas also notes that the changing social roles (and interests, obligations, and constraints) of modern women may lessen the supportive role of the family, since women have traditionally been the mainstays of family networks.

Finally, the emerging needs of future older people may have less to do with material needs and more to do with social and psychological needs--their position in the culture, the use of time, the availability of meaningful roles in ongoing community life. These are needs which are not effectively addressed by the extended family. Although the family can coalesce in times of need, it remains a diffuse social network which seems now to offer few meaningful or "meaty" roles for its older members. Social policies are needed which encourage flexibility and options throughout the life cycle--a "loosening up of life" (Butler, 1975)--so that people are prepared for the latter part of the life cycle, and entrance into old age is no longer so disruptive. Age peers comprise a potential social institution for addressing these new social needs, reducing social marginality, encouraging and supporting life style experimentation, and providing the bases for new self-conceptions as a reference group which provides meaningful role models (Ward, 1977b).

To conclude, the extended family is still an important social institution in modern societies. In terms of assistance to the aged, it is often the "first resort," and always serves as a material, social, and emotional insurance policy. Every effort should be made to support the family's role. But the family is poorly suited to meeting the chronic material, social, and psychological needs of older persons. Most importantly, it is not likely to provide the aged with meaningful roles and activities on an ongoing basis. For such purposes, we would do better to encourage and gather greater involvement among age peers.

The encouragement of supportive networks among older age peers partly implies greater use of age-segregated living arrangements. The clearest evidence that age-segregated residences can be beneficial for the aged comes from a national survey of older residents of public housing (Teaff, Lawton, Nahemow, & Carlson, 1978). The study found that age segregation was associated with higher morale, housing satisfaction, activity, and neighborhood mobility. This was attributed to increased feelings of personal security and the emergence of age-specific activity patterns and norms. The authors estimated that 1,250,000 older people would like to move and would prefer living with age peers--four times the number currently residing in housing for the elderly.

Specifically, age-segregated housing is not the only option, however, and many older people have no interest in such settings. There appears to be a more "natural" form of residential age segregation, whereby older persons tend to be concentrated in certain parts of metropolitan areas (LaGory, Ward, & Juravich, 1977). We need a better understanding of how social networks might develop among age peers in such situations, providing both direct support and serving as a referral network. There is also a need to better understand the factors which promote the emergence of social networks among older people outside of "old age" housing and the functions which such networks serve. Once this understanding is achieved, social policy can be more effectively directed at using networks of age peers to meet the psychological, social, and material needs of the aged. Service programs might then be able to tie into these ongoing networks, or find ways to encourage their more effective functioning. Local senior centers could also serve as mechanisms for encouraging and supporting social networks among age peers.

REFERENCE NOTE

1. LaGory, M., Ward, R., & Juravich, T. <u>The age segregation process in American cities: An ecological model</u>. Paper presented at Annual Meeting of the American Sociological Association, 1977.

B I B L I O G R A P H Y

Adams, B.

   1967   "Interaction Theory and the Social Net-Work." <u>Sociometry</u>, 30, 64-78.

   1970   "Isolation, Function, and Beyond: American Kinship in the 1960's." <u>Journal of Marriage and the Family</u>, 32, 575-597.

Arling, G.

   1976   "Resistance to Isolation Among Elderly Widows." <u>Aging and Human Development</u>, 7, 67-86.

Atchley, R.

   1977   <u>The Social Forces in Later Life</u>. Belmont, California: Wadsworth.

Beattie, W.

   1976   "Aging and the Social Services." In R. Binstock & E. Shanas (Eds.), <u>Handbook of Aging and the Social Sciences</u>. New York: Van Nostrand Reinhold.

Blau, Z.

   1973   <u>Old Age in a Changing Society</u>. New York: New Viewpoints.

Bultena, G., &
Wood, V.

1969   "The American Retirement Community:
            Bane or Blessing?" Journal of Geronto-
            logy, 24, 209-217.

Burgess, E.

1960   "Aging in Western Culture." In E.
            Burgess (Ed.), Aging in Western Socie-
            ties. Chicago: University of Chicago
            Press.

Butler, R.

1975   Why Survive?: Being Old in America.
            New York: Harper & Row.

Chevan, A., &
Korson, J.

1972   "The Widowed Who Live Alone: An Examin-
            ation of Social and Demographic Fac-
            tors." Social Forces, 51, 45-53.

Cowgill, D.

1974   "Aging and Modernization: A Revision
            of the Theory." In J. Gubrium (Ed.),
            Late Life: Communities and Environ-
            mental Policies. Springfield, Illi-
            nois: Thomas.

Cumming, E., &
Henry, W.

1961   Growing Old: The Process of Disen-
            gagement. New York: Basic.

Glick, I., Weiss, R. &
Parkes, C.

1974   The First Year of Bereavement. New
            York: Wiley-Interscience.

Goode, W.

1963 *World Revolution and Family Patterns.* Glencoe, Illinois: Free Press.

Hays, W., & Mindel, C.

1973 "Extended Kinship Relations in Black and White Families." *Journal of Marriage and the Family*, 35, 51-57.

Hess, B.

1972 "Friendship." In M. Riley, M. Johnson, & A. Foner (Eds.), *Aging and Society, Volume 3: A Sociology of Age Stratification.* New York: Russell Sage.

Hill, R.

1970 *Family Development in Three Generations.* Cambridge, Mass.: Schenkman.

Hochschild, A.

1973 *The Unexpected Community.* Englewood Cliffs, New Jersey: Prentice-Hall.

Jackson, J.

1971 "Aged Blacks: A Potpourri Towards the Reduction of Racial Inequalities." *Phylon*, 32, 260-280.

Jacobs, J.

1975 *Older Persons and Retirement Communities.* Springfield, Illinois: Thomas.

Kahana, E.

1970 "Grandparenthood From the Perspective of the Developing Grandchild." *Developmental Psychology*, 3, 98-105.

Kahana, E., &
Kahana, B.

1971   "Theoretical and Research Perspectives
            on Grandparenthood." <u>Aging and Human
            Development</u>, 2, 261-268.

Kastenbaum, R., &
Aisenberg, R.

1976   <u>The Psychology of Death: Concise
            Edition</u>. New York: Springer.

Lawton, M., &
Nahemow, L.

1973   "Ecology and the Aging Process." In C.
            Eisdorfer & M. Lawton (Eds.), <u>The
            Psychology of Adult Development and
            Aging</u>. Washington, D.C.: American
            Psychological Association.

Litwak, E., &
Szelenyi, L.

1969   "Primary Group Structures and Their
            Functions: Kin, Neighbors, and
            Friends." <u>American Sociologial Review</u>,
            34, 465-481.

Lopata, H.

1973(a)   <u>Widowhood in an American City</u>.
            Cambridge, Mass.: Schenkman.

1973(b)   "Social Relations of Black and White
            Women in a Northern Metropolis."
            <u>American Journal of Sociology</u>, 78,
            1003-1100.

Lowenthal, M., &
Haven, C.

1968   "Interaction and Adaptation: Intimacy
            as a Critical Variable." <u>American
            Sociological Review</u>, 33, 20-31.

Marshall, V.

1975   "Socialization for Impending Death in a
               Retirement Village." American Journal
               of Sociology, 80, 1124-1144.

Messer, M.

1967   "The Possibility of an Age-Concentrated
               Environment Becoming a Normative Sys-
               tem." The Gerontologist, 7, 1247-1250.

Neugarten, B., &
Weinstein, K.

1964   "The Changing American Grandparent."
               Journal of Marriage and the Family,
               26, 199-204.

Palmore, E.

1975   The Honorable Elders. Durham, N.C.:
               Duke University Press.

1976   "The Future Status of the Aged." The
               Gerontologist, 16, 297-302.

Parsons, T.

1959   "The Social structure of the Family."
               In R. Anshen (Ed.), The Family: Its
               Function and Destiny. New York:
               Harper.

Pasamanick, B., Scarpitti, F.,
& Dinitz, S.

1967   Schizophrenics in the Community: An
               Experimental Study in the Prevention
               of Hospitalization. New York: Apple-
               ton-Century-Crofts.

Pihlblad, C., &
Adams, D.

1972   "Widowhood, Social Participation and
               Life Satisfaction." Aging and Human
               Development, 3, 323-330.

Quarantelli, E.

1960   "A Note on the Protective Function of
                the Family in Disasters." Marriage and
                Family Living, 22, 263-264.

Riley, M. &
Foner, A.

1968   Aging and Society. Volume 1: An
                Inventory of Research Findings. New
                York: Russell Sage.

Robertson, J.

1976   "Significance of Grandparents: Percep-
                tions of Young Adult Grandchildren."
                The Gerontologist, 16, 137-140.

Rosenberg, G., &
Anspach, D.

1973   Working Class Kinship. Lexington,
                Mass.: Lexington Books.

Rosow, I.

1967   Social Integration of the Aged. New
                York: Free Press.

1974   Socialization to Old Age. Berkeley,
                Calif.: University of California Press.

Shanas, E., &
Maddox, G.

1976   "Aging, Health, and the Organization
                of Health Resources." In R. Binstock
                & E. Shanas (Eds.), Handbook of Aging
                and the Social Sciences. New York:
                Van Nostrand Reinhold.

Shanas, E., Townsend, P., Wedderburn, D., Henning,
F., Milhj, P., & Stehouwer, J. (Eds.)

1968   Old People in Three Industrial Socie-
                ties. New York: Atherton.

Sherman, S.

    1975(a)   "Patterns of Contacts for Residents of Age-Segregated and Age-Integrated Housing." Journal of Gerontology, 30, 103-107.

    1975(b)   "Mutual Assistance and Support in Retirement Housing." Journal of Geronotology, 30, 479-483.

Simmons, L.

    1960   "Aging in Preindustrial Societies." In C. Tibbits (Ed.), Handbook of Social Gerontology. Chicago: University of Chicago Press.

Sussman, M.

    1976   "The Family Life of Old People." In R. Binstock & E. Shanas (Eds.), Handbook of Aging and the Social Sciences. New York: Van Nostrand Reinhold.

Sussman, M., & Burchinal, L.

    1962   "Kin Family Network: Unheralded Structure in Current Conceptualizations of Family Functioning." Marriage and Family Living, 24, 231-240.

Teaff, J., Lawton, M., Nahemow, L., & Carlson, D.

    1978   "Impact of Age Integration on the Well-Being of Elderly Tenants in Public Housing." Journal of Gerontology, 33, 126-133.

Townsend, P.

    1965   "The Effects of Family Structure on the Likelihood of Admission to an Institution in Old Age." In E. Shanas & G. Streib (Eds.), Social Structure and

the Family: Generational Relations.
Englewood Cliffs, New Jersey: Prentice-Hall.

Treas, J.

1977   "Family Support Systems for the Aged:
            Some Social and Demograhic Considera-
            tions." The Gerontologist, 17, 486-491.

Troll, L.

1971   "The Family of Later Life: A Decade
            Review." Journal of Marriage and the
            Family, 33, 263-290.

Uhlenberg, P.

1977   "Changing Structure of the Older Popula-
            tion of the USA During the Twentieth
            Century." The Gerontologist, 17, 197-
            202.

Ward, R.

1977(a)   "Services for Older People: An Inte-
            grated Framework for Research." Jour-
            nal of Health and Social Behavior, 18,
            61-70.

1977(b)   "Aging Group Consciousness: Implica-
            tions in an Older Sample." Sociology
            and Social Research, 61, 496-519.

Wax, J.

1976   "It's Like Your Own Home Here." New
            York Times Magazine, November 21,
            1976, 38+.

Wood, V., &
Robertson, J.

1976   "The Significance of Grandparenthood."
            In J. Gubrium (Ed.), Time, Roles, and
            Self in Old Age. New York: Human
            Sciences.

Wylie, F.

1971   "Attitudes Toward Aging and the Aged
            Among Black Americans: Some Historical
            Perspectives." <u>Aging and Human Develop-
            ment</u>, 2, 66-70.

*Russell A. Ward is Assistant Professor, Department of
Sociology, State University of New York at Albany,
Albany, New York.

Reprinted from <u>The Family Coordinator</u>, Vol. 27 (October, 1978): 365-373. Copyrighted 1978 by the National
Council on Family Relations. Reprinted by permission.

CHAPTER 8

MEDIA AND THE FAMILY: A HOLISTIC APPROACH

Douglas B. Gutknecht*
and
Jerry Meints*

I. INTRODUCTION

This article explores the media and family from a holistic or systems perspective. Such a view emphasizes the interrelations of systems parts or subsystems which make up an integrated, fully functioning, holistic family system. The emphasis in family therapy, in our view, has too long focused on the muddied areas, the situations of mystification, distortion, disorganization (Cooper, 1970; Laing, 1969) and the so-called "death of family" life issues without trying to grasp the social structural and institutional system in which the family is embedded. Such conceptions of either ideal order and strength, or chaos and disorganization, both are over simplifications when applied to the complex realities of family systems. Our concern is how family systems interact with the media in a holistic, healthy, and critical manner to promote rather than detract from family well-being.

II. THE FAMILY AS A SYSTEM

The family functions as a complex system made up of component parts (i.e., roles) or subsystems, e.g., communication and decision making patterns. In addition, it functions as a subsystem of larger economic and communications systems. Systems theory is built upon the assumption that the parts are related in a network of reciprocal interactions and that the system is a relatively stable structure over a given period of time (Buckley, 1967). The key element is the idea of continuous interchange both within the system and between the system and its outer-environment.

The process model of social systems includes four assumptions: (1) that systems are complex and exist as a network of interdependent relations governed by feedback; (2) that systems are open or able to constantly evaluate and change; (3) that systems are adaptive to strain and tension; and (4) that systems are information processing systems (Kantor and Lehr, 1975:10-11).

Our focus is upon the ingredients of a healthy or holistic media-family system which orginates from the strengths of each component system. Our analysis rejects a functional view which emphasizes the arbitrary maintenance or stability functions of the family, the media, or any other system component. Such functional views ignore the variety of social system interactions and the multiple levels of systems involved (McIntyre, 1966). Our holistic systems view is not merely descriptive of what is, but is prescriptive regarding what should be (i.e., a normative view of the family system). This analysis does not assume that healthy social system interactions thrive on consensus alone but includes the dimensions of role bargaining, coalition formation, conflict and power of groups each trying to dominate or resist the other system and their component parts for their own ends. Each subsystem works to enhance its own freedom, meaning, goals, and interests thus strategically is capable of disruption and cooperation, withdrawal and bargaining, winner-take-all attitudes, as well as compromise.

It is our basic contention that the family system must interact more holistically and actively with all informational and media systems. Although we don't support a simplistic view of the "dominating media" and "passive family," the media system does often control and influence our viewing habits, cognitive picture of the world, consumption decisions, and leisure time choices. The influence of the media, though sometimes bordering on domination, is both pervasive and subtle in its effects. Our holistic view asserts the need for families to better articulate their own needs and interests and better evaluate the type, source, reliability, and amount of media information they receive. Part of the solution to the media monopoly, which stems from their tremendous resources, particularly to broadcast media, is for the family to function as a social and political force and to pressure media to recognize a legitimate role for the family in selecting and evaluating their own viewing habits and media experiences. Such a view doesn't sanction a conservative and censorship position but acknowledges that bargaining and pressure can be exerted by those interested in censorship, as well as

144

those interested in enlarging the scope and presentation of media. Our bias is toward the expansion of media to provide access and opportunities for families and communities to evaluate and utilize media information efficiently and productively in order to enhance family and individual informational needs and long term well-being. Such a view places primary emphasis on both media education and healthy family communication. We support public media awareness campaigns and educational programs that allow for a more interactive, open, critical, and interrogative use of the media. We need to focus on emphasizing what the family can do for itself rather than only what the media does to us.

The key element in our systems view is information. The family system that is capable of more critical assessment of information will be more healthy and promote a holistic sense of well-being. Thus, families who can maximize good communications within and between systems have more information and thus can better meet their own and their communities' needs, goals, and interests. Highly interactive and informed decentralized families, as well as political groups create a more viable and responsive pluralistic political democracy. Media concentration leads to a passive society and citizens.

Decentralized media involvement and critical evaluation as a family project instills lifelong developmental skills and techniques essential for a democratic electorate. Media concentration on cartoons leads to the dangerous situation of media saturation and the loss of discriminating viewing. We lose the ability to critically scan and responsibly select the sources and amount of information as we become habituated to passively turning on the T.V. or media source without asking ourselves what our media goals are or what we expect to gain out of participating in this media experience. Entertainment is certainly a worthy media goal for families when mixed with other information, educational, and dialog based media experiences. Dialog based media experiences means actively discussing a media presentation before, often during, and definitely after its completion.

Media concentration too often promotes habitual and passive viewing and the inability to feel we can select or can cope with the variety of informational

145

and media sources (e.g., T.V. cable, video cassette, radio, video conferencing) available. This situation leads to "information overload." Such overload results both from: (a) too much information that is not readily assimilated, therefore becoming noise, and (b) too few media skills on the part of the viewer or user of media. This situation produces "media burn-out," the inability to process information and reach informed decisions. In addition to attendant personal and family stress, anxiety, and often feelings of powerlessness, information overload leaves users of media more susceptible to manipulation.

We believe that lifelong and holistic learning can minimize informatin overload, increasing knowledge transfer and social involvement. In particular, we believe that the family must become a highly inter-active and participating unit, which evaluates critically all types of media presentations. The family must learn these roles and skills which help them to evaluate actively and critically and to confront media, various informational sources, and ultimately the powers behind media decision-making.

Such roles enable the family to assimilate good information which then can be used as a resource in family decision-making. In our view, a highly inter-active family environment facilitates lifelong education. This view supports the concept that autonomous learning modes and intense frequent interaction actually increases motivation to learn about public life and facilitates involvement in the lives of others, while promoting a concern with community, public ethics, and social health (Marks, 1977, 192-196; Spretzer, et al., 1979).

Even sophisticated consumers of information may require help in fostering crucial skills for under-standing and using media. This brief explanatory analysis concludes with an analysis of active and passive viewing and a discussion of a few skills that may help us facilitate active viewing for ourselves and our children.

III. ACTIVE VS. PASSIVE VIEWING

T.V. Zombies

Jerry Mander launched a critical and well docu-

mented attack upon television charging primarily that
television viewing produces passive zombies who uncritically and unavoidably allow information, ranging
from the best to the worst television has to offer,
to ooze past our otherwise discriminative cognitive
filtering process and pollute our consciousness. He
provided physiological evidence to suggest that television induces alpha wave states similar to those
states associated with boredom, daydreaming, medita-
tion, yoga, prayer, sensory deprivation experiments
and various states which transcend otherwise ordinary
consciousness. Often such ego states are associated
with higher levels of suggestibility (Mander, 1981).

Indeed certain cultic groups use these suggestive
states to program "happiness" (sic), group cohesion
and deindividuation. It is this potential loss of
autonomy and critical thinking which worries Mander
and motivates him to support the abolition of television.

In contrast to Mander's argument there is evidence to suggest that television actually requires
active viewer participation. While films consist of
literally millions of distinct still exposures shown
in rapid succession, video images are made up of
millions of tiny dots which then require the viewer to
perform "visual closure" to produce the "sense" of
moving action and image.

Experiments in Community Video also demonstrate
the viability of television as a powerful tool in
motivating community action and involvement (Meints,
1981). There is reason to believe that media formats,
including television, can promote family interaction.

The Media As Mediators

Family Therapists use terms such as pseudo-
mutuality, pseudo-hostility, conflict habituated, and
devitalized to describe dysfunctional family systems.
In such families, balance or homeostasis is facilitated by abberant devices such as the "troubled child"
or the family delinquent, any of which function to
simply take the attention away from the real causes
of family stress, e.g., troubled marriage, lack of
individuation, communication breakdowns, sexual dysfunction, etc. (Napier and Whitaker, 1981).

147

Television, the major in-home-media, is often used in the same way to reduce tension and cover up the "holes in reality" which threaten family homeostasis. The T.V. functions as the "triangled child" or the troubled teenager which draws attention away from the family's problems. If the media offered family programming emphasizing the value of nurturing, clear, effective communication, or the life passages and transformations we all face, or the techniques for managing a successful family business, then the media could function as a mediator and facilitator rather than as an escape.

Family Action

In contrast to passive viewing, families can take a wide variety of actions to facilitate a responsive and intentional relationship with the media: (1) The T.V. set is a voluntaristic object, i.e., it has an "off button;" (2) Responsible viewing entails consulting a viewing guide to insure discriminative choices; (3) Public television stations offer unique and varied programming plus subscriptions which provide viewing guides, supplementary reading and reference materials, textbooks, and audio adjuncts all of which further enhance the interactive and participatory experience of public television; (4) Cable stations offer a variety of locally oriented programs which present issues and information about matters that affect families and their immediate environment; (5) Movie channels offer a wide range of option to the viewing family including late run movies, rock concerts, foreign films, sports spectaculars, childrens festivals, etc.; and (6) Home video recording devices have recently become affordable to the average family and offer an incredible combination of viewing choices. Outstanding programs can be recorded anytime of the day or night with or without the viewer being present, given the new computer programming capabilities of most video devices.

While several studies show that television has reduced the interaction of family members this does not necessarily have to be the case (Brody et al., 1981; Belson, 1978). One study found that parents failed to offer more complete nutritional information to their children following their viewing television food commercials which promoted less nutritious foods (Brody et al., 1981). Not only does this result in the impression that the advertised foods are really nutritious, but parents also missed a great opportunity to teach children about good nutrition and wise consumerism.

Although novel as it may seem to most parents, watching television with the children offers parents valuable opportunities for shaping and modifying the socialization they receive from media. For example, after the program the family can discuss examples of cooperation, affection, or sharing that stood out for them. The family could play games such as "re-write the script" which invites family members to improve upon or humanize the program they just viewed to make the characters interact in more positive ways.

Educational television programs such as "Sneak Previews" by Roger Ebert and Gene Siskel provide humanistic and informative guidance towards more worthwhile movie going. Their format is conducive to post-preview viewer discussion and analysis which may lead to more discriminate movie choices.

The viewing choices made by family members may be flatly rejected. Another approach is to use them to provide an opportunity for dialogue among family members concerning the relative merits of the program, characters, script or themes. This approach invites learning, parenting, growth, and openness.

The message is clear: parents must be encouraged to use media as a tool for family socialization, not as an electronic baby sitter. Role modeling must be presented through academic journals, national magazines, newspaper articles, and public television that will encourage parents to take an active approach in using media as a resource for socialization and family communication.

BIBLIOGRAPHY

Belson, William A.

1959   "Effects of Television on the Interests
                and Initiative of Adult Viewers in
                Greater London." British Journal of
                Psychology, 50, 145-158.

Brody, Gene H., Stoneman, Zolinda,
Lane, T. Scott, Sanders, Alice K.

1981   "Television Food Commercials Aimed at
                Children, Family Grocery Shopping, and
                Mother-Child Interactions." Journal of
                Family Relations, 435-439.

Buckley, W.

1967   Sociology and Modern Systems Theory.
                Englewood Cliffs, N.J.:   Prentice-Hall.

Cooper, D.

1971   The Death of the Family.   New York:
                Vintage Rolls.

Kantor, D., &
Lehr, W.

1975   Inside the Family: Toward a Theory of
                Family Process.   New York: Harper/
                Colophon.

Laing, R.D. &
Esterson, A.

1964   Sanity, Madness and the Family.
                London: Tavistock Publications.

Mander, Jerry

1978   4 Arguments for the Abolition of Tele-
                vision.   New York: Morrow & Co.

Marks, S.

1977   "Multiple Roles and Role Strain: Some
                Notes on Human Energy, Time and Commit-

ment." <u>American Sociological Review,</u>
Dec., Vol. 42, 921-936.

McIntyre, J.

1966   "The Structure--Functional Approach to
               Family Study." In F.I. Nye and F.M.
               Bernardo (ed. 5) <u>Emerging Conceptual
               Frameworks in Family Analysis.</u> New
               York: MacMillan.

Meints, Jerry

1981   "Community Video As An Organizing Tool."
               <u>Humanity and Society</u>, March, Vol. 5,
               No. 1.

Napier, Augustus Y, &
Whitaker, Carl A.

1980   <u>The Family Crucible.</u> New York: Bantam
               Books.

Spreitzer, E., Snyder, E.,
& Larson, D.

1979   "Multiple Roles and Psychological Well-
               Being." <u>Sociological Focus</u>, Vol. 12,
               No. 2, 141-148.

*Department of Sociology, Chapman College, Orange,
California.

FAMILY SOCIAL PROBLEMS, POLICY AND THE FUTURE

Douglas B. Gutknecht*
and
Edgar W. Butler*

I. INTRODUCTION

One tragedy of our society is that there is a long time lag between recognizing the cultural realities of modern life and the pressures exerted on families. The traditional family has undergone four major changes: (1) functional losses, (2) increased personal mobility, (3) declining status ascription, and (4) the continued ascendancy of materialist values (Hobart, 1963). Further, it also is becoming more interdependent with other institutional sectors of society as its functions change (Edwards, 1967). There is conflict associated with the ascendancy of materialistic values in our society because some people believe that "individuals in our affluent society are becoming more important for what they are, rather than for what they are capable of doing" (Edwards, 1967:508). Further, "individual pleasure takes priority over communal solidarity" (Bosserman, 1977). Similarly, marriages appear to becoming predominantly utilitarian in nature. That is, persons are becoming more and more interested in what they will derive from that relationship with little concern for mutual sacrifice and sharing other than that which is essential to the maintenance of the marital bond.

II. CONTEMPORARY MARRIAGE THEMES AND THE FUTURE

A number of changes have occurred in U.S. families over the past three generations. First, there has been an emerging emphasis on developmental ideology with respect to childhood. Second, there has been an increasing stress on sharing household tasks and a concomitant decrease in specialization of husband-wife roles. Third, there appears to be more risk-taking by families. Fourth, there is more planning taking place now than previously in economic matters, family planning, and so on. Fifth, there is more open communication taking place, although it is accompanied by greater conflict. In an evaluation of these changes, Hill and his associates (1970) expli-

153

citly reject the notion that the family is disintegrating or becoming functionless.

Accompanying societal trends are a reduction in birth rate, morbidity, and mortality, and structural changes as follows:

1. More women are working for pay resulting in a loss or reduction of male power and dominance in the family.

2. Not only are more women working outside of the home, more of them are working in supervisory and higher level jobs.

3. More women are working at jobs not for survival but because they want to work outside of the home; there has been a decline in the economic dependence of women.

4. The government is increasingly providing services formerly provided by the family male.

5. There has been a steady increase in leisure time.

6. There is an increasing dispersion of leisure and social activities outside the family unit.

Structural changes have been accompanied by an increasing emphasis on human rights and individualism. Legal blocks to equality by race, sex, and age are being removed. Overall there has been a movement toward equalitarianism within society and in the family. As associated initial result has been the increasing number of marital separations, divorces, family violence, alcoholism, serial marriages, and alternative life styles. Child care increasingly takes place outside of the home unit, and children are having more early childhood experiences outside of the home, resulting in a broader world view. Marriage has been taking place at older ages than previously. One thus finds both positives and negatives resulting from such structural changes in family life.

Within the family, equalitarianism is growing, with more power accruing to females, and sexual standards are becoming more nearly equal for men and women.

154

There is increasingly less supervision of children by adults, especially regarding sexual activities. Fertility control, both by adults and younger people is becoming standard, and family planning of both the timing and number of children is the norm. Generally, even with all these trends it appears that the traditional nuclear family is here to stay, albeit with modified values, behaviors, and attitudes. The main reasons are that it is necessary for socialization, emotional security, and affectional needs. Other forms will emerge but probably with a minority of persons involved. There are several other main themes or threads that can be distinguished in contemporary marriage that need to be considered in discussing the future family. These themes are as follows:

1. With very few exceptions divorce is a painful and confusing experience; this is also true for professionals in the field.

2. There is universal dissatisfaction with the divorce process and its legal complications and procedures, which need simplification.

3. The choice of mate is often made when an individual does not have maturity and reason to make a good choice.

4. Current socialization practices in our society lead to expectations of marriage that are unrealistic. Partners expect too much of each other and are disappointed because their needs cannot be met through marriage.

5. Notwithstanding the increases in the divorce rate, the dissatisfaction of marriage, and the belief that it is a wretched institution, four out of five persons who get a divorce expect to remarry "within a reasonable time" (Otto, 1970:1-3)

Tyler (1975) suggests a simple plan that he believes would save marriage. Whether he is serious or not, his plan has merit since it would bring together people who are presumably sexually compatible. "At about 20-25 years of age, a man would contract his first marriage to a woman of 40-45 who is leaving her first marriage. A woman of 20-25 years of age would contract her first marriage to a man of 40-45 who is

leaving his first marriage. Presto! Revolving mates.
At 60-65 years of age, both men and women would leave
the system to marry each other in third marriages, if
they wish, or to enjoy retirement and well-earned
single bliss." There are substantial advantages to
this plan. First, it faces squarely sexual realities
as we now know them. That is, men appear to attain
their greatest sexual vigor at about the age of 20,
while women reach a sexual peak in their 40's. This
plan would match men and women at their sexual peaks.

Another possibility is companionate marriage
(Mead, 1966), which is based on earlier notions of
trial marriage (Lindsey and Evans, 1927; Russell,
1929). There would be two steps: (1) A simple ceremony would be followed by a trial marriage in which
members would have limited economic responsibilities,
easy access to divorce, and no children. (2) Couples
who were ready for the lifetime obligations of parenthood and economic interrelationships would enter a
parental marriage, which would be difficult to break
off and would entail continued responsibility for
children. A third step might be a legitimized cohabitation consisting of a short-term contractual arrangement which would precede the other two steps. This
trial relationship might be required for a year.
Such apprentice periods have been proposed so that
partners can explore each other before an actual
marriage takes place. Perhaps one of the most famous
trial marriage experiments was the fictional one proposed in the novel The Harrad Experiment; college
students lived with computer-selected roommates of
the opposite sex on a trial basis (Rimmer, 1966).

Progressive or serial monogamy may already be
substantially under way (Alpenfels, 1970). People
marrying, divorcing, and remarrying is a popular
pattern. While people may become unhappy with a
particular marriage, to be married is still a goal
that dominates the life of most men and women. The
basic structure and interaction networks in our
society are for couples, and people need a "steady"
that they go to functions with. These primary reasons
for progressive monogamy suggest that it will be a
viable future pattern.

In view of conflicting predictions, the safest
and most accurate assumption is that there will be
pluralistic models of the family in the future (Mor-

gan, 1975:229ff). There will be a variety of nuclear family forms, modified extended families, dual career families, open families, and loose or tight networks of families. In addition, communal experiments will continue to develop, ranging from completely economic self-sufficient communes with complex marriage and love relationships to looser and more temporary arrangements. In the immediate term such changes may suggest the family is failing but the situation is certainly more complex than simply relying on the obvious indicators of family disruption and disorganization like statistics on divorce, alcoholism, and violence.

III. CONCLUSION

We expect that the dominant family form in the future will continue to be the nuclear form as it now exists - a husband and wife and child or children. However, changes in society will alter many of the basic values, expectations, attitudes, and behaviors within these nuclear family units (Lasswell and Lobsenz, 1976). Similarly, many, if not most, of those who enter nuclear families probably will enter the nuclear family with a clearer notion of its advantages, disadvantages, and limitations.

The decline in family sex role differentiation will continue unabated, and while the basic tasks that need to be accomplished in the family unit will remain, who does each task will become less of a sex-linked characteristic and more of a personal preference by marital partners. The trend toward equalitarian families with shared powers and decision making is expected to grow as "personal growth" becomes a dominant value in our society. Associated with more democratic families will be more females working outside of the home. By virtue of this work, the female will accrue more power within the family unit and this will enhance the equalitarian marriage.

The growth of equality in sexual relations, both within and outside of the marriage, will profoundly affect the family of the future as well as all other human relations (Clavan, 1972). As equalitarianism becomes the mode and as power in the family becomes more equally distributed, the "open communication," so much revered by therapists and others, will become more of a reality, and it will strengthen rather than

157

weaken the marital bond. As this open communication becomes more extensively practiced, males will find themselves, of necessity, agreeing that their spouses should have the same freedoms that they do.

The future family is one that is evolutionary and still assumes that the nuclear family is the most effective unit for residential living, consumption, and social functions, as well as for raising children. It is a family that is not a radical departure from current forms and thus allows maintenance of the family unit for raising children, intimate relations, security, friendship, companionship, and sexual access (Constantine and Constantine, 1973:231).

In summary, the "reports of the death of marriage are, to paraphrase Mark Twain, greatly exaggerated" (Hunt, 1971). The evidence is overwhelming that old-fashioned marriage is not dying but that there is a continuing evolution and a rebellion against certain aspects of it (Toffler, 1970). The evolutionary aspects may be considered as patchwork modifications enabling marriage to serve the needs of contemporary people without being unduly costly or painful. In spite of the current divorce rates and the many problems involved with contemporary family, the future family may be as follows:

The marriage of the future will be a hetero-sexual friendship, a free and unconstrained union of a man and a woman or companions, partners, comrades, and sexual lovers. There will still be a certain degree of specialization within marriage, but by and large the daily business of living together--the talk, the meals, the going out to work and coming home again, spending their money, the love-making, the caring for children, even the in-dulgence or non-indulgence in outside affairs--will be governed by this fundamental relation-ship rather than by the lord-and-servant rela-tionship of a patriarchal marriage. Like all friendships, it will exist only as long as it is valid: it will rarely last a lifetime, yet each marriage, while it does last, will meet the needs of the men and women of the future as the earlier form of marriage could have. Yet, we who know the marriage today

158

will find it relatively unfamiliar, comprehensible - and very much alike (Hunt, 1971).

Changes taking place in marriage forms do not reflect immediate impulses on the part of married people but, instead, reflect genuine needs for growth and change in the family. There are basic needs that human beings have and these needs apparently are being expressed. The need for love, affection, recognition, respect, sexual satisfaction, and security remain vitally important for people in most marital relationships. This section will explore some of the problems, changes and projections regarding the future of the family in American society. Along the way we also hope to examine some policy issues that impact the health of the family and its ability to meet the stresses, strains, and challenges of the 1980's.

BIBLIOGRAPHY

Alpenfels, Ethel J.

1970   "Progressive Monogamy: An Alternate
                Pattern?"   In Herbert A. Otto (Ed.),
                The Family in Search of a Future.
                Englewood Cliffs, N.J.:   Prentice-Hall
                (Appleton), pp. 67-73.

Bosserman, Phillip

1977   "Changing Core Values in American So-
                ciety: 1876-1976," unpublished paper.
                Salisbury State College, Salisbury, MD.

Clavan, Sylvia

1972   "Changing Female Sexual Behavior and
                Future Family Structure." Pacific So-
                ciological Review, 15 (July): 295-308.

Constantine, Larry L., &
Constantine, Joan M.

1973   Group Marriage. New York: Macmillan.

Edwards, John N.

1967   "The Future of the Family Revisited."
                Journal of Marriage and the Family,
                29 (August): 506-511.

Hill, Reuben and
collaborators

1970   Family Development in Three Genera-
                tions. Cambridge, Mass.:   Schenkman
                Publishing.

Hobart, Charles W.

1963   "Commitment, Value Conflict, and the
                Future of the American Family."
                Marriage and Family Living, 25
                (November): 405-412.

Hunt, Morton

1971   "The Future of Marriage." Playboy,
            18 (August).

Lasswell, Marcia, &
Norman M. Lobsenz

1976   No-Fault Marriage. Garden City,
            N.Y.: Doubleday.

Lindsey, Ben B., &
Wainright Evans

1927   The Companionate Marriage. New York:
            Liveright.

Mead, Margaret

1966   "Marriage in Two Steps." Redbook,
            July.

Morgan, J.H.J.

1975   Social Theory and the Family. London:
            Routledge & Kegan, Paul.

Otto, Herbert A.

1970   "Introduction." In Herbert A. Otto
            (Ed.), The Family in Search of a
            Future. Englewood Cliffs, N.J.:
            Prentice-Hall (Appleton), pp. 1-9.

Rimmer, Robert H.

1966   The Harrad Experiment. Los Angeles:
            Sherbourne Press.

Russell, Bertrand

1929   Marriage and Morals. New York:
            Liveright.

Toffler, Alvin

1970   Future Shock. New York: Random House.

Tyler, Robert L.

1975   "The Two-Marriage Revolving-Mate
Generation-Bringing Plan to Save
Marriage." In Jack R. De Lora and
Joann De Lora (Eds.), <u>Intimate Life
Styles</u> (2nd ed.), Pacific Palisades,
Calif.: Goodyear, pp. 406-410.

*Doug Gutknecht, Department of Sociology, Chapman
College, Orange, California; Edgar W. Butler,
Department of Sociology, University of California,
Riverside, California.

CHAPTER 9

FACT AND FICTION IN MODERN DIVORCE:
DIMENSIONS AND ISSUES

Douglas B. Gutknecht*

I. INTRODUCTION

In keeping with one theme of this book regarding
the relationship between the private world of individuals in family life and the public and social world
tearing at the families fabric, the topic of divorce
takes on strategic meaning. The very survival or
viability of the family unit is brought into question
by those who cite recent statistics on divorce. However, the issue of the nature of the meaning of divorce and divorce statistics must be placed within a
larger social, historical, and public context. Furthermore, we cannot ignore the fact that families,
identical in many ways, choose completely different
ways of interpreting and coping with the strains and
stresses of modern life: one family chooses divorce
out of some compassion for the spouse or children,
another family chooses to stay together for the sake
of community appearance. Divorce statistics tell us
little about the nature of meanings and what makes
marital life satisfactory or unsatisfactory--thus
divorce statistics are not in themselves good indicators of marital health or disruption. Traditional
stereotypes and images of what makes families function, what effect divorce has on spouses and children,
must be evaluated in a manner that moves beyond a
simple view of marital disintegration fostered by an
uncritical reading of divorce statistics. The key
issues concern the meaning of marital life to partner,
the developmental stage of maturity of partners and
stage of the marriage, the destructiveness of the
marital setting, the involvement of children in the
divorce process, and degree of bitterness generated,
and what support systems the family can call upon in
time of need.

II. TRENDS IN DIVORCE: PITFALLS AND INTERPRETATION

In 1978 there were 2,243,000 marriages and
1,122,000 divorces. The marriage rate per 1,000 population was 10.3 and the divorce rate per 1,000 population was 5.1. For approximately every two marriages

163

in the U.S. there is one divorce (<u>Statistical Ab-stracts of the U.S.</u>, 1980:81). Do these negative statistics indicate that the family is falling apart?

Additional indications of the extent of the problem are revealed by the ratio of ever-divorced persons to persons who remain in intact marriages and also in statistics of separation. In the former case in 1960 there were 33 divorces per 1000 married whites with spouse present which increased to 83 by 1978; the statistics over the same time period for blacks is 62 to 194. The divorce rates also increased from 32 per 1000 married in 1960 to 59 in 1978. In addition, statistics on separation suggest that the number of women not divorced but separated and heading their household increased 54 percent to 1.5 million from 1970-79 (U.S. Department of Commerce Bureau of Census, 1979). These statistics along with the facts that many younger couples break up after living together and aren't counted as official divorces lead to the possibility that the current statistics on divorce are understated. Further, the idea of desertion, or the poor man's divorce, also contributes to problems of measurement. In addition, trend data indicate that long term divorce rates have risen from near 2% in mid 1850's to about 50% today (Plateris, 1973).

One might define the general issue as one of intentionally disintegrating or dissolving a marriage by one or both spouses which can be referred to by one of three social categories: separation, desertion, or divorce. Only the latter category is counted in official statistics. Separation may be viewed as a first step, the initial and informal resolve to start the process of disengagement. Although obvious psychological and emotional conflicts and bargaining proceeded this decision, the point is that separation moves the levels of discussion to a new, more serious, <u>social plane</u>. We will discuss the psychological stages in a later section. Such a step may provide temporary breathing space and time for reflection, leading to a temporary lessening of conflict and possibly eventual reconciliation. However, without assistance in defining why the problems accumulated in the first place, or why old coping strategies failed, a reconciliation merely lessens the negative stigma of divorce with friends and relatives. At this point in the process one often hears the refrain that, "at least I tried." Several repeat performances provide a measure of confidence on the part of spouses that the right decision was reached. However, for those convinced that divorce is the only viable and realistic option from an oppressive situation, separation only seems to prolong the uncertainty and agony of being in a provisional status, creating guilt, fear, and insecurity. One's old life cannot end and a new beginning tried within the old skins of misery, bitterness, and guilt.

The existence of desertion, often called the "poor man's" divorce is even more disturbing because, unlike separation and divorce, the split is sudden and total. The desertion itself is a rejection of the normative and institutional structure of society and prevents acceptance of any responsibility and the opportunity for the spouse to save face.

These statistics have to be placed in context, however. For example, most divorced persons remarry and the divorced are three times more likely to remarry than never married men are likely to enter their first marriage. Only about 6 percent of all adults over 18 were divorced in 1978 (Statistical Abstracts of the U.S., 1980:40). Although the divorce rate has risen sharply during the 1960's and 70's, the yearly percentage of the total population of marrieds divorcing is still relatively small. In addition, two of every three first marriages last a lifetime and about three-fourths of all who divorce remarry. Although 40% of all marriages will someday end in divorce, this statistic results from the fact that 44% of divorced individuals who remarry will divorce again, which pushes up the total percentage of marriages that will end in divorce in the long term. The fact that there is a small but increasing number of couples who marry three or more times adds to the distorted picture. Remember only a small percentage of the total population (e.g., 5 to 6%) actually divorce in any one year.

There are six separate ways that divorce rates can be calculated (Crosby, 1980:51-52). First, the percentage of divorces to weddings, compares the number of marriages (weddings) in a given year to divorces. If there were 100 weddings and 50 divorces, the divorce rate would be 50%. This method implies a high divorce rate and hence problem because of the fact that divorces in a given year result from mar-

riages in previous years and are then compared with
only the number of current year weddings. Second,
crude divorce rate is the ratio of number of divorces per 1,000 people. Remember that when many more
babies are born as during the post World War II baby
boom, adding to the total population, the divorce
rate goes down. Currently as the number of babies
born declines then the divorce rate goes up. Third,
a refined divorce rate compares the number of divorces
in any year to the number of married women. Fourth,
one can compare the number of marriages ending in
divorce with those ending because of the death of a
spouse. Fifth, age-specific divorce rates compare
the number of divorces per 1,000 married women in
various age categories. Sixth, a standardized divorce
rate summarizes age specific rates and divides this
number by the standardized size and multiplies the
result by 1,000. The adoption of certain methods of
calculating divorce statistics obviously biases our
impression of the extent of the problem of marital
dissolution.

Using divorce statistics as an indicator of
marital crisis or social disorganization also ignores
the historical evidence that marriage and family life
faced numerous disruptions and crises in the past.
For example, in the 19th century early death of a
spouse accounted for most marital disruptions and
dissolutions. The recent increase in the divorce rate
is less important for understanding satisfaction with
family life than the reasons that people give for
divorce which either "reflects a commitment to the
institution or a change to a quite different sort of
relationship" (Bane, 1976:22-23). Bane supports the
former assertion. The key element in her interpretation is that satisfaction is generally high but spread
out over longer years together as a result of an extended family life cycle (Bane, 1976:24). The question of how families readjust and cope with extended
years together has created short run strains as a
result of new patterns of work, leisure life, health
and illness, financial strains of retirement, and
death. Coping with these crises in the short run may
allow a better match between spouses, improved communication, changed sex role responsibilities, and
sharing of family tasks in the long run.

Numerous studies document that divorce is not a
uniform phenomena; it is distributed unevenly across

numerous social, political, and economic categories.
Divorce rates vary by regions of the country; they are
higher in the Western U.S. where social tolerance reduces the social stigma attached to divorce. Probabi-
lities of divorce after the first marriage increases
among men as their age at marriage, education, and
income decrease (Glick and Norton, 1971). The 1970
census indicated that among individuals who married
between 1901 and 1970, for those who married before
age 20, the divorce rate is twice as high as for those
who decided to postpone marriage until their late
20's. For women who married before 18, the divorce
rate is twice that of women who waited until their
early 20's for the first time. In addition, men who
earn more money generally have a lower divorce rate
and remarry more readily. Women who earn more money
often divorce more often and wait for longer periods
before they remarry. For females, however, the statistics are less certain because some divorced women,
who have a higher personal income, delay or remain
unmarried because they are supporting themselves
adequately. In addition, marital strain can be felt
because men feel threatened by financially independent
women (Bane, 1976:34). Indications are strong that
stability of income and employment both better explain
stability in marriage than simply the amount of income
earned.

> People are more accepting of divorce as a
> solution to an unsatisfactory marriage. But
> an increased tendency to end bad marriages
> probably does not in itself explain the rising
> divorce rate. The changing role of husbands
> and wives and new opportunities for women to
> be employed and independent also seem to con-
> tribute to the divorce rate...(Bane, 1976:36).

The larger public trends and social forces actually reinforce marital tensions and conflicts as
expectations for self-actualization, personal growth
and longing for a private haven from a heartless world
put excessive demands on the family (Lasch, 1978).
Demands for occupational success and public involvements often compete with needs for a private life and
family growth needs. Some ways to balance both dimensions are by having smaller families or no children,
or genuinely involving themselves in their careers and
social-community activities. However, the very fact
of success in the public sphere of career may create

167

strains on private life, unless each spouse is willing
to acknowledge contributions made by the other. Individuals with higher levels of education, occupational
status, and income may statistically divorce less, but
they also establish such high standards that the mundane reality of marriage often creates tensions and
disappointments. Likewise one may feel that one's
attributes and assets can yield better bargains in
the growing remarriage market-place, as more individuals divorce.

Divorce trends are made more tangible and reinforced in one's own experience if one finds more
divorces occurring in one's network of acquaintances.
Abstract statistics can't account for the brute realities of how people cope with the influential powers of
peers, and close friends, when interpreting or making
sense of the social world. Escalating divorce rates
itself creates a kind of momentum that stacks the deck
against a more reasoned, patient decision. The larger
eligible pool of partners made available in encounters, real or imagined, tempt one to ask oneself if
the grass is greener on the other side of the bed.
Whereas a smaller pool of eligible, re-marriage partners might make one more cautious about one's potential trade-in value in the marriage market or "flee"
market, as the case may be.

III. DIVORCE AND THE LAW

Let's examine some of the claims regarding the
increasing number of states with the easy out or "no
fault" divorce laws and the apparent increase in
divorce rates. Historically where divorce was legally
more difficult, alternatives to formal legal or dejure
divorce provided an escape hatch--de facto annulments
purchased from church courts for fees; separation if
fault could be proved; or the poor man or woman's option, desertion. Later, when ecclesiastical courts
lost the unconditional power to grant divorce, civil
courts stepped in to provide grounds--initially adultery, then physical or mental cruelty. Traditionally,
many individuals have stayed together because of
economic necessity. However, involuntay separation,
via early death of spouses, created so-called "broken
homes," necessitating orphanages and charity homes for
children (Bane, 1976). The key question, however,
still seems whether or not no fault divorce laws are
the key cause of increasing divorce rates in the U.S.

No fault divorce laws first became legally binding in
January 1970 in California as a result of the passage
of the California Family Law Act of 1969. Several
states earlier developed aspects of a no fault law
but only California passed a comprehensive and comp-
plete law. In several instances the no fault grounds
only included statutes that specifed one ground for
divorce, defined as irretrievably broken marriages
or breakdown of marriage relations. These grounds
prevented the use of the concept of fault in the proceedings. Traditional fault grounds estabishing guilt
or innocent included physical cruelty, adultery, etc.
In addition, several states (i.e., Connecticut, Idaho,
Rhode Island, New Hampshire, and Texas), added no
fault laws to traditional grounds for divorce. In
these states fault grounds such as adultery can be
used to establish custody rights. In addition to no
fault, grounds of incompatibility or irreconcilable
differences is still used where no guilt is established.

The idea that permissive no fault laws creates
a drastic increase in divorces stems from a set of
assumptions embedded in the nature of Anglo-Saxon
law. This view recognizes fault as the only grounds
for divorce and adversary legal proceedings as the
main opportunity to establish fault. The court room
becomes a battleground for character assassination
and psychological retribution, often creating excessive guilt and lowering the self esteem of the beaten
party. In this traditional view of divorce one spouse
must be blamed because someone is guilty of disrupting
the marriage. Many traditionalists believe that divorce must be made traumatic and difficult in order to
protect families from the social disorganization in
society (i.e., suicide, crime, mental illness) which
comes from high divorce rates. Many family writers
have questioned this hypothetical relationship between
high divorce rates and social disorganization.

Since 1968 the divorce rate has increased in conjunction with the liberalization of divorce laws by
numerous states (i.e., about two-thirds). However,
the argument that no fault divorce laws have caused
this increase in divorce rates ignores the complex
realities of the modern world. The law itself seems
to have little impact, in that people can end relationships in a variety of ways, which indicate the
pressure of the law is not working. Divorce and mari-

169

tal breakups are complex processes. Even when the law is punitive and stringent and the costs high (e.g., costs may include social stigma, loss of reputation, falling out with family, alimony, child support, possibility of resource loss, diminished income or standards of living, loss of social status), it is still the case that punitive laws were not effective in deterring divorce.

The argument itself ignores the complex personal and public realities of the modern world. The private world of two individuals trying to create intimate emotional bonds and satisfactory communication in a world of constant disruptions, interruptions, and turmoil indicates that both parties are trying to make sense of their lives together. Both parties are thus responsible for the success or failure of their relationship. The idea of fault by only one guilty party ignores both the psychological and social context of the interdependent family which requires many role adjustments, internally and externally. Divorce, marital conflict, violence, adultery, and other family problems and hassles are more a symptom or result of these larger forces, rather than a cause of marital disruption itself.

There are four limitations of the fault system in need of reform beyond the traditional criticisms of the time and money it costs society by overloading the courts. The fault or guilt system: (1) ignores the more complex reasons for marital split ups; (2) forces individuals to lie to one another and the court creating additional guilt; (3) frustrates societies' interest in maintaining marital relationships which support stable families; (4) promotes aggressive behavior, bitterness and unforgiving attitudes that might even continue in the custody hearing and ultimate arrangements (Reppy, 1970).

Families may benefit by staying together at all costs, by relying on traditional remedies. Without more adequate understanding of the psychological realities and social pressures that caused the problem in the first place, the climate of bitterness may only increase the living hell for all family members. Much evidence exists to suggest that constant and unresolved conflicts create more damaged children than by making a clean break (Nye, 1957). Since so many remarry successfully, over 50% of second marriages are successful, children receive adequate care and socialization. The suggestion that divorce causes other social problems and breakdowns in society results from an inadequate understanding of the problem. Divorce and crime don't correlate highly with easy divorce laws. Broken relationships more often result from poverty, which causes both crime and divorce. It is more accurate to look at larger public issues and structural problems which may cause psychological problems and pressures on individuals. Many families experience financial difficulties during recessions or times of economic instability, but the poor experience these problems constantly, which compounds them into multi-dimensional problems, affecting numerous spheres of living involving work, family, health, leisure, or lack of it.

IV. CHILDREN, CUSTODY AND DIVORCE

The film, "Kramer vs. Kramer" told the story of a custody fight and the traditional stereotypes associated with standard divorce law, where the mother is assumed to have the inside track as the best parent to guide the child's future. This media portrayal of a dedicated father fighting for custody rights only publicly established what has been found on a mass scale in courts and states, by both men and women, often as allies, throughout the decade of the 1970's. In the 1970's states like Florida and Kentucky adopted more humane and fair requirements for the situation of fathers in custody cases. In both Iowa and Washington, lawyers are court appointed to represent the interests of minor children regarding issues of custody, visitation, and child support. Yet even today several no fault states, like California and Oregon, still consider the issue of spousal misconduct as grounds for custody decisions. This troubling situation often restages the damaging court room battles of the pre- no fault legal climate. However, no fault laws have taken some bitterness out of custody battles and allowed more humane options; like joint custody, to become viable options; one even encouraged by many courts attorneys, family counseling services, and expert witnesses.

The question of divorce, although a private matter, obviously disturbs many because of its public ramifications and consequences; particularly those issues which influence our next generation of citizens, today's children. The question of who will socialize and take care of our children and the quality of such care, becomes one of concern to all those interested in the potential negative effects of broken families upon children and society.

Current guestimates indicate that about 40% of the children born in the mid-1970's will live in one-parent families at least some time before they are eighteen. About 10% of those now living with a two-parent family are living with a step-parent because the remarriage rate for divorced parents is high. The average number of children, including young ones, per divorce has decreased, so by the late 1970's, fifty-two percent of those households headed by divorced or separated women involved no children. One-parent families in 1979 accounted for 13% of all households. The question of the quality of single-parent families certainly requires some reflection. Two out of three children are living with their natural parents as of 1978; 19% are living with one parent and 4% are living with neither parent for a total of 23% not living with two parents (U.S. Dept. of Commerce, Bureau of Census, Series P. 20, No. 338, 1979).

The impact of divorce on children is difficult to assess because of the numerous complex variables that affect well-being and development needs at different stages in life. The conventional view and strongest argument against divorce is that children in broken homes will move through life at a disadvantage compared with children from a two-parent intact home. The argument asserts that a child from a broken home will experience reduced psychological well-being, and often inadequate personality development, both essential for coping with life's future stresses. However, the evidence seems to point to the importance of comparing children from broken homes and unbroken homes on factors related to the quality of home life and degree of happiness before the divorce.

When comparisons are made of children from disrupted marriages with children from unhappy but broken homes, the slight disadvantage that broken homes have, when compared to happy intact homes, disappears (Nye, 1957). One-parent homes show no significant differ-

172

ence in school achievement, social adjustment, and delinquent behavior when compared with two-parent families of similar economic status (Murchison, 1974).
This research argues against the idea that unhappy
marriages need to be retained for the sake of children
and supports the idea that good relations are essential in familial life, no matter how many parents are
involved. Likewise, such evidence discounts the false
idea that liberalized or no fault divorce laws cause
bad marriages and produce conflict, which may lead to
problems for children.

The latest research at the Harvard Medical
School's Laboratory of Community Psychiatry points up
the strengths of children of divorce, separation and
widowhood:

> "They tend to be more mature, responsible,
> independent and self-reliant than kids from
> two-parent families. They often also have
> special skills and abilities unusual for
> their age, and unusual self-assurance"
> (Graves, 1982:47).

This evidence should not lead us to assume that
one-parent families don't experience problems, particularly economic, and that children don't experience
some form of initial separation anxiety and distress
as a result of parental separation. Bane (1976:112)
summarizes the issues that suggest that divorce
seems to impact more negatively upon female single
parents, creating stress and strain as a result of
the following conditions:

> loss of economics of scale; greater preva-
> lence of divorce and death among poor fami-
> lies; low and irregular levels of alimony,
> child support, and public assistance; fewer
> adult earners, fewer opportunities for fe-
> male heads of families to work; lower wages
> than men when they do work.

Weiss (1976:140) calls attention to issues of separation distress even for children who adjust well in the
long run to lost attachments:

> One list of reactions among children to a
> loss of a parent includes, among others,
> rage and protest over loss, maintenance of

173

an intense fantasy relationship with the
lost parent, persistent efforts at reunion,
anxiety, and a strong sense of narcisstic
injury.

While some children actually experience a euphoric increase in self-confidence and self-esteem, the more
likely pattern, even for these individuals, were periods of alternating euphoria and separation distress.

Children are more resilient than once thought,
although the life of emotions contains many periods
of ambivalence and emotional backtracking. We seldom
move through fixed emotional stages once and for all
without backtracking. Children may move from subordinate role to junior parent or helper role in the new
family configuration. Single parents often treat
their adolescents as peers and turn to them as a substitute spouse for companionship, understanding, and
support (Graves, 1982:47). This new and intense
closeness may, however, create paradoxical problems
because the child as parental supporter may mature
too quickly and feel both sympathy and painful awareness of parental weakness and fallibility. The
ambivalence relates to pride in their own maturity
and self-reliance, mixed with a wistful emotion that
they may have missed some of the fun and luxury of a
truly dependent childhood. Such ambivalence may become anger or bitterness in some cases, where one's
network of friends all live with two-parent families.
Again the importance of support networks and exposure
to successful models of alternative family styles
may be the most important variable. Likewise, we
find today that most children appear more grown up
and mature in their attitudes at earlier ages.

V.   FACTORS CONTRIBUTING TO DIVORCE

Let's briefly focus on a social-psychological
model built upon exchange theory that views the conditions that lead to divorce in order to call attention to factors that couples, even in intact relationships, might reflect upon (Levinger, 1976). This
theory asserts that people make choices or exchanges
in all areas of life. Exchange theory tries to measure the cost and benefits of behaviors by arguing
that behaviors will be continued when benefits outweigh the costs (Heath, 1976).

The exchange perspective applies cost-benefit
analysis to divorce--when cohesiveness is strong,
then benefits are greater and vice versa. Pair cohesiveness is increased when partners present greater
attractions and fewer barriers to each other inside
the relationship and more barriers separating one's
relationship to outside world. When inducements or
benefits to remain in a relationship increase they
become attractions or gratifications to remain and
not divorce. Likewise, the strength of restraints
or barriers for leaving a relationship increases with
perceived rewards and decreases in perceived costs.
The probability of evaluating rewards and costs thus
relates to how we perceive our situation at a given
time. Rewards are associated with positive outcomes
and might include love, friendship, companionship,
status, information, goods, services, money, property,
sex, children, support, security, validation of self.
Costs might include perceived or real rejection, energy, time, loss of pleasure, lack of sexual variety,
vulnerability of ego exposure, or anything that might
be defined as an expenditure demanded from staying in
the relationship.

Individuals are more likely to stay in a relationship, marital or dating, and reject a divorce or
break-up, when the subjective probability of gaining
rewards exceeds the costs. Often the objective reality is difficult to measure and one's arbitrary and
perceptual calculation becomes our guide to behavior.
Individuals divorce or leave, in many cases, when
costs exceed rewards from the relationship over a
given period of time. Generally longer periods of
deprivation or costs lead us to hypothesize the
probability of marital or dating disruption. However,
numerous factors are often ignored in exchange theories. For example, some additional important variables
that are often ignored are self-esteem, understanding
the reasons for disruptions of rewards, spouses'
ability or potential to change or develop, knowledge
of the cycles of disenchantment and life crises,
compassion, spiritual and humanistic values. A strict
cost benefit analysis oftentimes appears to imply a
model of man as a machine devoid of consciousness, intention, sense of community, spirit, values, or history. However, it does provide many pertinent insights into the realities of relationships after the
romantic glow of early courtship fades.

175

There are barriers or restraining forces which can
reinforce a relationship and actually keep people
together (Levinger, 1976:25): A strong barrier results from a strong commitment to each other, brought
about by being of the same religion, sharing the same
economic, social, educational, class, or ethnic
experiences. Alternative attractions also detract
from one's primary relationship. For example, other
role-partners, work, friends, former spouse or
children, travel schedule, may provide options that
make one's perceived relationship less likely of
providing inducements.

Alternative attractions demand time and energy
which can draw emotional energy away from the primary
relationship or marriage. For example, relationships
where spouses constantly exclude the other spouse may
threaten the bond and create jealousy and increase negative emotions and costs for both parties. However,
when both spouses participate in the alternate attractions there is less danger of costs exceeding rewards
for only one spouse or partner. Again it is the perception of accumulating alternatives as attractions
that is most important. For example, relationships
outside the primary bond may be attractive but less
attractive than a fully functioning, primary relationship. In addition, alternative attractions, like
friends, may create a stronger primary bond if a
spouse feels more self-esteem and thus provides an
added inducement in self-esteem.

The exchange theory of divorce provides an interesting perspective for reflection about one's relationships and how both spouses perceive each other's
strengths and weaknesses, costs and rewards. This
theory can stimulate some critical analyses and application to each person's own life.

VI. THE PROCESS OF DIVORCE

A divorce is an ending but it does not end everything about marriage. Although the legal contract is
broken, the emotional and psychological relationship
between partners often continues. Likewise, an individual may or may not divorce legally, but still experiences the trauma of emotional divorce.

Divorce involves six stages (Bohannan, 1970).
First is the emotional divorce, which centers on the

important, often traumatic recognition that spouses are no longer nurturing or supporting each other, providing good feedback and building a sense of a common purpose. People emotionally divorce when they grow as individuals yet find no common tasks or projects which allow them to grow interdependently as a team or couple. Second, is legal divorce which means by law. Legal reasons often diverge from the real reasons for divorce, which are often psychological or emotional. Third, is economic divorce which includes the dissolution of the family as an economic unit. Assets must be divided for child support and alimony must be settled. Fourth, is the co-parent divorce in which the issue of custody must be settled. The fifth stage of the divorce process involves a change in status recognized by one's community of friends, neighbors, or family. The sixth and last stage is psychic divorce in which one's autonomy or sense of being as a person is separated from one's partner. The maintenance of autonomy is more difficult when spouses exhibited great dependence on one's mate and the divorce was initiated by the other partner. However, even in such a case where the emotions of loving, even liking may be absent, the sense of attachment proves difficult to eradicate (Weiss, 1976). Such attachments to those we've once cared deeply about point to the emotional complexities of loss and change, divorce and separation.

VII. CONCLUSIONS

Divorce involves some of the most complex elements in understanding the modern dimensions of marriage and family life. The emotional and psychic aspects are more important than the legal realities. Often we reduce marital problems to arbitrary legal definitions and solutions. Divorce is not an easy process, even though popular manuals speak of the joys of "creative" divorce. Mel Krantzler (1982), author of a book on the process of creative divorce, has since remarried and written a new book on the several stages of marriage called Creative Marriage. Weiss (1976:144) calls our attention to those ambivalent feelings that are part of any divorce:

Ambivalence makes separated individuals uncomfortable with any resolution of their separated state. Reconciliation may result not only in relief at the ending of separa-

tion distress, but also in dismay at the
return to an unsatisfactory relationship.
The decision to divorce may also have mixed
implications: not only gratification that
freedom appears within grasp but also sorrow
that the spouse will be irretrievably lost.

The ambivalent responses of partners to marital
disruption is understandable if we view emotions as
being important. Psychic disruption and loss or
separation is an important dimension of life that
individuals often seem unprepared to deal with. Somehow modern men and women assume that breaking bonds
of love, friendship, family, community, can be made
painless by reliance on rules, contracts, modern
attitudes. It is apparent that deep feelings of
attachment remind us of our capacity for caring even
when our imperfections and the strains of the modern
world pull and tug at us. Regardless of our sophistication, the lack of institutional supports give us
little emotonal help to face an often heartless world.

"Whatever they decide - whether it is to
reconcile or to continue their separation,
and, perhaps, move on to divorce - they
will leave one set of feelings unsatisfied"
(Weiss, 1976:146).

BIBLIOGRAPHY

Bane, Mary Jo

    1976   "Marital Disruption and the Lives of
                    Children." Journal of Social Issues,
                    Vol. 32, No. 1.

Bohannan, P.

    1970   Divorce and After. New York: Double-
                    day and Co.

Crosby,

    1980   "A Critique of Divorce Statistics and
                    Their Interpretation." Family Rela-
                    tions, Vol. 29, p. 51-58.

Glick, P. &
A. Norton

    1971   "Frequency, Duration and Probability of
                    Marriage and Divorce." Journal of
                    Marriage and the Family, Vol. 33, p.
                    307-317.

Graves,

    1982   "Growing Up Quicker If Not Better:
                    Kids in Single-Parent Families Have
                    Some Advantages." American Health,
                    May/June.

Heath, A.

    1976   Rational Choice and Social Exchange,
                    Cambridge, England: Cambridge Univer-
                    sity Press.

Krantzler, Mel

    1982   Creative Marriage. New York: McGraw
                    Hill.

Levinger, G.

1976   "A Social Psychological Perspective on
            Marital Dissolution." Journal of
            Social Issues, Vol. 32, No. 1

Murchison, N.

1974   "Illustration of the Difficulties of
            Some Children in One-Parent Families."
            In M. Finer (Ed.), Report of the
            Committee on One-Parent Families, Lon-
            don: Her Majesty's Stationary Office.

Nye, F.I.

1957   "Child Adjustment in Broken and Unhappy
            Homes." Marriage and Family Living,
            Vol. 19.

Plateris, A.

1973   "100 Years of Marriage and Divorce Sta-
            tistics: 1867-1967." U.S. National
            Center for Health Statistics, Vital and
            Health Statistics, Series 21, No. 24.

Reppy, Susan

1970   "The End of Innocence: Elimination of
            Fault in California Divorce Law."
            U.C.L.A. Law Review, XVII (June), p.
            1306-1332.

1980   U.S. Bureau of the Census, Statistical
            Abstracts of the U.S., 1980, 101,
            (ed.), Washington, D.C.

1979   U.S. Dept. of Commerce, Bureau of
            Census, Series P. 20, No. 338, Marital
            States and Living Arrangements: Manual
            1978 (Washington D.C.: Government
            Printing Office.

Weiss, R.

1976   "The Emotional Impact of Marital Separa-
            tion." <u>Journal of Social Issues</u>, Vol.
            32, No. 1.

*Department of Sociology, Chapman College, Orange,
California.

CHAPTER 10

ALCOHOL ABUSE AND FAMILY STRUCTURE

Peter M. Nardi*

I. INTRODUCTION

To conceive of the family as a social system is to focus on rules, roles, and relationships. The social structure of a family is its configuration of roles bound together in relationships according to a set of rules evolved by the larger society and by a particular family. For purposes of this discussion, a "family" is any set of people defining themselves as a social, emotional, and economic unit, regardless of legal status, and creating for themselves a set of roles, rules, and relationships. Thus, "family" includes two or more unmarried adults living together with or without children, heterosexual or homosexual, as well as the traditional nuclear family unit of legally married adults and children. It is important to define family this way since alcohol abuse affects all kinds of families without regard to the dominant legal or social norms of a culture.

An analysis of an alcoholic family must, therefore, begin with its structure and the meanings that family creates about alcohol and its use. For every family there exists a set of sociodemographic characteristics which contribute to its social structure and definitions. Socioeconomic status, ethnicity, race, religion, and regional variations (such as urban/rural, north/south, east/west) contribute customs, norms, and rituals to a family's structure. These characteristics are also highly related to customs, norms, and rituals surrounding the definitions and uses of alcohol. For example, a working class Mexican-American Catholic family living in the rural southwest has traditional family rules which stress the power role of the male in decision-making, has religious customs valuing authoritarianism, and has an ethnic tradition of machismo which encourages men to drink heavily. It often becomes difficult, then, for children or wives to confront a problem-drinking father/husband, given the ethnic, class, and religious rules regulating relationships and roles.

In short, the investigation of family structure
and alcohol use must begin with an analysis of relevant sociodemographic characteristics and how they
relate to that particular family's dynamics and its
definitions regarding alcohol use. Most work on
families and alcohol use has not done so systematically.

In more general terms, all families develop a
set of interlocking roles performing functions necessary for the family unit's emotional, economic, and
social survival. Some roles are defined as having
higher status (adult roles over children roles) and
some roles as having more power (traditionally the
males over the females). According to custom, age,
and gender, the roles within the family are given
meaning and defined. In a healthy functioning family,
there exists a reciprocity of power and control; within a problem family, competition for power and control
is prevalent and roles begin to shift to accommodate
to changes in status and power.

Thus, conceiving the family as a dynamic social
system of interlocking roles, defined in part by
ascribed characteristics and by the culture's rules,
is a useful model when attempting to understand the
effects on and dynamics within a family troubled by
alcohol abuse. All families change in their definitions of rules, roles, and relationships as members
adjust to shifts in age, occupational status, educational level, and economic conditions. But the
shifts brought on by alcohol abuse yield effects
and produce processes which may lead to the intergenerational transmission of alcohol abuse and related
mental health problems. It is this aspect of family
structure and dynamics that will be the focus of this
paper.

II. ALCOHOL USE AND FAMILY ROLES

It is estimated (NIAAA, 1981) that about two-
thirds of the adult population are consumers of alcohol and that about 10 percent have serious problems
with alcohol. Each one of these approximately 15
million alcoholics affects about 5 million other
people directly or indirectly. Most of these are
family members who rarely receive professional attention or treatment. Growing evidence exists, however,
that many of these people also have problems with

alcohol or drugs, develop related mental health problems, and may experience family violence and abuse.
It is becoming increasingly clear that it is not only
the alcoholic who needs treatment but also every member of the family unit. For in order to cope with
the alcohol abusing member, others in the family take
on roles which appear functionally necessary at the
time but often prove to be emotionally and personally
dysfunctional in the long term.

Children's Roles

In a traditional, non-problem family, children
in our culture usually take on dependent, powerless
roles. Decisions and choices are normally structured
by adults. Children are expected to be nonresponsible
when it comes to making decisions or family policy;
they are expected to be dependent on their parents.
Children essentially are in compulsory relationships
with parents while a spouse is in a volitional one
(Greenleaf, 1981).

In the alcoholic family, however, role reversal
is a common event (Nardi, 1981). As the family system accommodates to shifts in parental drinking patterns, children's roles alter. Children of alcoholic
parents often take on roles of responsibility in which
they become the parent to the alcoholic who is acting
like a child (i.e., non-responsible, dependent, and
powerless). These children sometimes care for younger
siblings, cook and clean, run household errands, and
even balance checking accounts, all above and beyond
the normally expected sharing of family tasks. These
children increasingly adopt adult-type roles of responsibility within the family system, thus leading to
changes in relationships between adults and children.

In other families, children cope with family role
disruption by adopting placating and adjuster roles
(Black, 1980). They begin to act as mediators between
arguing parents or they learn consistently to give in
to situational demands and to others' feelings. In
these situations, children of alcoholics have received
a clear message that it is not important to discuss
their own feelings, but to spend the time dealing with
their alcoholic parent's problems and, in many cases,
with their non-alcoholic parent's needs. It is not
uncommon to find children in surrogate spouse roles
in addition to surrogate parent roles.

185

In some families, children of alcoholics become scapegoats, receiving the message that they are the cause of their parent's drinking problems (Seixas, 1977). Often this is exhibited by physical and emotional neglect or by physical and sexual abuse (NIAAA, 1981). Some of these children cope by acting out and taking on delinquent roles.

In Cork's (1969) study of children of alcoholics, the alcoholic family appears to be characterized by shame, resentment, anger, and inconsistency. Children were often confused about the rules and their role expectations. They were isolated, lacking in self-confidence, anxious, and ashamed. Their relationship with the non-alcoholic parent was also strained and tense.

In short, when alcohol problems produce dysfunctioning parental roles, children often adopt functional parental roles in order to cope with the family problems and to fulfill necessary family tasks. While learning to be more responsible and adult-like, these children also receive a message that their feelings are secondary. As these overly responsible children (and those who become scapegoats, adjusters, placators, or were abused or neglected) become adults, they carry with them into their adult relationships (at home and work) the anger, resentment, guilt, lack of trust, and low self-esteem they developed as children. They also realize that the roles they took on to cope with shifts in the family system are no longer functional in adult relationships. Not dealing with one's own feelings, consistently doing other people's work, rescuing other people from their problems, and constantly doing what one thinks the other wants are not mentally and physically healthy behaviors in adulthood. Children of alcoholics, as adults, have failed to learn how to identify their own feelings and to deal with them once discovered. They continue to be overly responsible and to conceal the mental and physical scars of abuse or neglect. It is when they turn to some form of compulsive behavior, such as excessive alcohol use, that the outcomes of growing up in an alcoholic family become evident.

Shifts in children's roles to accommodate alcohol problems in the family system, while positive and necessary at the time, may later in life lead to continuation of alcohol abuse unless identified and treated early on. Hence the need to focus on the entire family system and the changing rules, roles, and relationships that accompany disruption of the family structure. By understanding alcoholism as a family problem and by viewing the family as a system of shifting roles and relationships, the intergenerational transmission of alcohol abuse may begin to be halted.

It is also important for specialists involved with family problems to look at the positive outcomes that may result from growing up in an alcoholic family. Not all children of alcoholics are delinquent or alcohol abusers. Many enter helping professions and service-oriented occupations. Anecdotal evidence suggests that some become good listeners, altruistic, and empathetic. In other words, many children of alcoholics may have adopted coping roles which demonstrate healthy adjustment and positive outcomes. No research has yet focused on this dimension.

Whatever the effects may be, there is a necessity to differentiate impact of alcoholic parents on child-rearing according to variations that exist among families and the other social systems of which they are a part. As mentioned in the Introduction, family dynamics are also a function of such demographic characteristics as ethnicity and race, religious traits, family size, socioeconomic status, and regionality. For example, it is difficult for children raised in authoritarian families (often related to religiosity and ethnicity) to confront their parent's drinking problems, for lower income families to afford extra support services (such as housekeeprs and private mental health programs) or for one-parent families to cope in as smooth a way as a two-parent family might.

Little research exists that focuses on the mediating effects sociodemographic variables may have on the outcomes of growing up in an alcoholic family. Yet it is likely that these variables will contribute something to how a family defines the problem in the first place and to how it responds by changing the rules, roles, and relationships of the system.

Significant Others' Roles

Whether the alcoholic's partner in a close rela-

tionship is the legal spouse, a same-sex or opposite
sex lover, or simply a roommate, that person must
learn to adjust to the alcoholic's problems and the
disruption of the family system. Within such a system, the rules, roles, and relationships between a
significant other and the alcoholic shift to accommodate the new disruptive behaviors. The responses
the significant other makes not only affect the alcoholic's behavior and feelings, but also contribute
to those of the significant other. Like children in
the family system, partners take on roles to meet
family tasks and adopt relationships which may seem
situationally functional but may prove in the long run
to be mentally and physically unhealthy for everyone
within the family system.

Jackson (1954) has argued that wives of male
alcoholics go through seven stages in adjusting to the
alcoholic situation. Initially, attempts are made to
deny the problem and to create the illusion of a normal relationship. While concern is expressed about
excessive drinking, both partners avoid the strains
and issues related to drinking. In stage 2, attempts
are made to eliminate the problem when the family
begins to experience social isolation due to drinking
incidents. The wife begins to feel self-pity, a loss
of self-confidence, and inadequate. Yet attempts are
made to cover up and to maintain the family structure
of roles and relationships. Disorganization characterizes stage 3 when the family gives up attempts to
control alcohol use. The duties and responsibilities
of family roles are no longer being enacted by appropriate persons. The alcoholic's spouse has lost almost all self-assurance and experiences guilt and a
further loss of self-respect. Violence, role rever-
sals, and role conflict can occur at this stage. In
stage 4, attempts are begun to reorganize the family
system in response to a crisis situation. The spouse
has taken over the alcoholic's roles and the alcoholic
is increasingly viewed as a dependent child. For the
woman of a male alcoholic, this usually signifies a
gain of status and power in a traditional family system of male dominance. By bringing some order and
stability back to the system, the spouse begins to
regain self-esteem and assurance. For many, however,
leaving the family system or developing an alcohol
problem signifies stage 5. Some begin to depend on
alcohol as the only apparently viable means to cope
with the alcoholic partner and the concomitant chaos

while others have found the newly acquired self-confidence and power roles comfortable enough to believe they can make it on their own and leave the disruptive situation.

In stage 6, the family reorganizes, often without the alcoholic spouse. At times the alcoholic makes attempts to return to the family system by playing on guilt feelings. Stage 7 is the reorganization of the entire family if the alcoholic returns having achieved sobriety. Problems usually occur when attempting to alter roles and relationships once again. For the woman, newly achieved power and control become difficult to relinquish and some tension exists in accommodating to a sober husband's revitalized roles. Slowly the family system adjusts to include a recovering alcoholic and some degree of stability is achieved.

Recently, the term "co-alcoholic" has been developed to describe the non-alcoholic significant other. It incorporates the concept of the partner evolving in similar ways to the alcoholic. That is, it emphasizes the idea that the significant other goes through stages similar to the development in an alcoholic: denial, loss of trust, diminishing sexual interaction, low self-esteem, low self-confidence, and helplessness. In other words, the non-alcoholic partner begins to share the problems and loss of control the alcoholic experiences.

Often the non-alcoholic partner inadvertently enables the alcoholic to continue drinking. As the significnat other increasingly enacts the duties of the alcoholic's roles and takes control of the family system, the alcoholic is alleviated from responsibilities and shielded from the problems due to alcohol abuse. This results in the family members becoming accustomed to the new roles, rules, and relationships, often enabling the alcoholic to continue drinking without further serious consequences (Hanson & Estes, 1977).

In same-sex relationships (lovers or roommates) other issues may emerge. Power is potentially distributed more equally in these relationships, unlike traditional heterosexual ones in which power is distributed according to gender differences. When alcohol problems are introduced in same-sex relationships, shifts in power between two potential equals create added tensions (Nardi, 1982a). Homosexual "families" must also deal with the values of significant others who make up an extended family of close gay friends. Confronting the positive meanings of alcohol and drinking within the gay community, gays and lesbians must reconcile their problem drinking patterns with their extended family's emphasis on social drinking. The role of such family systems and significant others takes on added meaning for gay people since they require these communities to maintain and legitimate their identities in the context of an often hostile society (Nardi, 1982b).

In sum, regardless of the nature of the family system, alcoholics influence the emotional and physical lives of their significant others (spouses, lovers, partners, or extended families of close friends). The violence which may occur, the tensions and arguments which do occur, and the concomitant feelings of guilt, fear, despair, low self-esteem, and low self-assurance need to be addressed. As members of a family social system, the significant others are continuously modifying their roles and relationships to accommodate to shifts in the alcoholic's behavior. While the attention is focused on the problem drinker, the partner is developing undetected his or her own problems and mechanisms for coping. Some take on new power and control, some develop denial and enabling techniques, and others begin to cope as the alcoholic has done--with alcohol.

As with children of alcoholics, the significant others do not emerge from a dysfunctioning family system untouched. Reaching out to them and giving them more positive and less destructive ways to cope with the problem drinker and their own feelings of inadequacy and fear become the goals of family-oriented treatment.

III. TREATMENT IMPLICATIONS

Viewing the family as a social system of inter-locking roles, rules, and relationships and recognizing that reorganization occurs in times of problems lead to important treatment and prevention strategies. Wolin, Bennett, Noonan, and Teitelbaum (1980) have discovered that family rituals enacted in the family system have salient implications for treatment and prevention of alcohol abuse. Family rituals (symbolic forms of communication repeatedly acted out in systematic fashion over time) "contribute significantly to the establishment and preservation of a family's collective sense of itself" (Wolin, et al., 1980:201). Rituals clarify roles, delineate relationships, and define rules for a particular family system. The researchers found that in those families in which rituals were substantially altered during times of heaviest parental drinking, the transmission of alcohol problems to the children's generation occurred. During such rituals as family dinners, holidays, and weekends, the alcoholic parent in these families usually drank and got drunk while the families accepted this behavior by failing to respond to it.

In those families in which family rituals remained relatively unchanged during periods of heaviest parental drinking, there existed a lack of transmission of alcohol problems to the children's generation. These families rejected the alcoholic parent's drunken behavior by confronting the parent or by talking negatively about it among themselves. They tended to keep their holiday rituals intact.

This research indicates the importance of maintaining a structure to the family system and the relevancy of focusing on all the members in prevention and treatment programs. Many programs emphasize the interactional and communication patterns of the family, not simply the problem drinking (NIAAA, 1981). Treatment programs usually work with the alcoholic alone and in family sessions. Yet, despite the growing recognition of family dynamics influencing individual alcohol behavior, relatively few alcoholics are treated in family therapy (NIAAA, 1981).

When family treatment does occur, the first stage is to identify how the alcoholism is perpetuating the family system. In what ways does the family accommodate to the changes in roles, rules, and relationships brought on by the problem drinking? Once the dynamics and interactions among the partners and children are identified, treatment can begin with each family member individually and then together. It is important to allow situations in which the children can discuss their feelings without their parents being present and for the significant others to express their issues without their alcoholic partner. Then, it becomes therapeutically relevant to bring the family members

together in a group session to work out the dysfunctional ways they may be using to cope with the problem
and to learn better methods in dealing with it.

As Janzen (1978:139) states,

> Regardless of who the patient is, the important
> thing in treatment is to clarify the nature of
> the interaction among the dyads and triads in
> the family group. In this way, previously
> established destructive patterns can be inter-
> rupted and changed. Since conflict in a family
> is to be expected, the goal of therapy is to
> help family members find new ways of resolving
> such conflict.

IV. CONCLUSIONS

If there is one way of summarizing the dynamics
of alcoholism and the system of family roles, it is
with the concepts of power and control. It should be
recognized that the struggles for control within a
relationship may lead to alcohol problems as well as be
the results of alcohol abuse. The relationship between
the alcoholic and other family members is a competitive
struggle among people driven by strong dependency needs
and who usually seek to maintain drinking patterns in
order to continue control (Shapiro, 1977). The request
for help by the alcoholic (a statement of loss of control) is answered by the partner and children who attempt to control the alcoholic's drinking and to maintain family stability. By taking on new roles and
relationships of power and control, family members
often find themselves liking these new positions of
responsibility and develop a need to maintain control
even when the alcoholic achieves sobriety. Herein
lies the struggle for power and control and the dynamics of enabling and cover-up behaviors.

The struggle for power and control is also exhibited in the alcoholic's attempts not to lose control
and to maintain power in the family system. While
announcing the need for help, the alcoholic is simultaneously asserting the reluctance to be helped. This
contradiction and the helpless, inadequate feelings
this engenders in non-alcoholic family members can
lead to unhealthy coping devices adopted by partners
and children.

By focusing on the family as a system in which control and power shift and in which struggles to maintain stability are common, we can learn much about the dynamics of families in general and about the unique dimensions that accompany family suffering from the disruptions brought on by problems of alcohol abuse. We can also develop better techniques and strategies more specifically geared to the treatment of alcohol problems and to the prevention of the intergenerational transmission of alcoholism.

BIBLIOGRAPHY

Black, Claudia

  1979   "Children of Alcoholics." Alcohol
              Health and Research World, 4, pp. 23-37.

Cork, Margaret

  1969   The Forgotten Children. Don Mills,
              Canada: Paperjacks.

Greenleaf, Jael

  1981   "Co-Alcoholic/Para-Alcoholic: Who's
              Who and What's the Difference."
              Presented at National Council on Alco-
              holism annual forum, New Orleans.

Hanson, Kathye &
Nada Estes

  1977   "Dynamics of Alcoholic Families."
              In Nada Estes and Edith Heinemann
              (Eds.), Alcoholism, pp. 67-75.
              St. Louis: Mosby.

Jackson, Joan

  1954   "The Adjustment of the Family to the
              Crisis of Alcoholism." Quarterly
              Journal of Studies on Alcohol, 15:4,
              December, pp. 562-586.

Janzen, Curtis

  1978   "Family Treatment for Alcoholism: A
              Review. Social Work, March, pp.
              135-141.

Nardi, Peter M.

  1981   "Children of Alcoholics: A Role
              Theoretical Perspective." Journal of
              Social Psychology, 115, pp. 237-245.

Nardi, Peter M.

    1982a   "Alcohol Treatment and the Non-Traditional Family Structures of Gays and Lesbians." <u>Journal of Alcohol and Drug Education</u>, 27:2, Winter.

    1982b   "Alcoholism and Homosexuality: A Theoretical Perspective." <u>Journal of Homosexuality</u>, 7:4, Summer.

National Institute on
Alcohol Abuse and
Alcoholism (NIAAA)

    1981   Fourth Special Report to the US Congress on Alcohol and Health. Reprinted in <u>Alcohol Health and Research World</u>, 5:3, Spring, pp. 2-65.

Seixas, Judith

    1977   "Children from Alcoholic Families." In N. Estes and E. Heinemann (Eds.), <u>Alcoholism</u>, pp. 153-161. St. Louis: Mosby.

Shapiro, Rodney

    1977   "A Family Therapy Approach to Alcoholism." <u>Journal of Marriage and Family Counseling</u>, 3:4, October, pp. 71-78.

Wolin, Steven, Linda Bennett,
Denise Noonan, Martha Teitelbaum

    1980   "Disrupted Family Rituals: A Factor in the Intergenerational Transmission of Alcoholism." <u>Journal of Studies on Alcohol</u>, 41:3, pp. 199-214.

*Peter M. Nardi, Department of Sociology, Pitzer College, Claremont, California 91711.

CHAPTER 11

THE IMPACT OF CRIME UPON FAMILY LIFE IN THE INNER CITY

John Gruber*

I. INTRODUCTION

The impact of crime pervades all stratas of our
society. Crime has no boundaries with regard to age,
sex, race, social, or economic status. Yet both the
short and long term effect of crime upon individual
victims and its contribution to family disorganization
is often glossed over. The fear of crime alone impacts family life style, mobility, recreation, and
interactions within our society.

While Americans are repulsed by crime, many feel
powerless to do much about it. Forty-one percent of
those in high crime areas will not go out at night,
35 percent will not speak to strangers, 20 percent
have watchdogs in their homes, and more than a third
keep firearms for their protection.

Though the chances of being assaulted are considerably less than 1,000 to 1, last year alone, more
than 200,000 people in the United States experienced
violent attacks. Their injuries ranged from a de-
flated ego or bruised lip, to irreparable damage, or
even death.

Both in terms of physical and monetary loss,
national statistics in the FBI Uniform Crime Reports
are staggering. One violent crime occurs every 31
seconds; one property crime every three seconds;
one murder every 27 minutes; one forcible rape every
eight minutes; and one robbery every 78 seconds. In
addition, one aggravated assault occurs every minute;
one burglary, every 10 seconds; one larceny/theft
every five seconds; and one motor vehicle theft every
33 seconds.

How families perceive crime (especially in the
inner city where it is the highest) greatly affects
how they live their lives. A study conducted by the
U.S. Department of Justice in 8 selected cities concerning the public's attitude towards crime showed
that 82% perceived national crime as rapidly escalating, particularly crimes of violence as well as pro-

197

perty crime. Most citizens felt that their chance of
being attacked or robbed had increased. Sixty-four
percent of those who felt that their chances of attack
had increased had a member of their household victimized by a personal crime. One out of five questioned
were afraid to go to some parts of metropolitan areas
during the day. Thirty-six percent would not go to
those same areas at night. An incredible 97% of those
questioned felt that their activities were generally
limited because of crime. Thirty percent of those
questioned under the age of 35 who were members of
victimized household indicated that they have either
limited or changed their activities because of crime.
Half of the respondents over the age of 35 limited or
changed their activities due to crime. Thirty-four
percent of those responding indicated that they were
going out less in the evening compared to a year or
two ago.

Crime in the form of attack upon individual family members not only causes severe disorganization in
the family unit, but all too often disintegration to
the unit due to death. Let us for a moment focus upon
an individual victim's plight leading to this disorganization.

Behind the grim figures are the legions referred
to by many as the "forgotten victims." U.S. Senator
S.I. Hayakawa once commented, "Much has been said in
these chambers about the rights of criminals to a fair
trial. How often do we hear about the rights of their
victims?"

The California District Attorneys Association is
disturbed by the national lack of concern for victims
of crime. In an effort to overcome that apathy, in
1977, it initiated Forgotten Victims Week, dedicated
"to the thousands of Californians senselessly murdered
and to the tens of thousands injured, maimed, and de-
formed by crime."

But where there appears to be growing support for
a movement to protect victims' rights, one step back-
wards is taken for each step forward. Partly to blame
for this situation is the nation's legal system, which
often complicates and intensifies the victim's plight.

In property loss cases, for the duration of the
trial, owners are deprived of stolen items being held

as evidence. Occasionally, either because identification is faulty or ownership is unclear, confiscated property is never returned. The impact upon the family in cases where property has been lost can be great. To an inner city lower income family the loss of a television set may disproportionately affect their lives if television was their major form of recreation.

In assault cases, the aggrieved often is pressured into admitting complicity in attack, which is often embarrassing and morally damaging to the family as well as the individual victim. Moreover, the victim loses time from work - generally without pay - to testify against the attacker. The loss of work time to either recover from attack and/or to testify against the attacker impacts the entire family financially.

To compound the problem, defense attorneys frequently discourage victims and witnesses from testifying by frequently asking for trial date postponements. As a result, those with key testimony often stop cooperating with the prosecution. In the past few years, victim/witness assistance programs have lightened the load to some degree. In fact, where available, this aid has been quite beneficial in maintaining the family's stability while going through such an ordeal. However, many jurisdictions still do not offer such help and in some that do, funds are insufficient.

II. HISTORY OF THE GOLDEN AGE OF THE VICTIM

Stephen Schafer, in his book, Victimology: The Victim and His Criminal refers to certain periods of history known as The Golden Age of Victims. Needless to say, we are not presently in one of those Golden Ages. During the last Golden Age, which extended from about the 5th to the 15th centuries, victims had "almost dictatorial power over the settlement of the criminal case," according to Schafer.

". . . During this period, criminal procedure was the private or personal domain of the victim or his family and was largely under their control. The injury, harm, or other wrong done to the victim was not only the main or essential issue of the Criminal case; it was the only issue." While the harmful act was probably quite disruptive to the family, revenge by the family of the aggrieved upon the family of the offender had an equalizing effect. "An eye for an eye and a tooth for a tooth" helped balance the books (i.e., the Hatfield and the McCoys).

Fortified by this concept, victims of the Middle Ages extracted personal revenge and restitution. There was no cross-examiner to confuse and compound; "justice" was pure and simple. For each harm, reparation must be made to the offender or the offender's family. "In the case of the rape of a married woman by a married man" Schafer points out, "both her own and her husband's kin groups were offended. Each collected damages equivalent to those paid in cases of aggravated adultery. If the rapist was married, he paid these damages not only to the women's and her husband's but also to his wife's kin. In Athens it was the duty of the family to obtain vengeance or retribution and to fail to do so was a disgrace."

The Golden Age of the Victim began to wane when arbitrators between the wrongdoers and the wronged started to charge a fee. Slowly - rulers took over reconciliation functions and as the commission for their service became larger, the share going to the victim became smaller. Eventually, the entire amount went to the authorities and victims lost their rights to retribution.

III.   LACK OF RESPONSE TO THE FAMILY UNIT BY PUBLIC
        AGENCIES IN COMPENSATING THE VICTIMS OF CRIME

The fate of contemporary victims is not too different. They cannot take the law into their own hands because the state protects the public against crime. At the same time, they are left holding the bad because the state assumes little responsibility for reparation when a loss occurs. To make matters more equitable, the state therefore must start entering cases as a third party to compensate victims through the use of public funds.

Instituted in England, crime victim compensation programs have operated successfully throughout the British Commonwealth for a considerable length of time and to a lesser extent on a successful basis in the United States since 1965. These programs evolved when it became obvious that the offender seldom is in

200

a financial position to compensate the victim - particularly when any earning power the criminal has is taken away during imprisonment.

Most of the 29 states with victim compensation programs fix the limit at either $10,000 or $15,000, which covers only basic expenses during inflationary times. Even in Ohio and Texas, where the upper limit is $50,000 per claim, the maximum amount spread over a period of years would not go very far for survivors of a murder victim.

For example, Michael Collins, a computer programmer in New York City was knifed to death in the presence of his family by some young hoodlums he was attempting to eject from a subway train while they were harrassing a group of senior citizens. This case occurred in the early 1960's prior to any legislation to aid victims injured or killed during an act of being a "good samaritan." Had the state not stepped in to compensate his surviving family they would have had to go on welfare. Special legislation was enacted by the New York State Legislature to compensate the family by the amount of $6,000 per annum. While the amount seemed adequate in the 1960's it became extremely inadequate in the inflationary 1980's.

To be eligible for compensation, claimants usually must prove financial hardship. This provision offends sociologist Marvin Wolfgang, who insists that "compensation should be provided as an assertion of an individual's (and family's) rights and (of) a social obligation - not a form of charity."

Without realistic compensation programs, victims generally must endure crime consequences alone - often suffering severe financial hardship. Offenders, on the other hand, are "punished" by being clothed, housed, fed, doctored, educated, and counseled, while their families often are on welfare.

There also are other precedents for instituting victim compensation programs. Provisions had long existed for compensating those injured in wars, riots, accidents, or by negligence. Surely if the state can provide aid in those cases, it also can provide it for victims of criminal acts and their families.

Given current anxiety over crime in the streets, one might assume elected officials would be enthusiastic about victim compensation programs if only to prevent family disorganization and disintegration, not to mention political gain. However, when they have done so at all, politicians seem to have acted more to mollify voters than to provide significant benefits.

For example, Louisiana passed a victim compensation statute in 1972. They did not fund that law in 1976 when convinced the federal government wouldn't supply a subsidy. This instance and others like it suggest there is considerable disparity between society's humanitarian instincts and its delivery commitment.

Be that as it may, it would be argued that since the state has failed to provide protection against violent crime, it is obliged to compensate victims for personal injury or productive loss. What is needed is a system under which all victims would be treated fairly, would be compensated on a meaningful basis, and would be able to preserve their dignity and that of their families while accepting renumeration.

IV. FOCUS ON SPECIAL PROBLEMS OF THE ELDERLY LIVING IN THE INNER CITY

In the past three decades, the composition of inner cities of our country has changed drastically. The post-war baby boom children raised in the city moved to the suburbs to marry and raise their own families. In doing so they left their distinctively rich and culturally ethnic neighborhoods in favor of anonymous tract homes. Growing up in the inner city apartments these children often lived in small cramped quarters, never having the luxury of privacy, and often sharing not only their rooms, but their beds with other siblings. Parents often slept in the living room or the "Castro convertible Couch." More than likely grandparents, aunts, uncles, and cousins lived either in the same apartment building if not the same apartment.

Over the years this extended family started to disappear. The three generations (grandparents, parents, children) which so warmly insulated, protected, and supported its individual family members started to break up. First one grandparent died, then the other.

Later, an aunt or uncle died. Cousins married and moved either out of state or to the suburbs to seek a better life. Within a generation or two, suddenly the surviving parents saw their children moving away and their own parents gone. The inner city is still home to them. The surroundings are filled with memories which they are not prepared to discard. They are now the inner-city elderly.

Yet the memories the elderly are so desperately attempting to hold on to, are just that - memories. The city has changed around them. The community that has supported them for years is gone and suddenly alien to them. They are left behind in the deteriorating inner-city with all the other unfortunates. The more isolated they feel the more they allow their fears to take over their feelings. The inner city elderly fear their vulnerabilities because they are indeed vulnerable. Often they lock themselves in their apartments, going out only when absolutely necessary. A few even resort to storing their garbage in unneeded bedrooms just so they won't have to go out. They have all their shopping done for them and are almost completely out of touch with the world outside. One elderly New York couple laid out clothes to be buried in and left a note saying, "We don't want to live in fear anymore," and committed suicide.

One of their greatest fears is that they will be seriously injured if they are attacked. They often can deal with death as inevitable. What they really fear is that they will be badly injured and may suffer a long agonizing painful death or that they will lose their independence as a result of a criminal act and have to move to a convalescent hospital. The reality is that at their age injuries are rarely minor because of their physical condition. "Crime in the street... is often directed at the elderly because they are relatively defenseless and are most often alone" (Adkins, 1975:40). Nearly one third (29.8%) of all crimes are perpetuated upon people aged 65 and over.

There are seven primary problems people face as they become 'elders': (1) a change in physical appearance, (2) partial or total retirement from active duties, (3) lower energy level, (4) greater possibility of ill health, (5) greater possibility of need for help, (6) changes in cognitive and intellectual functioning, (7) greater uncertainty about the duration of life (Clark and Anderson, 1967:60). When all these problems are combined with the trauma of victimization, the psychological effects can be devastating" (Malinchak, 1980). Whether the victimization is real or perceived the psychological effect can be equally damaging. Stories about "crib jobs" quickly spread throughout the inner city neighborhood. "Crib jobs" are young hoodlums on the prey in predatory gangs. While there are specific instances of such attacks occurring, sensationalizing newspapers sometimes overplay the gravity of the situation, creating severe anxieties among elders. This makes them retreat further into their old world of memories. One elder said, "Living in terror is a terrible thing for older people while they are passing their last days."

Elderly victims also generally do not report their attacks to the police. This happens for two reasons: (1) they fear retribution from those who attacked them; (2) they feel that the police can't really do anything about the crime problem which has run amok. Even if they do report the crime, they generally tend to make poor witnesses in court. Because of advanced age they sometimes tend to be easily confused about their testimony, and are a poor match for aggressive defense attorneys who take full advantage of the situation.

Obviously the problem of lack of respect for the elderly by the young is not a new one. Famous mystery novelist Agatha Christie wrote, "It frightens me nobody seems to care about the innocent. When you read about a murder case, nobody seems to be horrified by the picture, say of a fragile old woman in a small cigarette shop, turning away to get a packet of cigarettes for a young thing and being attacked and battered to death. No one seems to care about her terror and her pain and the final merciful unconsciousness. Nobody seems to go through the agony of the victim."

V. CONCLUSIONS

In this chapter we have taken a look at the impact of crime upon family life with particular focus upon the elderly. The contemporary picture for victims is not a pretty one. We have moved from the Golden Age of the victim in which settlement for wrongdoing was between the victim and his perpetrator, to where victims are left to fend for themselves. It is possible that the pendulum will again swing back to another Golden Age for victims and their families.

Only then can we hope that victims will receive justice under the law.

BIBLIOGRAPHY

Adkins, Ottie

    1975   "Crime Against the Elderly." The
                    Police Chief (January) p. 40.

Clark, Margaret &
Barbara G. Anderson

    1967   Culture and Aging: An Anthropological
                    Study of Older Americans. Charles C.
                    Thomas, Springfield, Illinois.

Malincheck, Alan A.

    1980   Crime and Gerontology. Englewood
                    Cliffs, New Jersey: Prentice-Hall.

Schaefer, Stephen

    1977   Victimology: The Victim and His
                    Criminal. Reston, Virginia: Reston
                    Publishing Company.

*John Gruber is an Associate Professor of Criminal
Justice and Director of the Criminal Justice Institute, Chapman College, Orange, California.

CHAPTER 12

THE FAMILY FACING THE FUTURE

Jessie Bernard*

Despite the legitimacy of the view that historical "periodization" reflects subjective judgment, the
early 1970s nonetheless seem to have constituted a
crucial moment--demographically, psycho-economically,
and politically--for marriage and family in our society. These years were the midpoint in a decade-
long crisis reflected in marriage, divorce, and fertility rates; the point in time when the postwar
labor-force participation rate for married women living with their husbands--in what Ralph Smith has
aptly called a "subtle revolution"--had doubled, from
20.0 to 40.8 percent; and the time when the "politics"
of marriage and family veered in a direction notably
different from that of the past.

The great turmoil that characterized our society
in the late 1960s and early-to-mid 1970s left no corner of its structure untouched, certainly not marriage
and the family. There was enormous concern about
their future, and the Chicken Little syndrome was
widespread. The demise of family life was regularly
reported in the media. Even Margaret Mead, whose social antennae were more sensitive than most people's,
was asking if the American family could survive.
There seemed to be reason to reply in the negative.
Nineteen seventy-two may be said to correspond with
the midpoint of a genuine family crisis, manifesting
itself in the three "vital signs" of a society--
marriage, divorce, and fertility rates--which all con-
verged in that year.

Monitoring Vital Signs

The first-marriage rate of women declined from a
high of 109 per 1,000 in 1969-1971 to 85 in 1975-1977.
The remarriage rate also began to drop in the late
1960s, precipitously so in the early 1970s (from 166
in 1966-1968 to 134 in 1975-1977). In the case of
some young women, the declining marriage rate meant
only a delay in marriage. For some it meant no marriage at all; we know that the longer young adults
delay marriage, the greater the chance they will never

207

marry. Paul Glick estimates that the proportion of
young adults now in their twenties who will never
marry may be twice as large (8 or 9 percent) as the
proportion of those now about fifty who have never
married (4 or 5 percent).

The apparent reluctance to enter marriage was
paralleled by a growing willingness among the
married to leave it. Divorce rates revealed the same
kind of disaffection with marriage as did the marriage
rates. Whatever the actual divorce rate may be at any
particular time, it always seems to be soaring. Actually in the 40 years between 1920 and 1960--with the
exception of the 1946 dissolution of wartime mar-
riages--the increase had been fairly moderate, even
reaching a relatively low point in 1958. Thereafter,
however, the ever-present concern about high divorce
rates was validated. The divorce rate began to rise.
Between 1963-1965 and 1975-1977 it rose spectacularly,
more than doubling from 17 to 37 per 1,000 married
women.

Marriage used to mean having children as a matter
of course. The research questions had to do not with
whether one planned to have children, but with how
many one planned to have. Wherever records have been
kept, the long-time secular trend in fertility has
been down. There have been fluctuations related to
crops, wars, economic conditions, and the like, but
the number of families with five or more children has
--with exceptions like the 1950s--declined. What was
notable in the 1970s was the increase in the proportion of young women who planned to have no children
at all. The figures themselves were still low--only
11 percent of women 18-34 in 1978--but the trend
seemed to be up. Thus, for example, among 18-19 year-
olds, 13.5 percent expected to have no children. At
the other extreme, among women 18-34 with postgraduate
education, 21 percent did not expect to have children.
The positive social pressures to have children at all
were apparently subsiding, and the environmental and
ecological movements were exerting negative pressures
on many young people. There were even organizational
supports--such as the National Alliance for Optional
Parenthood--for those who wished to remain childless.
A new term--child-free--was even created to remove the
implicit disapproval in the term childless.

Among currently married women, the average number of expected children in 1967 was 3.1; in 1978, 2.3; among women 18-34, 2.1. The Roper poll of 1980 found that the 2 children women said they wanted was half the number they had said they wanted in 1970. The number of children under the age of 5 dropped 9 percent between 1970 and 1979.

There seem always to be people who view such declines with alarm. Theodore Roosevelt spoke of race suicide; and the reduction of the birthrate as rural migrants came to the city was already being spoken of as folk depletion early in the century. There was little such alarm in the 1970s, when many were urging zero population growth and growth itself became a political issue. Still, there were some like the man quoted in the Wall Street Journal to the effect that we might need a $2,000 bonus for every baby in order to keep the economy strong.

None of the three trends alone would justify using the term crisis. Declines in the marriage rate have occurred many times. Taken alone, neither the increasing divorce rate nor declining fertility trends would qualify as a crisis. More to the point was not the mere convergence of these trends but the accompanying changes in attitudes toward marriage and parenthood that surveys were reporting. Whatever it was in the turbulent late sixties and early seventies that directed the demographic trends, it seemed to find expression in the way people felt about marriage and parenthood. Or the way they felt may have influenced the way they behaved demographically.

Durkheim pointed out in 1897 that marriage was a less auspicious relationship for women than for men, and a not inconsiderable body of writing after that traced the deteriorating effect the wife's occupation --housewifery--had on her character, her mind, and her mental health. In the late sixties and early seventies a corpus of research gave substantial support to this thinking and later work, especialy on female depression, corroborated the earlier findings. Marriage, which had always been portrayed to young women in a glowing haze, seemed to retain this aura for fewer and fewer of them.

Elizabeth Douvan has documented these attitudinal changes on the basis of two national surveys, the first in 1957 and the second in 1976. Almost without exception, positive attitudes toward both marriage and parenthood declined between 1957 and 1976 in all sex-marital-status categories, and negative attitudes increased. Most notable were the changes among single women, where both the declines in positive attitudes and the rise in negative ones were spectacular. Fewer than half as many in 1976 as in 1957 had positive attitudes toward marriage, and twice as many viewed it as all burdens and restrictions. Similar changes were registered with respect to parenthood. It does, indeed, seem legitimate to label as a crisis a situation in which so few single women have a positive attitude toward marriage (17 percent) and parenthood (23 percent); in which, conversely, almost three-fourths define marriage as burdensome and restrictive and three-fifths feel the same way about parenthood.

There is now, however, some evidence that the turmoil-generated crisis in marriage and family of the late sixties and early-to-mid seventies is coming to an end. The most important news about marriage and family at this time may be that we are now emerging from that crisis. The overall marriage rate for 1979 (10.5) was higher than it had been for any year since 1974. Nineteen seventy-seven was the first year in which there was no increase in the divorce rate; and when it did begin to rise, it was at a decelerated rate. In 19 jurisdictions the number of divorces began to decline in 1977. In 21 jurisdictions the rate itself declined in that year. Comparable evidence for the end of the crisis may be found also in attitudinal clues. In a widely heralded talk at a 1979 NOW conference, the future of the family was pronounced to be an overriding feminist issue. It is always hazardous to project the future. A resumption of the draft, let alone the actual occurrence of war, slowness in mastering the energy crunch, failure to control inflation, a serious, long-lasting recession could cause serious derailing of all trends. With all these hedges, it nevertheless seems legitimate to conclude that the crisis delineated here is just about over.

Assuming, then, that the crisis is in fact over, what kinds of marriages and families are young people entering, or returning to? Certainly not to the so-called traditional family. People are experimenting with a variety of family types. They reflect, in one way or another, the impact of the subtle revolution.

Its concomitants are still far from having been fully traced vis-à-vis their effects on female marital roles, male marital roles, and parental roles.

The Subtle Revolution

Did the women's movement have anything to do with the subtle revolution? Can the movement be "blamed" for the subtle revolution's effect on marriage and family? Was the subtle revolution a revolt of women against the fundamental underpinning of the traditional family, the belief that woman's place is in the home? Although there was a long feminist rejection of that traditional ideology, the enormous surge of married women and mothers into the labor force began before the current feminist movement did. They entered the labor force because they were needed there; even, in many cases, against their own preferences. Their entry was not a response to feminism but to the needs of the labor force and, indirectly, of their families. There was, nonetheless, a rationale for it in the concept of women's two roles.

At mid-century, a Royal Commission in Great Britain gave official recognition to the two-role ideology for women. President Kennedy also did so when he appointed his Commission on the Status of Women in 1961. Alva Myrdal and Viola Klein supplied the social science research to validate it in 1956. In all three instances creation of supporting services to make possible the two-role pattern was recommended. In reality, the subtle revolution was already in progress.

The astonishing rise in labor-force participation by married women living with their husbands, including mothers of young children, had started earlier. Between 1947 and 1976--including the post-World War II period when married women were supposedly returning home from their war-time jobs--the proportion of married women, husbands present, who were in the labor force more than doubled, from 20.0 to 45.0 percent. By the mid-seventies, a "tipping point" was reached, when half of this population were in the labor force. By 1978 well over half (55.4 percent) of those aged 16-54 were in the labor force. Ralph Smith projects the 1990 figure to be 66.7 percent. The concomitants of this subtle revolution have been pervasive, especially with respect to the roles of both husbands and wives.

211

The needed re-structuring of traditional marital and parental roles is proving harder to achieve than had been anticipated. It involves many aspects, including the industrial-engineering, having to do with re-scheduling of work to accommodate more flexible hours; the economic, having to do with reducing the wage and salary differentials which often make it too expensive to use male time for homemaking contributions and child care; and, most especially, the social-psychological, having to do with sexual or gender identity itself. The roadblocks for both sexes are greater than earlier research had anticipated.

For women, one of the most salient results of the subtle revolution has been overload. The two-role ideology as originally conceived presupposed supporting services to accompany the two roles. The supporting services have not been forthcoming, and the two-role pattern has boomeranged. The result in many cases, well documented in the research literature not only in our country but all over the world, in communist and capitalist systems alike, is overload for women.

Despite this overload, the proportion of married women who prefer to have jobs has been rising, from a third (35 percent) of those polled by Roper in 1974 to almost half (46 percent) in 1980. The preferences vary considerably by age. More than half (57 percent) of the women aged 18 to 29 prefer jobs; only a little over a third (36 percent) of women aged 50 and over do. The new reality seems to be one of women continuing to enter the labor force soon after they complete their schooling and remaining for many years, with or without breaks to have children. As yet unresolved is the best way to supply the supports needed to help them carry the extra load the new pattern generates.

Whatever the preferences or cost in the form of overload, the potential for women's economic independence inherent in their labor-force participation has great impact on family relationships. There is documentation from colonial times to the present that whenever there have been alternatives to unsatisfactory marriages, women have taken advantage of them. The recent surfacing of so much wife abuse suggests the number of women who have remained in destructive marriages for lack of feasible alternatives. Ability to earn money and availability of jobs offer such an alternative to those who want it.

The subtle revolution also permits women to have more say in the kinds of marriages they will enter. Increasingly one of the specifications is that the marriage be an egalitarian relationship. Although many women (42 percent) still said in the 1980 Roper poll that they preferred a traditional marriage, considerably more (52 percent) said they preferred an egalitarian one, reversing the 1974 situation, when slightly more preferred the traditional and slightly fewer the egalitarian (50 percent and 46 percent). This trend is also reflected in the difference between older and younger women. More than twice as many older as young women were traditional in their preferences; only three-fifths as many were egalitarian. The trend seems to be unequivocally in the egalitarian direction and is almost certainly related to the subtle revolution. When women enter into formal marriage contracts, they tend to specify that the marriage be a partnership rather than a hierarchy; that assets be viewed as common property; and that there be a sharing of responsibility for both economic support and home-making tasks (in contrast to the legal assignment of these duties on the basis of sex).

For the sizeable number of wives in the labor force who are career women rather than job holders, there are special problems involved in the greater commitment implied. The results of a considerable body of research show that change has not proceeded very quickly. The career wife continues to contribute more than her husband to running the household, and if there has to be a choice between her husband's career and her own, his will be favored. She and her husband negotiate a distribution of family contributions in which she tries to compensate with child care for time spent away from the children and he undertakes the family work that is less threatening to his masculinity. Parenthetically, just as there are now couples who live together without marriage, the research literature shows there are now married couples who do not live together, such as those in commuter marriages and two-location families. As an indication of the problems arising in dual-career marriages, they are now common enough to call for special therapy.

For men, the subtle revolution has undermined the good-provider role, central in the traditional family. This role had only a relatively brief history in our society. Its rise may be dated roughly in the 1830s, when Tocqueville was commenting on the importance of work in men's lives, and its demise, April 1, 1980, when the U.S. Census stopped assuming automatically that the male in the household was its head. Although there had always been nonconformists--deserters, tramps, bums, and hoboes, some of whom were "conscientious objectors" to the role--most men had accepted it; for those who were successful in it there were valuable rewards, not the least of which were the power of the purse within the family and dispensation from other economic obligations. In the community, success earned kudos. Men commonly resisted women's infringement on this role not only because it reduced their financial power within the household but also because it lowered their status in the community. If a man's wife "had to work," it reflected on his success as a good provider. A good deal rode on success in that role.

One of the most serious defects of the traditional family was, in fact, that the well-being of the whole unit depended on the father's earnings and made those earnings dependent on forces far beyond his control. Unemployment could be as devastating to families as famines, plagues, and other acts of God had been in the past, and equally outside of their realm of control. Recently the role has also been challenged to another front. There have been rumblings of dissatisfaction with its requirements. Many men feel boxed into jobs and/or careers that allow them no escape. Not deserters, tramps, or bums, these are men with impeccable work histories. For them, the subtle revolution offers surcease. The employment of wives lightens their load. Some feel free to change jobs or careers even if it means lower income. Others feel free to slow their pace or even to reverse marital roles.

Such role changes, however, are seriously penalized. A Roper poll shows that a considerable proportion of both men and women condemn or denigrate men who are willing to assume any part of the traditional homemaking and childrearing roles. The experience of men who attempt to combine the provider and the homemaker-and-father roles supports the poll's findings.

214

One reports that he finds "silence and, at times, contemptuous looks." Why is he the only man at the swimming pool? Why is he ignored at the nursery school? He feels isolated, even excluded. "You are not a man either." He feels bereft of his male identity. Another man who experimented with part-time work so he could share in homemaking chores and child care felt strong social pressures from co-workers; part-time work, he was pointedly reminded, was not good for his career. A study of hard-hat workers found that the man who admitted to helping his wife in household activities and child care was derisively called a scab.

One informant, quoted by Laura Lein in "Responsibility on the Allocation of Tasks," put her finger on the gender-related aspects of the good-provider role: "He probably wouldn't admit this, but he is real old-fashioned in the way he thinks, that a man should work and a woman should be at home... He would never say that a woman is equal to a man... He feels that if I am working, I am going to expect him to do certain things that in his mind a man shouldn't do. A woman should do...housework, dishes, and things like that... He'll take the kids out and take them for a ride and get lost rather than help me make a bed or something like that." The gender-related aspects of roles in the traditional family are going to be far harder to change than we once thought.

Still, these attitudes may be diminishing. In 1970, two-thirds of the women polled (68 percent) and almost two-fifths of the men (58 percent) said they would lose respect for a male homemaker; in 1980, only two-fifths of both men and women said they would lose respect for him. There is a convergence between men and women here: the difference between them was 10 percentage points in 1970, only 1 in 1980.

"Any policy," wrote Heather Ross and Isabel Sawhill in Time of Transition: The Growth of Families Headed by Women, "which treats persons differently based on their marital status, or which alters the costs or benefits of living in a particular status, can affect the way people choose to group themselves in family units. The fact that such effects are largely unintended does not mean that they are necessarily unimportant." Opening up credit resources to single women, for example, means they can buy their

own homes; the so-called "marriage penalty" tax may
discourage marriage and encourage cohabitation. New
kinds of "families" and households flourish.

When Jimmy Carter in 1976 promised to call a
White House Conference on the Family, the organizers
found that the definition of the term itself became an
issue. The title was changed to White House Conference on Families. For, along with the subtle revolution, there had burgeoned a variety of relationships
and households, all of which considered themselves
entitled to recognition as families.

One of these so-called alternative life styles,
known as "cohabitation," shows up in statistical reports as "households of unrelated individuals," and
they have been increasing spectacularly. Although
relatively few, the number doubled between 1970 and
1978, from 530,000 couples to 1,137,000 or from 1.1
million adults to 2.3 million. In just one year from
1977 to 1978, the number rose 19 percent. Still, even
with this rise, only 2.3 percent of couple-households
consisted of unmarried adults. Whether the United
States will reach the Swedish figure--15 percent of
all couples living together are not married to one
another--is not discernible as yet, but the trend is
in that direction. Paul Glick thinks it may actually
exceed the Swedish level. Cohabiting couples tend to
be younger than married couples, as well as less
religious and more likely to be divorced when entering
the relationship; the relationships are of shorter
duration.

An alternative life style, intermediate between
official marriage and cohabitation, is represented by
a bill proposed in the Alaska legislature. It would
permit men and women to marry for a specific period of
time agreed upon in advance; and unless the marriage
was then renewed, it would expire. The advance agreement would spell out the arrangements to be made about
assets and child custody if the marriage were not renewed.

So far as the relationship itself is concerned,
there do not seem to be many differences between co-
habitating and married couples that can be detected
and measured by standard research methods. Still,
many cohabiting partners claim there is a difference
between the two relationships. Some cohabiting part-

ners who later marry say that marriage changes the
relationship. The precise nature of the change has
yet to be precisely determined.

In some cases, the households of unrelated individuals are just that--cooperative households in which
men and women simply share the expenses. They are
presumably congenial but not necessarily bound by
emotional ties. The arrangement is basically an
economic one in which duties and responsibilities are
formally structured. In Washington, D.C., there are
several referral services which specialize in households for those seeking this life style. In some
cases, male-female couples or groups of friends join
together and purchase homes they could not afford
individually. Changes in credit practices have made
this pattern available even for groups of unmarried
women. In some cities, the increasing value of real
estate minimizes the importance of the joint legal
commitment. One can always renege and sell one's
share at a profit. Despite these alternative life
styles, in and out of marriage, most people in this
country still live in households of husband, wife, and
at least one child. In 1977, more than three-fourths
of the population--77 percent--lives in such households. It is the ways the members relate to one
another within these households that have been changing under the influence of the subtle revolution.

Although we may say with a modicum of confidence
that the crisis of the 1970s has passed, the same
cannot be said of the subtle revolution. We are still
accumulating research data, and there is much left to
learn. By the time the rate of married women's labor-
force participation has reached its probable ceiling--
perhaps in the 1990s--we may know enough about what it
does to marital and parental roles to deal with it,
and this type of family will become the stable pattern
until the next crisis or revolution. In the meanwhile, Sandra Hofferth and Kristin Moore have summarized the research to date on the effect of the subtle
revolution on marriage and children, and they arrive
at certain policy implications. With respect to
marriage, implications include equal pay and equal
job opportunities for both sexes, flexible work schedules to allow more participation in family life by
men, changed attitudes towards women's and men's
work, changes in the Social Security system to recognize wives' contributions, and modification in tax

laws. The chief implication with respect to children, in addition to the above, is relief of work overload by improved support services, especially with respect to child care, which should facilitate "maximum choice and quality with minimum cost and red tape."

A great deal of the academic research on the subtle revolution deals with husband-wife families. But there is another stream of research, far older, which has long engaged the attention of policy makers, the so-called female-headed families, long noted in the social-work literature as "broken" families. It had shaped the "politics of marriage and family" for centuries. In the early 1970s, as noted earlier, the "politics of marriage and family" took a quite new direction.

Widows and orphans--female-headed families--have been a charge on the community from at least Biblical times. The church had assumed part of the burden and, in the early seventeenth century in England, community responsibility for the poor was spelled out in the Poor Laws. For the well-to-do, where property or inheritance or paternity was concerned, the state had some interest, but domestic law had rarely become a political issue. For the poor, however, the family early became "politicized" in issues related to the administration of the Poor Laws. In essence, the issue boiled down to this: should the dole be made so humiliating and degrading that it would discourage people from asking for it, or should it be generous and rehabilitative? In one form or another, the issue has remained. It is still unresolved. Political positions on "the welfare mess" reflect it to this day. Although this old issue remains, a new one has emerged--abortion. It is not primarily an economic issue, as the old one had been. It is a moral issue. As such, it is able to--and does--elicit powerful emotional response.

Old and New Issues

When political parties had more power in operating the political machine, family-related issues--except in connection with the "welfare mess"--did not have much likelihood of getting widespread political salience. They were too sensitive. But when a series of reforms in party organization in the late sixties opened up the system, the so-called single-issue

218

groups found channels through which to bypass party discipline and press their points of view. One of them, the so-called pro-life movement, proved to be a sleeper. It had enormous clout and could carry a heavy political load. It became the centerpiece of a coalition of supporters of a wide gamut of conservative economic and political as well as family-related issues. Pro-life--or pro-family--became a code term for opposition to big government, labor in general, and labor-force participation by women. It also became a code word for right-to-work laws, private enterprise, public support for private schools, prayer in schools, and censorship. Along with these non-family issues, pro-life became a code term for its own concerns in addition to its anti-choice position vis-àvis abortion; namely, opposition to contraception, sex education, homosexuality, cohabitation, shelters for battered women, child care, the ERA, and divorce. In effect, pro-life was like a Trojan horse that could carry troops converging from many directions.

The surfacing of the abortion issue in the mid-1970s was a reaction against another series of events. In 1959 the American Law Institute had recommended, as part of a modified penal code, that abortion be legalized. In 1973, the Report of the Commission on Population Growth and the American Future made several recommendations on the subject of abortion. The Report was based on almost a hundred commissioned research papers; its tone was measured, nonhysterical, calm. It reflected the best thinking of academic and specialized researchers. Most reviewers considered it an excellent statement of what was thought to represent a general consensus. A year later, in January 1973, a Supreme Court decision set the seal of approval on the Report's recommendations. It looked as though the right of women to reproductive control of their bodies had won a victory.

As it turned out, the victory, if it was one, was Pyrrhic. It galvanized opponents to the decision, and a strong coalition of forces began a campaign to undo it. Each court victory for pro-choice stimulated renewed vigor in the New Right. Well financed and increasingly sophisticated in its political activities, the New Right greatly increased its power. Three cases-in-point illustrate the form the politics of the family is taking at the present time: sophis-

ticated use of standard political processes, the
White House Conference on Families, and the electronic
church.

In 1980, the pro-life group drew up a "hit list"
--their term--of candidates targeted for defeat solely
on the basis of their votes on abortion issues. They
also mounted a movement for a Constitutional conven-
tion to work for an anti-abortion amendment. In
September 1979, Republican Senator Paul Laxalt from
Nevada introduced into the Senate an omnibus Family
Protection Bill (S.1808), with 24 sections, which
frowns on reproductive choice, gay rights, fornica-
tion, humanism, divorce, women's rights, school dese-
gregation, pornography, homosexuality, and voluntary--
rather than required--prayer in the schools. The so-
called Moral Majority says the bill "is designed to
strengthen parental authority, encourage families to
stay together, encourage mothers to stay at home with
young children, encourage families to take care of the
elderly and disabled, and to protect the right of
Christian institutions and Christian parents to rear
their children." Federal funds would be denied for
the purchase of textbooks or materials which "would
tend to denigrate, diminish, or deny the role differences between the sexes as it has been historically
understood in the U.S."

Politics of the New Right

In 1976 Jimmy Carter had made a campaign promise
to convene a White House Conference on the Family to
explore its strengths and ways government policy could
help maintain them. From the very beginning, the old
and new issues in the politics of the family confronted one another. At the early planning meetings, there
was a great brouhaha about the definition of the term
family, objection to including divorced persons on the
staff, and objection to the whole idea on the grounds
that family values were a private matter, not appropriate for public discussion. "Family" in the original call became "families" in order to recognize the
pluralistic nature of our society and the diversity
among family units. After months of delay, plans were
finally arrived at. They included state conferences,
widespread hearings, and three regional conferences in
Baltimore, Minneapolis, and Los Angeles, whose recommendations would be consolidated in a final report in
the fall of 1980. From the beginning, the state con-

ferences became, as one report put it, backdrops for a family feud that made the Hatfields and McCoys seem like kissing cousins.

On one side there were the old issues: improved health care, better social services, employment for low-income families, revised welfare practices, Social Security and pension reforms--the gamut. On the other side were the new issues: first and foremost abortion, but also homosexual rights, ERA--again, the gamut. On one side, 54 groups organized into a National Coalition on the White House Conference on Families; on the other side, 150 groups organized into a National Pro-Family Coalition. The first included government professionals in social programs, social workers, and social-welfare workers; the second, agonized protesters who saw their opponents as undermining the traditional family and as self-serving bureaucrats interested only in saving their jobs.

As it turned out, the abortion issue appeared in the final recommendations of only two of the three regional conferences where support for choice was passed (in Baltimore by 65 percent of the delegates; in Los Angeles, by 62 percent). In all three conferences there were, however, minority reports opposing abortion; in Minneapolis, in fact, a recommendation for a constitutional ban on abortion was narrowly defeated. The minority reports of all three conferences also contained recommendations opposing discrimination against homosexuals. Recommendations in support of ERA came out of the Baltimore and Los Angeles conferences, but so also did endorsement of the Laxalt Family Protection Bill. There was widespread endorsement of more education about alcohol and drugs, help with in-home services for the elderly, and recognition of the social and economic value of the homemaker. Support for experimental forms of marriage was rejected.

Although the abortion issue was the most dramatic, the White House Conference on Families may be remembered finally as the first national recognition of the passing of the old traditional family and the legitimacy of the families resulting from the subtle revolution. Many of its resolutions were addressed to their needs. Endorsed, for example were: upgrading of child-care programs; variable working hours for employed parents, such as flexitime; help with

medical and income problems for women in the labor
force; parental leave policies; authorization for
husbands and wives to split their social security
credits regardless of who earned the income; free
social security credits for periods of childrearing;
and abolition of the marriage penalty tax, which
falls heavily on two-earner families. All of these
resolutions, designed to overcome the difficulties
associated with the subtle revolution, garnered wide,
if not unanimous, support.

But the new issues will not go away. The abortion issue seems to be one of the few places defenders
of the traditional family can make themselves felt
politically. They may not be able to restore sexual
discipline, but they can try to see to it that attempts at non-reproductive sexuality do not escape
their consequences. Let women who engage in sexual
relations pay the price; do not let them go scot-free.
This issue provides a last-ditch stand in behalf of
the traditional family. It may take the demise of a
whole generation before it wholly disappears. Meanwhile, it has the backing of a growing power, that of
the so-called electronic church.

When church bodies talk about international peace
or industrial peace or justice or poverty or the
rights of ethnic and racial minorities, there are
rarely church-state issues involved. But when they
talk about issues relating to marriage and family,
there frequently are, for these issues have traditionally been part of the churches' domain. For
defenders of the traditional family, that is where
they belong. As opposed to the bureaucrats who think
they know what is best for families, "there is," wrote
Carl F. Middledorf in a letter to the Washington Post,
"the time-tested philosophy that the family is truly
the basic unit in our society, ordained by God....
Therein lies the conflict. The destiny of our nation
will be decided by its outcome."

A considerable part of the argument used against
abortion is based on Biblical grounds. There is an
erroneous assumption that our government was founded
in Christian principles and should abide by them. The
affinity between some Christian churches and the New
Right is therefore understandable. What is new is the
growing political sophistication of its leaders and

its burgeoning power resulting from use of the electronic media.

There was a time when the Bible-based political and moral positions of religious groups could be discounted. H.L. Mencken had great sport with the boobocracy of the Bible Belt whose intelligence it was impossible to underestimate. It was an unequal match. There were few able to take up cudgels against him. But the scene has changed. As Michael Novak reminds us, "the Bible Belt has been becoming more sophisticated, experienced, and realistic. Millions of evangelicals have gone to college, entered the professions, tasted power and wealth and responsibility. They are no longer innocent." Today there are few rollicking Menckens to take them on.

Sophisticated in the skills of lobbying and campaigning, the new evangelicals organized to defeat candidates for political office in 1980 based solely on their position on abortion. They organized a Week of Prayer to bring 200,000 Christians to Washington in April, 1980. It was ostensibly a great religious revival. Still, wrote Paul Valentine and Marjorie Hyer in the Washington Post, "speaker after speaker denounced abortion, divorce, pornography, homosexuality and other sensitive political issues and prayed earnestly for national delivery." As one participant put it, "the rally may have some effect in outlawing abortion." Or getting prayer back in school. Delegates from each of the 50 states visited every member of Congress "to assure the officials that in accordance with the Bible, many people in the various states are committed to praying for them, and to urge the senators and representatives to carry out their responsibilities in keeping with Biblical standards of right and wrong."

Especially crucial is the use by this new generation of religious leaders of the electronic media, which become a great resource for the exertion of power. The issues in this decade-long religious revival range the usual gamut, with heavy emphasis on the so-called moral ones. These religious leaders are confident that they represent the political wave of the future: "We have enough votes to run the country and when the people say, 'We've had enough,' we are going to take over." Even dissenters concede that "this sleeping giant...can be roused on moral issues."

According to Garrett Epps in the Washington Post, the "continued talk about political action is beginning to accustom many evangelicals to the idea that they are a potential voting bloc," even though they are aware of the possibility of being used by shyster politicians and phonies.

Reassembling the Pieces

The crisis of the 1970s seems to be over. The subtle revolution may take many years yet to run its course, but in time it will. The prospect that the coalition of single-issue groups will succeed in restoring the traditional family, however, is not bright, for the circumstances that created it have passed. Its components--highly disciplined sexuality which meant virginity before marriage, preferably for both sexes but certainly for women; chastity after marriage; the good-provider husband-father as head of the household with commensurate power and authority and wife-mother as homemaker; permanence, until death parted its members--have all become attenuated. Little by little they have been chipped away at, until few remain in pristine form. Non-marital sexuality is condemned by fewer and fewer people, flouted by more and more. No one seems to be punished for anything anymore. The independence of wives downgrades the status of husbands. Divorce rather than death ends more and more marriages. There have been protests against each of these changes; but no more than Canute can decriers of change sweep back the waves.

The collapse of an ancient regime of any kind leaves a lot of sociological debris. There can be little doubt that the passing of the traditional family has left a great many traumas, a great deal of suffering, a great many loose ends. It will take considerable re-thinking, searching and re-searching, and balancing of costs and benefits before these problems can be dealt with optimally. It will take much painful re-evaluation of the pursuit of happiness. If the 1970s were a time of crisis, revolution, and moral political issues, the 1980s will be a time of putting the pieces together to develop family structures suitable for this time and place, this day and age.

READINGS SUGGESTED BY THE AUTHOR:

Lein, Laura

1979   "Responsibility on the Allocation of
              Tasks." The Family Coordinator, 28,
              489-96.

Myrdal, Alva &
Kelin, Viola

1956   Women's Two Roles. London: Routledge
              and Kegan Paul.

Ross, Heather &
Sawhill, Isabel V.

1979   Time of Transition: The Growth of
              Families Headed by Women. Washington,
              D.C.: The Urban Institute.

Smith, Ralph E. (ed.)

1979   The Subtle Revolution: Women at Work.
              Washington, D.C.: The Urban Institute.

White House Conference on Families

1980   Listening to America's Families, Action
              for the 80s: The Report to the Presi-
              dent, Congress and Families of the Na-
              tion. Washington, D.C.: White House
              Conference on Families.

*Jessie Bernard is Research Scholar Honoris Causa,
Pennsylvania State University.

Reprinted from Society, January/February, 1981: 53-59.
Copyright 1981 by Transaction, Inc. Reprinted by permission.

CHAPTER 13

THE AMERICAN FAMILY OF THE FUTURE: WHAT CHOICES WILL WE HAVE?

Stephen R. Jorgensen*

I. INTRODUCTION

It seems that every few years social scientists feel compelled to go through a social forecasting exercise which focuses on the status, well-being, and future of the American family. "Is the family alive and well, or is it sick, in trouble, or dying?" "Are we moving away from a nuclear family system to one where no modal category or structural norm exists?" "Will marriage and family life in the future have positive, adverse, or neutral influences on the physi-cal, emotional, and psychological health of the indi-vidual family member?" "What major social functions will the family have 20, 30, or 40 years from now?" These questions typify the concerns of social scien-tists and other observers (politicians, clergy, and mass media writers) who have an interest in the future of the family.

Social scientists have experienced considerable difficulty in predicting with any degree of accuracy societal, economic, or political trends of the future (beyond one or two years, at least). Moreover the greater the distance into the future one predicts, the lower the degree of predictive accuracy. This is especially so for family sociologists, given that we must rely on rather limited and sometimes questionable data banks, that human values and behavior related to family life have often taken unanticipated and seem-ingly non-logical twists and turns, and what people say they will do or how they intend to behave in the future often does not correspond to their actual be-havior.

II. SOME DEFINITIONS

It is critical to this discussion that two impor-tant concepts be operationalized so that we have a common ground for discussion: (1) future and (2) family. By future I mean the next 20 to 30 years, which would take us through the years 2002 to 2012.

227

This operationalization was selected for two reasons. First, it carries far enough into the future to make the discussion interesting, but not so far that our level of predictive accuracy and confidence assume miniscule proportions. Second, most who read this article will live long enough to see if these predictions actually hold true. Hence, it is entirely possible for anyone to "test" these predictions as hypotheses in future research.

Defining the _family_ is a more arduous task, however. Take any fifty family sociologists and you are likely to get nearly as many definitions of "family." I will therefore short-circuit any definitional debate by pointing out that there is probably no single acceptable "definition of consensus" in the scientific community of family scholars. There are many types of family structures, and families can be studied from any of a number of levels of analyses (micro, macro; sociological, anthropological, social-psychological, legal, psychological; nuclear, extended; etc.). I will limit the discussion here to those _primary groups in society where members are related by kinship ties (affinal, adoptive, or consanguineal), where children (if present) receive nurturant socialization, and which link generations through expressive and instrumental means._ This operational definition of family includes the _traditional nuclear family model_, composed of a husband-wife couple, children, husband working outside of the home with the wife at home with primary responsibilities for child care and household chores, as well as emergent structures of single parent families, childless married couples, extended families (or "modified extended") and reconstituted (blended) families. Excluded from this definition are single-person households, dating and engaged partners, and cohabiting couples. However, behavioral trends and values relating to these latter categories are closely related in a reciprocal fashion to trends and values in the family system.

III. THE SOCIAL AND ECONOMIC WORLD OF 2002 TO 2012

A projection of where the family in America will be 20 to 30 years from now requires a prior understanding of what the societal and socioeconomic context of the family will be at that time. Knowing what we do about the aspects of that environment which have

the greatest impact upon families and contribute most
to the shaping of family structure, function, and process, it is evident that four interrelated domains
deserve special attention: (1) the economy, (2) the
polity, (3) the physical environment, and (4) the
sociocultural environment.

(1)   The Economy

The economic woes experienced in our society in
the 1970s and early 1980s are likely to be with us for
some time to come. Although economic projections are
extremely difficult to make with a great deal of accuracy, most economists agree that we will continue to
see slow economic growth marked by periods of recession. Inflation will continue, eroding the purchasing
power of many families, especially those on fixed
incomes and the poor. Recessionary-induced unemployment will continue as long as government attempts to
reduce the inflation rate with tight money policies.
High interest rates owing to a tight money supply and
a burgeoning national debt will keep the housing
market depressed for quite a few years, making it
extremely difficult for young couples and families
to own their own homes. These interrelated economic
stresses will place an increasing pressure on married
couples to have both spouses working outside of the
home.

(2) The Polity

It is by now common knowledge that a conservative
wave of political and social thinking is gaining favor
in many segments of the society in the 1980s. Just
how extensive the impact of this wave will be by the
years 2002 to 2012 is highly speculative at this
point. If it continues, the impact will be felt most
in the legal system and those aspects of family life
most affected by it. The legal status and acceptability of certain structural alternatives to the
traditional nuclear family model could be affected,
such as homosexual rights and relationships, communal
arrangements, and cooperative households. Laws such
as the Family Protection Act and its many subparts,
if passed, will have a profound potential impact on
families. For example, the following are just some of
the ways in which the new conservatism can legally
impact on families:

1) requiring parental notification for minors seeking contraceptive health care or abortion;

2) removing the federal government's jurisdiction in juvenile delinquency, child abuse, and spouse abuse;

3) allowing a tax credit or exemption for households with a dependent member age 65 or older;

4) additional tax exemptions for children born;

5) denying access of low income women to abortion or contraceptive health care services by withdrawing federal subsidization of such activities; and

6) removing federal support for reducing sexism in school textbooks.

Finally, the "new federalism" and its introduction of block grants to states means that many lower income and working class families in the future will be denied access to social and economic support services that they otherwise would have received in an economy that will continue to be strained by inflation and slow economic growth. The AFDC, day care support, and unemployment compensation pies will be smaller in the future, and many families will feel the effects.

(3)   The Physical Environment

Families in the future will be living in a different environment than did families of the past. We will find ourselves in an environment with dwindling natural resources, especially energy and water in many areas. We will see continuing increases in human-made chemical pollution of air, water, and land, with critical decisions being made in regard to alternative energy sources, such as nuclear and solar. Moreover, U.S. households are expected to increase per capita consumption of energy, and will be paying higher and higher prices for each unit of energy consumed. We also became more reliant on new technological developments, and families will be influenced by them. For example, one of the fastest growing markets in the United States today is the home computer industry. By the year 2,000, computers should be commonplace in the typical American home.

Also, optical fiber development and use will greatly increase our ability to communicate with each other verbally and visually, and more advanced means of high speed air and rail transportation are likely to bring us closer together than ever before.

(4) The Sociocultural Environment

Many parts of the world in 2012 will be suffering from the effects of high fertility rates. The population explosion and rural-to-urban migration is going to more than double the populations of several regions by that time, including several in Latin America and in the Middle East. In the United States the pinch will not be as severe, but the distribution of population into already congested urban areas and ghettos will increase the stress and pressures currently building from an uncertain and faltering economy.

Our society will also be growing older due to the low birth rates of the late 1960s and 1970s and the increased lifespan of our population. The aging population will become an increasingly potent political and economic force with which to contend.

In regard to child rearing and the social/cognitive development of future generations, we can expect video games and home computers to replace (in part) television viewing among youth. Young people will also find themselves placed more in position of self-reliance and self-direction than in the past due to parents being in the labor force full time. The potential implications of this situation will be discussed below.

Finally, another important feature of the sociocultural environment of the future will be the continuing in-migration of ethnic minorities, particularly Hispanics. Such minorities are overrepresented in the lower socioeconomic strata as well as having high rates of fertility. This situation will have important implications for family and individual well-being within these groups and among others, especially if they add to the burden of governmental assistance and support due to their own income status. Hispanics already have had a profound impact on education, social and political life and this impact will grow in the future as their population continues to expand

231

due to the expected continuation of migration and fertility trends.

IV. THE AMERICAN FAMILY OF THE FUTURE

During the 1960s and 1970s, the major change in the American family system was the growth in the number of alternatives to the traditional family model viewed as legitimate by the mainstream society. Although never practiced to any significant degree, permanent singlehood and childlessness, sexually open marriages, group marriages, and communes became at least tolerated in most quarters, if not actively supported. Cohabitation, premarital sexual intercourse, and dual earner families have come to be viewed as legitimate choices as well as becoming popular activities among many. The legitimation of choice in the family system has been accompanied by an "emphasis on experimentation" where people are able to try out different life styles and settle on the one that best fits their needs (Reiss, 1980: 466-467). The traditional nuclear family model is no longer viewed as the "only right way" to manage one's life, as norms have become tolerant of a range and variety of choices. This range of choices is likely to continue into the future, and experimentation with even more alternatives is likely to take place (such as "gay marriages" or long term homosexual commitments). This will occur in spite of the apparent shift toward a conservative political and social climate noted above. I predict that the actual frequency of most of them will continue to be quite low, especially permanent singlehood, voluntary childlessness, and such structural alternatives as group marriage or communes, and that this will result from personal preference rather than a conservative political ideology or public policy. Others will continue to increase gradually in relation to the traditional nuclear family model, including cohabitation and dual-earner families. However, several major vestiges of the traditional nuclear family model will continue to thrive into the future.

1. Marriage Rates

Although the marriage rate in American society declined notably during the early 1970s, this trend reversed itself in 1976 as the marriage rate increased in each succeeding year through 1981. Marriage will

232

continue to be a popular choice in the future. The proportion of American adults marrying at least once will continue to hover around the 92 percent level through the 1980s, and may actually rise again in the 1990s (Glick, 1979). In a societal, economic, and environmental context pervaded by uncertainty and a heretofore unknown level of stress on the well-being of the individual, the commitment and stability in a long-term relationship such as marriage will remain a highly valued enterprise. Permanent singlehood will not, I predict, be any more popular in the future than it is now. The rate is unlikely to exceed 10 percent for adults now in their 20s, and in all like-lihood will peak at 7 or 8 percent. However, it will be a legitimate choice for those who prefer that type of life style.

2. Birth Rates

Birth rates, like marriage rates, demonstrated a significant (albeit sharper) decline during the late 1960s and into the mid-1970s. The birth rate in our society reached its lowest point of the century in 1975 and 1976. Beginning in 1977, however, the trend was reversed and we have seen gradual increases in the birth rate each succeeding year (comprising a 9.4 percent increase between 1976 and 1980).

I predict a continuing moderate increase in the birth rate for the next 5 to 10 years, followed by a leveling off with minor fluctuations thereafter. Parenthood will continue to be a popular choice in the future. I do not expect to see a significant rise in the crude birth or fertility rates, however,

> ...the decline in the U.S. birth rate
> from the peak it reached two decades ago
> has provided much of the momentum for a
> variety of other changes, and this de-
> cline has gone about as far as it can go.
> Most demographers do not expect the birth
> rate to rise very significantly in the
> next decade or two...(emphasis added),
> (Glick, 1979:2).

Neither do I expect to see a significant increase in the rate of voluntary childlessness. Only 4 percent of all wives in 1976 expected to be childless, with only 5.3 percent of all wives aged 22-24 in 1976 ex-

pecting childlessness (Blake, 1979). The continuing
negative social climate vis a vis voluntary childlessness, coupled with the increases in birth rate over
the past few years, lead me to speculate that permanent voluntary childlessness will not exceed 10 percent
in the next two or three decades, and probably will be
less. However, as with permanent singlehood, societal
attitudes and norms toward the voluntarily childless
person or couple should continue to be relaxed so that
it becomes an increasingly viable status that is
viewed as legitimate in most segments of the society.

There is certainly some serious disagreement with
this prediction. Veevers (1980) predicts that permanent childlessness women in the younger age cohorts
leads to the prediction that 31 percent of young women
in the United States will remain permanently childless
(given the continuation of current trends). This latter assumption is a critical one, however, in view of
the empirically generated knowledge that behavioral
intentions often do not correspond with actual subsequent family planning behavior (Davidson and Jaccard,
1979; Fishbein and Jaccard, 1973). In view of recent
birth rate increases, it appears as if some women, at
least, are changing their future childbearing intentions, perhaps from "zero" to "one or more," and that
children are still highly valued as important social
investments (Blake, 1979).

At the other extreme are social economists predicting a "baby boom" by the 1990s. There are two
arguments at the base of this prediction. First, the
"birth dearth" of the 1960s and 1970s created such a
smaller number of babies that they have taken on a
certain degree of "scarcity value." A natural response to the shrinking quantity of any valued commodity is to attempt to increase the supply; that is,
to produce more babies. Second, it is argued that the
low birth rate of the 1930s, high rates of the late
1940s and 1950s, and low rates of the 1960s and 1970s
have created a cyclical and compatible interchange
between the size of certain cohorts in the childbearing age ranges and the employment market. When the
few babies born during the Great Depression of the
1930s grew into adulthood and saw relatively little
competition for employment in the 1950s, thereby
sensing economic good times, they produced many children. This large cohort of children in turn grew into
young adulthood in the 1970s and, seeing much compe-

tition for jobs, lowered their fertility to adjust to economic hard times. By the time this small cohort of 1970s babies grows to maturity in the 1990s, they again will see little competition (as did the 1930s cohort) and, it is predicted, will produce many babies.

There are serious difficulties with this prediction as well. Beyond the fact that children are viewed as "socially instrumental investments" rather than as "consumption goods in an economic marketplace" (Blake, 1979), this model does not take into account the wide-sweeping value and gender role changes which have pushed us toward a two-child norm (Buckhout, 1972), and which are unlikely to change drastically in the future. In this case, social considerations will outweigh economic ones. Nor does this model consider the likelihood that economic hard times and uncertainty in the form of recession, unemployment, inflation, and high interest rates will continue into the future. The 1930s cohort entered their childbearing years during an economic growth and expansion period in our society. It is my prediction that history will not repeat itself in this case, and that average family sizes will continue to be kept small due to this combination of social and economic conditions.

3. Divorce Rates

I predict that we have seen the zenith of the recent divorce rate acceleration. The divorce rate will probably continue to remain about the same for some time to come. The primary effects of the gender role changes of the 1960s and 1970s have been felt, divorce laws have been eased about as much as they can be in many states, and the belief in the importance of personal happiness versus commitment to unfulfilling relationships realized as much as it is going to be. It is predicted that 62 percent of those who married for the first time in the late 1970s will survive without divorce, somewhat lower than for previous generations (Glick and Norton, 1977).

The net effect of this new divorce rate plateau will continue to be felt: a large pool of divorced adults (around 3,000,000 each year) and a sizeable number of single-parent households created among divorcees with dependent children. Given the con-

tinuing popularity of marriage (and remarriage), as
predicted above, this means that a major transformation in the traditional nuclear family model will be
with us: reconstituted, or blended, families composed
of remarried adults and/or children from previous
nuclear family situations. By 1990 more than one-half
of all children will spend some time in a single parent family or household by the time they reach their
18th birthdays (Glick, 1979:4). Regardless of this
fact, the number who live in such a family at any one
time will continue to remain quite moderate, probably
around 20 percent. The high rate of remarriage means
that living in a single parent household for most will
continue to be a temporary situation, but we will also
see a continuing increase in the number of blended
families commensurate with any future increases in the
divorce rate.

As with voluntary childlessness and permanent
singlehood, divorce will be viewed in the future as a
legitimate alternative to the traditional nuclear
family model. More than today, it will be viewed as
a rational means for removing one's self and children
from an untenable marital situation, rather than remaining in a home marked by hostility, alienation,
and negative affect. This will occur in a future
society where marriage maintains its popularity--even
among the divorced population.

4. Ethnic, Racial, and Social Class Variations in Birth and Divorce Rates

Ours is a multi-ethnic and racially diverse
society. All of the evidence suggests that major
differences between the Anglo majority family and ethnic or racial minority families will persist into the
future. Especially among Blacks and Hispanics, the
latter group revealing significant population gains
in the last decade, the differences will be stark.
Blacks and Hispanics will continue to have higher
fertility rates, with Mexican-American rates remaining
the highest of all. These groups will also continue
to have higher rates of marital instability in the
future, yielding a higher proportion of single parent
families. The basis of this prediction is knowledge
derived from a large body of marriage, divorce, and
family planning research literature which shows an
inverse relationship between socioeconomic status
(SES) and divorce, and SES and fertility. Relative

to their number in the population, Blacks and Hispanics are overrepresented at the lower end of the socioeconomic spectrum and are not expected to make significant gains in the future. Hence, for Blacks and Hispanics it is particularly the case that those who can least afford it will continue to have the most children and experience highest rates of marital separation and divorce. The proportion of single parent, usually female-headed, families that are Black or Hispanic will continue to exceed by far the proportion of these groups in the total population. The most poverty-prone and unemployment-prone group of families in the United States are female-headed single-parent families in racial or ethnic minority groups, and the outlook for improvement in this situation is not favorable (Chilman, 1975; Bianchi and Farley, 1979; Moen, 1975).

5. Premarital Sexual Activity and Cohabitation

Our society is rapidly moving toward one in which nearly all young people will have had premarital sexual intercourse. Although valid estimates are hard to come by, most experts agree that the proportion of premaritally experienced males will be over 90 percent and females over 75 percent in the near future (Reiss, 1980; Hunt, 1974). Unless contraceptive behavior of teenagers and young adults improves in the future, this means we should see a continuing growth in the rate of adolescent pregnancies. In predicting this, it is instructive to examine the findings of national studies conducted by Zelnik and Kantner (1980) in 1971, 1976, and again in 1979. The proportion of 15-to-19 year old girls experiencing a pregnancy grew from 1-in-11, to 1-in-8, to 1-in-6 during that time period. This is not surprising in view of the dramatic increases in adolescent sexual intercourse and actual decreases in effective contraceptive use found in their samples.

In regard to cohabitation, the continuing popularity of marriage means that "living together" will never be more than a temporary stage in the premarital courtship process. It will not become a permanent alternative to marriage. Cohabitation in the future will be viewed as a logical step in making progress through the premarital relationship development process, as a couple moves from low to high intimacy types of activities. Glick (1979:4) predicts that the frequency of cohabitation before marriage will con-

237

tinue to increase, perhaps exceeding the level in
Sweden where 15 percent of all heterosexual couples
currently living together are unmarried (it was 2.3
percent in the United States in 1978). I agree that
cohabitation will increase in frequency, but it will
not increase as rapidly as we once might have predicted in the middle 1970s.

6. Communes, Group Marriages, Cooperative Households, and Other Structural Alternatives

There does not at present seem to be the kind of
normative support or ideology necessary to increase
the popularity of these alternatives in the future.
However, if the current situation relating to high
interest rates and a sluggish housing market persists
into the future (as predicted above), then it is likely that families will begin sharing housing facilities
in some type of communal or cooperative arrangement
out of economic necessity. I do not believe any conditions other than economic will prompt a noticeable
increase in these arrangements. Nonetheless, they
will be accepted in most segments of society as legitimate alternatives in the future for those who believe that their needs can best be met by them.

7. The Future of Individual Well-Being in the Family

This is clearly the most difficult prediction to
make because existing data on this issue are inconsistent (Glenn, 1975; Radloff, 1975). The nuclear family
structure, whether in its original, single-parent, or
reconstituted form, is likely to be the primary means
for satisfying psychological needs for emotional
attachment, intimacy, and belonging. As other segments of society become increasingly unpredictable and
volatile, such as the economy or political conditions,
the family unit will assume an even greater role in
nurturing and supporting its members. Perhaps para-
doxically, however, worsening economic and social
conditions are also associated with heightened levels
of family violence owing to the higher stress levels
placed on family members.

Perhaps the key mediating variable in determining
which effect, favorable or unfavorable, the family
will have on its members in the future is the availability of family support networks. Formal support
networks, such as governmental or community services,

and informal networks, such as friendship or kinship ties, will play a key role in supporting the family's efforts to provide for the instrumental and expressive needs of its members. Without such support, many families will be either too unskilled or will simply lack the necessary resources for adequately meeting the needs of its members. Reuben Hill's (1958) classic description of the inherent frailty of the family will be just as apropos 25 years from now as it was 25 years ago when he stated:

> Compared with other associations in the society, the average family is badly handicapped organizationally. Its age composition is heavily weighted with dependents, and it cannot freely reject its weak members and recruit more competent team mates. Its members receive an unearned acceptance; there is no price for belonging. Because of its unusual age composition and its uncertain sex composition, it is intrinsicallly a puny work group and an awkward decision-making group. This group is not ideally manned to withstand stress, yet society has assigned to it the heaviest of responsibilities: the socialization and orientation of the young, and the meeting of the major emotional needs of all citizens, young and old. (140)

This is one area in which the "new federalism" and wave of conservative social thought can have serious effects on the well-being of families. As federal programs and economic support are made increasingly inaccessible to low income and working-class poor families, their ability to thrive and provide minimally for the instrumental and expressive needs of their members will be threatened. At the same time that our future society will be mandating increased support for families, our political and social systems are moving in a direction that would provide less support for families both socially and economically.

8. Women in the Labor Force

It is predicted that by 1990 nearly 70 percent of all wives and mothers will be working outside of the home (Smith, 1979). This will be due to the continuing necessity for such an arrangement brought on by an uncertain economy, coupled with a gradual increase in the number of women socialized to be career or work oriented in adulthood. Such women will work for personal fulfillment reasons regardless of financial necessity. In addition, if the divorce rate continues to rise, even as slowly as expected, the numbers of single parent mothers working to support their families will increase as well. By the year 2012, this proportion of working wives and mothers will be even greater, perhaps 80 to 85 percent.

The significance of this trend lies in the expectation that such women will continue to bear children, on the average of 2 to 3, thereby combining occupational and parental careers. However, there is not yet any sign that husbands and other male partners are going to withdraw from the labor force to care for home and children while the female works. Although sharing of child care and child socialization roles is likely to continue its current pattern of growth, women are unlikely to get much relief from their male partners if they should wish to pursue a career. The net effect of this is going to be a massive increased demand for substitute child care to accommodate the expected increased number of preschool and school-age children whose parents are working. It will be critical, moreover, that such child care be not prohibitively expensive. At this point it is doubtful that governmental, corporate, or private day care facilities will be able to meet the child care demands we are likely to face (Hofferth, 1979). The result may well be families with a large number of "latch-key" children--children who must assume responsibility for their own behavior and take care of themselves for several hours during the day while parents are working. The consequences for child development can be either positive or negative under these circumstances. Some children who do not receive parental supervision might experience problems related to juvenile delinquency or other non-productive involvements (such as excessive television viewing or "video game addiction"), while others may develop skills of self-reliance and dependability under the same circumstances. The nature of the consequences will probably depend on the social climate of the home and neighborhood, as well as the maturity level of the child who must fend for him/herself.

In addition to problems associated with blending occupational and parental careers, families of the future will also experience problems relating to marriages in which both partners work outside of the home. Decision-making when one partner is offered a promotion or better job in another city when the other may find it difficult to secure employment there; compromises in career advancement made due to the demands of home and children and the time demands of the job; and conflicting work schedules of spouses which prohibit their being together for any extended time period in their waking hours, have all been identified as contributing to the role strain and psychological stress in dual-earner marriages (Hood and Golden, 1979; Keith and Schaefer, 1980; Skinner, 1980). These stresses will increase as the flow of women into the labor market increases, and the outcomes for individual and family well-being will depend on the ability of family members to cope with and adjust to the demands of the situation.

On the other hand, the gains realized from this emergent dual earner life style may outweigh the strains. The higher income and standard of living which dual-earner families are able to enjoy; the personal gratification and sense of contribution experienced by both partners working outside the home; the mutual satisfaction gained in marital partners' seeing each other growing in a career; and the enriched environment for marital and parental relationships allowed by their continually developing life styles, are all features of dual-earner situations which promote fulfillment in the eyes of the participants. The dual-earner family of the future, therefore, might experience a counterbalancing of rewards along with increased tensions, resulting in increased stability and personal satisfaction.

9. The Burden of an Aging Population

As pointed out above, a result of the 1970s "birth dearth" and the increasing longevity of the human lifespan has been the "graying of America." The age structure of our society is increasing rather significantly, and this will have a profound impact on the family of the future. An increasing number of families will be maintaining relationships with aging kin, both interpersonally and instrumentally. Increased stress on families will result to the extent

241

that aging members become viewed as psychological and/
or economic burdens. Other issues relating to sexual
expression and fulfillment of sexual needs will become
paramount as we become an older population. Economic
stress on the elderly will also continue to grow as
the number of elderly increases. The Social Security
system has already showed signs of faltering, and
those who would have relied to a large extent on Social Security benefits in the past will be forced to
look elsewhere for support--probably to the families
of their adult children. It is unclear at this point
what the result will be for family well-being. Nonetheless, it is safe to say that this phenomenon will
add to the already heightened levels of stress that
will be confronting families of the future, a level of
stress that many may find too overwhelming to cope
with adequately.

V. SUMMARY AND CONCLUSIONS

So what choices will we have in the American family of the future? The best answer to this question
at this point is, "More than we have had in the past."
Choice is the key word for the future. A variety of
structural and functional alternatives to the traditional nuclear family model will be available as
legitimate options in the future. However, it is
doubtful that more than a few will gain significantly
in either active endorsement or popularity. The most
likely candidates for growth in popularity are: (1)
dual-earner couples, (2) unmarried cohabitation (but
not as a permanent alternative to marriage) and premarital sexual experimentation, and (3) reconstituted,
or blended, families. Continuing to be highly popular
choices will be: (1) marriage, (2) parenthood, and
(3) divorce (for unfulfilling marriages). The number
of single-parent families and children reared under
such conditions will continue to grow as the divorce
rate creeps upward, but these will not be permanent
or preferred arrangements for most. Remarriage rates
will remain high, and the single-parent situation will
only be a temporary stage for all but a small minority
(probably 25 percent or less). Group marriage, swinging, cooperative households, voluntary permanent
childlessness, communes, and permanent singlehood are
all alternative structures which are unlikely to grow
significantly in the future American family system,
although they will be available to those who find that
these alternatives best meet their needs.

242

BIBLIOGRAPHY

Bianchi, S.M. &
R. Farley

1979   "Racial Differences in Family Living
            Arrangements and Economic Well-Being:
            An Analysis of Recent Trends." Jour-
            nal of Marriage and the Family, 41 (3):
            537-551.

Blake, J.

1979   "Is Zero Preferred? American Attitudes
            Toward Childlessness in the 1970s."
            Journal of Marriage and the Family, 41
            (2): 245-257.

Bloom, D.E.

1981   "What's Happening to the Age at First
            Birth in the United States? A Study of
            Recent White and Nonwhite Cohorts."
            Paper presented at the annual meeting
            of the Population Association of Amer-
            ica, Washington, D.C., March 26-28.

Buckhout, R.

1972   "Toward a Two-Child Norm: Changing
            Family Planning Attitudes." American
            Psychologist, 27 (1): 16-26.

Chilman, C.S.

1975   "Families in Poverty in the Early
            1970's: Rates, Associated Factors, Some
            Implications." Journal of Marriage and
            the Family, 37 (1): 49-60.

Davidson, A.R. &
J.J. Jaccard

1979   "Variables that Moderate the Attitude-
            Behavior Relation: Results of a
            Longitudinal Survey." Journal of
            Personality and Social Psychology, 37
            (8): 1364-1376.

243

Fishbein, J. &
J.J. Jaccard

1973   "Theoretical and Methodological Considerations in the Prediction of Family Planning Intentions and Behavior."
Representative Research in Social
Psychology, 4 (1): 37-51.

Glenn, N.D.

1975   "The Contribution of Marriage to the
Psychological Well-Being of Males and
Females." Journal of Marriage and
the Family, 37 (3): 594-600.

Glick, P.C.

1979   "Future American Families." The Washington COFO Memo, 2 (3): 2-5.

Glick, P.C. &
A. J. Norton

1977   "Marrying, Divorcing, and Living
Together in the U.S." Population
Bulletin, 32 (October): 1-39.

Hill, R.

1958   "Social Stresses on the Family: 1.
Generic Features of Families Under
Stress." Social Casework, 39 (1):
139-150.

Hofferth, S.

1979   "Day Care in the Next Decade: 1980-
1990." Journal of Marriage and the
Family, 41 (3): 649-658.

Hood, J. &
S. Golden

1979   "Beating Time/Making Tune: The Impact
of Work Scheduling on Men's Family
Roles." Family Coordinator, 28 (4):
575-582.

Hunt, M.M.

1974   *Sexual Behavior in the 1970s.* Chicago:
                Playboy Press.

Keith, P.M. &
R.B. Schafer

1980   "Role Strain and Depression in Two-Job
                Families." *Family Relations*, 29 (4):
                483-488.

Moen, P.

1979   "Family Impacts of the 1975 Recession:
                Duration of Unemployment." *Journal of
                Marriage and the Family*, 41 (3): 561-
                572.

Radloff, L.

1975   "Sex Differences in Depression: The
                Effects of Occupation and Marital
                Status." *Sex Roles*, 1 (3): 249-265.

Reiss, I.L.

1980   *Family Systems in America* (3rd Ed.).
                New York: Holt, Rinehart and Winston.

Skinner, D.

1980   "Dual-Career Family Stress and Coping:
                A Literature Review." *Family Rela-
                tions*, 29 (4): 473-481.

Smith, R.E. (Ed.)

1979   *The Subtle Revolution: Women at Work.*
                Washington, D.C.: The Urban Institute.

Zelnik, M. & J.C. Kantner

1980   "Sexual Activity, Contraceptive Use
                and Pregnancy Among Metropolitan-Area
                Teenagers: 1971-1979." *Family Plan-
                ning Perspectives*, 12 (5): 230-237.

*Associate Dean, Texas Technological University.

CHAPTER 14

FAMILY POLICY: ISSUES AND PROGRAMS

Leo Hawkins*
and
Frances T. Wagner*

I. INTRODUCTION

This paper reviews some efforts to develop national policies for families, list policies that have
helped families, policies that have burdened families,
and discusses recent policy recommendations that have
been made to support families. The attempt to have
no family policy is rejected in favor of a deliberate
search for better policy-making and wiser policies.
The basis for such a position is that government,
business, and industry are deeply and permanently
involved in making policies that impact upon families.

Keister and Garner explained in beautiful language why family life educators are interested in
public and private decisions and how these decisions
impact upon families.

> Families that perform their appropriate
> functions effectively in today's world
> weave strength into the fabric of their
> society. Because human society will
> never be without crises and stress, will
> never be free of natural and man-made
> catastrophes, it must always value those
> of its families that perform well the
> important roles assigned them.
>
> A strong and healthy society is one where:
> individual potential is encouraged and
>   realized
> human sexuality is respected and lent
>   dignity
> children are wanted and nurtured
> life is enriched by moral, spiritual,
>   and social values
> members grow and live in relationships
>   that ensure a sense of personal worth
>   and purpose and commitment to worthwhile
>   cultural values

And it may be said that it is the family
more than any other agent in society that
provides the setting for these experiences,
these learnings and values that so enrich
a society.

Because of present-day stresses in our
society it is difficult for families to
function effectively, and more families
need more help than in the past to carry
out well the responsibilities assigned
to them, to transmit their stabilizing
values to the new generation, to continue
to be society's anchor in a turbulent
world. (Keister and Garner, Note 2)

Novak (1976) affirmed that "every" avenue of
social research leads to the family, citing educational achievement, nutrition, mental health, economic
skills and attitudes, unemployment, sex-role identification, aspirations and religious seriousness.

The Search for A National Policy For Families

Our discussion assumes a general agreement with
the position that families are essential, primary, or
basic to American industrial society. Further, it is
necessary in this context to accept a very broad definition of "family." Acknowledging that there is no
perfect definition of "family," our purpose seems to
be served by following the American Home Economics
Association. "AHEA defines the family unit as two or
more persons who share resources, share responsibility
for decisions, share values and goals and have commitment to one another over time. The family is that
climate that one 'comes home to' and it is this network of sharing and commitments that more accurately
describes the family unit, regardless of blood, legal
ties, adoption, or marriage" (Note 1).

Having accepted the importance of families, many
students of the family have advocated a national policy for families. From 1948 till now there has been
intermittent discussion concerning the formation of
such a policy (Frank, 1948, and "Report of National
Conference on Family Life," 1948). These early efforts boldly recommend a Federal Department of Family
Life and they strongly support public and private
community programs related to family income, counsel-

ing and guidance, education, recreation, housing, legal help and training for leadership.

A comprehensive coverage of attempts to formulate public family policy is far beyond the purpose of this paper. However, any person who wishes to gain some knowledge of what was discussed from about 1960 until the present may wish to refer to Schorr (1962), Cohen (1967), and Rue (1973). These authors were realistic in attempting to face the complexity of forming a national policy for families. At the same time they strongly affirmed their belief that families should be a central concern of government and business, that social and economic goals for families can make such policies possible and that a U.S. Department of Marriage and the Family is needed on a cabinet status.

The latest serious effort to inspire a national policy related to families was a study by the National Research Council, Advisory Committee on Child Development (Toward a National Policy for Children and Families, 1976). The committee report described the problems of American children and families and made thirteen recommendations related to family income, health care, child care, special services, techniques for the delivery of services and future research.

The Attempt to Have No Policy

In discussing "policy" a simple definition is helpful. Moynihan (1970) said that many government efforts at social improvement have failed because of a tendency to define policy in terms of programs. "Programs" he defined as efforts that relate to a single part of the system. "Policy" for Moynihan responds to the entire system. Further, the government has some social policy related to all social interests even if these are "hidden policies" with negative impact. For this paper a policy is a decision related to the entire social system. The decision becomes a definite course of action selected from alternatives to guide and determine present and future decisions.

A. Sidney Johnson (Note 3) discussed the assumption that the USA is neutral, having no policy related to families. That assumption is true, he said, in the sense of a conscious, explicit and consistent public policy. He quoted Colman McCarthy from the Washington Post, October 12, 1974:

> To say that the government has no family policy is not entirely accurate. To ignore the pressures on families, to look away from the immense costs--both in terms of public money and personal suffering--to mistakenly believe that families can make it on their own: that becomes the national policy.

The same type of statement could be made concerning many business and non-profit organizations. They do not enter into a conspiracy to weaken families. They merely go about working at their primary purpose without seriously considering the impact of what they do on family life. Thus for many public and private policies that provide support for families there are usually an equal number of policies that become burdensome.

The Need for Wise Family Policies

Urie Bronfenbrenner, who has been called "The Family Man," said that before we can tell where to go in family programs we need to give at least as much attention to social policy as we give to material technology. For moon trips we test carefully and try all the components of the blueprint. Then we send a rocket without anyone in it to avoid the possibility of hurting someone. What about "social vehicles?" he asked. "No pretesting, no trying out the parts, nothing. Just send it out there with people in it. And people get hurt, especially women and children. The welfare system is a case in point" (Bronfenbrenner, 1977, p. 47). With his usual vigor and directness Bronfenbrenner affirmed that if we put family and children first we will "rediscover the wheel" and find that families are really very efficient.

Clark Vincent (1967, p. 38) attempted to keep a balance in the discussion of family policies by saying that in many ways the absence of a national policy for families may be a blessing. His point is that the family's greatest contribution to society may be its adaptability. Attempts to formulate "a" national policy quickly encounter many values which place individualism ahead of families. We cannot assume that

250

all families or family support programs are good for individuals. Legislation to support broken families, he says, may amount to a punishment for intact families.

Catherine Chilman (1976) represented the many family educators who through almost a generation have stressed the need for better policy-making for families. The choice is between wise or unwise policy, not between policy or no policy. Families, she contended, are actually weak in comparison with organized corporate interests. The capacity of the business-industrial-communications complex to control people's lives is enormous. Thus many freedoms are illusory and many opportunities for making decisions are restricted.

Families have no special lobby. The average family member cannot hope to influence corporate power. With government the average citizen can at least hope to have some influence through political activity and voting. Thus Chilman was saying that all business and industry as well as government must be considered when family policies are being made.

Turning back to government, Chilman said that many government policies produce partial, inexpensive programs designed to change people rather than systems (Chilman, 1976, pp. 215-223). Such programs, she said, cannot meet the problems of a technological society. Many social systems unfairly and adversely affect families. She called for broad policies that deal with the whole of society. "As these policies are developed, the needs and characteristics of a diversity of families and family members should be taken into account" (Chilman, 1976, p. 216). The more powerful systems in society are called upon to protect and support families as complex units, rather than demanding that families be strained and broken in attempting to deal with business, industry and government.

The Advisory Committee on Child Development, National Research Council (1976, p. 4) summarized the need for wiser policy decisions in relation to families regardless of how complex or difficult.

> The difficulties faced by many families result largely from social and economic

forces beyond their immediate control.
It is therefore not enough to exhort
parents to do a better job of caring
for their children. Courses in parent
education, while helpful, will not resolve the dilemma faced by a single
parent who must work full time and who
cannot make adequate substitute child
care arrangements without sacrificing a
reasonable standard of living.... Even
increased income and opportunities for
the employment of women, minorities and
the poor will go only part way toward
resolving problems faced by many families
in America.

....Without outside support, therefore,
it seems likely that the problems faced
by families and children will increase
in severity and that the rates of child
abuse, crime, drug dependency, failure
rate in school and other indicators of
our inattention to the problems of children and families will also grow.

II. SOCIAL PRESSURES ON AMERICAN FAMILIES

Most American families are strong and healthy.
Such a positive position was supported by a recent
report by Paul C. Glick (1977, p. 12). His report
indicated that in 1975:

- 84 percent of all families were husband-wife
  intact families.
- In seven of eight families the husband was
  still in a first marriage.
- Only a fraction of one percent of all couples
  were living in an informal relationship.
- Two of every three couples will have intact
  marriages throughout their joint survival.
- Three-fourths of women and five-sixths of men
  who become divorced will remarry within an
  average of three years.
- Between one-half and two-thirds of those who
  remarry will remain married as long as both
  partners live.

However, along with this positive picture there
are urgent warning signals produced by the pressures

of social change. Families are generally left to
survive without needed support from larger social systems such as business, industry and government on all
levels.

Some indicators that show the profound effect of
social change on American families are:

- As of March, 1976, 52 percent of married
  women with children aged 6-17 were working
  or looking for work. Since the early 1950's
  married women with children 6-17 have been
  more likely to work than married women without children under 18.
- During the past 25 years there has been a
  marked rise in the proportion of families
  with only one parent present; this rise
  being sharpest during the past 10 years.
  In 1975 more than one in every six children
  under 18 was living in a single-parent
  family. This rate is double that of 1950.
- For one-parent families in 1975, 72 percent
  of those mothers with children 6-17 and 56
  percent of those with children under six were
  in the labor force, with over 80 percent of
  those employed being full time workers.
- Since the late 1950's the rate of divorce for
  couples with children has been higher than
  that for childless couples. By 1975 over a
  million children were involved in some type
  of divorce action and half that number were
  involved in a remarriage.
- As the percentage of unmarried women of childbearing age becomes larger the proportion of
  unmarried women having children also grows.
  Over 80 percent of all children born out of
  wedlock are born to young women under the age
  of 25.
- Among preschool children, one in six lives in
  a family below the poverty line, and one in
  eight lives in a family barely above it.
  Thus, nearly 30 percent of America's youngest
  children live in families whose ability to
  rear them is severely crippled by lack of
  money.
- In 1975, 15 developed countries had infant
  mortality rates lower than that of the United
  States. Further, the mortality rates for in-
  fants varied greatly between regions of the

nation, and the rate for nonwhites was double that of whites.
. More than 1 million school-age children, and probably far more, have no formal care at all between the hours of school closing and the parental return from work.
. Other indicators of pressure upon American families are the rising number of reported cases of child abuse, the 95,000 children who live in residential hospitals for mentally retarded people, the 78,000 who live in residential centers for emotionally disturbed, and the 150,000 children in detention centers and training schools for delinquents. Many of these latter children have committed no offenses, but are children who are in need of supervision. (Advisory Committee on Child Development, National Research Council, 1976).

Still other indicators are listed by various authors to indicate family pressures or their results:

. Residential mobility rates reveal that the average American family moves fourteen times in a lifetime and that 20 percent of our population moves each year (Califano, 1976, p. 4).
. The average child by age 16 now spends more hours watching TV than in attending school and the average child between ages 5 and 15 views the killing of over 13,000 persons on television (Califano, p. 4).
. Costs for the hospitalization of a mental patient can easily reach $50,000 per year (Eldridge, p. 275).
. Deaths from homicide have risen steadily in the U.S. since the late 1950's. In 1975 the homicide rate of 10.0 per 100,000 was almost double the rate of ten years earlier. Crime reports indicate that about one quarter of all the 21,300 homicides in 1975 occurred within families. Half of the family killings involved a spouse, an eighth involved parents killing children, and a third were killings among relatives (Recent trends in homicide, 1977, pp. 3-4).

Kenneth Kenniston jointed with Bronfenbrenner in pointing out the seriousness of what he called the "depopulation of the family" (Kenniston, 1976, p. 236)

By this he meant: 1) One-third of all children under six have mothers working outside the home, 2) For the first time in our history most children have mothers who are in the labor force, and 3) Separated, divorced and unwed parents have helped to create one-parent families for one out of seven children by 1973. Kenniston pointed out that television, the peer group, and school have replaced adults in the family. In the end he traced the cause back to economic pressure on families. "Children," he said, "are born in the cellar of our society and systematically brought up to remain there" (Kenniston, 1976, p. 243).

Kenniston also joined many educators who discussed noneconomic pressures on families. He believed we are witnessing a "growing emphasis upon the child as a brain," the cultivation of narrowly defined cognitive skills. The value of a child is being judged by his progress in relation to IQ tests, reading readiness, and school achievement. Being ignored are fantasies, imagination, industry, artistic capacities, physical grace, social relationships, cooperation, initiative, love, and joy (Kenniston, 1976, p. 239).

III. POLICIES AND PROGRAMS THAT HELP

There is considerable evidence that a number of government economic policies and programs have been helpful to families. Schottland (1967, p. 123) offered a list of five indicators of such help:

- A continued rise in American family income.
- Rapid growth of public and private income maintenance programs.
- Medical insurance programs for the elderly.
- The objective of national medical care for needy people.
- An increase in minimum wages.

From a long list of specific programs Schottland picked the following as being definitely helpful to families:

- National school lunch.
- Special milk program.
- Government savings programs.
- Housing programs, in spite of many problems, and rent subsidies.

. Veteran's programs.
. Food stamp program.

To make a complete list of public and private
programs that help families would be difficult because
of the length and also because of having to gather
evidence to indicate whether a program is helpful or
burdensome. To indicate how long such a list may
become, the following is from A. Sidney Johnson (Note
3).

> Aid to Families of Dependent Children (AFDC);
> Unemployment Compensation; a variety of child
> programs including Head Start, Homestart and
> day care under Title XX of the Social Security
> Act and income tax deductions for child care;
> disability, survivors, and retirement insurance
> under Social Security; housing support through a
> variety of subsidy programs ranging from public
> housing to mortgage and interest deductions in
> the income tax code; public education programs;
> maternal and child health projects; food and
> nutrition programs; child abuse prevention and
> treatment programs; public support for provision
> of homemakers; home economic services through
> the Agricultural Extension Service,....

In the area of housing one may turn to Glazer
(1967) who described the traditional bias of American
housing policy towards single housing units built for
one family. He also showed how difficult it is to
have multiple family units and still create good
communities. For governmental health programs one may
begin with Roemer (1967) who affirmed that many such
programs are helpful in spite of gaps that need to be
filled.

It is appropriate in this section to mention the
family life programs that have been conducted through
the years by the Home Economics Departments of the
Cooperative Extension Service. These programs are
unique efforts to meet the various problems of families in a changing society. To gain an introduction
to such programs and to realize their great variety
one may refer to Arthur McArthur of Missouri (1967)
and Roberta Frasier of Oregon (1971).

One great advantage of Extension family life
programs is that they provide for planning and follow-

256

through over a period of years. Short-term educational and service programs that are funded for only one
to three years are likely to create a great deal of
frustration due to raised hopes that cannot be realized. Many times the people who inspire the hopes
have to move on to another job within one year and
the clients don't even have someone with whom to
discuss their frustrated hopes.

An encouraging trend is for individuals and
agencies in government and business to change some
outworn concepts. One illustration was reported by
Sylvia Porter (1977) when she wrote that for the first
time in July, 1977, the Bureau of Labor Statistics
will publish data on the status of family members
without designating either husband or wife as the head
of household. The new approach is to present data on
individuals in relation to the people with whom they
live," the "person in the family." A second meaning
of the new approach is that the government is finally
recognizing that there is no "typical" family. When
making vital decisions or policies about such things
as social security, welfare reform, income maintenance, and job programs, the needs of a great variety
of families must be taken into account. Porter added
that only 6 percent of family types now include a
husband, a full time homemaker wife, and two young
children, although many families fit this category
for a short time in their family history.

It would be appropriate here to mention two of
the many other encouraging developments. One is the
increasing number of studies of policies and programs
that impact on families. Family impact analysts are
now being trained. A few of the groups working specifically on family impact analysis are Family Impact
Seminar, The George Washington University, Minnesota
Family Study Center, University of Minnesota, The
National Conference on Social Welfare, and the U.S.
Department of Health, Education, and Welfare through
grants to various organizations and universities (The
American Family, Vol. 1, No. 1. R. Wakefield, ed.,
1129 20th St., N.W. Suite 511, Wash., D.C. 20036).

The second development is the public notice in a
number of places by Vice President Walter Mondale
about the 1981 White House Conference on Families.
Other such conferences in this century have done some
great work in leading our nation toward awareness of

the needs of family members of all ages. The 1981
White House Conference may well show the way toward
better policies for all types of families.

IV. POLICIES AND PROGRAMS WITH ADVERSE IMPACT

Califano (Note 4) quoted Dr. Edward Zigler as
saying, "We can and should demand the rejection of
apathy and negativism and expect a renewed commitment to the proposition that families are indeed
important and that it is the Federal Government's
role to help reduce the stresses and to meet the
problems confronting families."

Government Policies and Programs

Extreme individualism is a government policy
considered by many writers to be harmful to families.
Cox (1974) mentioned old age, survivors and disability
insurance, AFDC, public assistance programs, and
Medicare as examples. Except for housing, she said,
no programs define a family as an eligible unit.
Further, there is great variation in eligible persons,
treatment of incomes, work requirements, disregarded
earnings, etc. The result is overlapping and great
inconsistencies in the treatment of families.

Lerman (1972) studied 13 income transfer programs
and criticized policymakers for concentrating on who
gets benefits without examining the impact of the
rules on work incentives. He reported the case of
one recipient who earned from $200 to $300 per month
above benefits and could keep only $11 of that amount.

Aid to Families of Dependent Children has been
one of the most discussed of all government programs
and most writers agree that policies related to work
incentives should be improved. Honig (1974) used
studies of 44 metropolitan areas made in 1960 and 1970
and concluded that support levels for two-parent families should be as high as for one-parent families.
The reason given is that higher levels of support for
one-parent families helps to create more families
headed by women. Other studies (Cutright and Scanzoni,
1974) concluded that AFDC payments had no effect on
family characteristics such as one-parent or two-
parent composition. However, these authors still
favor income supplements for intact families, saying
that this help would not cause splitting. In short,

258

families need to be helped because of need and not because the government wants to determine family characteristics.

Catherine Chilman (1973) said that the major public policy harmful to families is to ignore the problem of inadequate income for poor families. By the summer of 1977 there was evidence that the problem was at least being touched. Network news broadcasts were reporting (7-15-77) that government reports show that the percent of families below the poverty level had dropped to just above eight percent if consideration is given to all income from such benefits as food stamps and social service help. The truth of such reports does not change the fact that poverty families are made up largely of elderly families, families with young children, one-parent families, and inner-city black families. Such families need all the work incentives they can find.

Health Programs, Public and Private

National Health Insurance, according to Bruce Stuart (1972) is primarily designed to serve provider groups. Stuart used a 1970 President's plan and expenditure data from Michigan. He concluded that poor families in Michigan would gain, but that families in most other state would lose. As a national health plan continues to be debated in Congress and in the news media it can at least be said that the impact upon families is being considered.

Turning to private medicine, Dr. Lewis Thomas (1976) stated that policies of the medical profession in the U.S.A. tend to guide a very large proportion of time and money toward dealing with dramatic efforts such as the transplantation of hearts, kidneys, or livers and the invention of artificial organs. These, said Thomas, are makeshift procedures that tend to take time and money away from more basic research in biological science. Similarly, an enormous effort is being put into intractable cancer, severe rheumatoid arthritis, multiple sclerosis, stroke, advanced cirrhosis, and other such diseases. In the absence of effective technology there are many varieties of non-technology and half-way technology. Under such influences the health care system is in danger of being bankrupt by efforts that do little good. High priority should be placed in the areas where basic biological research and effective technology can have hope of success. Such efforts have conquered typhoid fever, polio, pulmonary tuberculosis and other diseases after physicians were bogged down in makeshift procedures for generations.

Dr. Thomas was also critical of government policy in the recent past for the tendency to back away from educational programs related to amniocentesis (the procedure that detects mongolism and other abnormalities), abortion, and even birth control. Since important studies of these procedures are being conducted there is a pressing need to design a major detailed educational program to help citizens know the results of such studies and to face their implications. Interested citizens need to be informed about who will be tested, what the tests will be used for, what the costs will be and how people who need such services can be reached.

Back to popular government programs, Califano (Note 4) pointed out that medical benefits under Medicaid and Medicare are often restricted to a very narrow range of families. Such restrictions make it difficult to support programs that are designed to reach families with the greatest needs. In some states medicaid programs are denied to first-time mothers in spite of the greater risk for this group.

Business and Industry

One of the policies of business and industry that seems to have directly negative impact on some families is the policy of nonflexible hours of work. Bronfenbrenner (Note 5) reported on the efforts of a state legislator to put through a bill prohibiting discrimination against parents who sought or held part-time jobs. The legislator not only failed to get a part-time provision, the amended bill setting a 40 hour or full time limit also failed! The pressure from business and industry, said the legislator, was just too great. They did not want any limits upon how many hours a parent could be required to work. Bronfenbrenner also reported that this issue is now being considered by one of the largest labor unions.

The requirement of mobility is cited by many family advocates as having a very adverse impact upon families. Novak (1976) named great corporations, foundations, newspapers and the film industry as among those whose moving policies for employees help to diminish the moral and economic importance of families. All of these demand travel and frequent change of residence, thus dissolving attachments and loyalties of family members.

The mobile home industry, according to The Center for Auto Safety (1975), is one specific illustration of a broad enterprise that has followed policies that tend to harm families. This industry has sold 95 percent of the single family dwellings under $15,000. At the same time mobile home construction leaves the dweller a likely victim of personal injury from physical defects in the dwelling. A study shows that in general the industry has failed to produce homes that are consistently safe or of reasonable quality. The study's author recommended a new governmental agency to set product standards.

V. THE EDUCATIONAL SYSTEM

The public school system is probably the scapegoat of American society. Families, churches, and the legal system have all attempted to turn over to public schools some of their traditional roles. Then when young people are not successful, religious, or law-abiding, many citizens will look quickly at the schools. Michael Novak (1976, p. 46) stressed the point that, "Economic and educational discipline are learned in the home and, if not there, hardly at all." He believed that most disciplined hard workers of this generation, both black and white, came from families where parents watched over and supervised children, making discipline, hard work and education become serious pursuits for the family. Novak wondered why American society always picks the schools to help when schools cannot reach young people unless families have already opened the doors to young minds. "The provision of books and newspapers in the home, and sessions to assist parents in teaching their children, might be more profitable than efforts in the school."

Whether or not the schools are overloaded with roles, it can be said that many policies in almost every section of the nation's schools have made it more difficult for families to perform their basic functions. Chilman (1976, p. 218) said that schools may ask a parent without a car to come many miles to

261

participate in parent-teacher conferences or other activities. Other conditions, such as the mother working full time or other children being sick, may not be known.

More seriously, it is a well-documented fact that public schools have been used by American society as tools of segregation and the perpetuation of exclusion and status. In almost every county and city, a new citizen could learn in a year or two exactly where each school was placed on the hierarchy of status. Equipment, money, better trained teachers, new buildings, and principals were usually assigned with status in mind. Local school boards and committees have resisted basic changes step by step until many experienced court orders and legal sanctions. Even today when most school systems spend an equal amount of money on all pupils the more affluent neighborhoods are likely to raise money on the side in order to have popular status items such as marching bands and new uniforms for athletes.

Public schools are reflections of American Society. Their proper role is to help families to promote the total development of children. With successful families the schools will only need to supplement and broaden what the family has started. With weaker families the schools must have policies that support whatever is strong in the family. Many research studies and long experience seem to indicate that any attempt to "take the place" of the family is doomed to failure.

VI. RECOMMENDATIONS

Recommendations for public and private family policies and programs appear to be endless. The purpose of this discussion is to briefly present the major recommendations that seem to be directly related to family policies. Such policies may help to guide planning and programs in the future.

Families as a Central Concern

Most recommendations about family policies either discuss or take for granted that families should be made a central concern of government and that the private world of business and industry will follow. Cohen (1967) had a convincing discussion of government concern, saying that such a general interest must be "active, comprehensive, and habilitative rather than residual, restrictive, and rehabilitative."

A Minimum Family Income

If there is any one specific recommendation that all writers and committee reports agree upon it is that families cannot fulfill their assigned roles in America without a minimum family income. The Advisory Committee on Child Development, National Research Council (1976) seemed to voice the general concern in recommending that no child should live for a long period in a family with an income lower than half the median family income level and never under the government level of poverty.

The same Advisory Committee (p. 46) reported that a majority of poor people are struggling to earn as much as they can. Generally they use their money in an attempt to obtain what other Americans have. Their management skills vary, but many poor family members show ingenuity and skill. Kenneth Kenniston (1976, p. 248) spoke for advocates of families in saying, "Some of what we need to do, like income support, could easily be done, had we the national commitment and will to do it." There is also an agreement on the position that income alone will not do the whole job. The point is that nothing else seems to work without a base level of family income.

Marriage as a Health Speciality

A basic and far-reaching recommendation that has caught too little public and scholarly attention is that marriage should become a medical specialty on a level with an area such as dental health (Vincent, 1967, 1973). We have largely forgotten, said Clark Vincent (1973, p. 260), that couples continue to be the backbone of American society. Our highly urbanized and industrialized society demands more of married couples than ever before. Leadership of many kinds depends upon couples who are willing to keep up with very busy and demanding time schedules. The "megaversity," factory, corporation, church and hospital still hold on to impersonalism, alienation, dehumanization. For most leaders in such a system the marriage relationship is almost the only long-term relationship that has the time and tolerance to create an atmosphere in which needs can be expressed. Being emotionally honest in a marriage relationship "does not disrupt the production line, the board meeting, or the transportation schedule."

Clark Vincent (1967, pp. 36-37) spoke for a growing number of family scholars in relating many types of mental problems to negative relationships between parents and children, and these were traced to a malfunctioning marriage. He went further and recommended a National Commission on Marriage as part of the National Institute of Mental Health for the purposes of pointing out gaps in research and publicizing what is known.

A U.S. Department of Marriage and the Family

One of the strongets cases during recent years for the establishment of a U.S. Department of Marriage and the Family was made by Vincent Rue (1973). In spite of large spending for H.E.W. and H.U.D., the government, said Rue, has not paid direct attention to families. Further, "The institution of marriage has been nearly excluded from concern." Rue presented a discussion of the rationale for such a department, a discussion of the constitutionality, and a listing of the following functions: 1) Interagency coordination and liaison, 2) Educational development, 3) Advocacy, 4) Environmental planning development and demonstration, 5) Management and administration of service delivery systems, 6) Manpower recruitment and education, 7) Regulation, and 8) Research and evaluation.

The author attempted to be realistic in facing constraints to a national department on families: bureaucracy and ineptness of policy makers, different values, and the danger of growing toward drabness, restriction and totalitarianism. In spite of such negative considerations Rue believed the nation should move ahead with the idea and support variability of families and life styles as a policy in a U.S. Department of Marriage and the Family.

Policies for Minority Families

Families from any racial or ethnic group may be pushed into poverty by such unpredictable difficulties as long-term illness or death of a spouse when the

family has several young children. Robert Staples
(1973) said that the government's effort to strength-
en black families have been sporatic, misguided and
ineffective. He suggested six policies that are
specific enough to be called programs: 1) Guaranteed
income, 2) Elimination of sexist discrimination in
employment opportunities, 3) Community controlled
child care centers, 4) A child development program,
especially for preschool children, 5) Subsidized
adoption, and 6) Family planning and abortion services.

Stack and Semmel (1974), also dealing with Black
families, maintained that the government should not
make a large scale effort to obtain child support
contributions from the fathers in AFDC families. Such
a policy may cause poor children to lose some financial and psychological support. Instead they recommended that two-thirds of a father's support not be
counted as income in determining a family's AFDC
grant. This policy, the authors said, would reduce
the tendency of the fathers to fail to support a family in order to avoid reduction in the AFDC stipend.

Alan Sorkin (1971) made a study of American Indians and federal aid and came to the conclusion that
most reservations were "open-air slums" in spite of
government programs for education, vocational training, health services, low-cost housing, and aid to
industry and agriculture. Sorkin's recommendations
include: 1) More complete freedom and opportunity to
go and come; 2) The privilege to keep local tribes
and customs, and 3) Training and support in learning
skills to manage independent business.

The Bronfenbrenner List of Recommendations

Since Urie Bronfenbrenner has attempted for a
generation to influence policies and programs for
families it seems appropriate to list his recommendations in brief form (Note 5).

1. Welfare and work legislation should be revised so that no single parent of young children
should be forced to work full time or more in order
to provide an income at or below the poverty level.

2. Tax incentives should be extended to busi-
nesses, industries, and a great variety of community

organizations when they set up family and child services for any families in the community.

3. Family impact assessment should be undertaken
by both houses of Congress and by state legislatures
in order to monitor all legislation for possible impact on families.

4. Homemaker services should be provided when
needed for disadvantaged families in order to allow
parents to spend more time with their children.

5. Group day care should be provided for families and the eligibility rules should be very broad
and flexible.

6. Training programs for child care workers
should be available at high schools, community colleges, and universities.

7. Commissions for children and families should
be established on local neighborhood or community
levels. Such commissions should give attention to
the total environment of families and should develop
and monitor programs in addition to making recommendations.

8. Research should be supported in order to
focus on specific components of particular programs
in addition to massive surveys used in the past.

9. The Federal Government should adopt a family-
centered employment policy and set an example by
adopting the policies and practices in these recommendations.

Another excellent list of recommendations was
produced by the Advisory Committee on Child Development, National Research Council (1976) in their report, Toward a National Policy for Children and Families. Their list is not being included here because
it is in all essentials almost totally in agreement
with the Bronfenbrenner list, an understandable situation because Bronfenbrenner was part of the Committee.

Recommendations for Business and Industry

Eugene Koprowski (1973) saw families and industry
as complementing each other within society, the fami-

266

lies supplying people with talent, discipline, skills, and necessary values. Industry seeks production and wants to overcome apathy, alienation, militancy and withdrawal into worker organizations. Koprowski offered the following suggestions for industry as ways to bring about a reality of families and industry complementing each other. He said industry should:

1) Shorten the work week to allow parents more time with their children and should adjust work schedules for the same purposes.

2) Consider families when planning new communities in order to make work an integral part of the organic life system.

3) Try to minimize major relocations of families, and when moves are necessary plan them around natural growth cycles in the life of a particular family.

4) Whenever possible eliminate working conditions that are especially frustrating or that cause great tension.

5) Allow employees to take home some creative energy by cutting out overtime when possible and by rotating very tough jobs among all the staff.

6) Try to make jobs more enriching and more challenging whenever possible. Rotate leadership and rotate men and women jobs. The job itself needs to be made important in order to protect self-esteem.

7) Review more closely the value systems and problem solving techniques of programs and advertisements sponsored on television.

VII. DISCUSSION

After some study of the impact of policy decisions on families it is hard to escape a defeatest attitude. Staples (1973), Stack (1974), Sorkin (1971) and many others pointed out the misguided and ineffective aspects of many programs designed to help families. Even Rue (1973), who advocated a U.S. Department of Marriage and Family, admitted that a lot of impersonal bureaucracy and misguided programs are unavoidable.

267

A study of policy decisions and families is also
likely to convince one that government, along with
business and industry, is deeply and permanently involved in policies that impact upon families. There
is no evidence that government or industry will pull
back and leave families alone. The question becomes,
"Shall the policy decisions that are made by government and industry be wise policies that create helpful
programs, or will policies continue to be non-family
oriented, individualistic, and sometimes inhuman and
harmful?"

A very helpful and balanced view is that of Otto
Pollak (1967) who agreed that government services may
help solve many family problems in health care, education, and welfare. However, he said, by doing so a
great many problems are necessarily created. Our
civilization, for better or worse, is geared to corporate organizations. The individual must be replace-
able and thus a conformist. He must be willing to be
transferred from one location to another. His local
ties cannot be too strong.

In this situation, said Pollak, the family is
more essential than ever. Only within a family can
most people be human, expressing hostility and weakness. Families serve as counterparts to bureaucratic
adaptation. "The family becomes a community of suf-
ferers who understand one another and an organization
of self-help and regeneration for the battles of
bureaucratic existence" (1967, p. 199). Pollak's
final summary is realistic but optimistic.

> In the final sense the impact of govern-
> ment upon the family is the impact of
> large-scale organization upon small-
> scale organization, the impact of stand-
> ardization upon autonomy, the impact of
> security upon risk, and the impact of
> the professional upon the layman. From
> the vantage point of the past, this
> appears to be invasion and limitation.
> From the vantage point of the future,
> the following reformulation may be in
> order: In the ups and downs of social
> change, the impact of government upon
> the family is followed by the impact of
> the family on the government. Seen in
> this light it is the impact of autonomy

268

upon standardization, the impact of
courage upon security, and the impact
of individualism upon depersonaliza-
tion in a maintained state of point
and counterpoint (p. 205).

REFERENCE NOTES

1. "A Force for Families," a pamphlet by American Home Economics Association, 2010 Massachusetts Ave., N.W., Washington, D.C. 20036.

2. Keister, M.E. and Garner, K. " Healthy Families: Society's Anchor in a Turbulent World." A Proposal for Funding, N.C. Family Life Council, 1971, unpublished.

3. Johnson, A.A. "Toward Family Impact Analysis: Some First Steps." Unpublished paper, 1976. Family Impact Seminar, The George Washington University.

4. Califano, A., Jr. "American Families: Trends, Pressures, and Recommendations." A Preliminary Report to Governor Jimmy Carter, 1976, unpublished paper.

5. Bronfenbrenner, U. Testimony Before the Senate Subcommittee on Children and Youth. September 25, 1973.

B I B L I O G R A P H Y

Advisory Committee on Child Development,
National Research Council

1976   Toward a National Policy for Children
                and Families. Washington, D.C.:
                National Academy of Sciences.

Bronfenbrenner, U.

1977   "Nobody Home: The Erosion of the
                American Family." Psychology Today,
                May, pp. 42-47.

Chilman, C.S.

1976   "Public Social Policy and Families in
                the 1970's." In El. Eldridge & N.
                Meredith (Eds.), Environmental Issues:
                Family Impact. Minneapolis: Burgess.

Cohan, N.C. &
Connery, M.C.

1967   "Government Policy and the Family."
                Journal of Marriage and the Family,
                29: 6-17.

Cox, I.

1974   "Treatment of Families Under Income
                Transfer Programs." The Family, Pover-
                ty, and Welfare Programs: Household
                Patterns and Government Policies.
                (U.S. Congress, Joint Economic Commit-
                tee. Studies in Public Welfare. Paper
                No. 12, Part II.) Washington, D.C.:
                The Government Printing Office.

Cutright, P. &
Scanzoni, J.

1974   "Income Supplements and the American
                Family." The Family, Poverty, and
                Welfare Programs: Household Patterns
                and Government Policies. (U.S. Con-
                gress, Joint Economic Committee.

Studies in Public Welfare. Paper
No. 12, Part I.) Washington, D.C.:
The Government Printing Office.

Eldridge, E.

1976   "Health Care Policy." In E. Eldridge &
N. Meredith (Eds.), Environmental Issues
Family Impact. Minneapolis: Burgess.

Frank, L.K.

1948   "A National Policy for the Family."
Marriage and Family Living, 10: 1-4.

Frasier, R.C.

1971   "Meeting the Problems of Today's Families Through Extension Programs." The
Family Coordinator, 20: 337-340.

Glazer, N.

1967   "Housing Policy and the Family." Journal
of Marriage and the Family, 39: 5-13.

Honig, M.

1974   "The Impact of Welfare Payment Levels
on Family Stability." The Family,
Poverty, and Welfare Programs: House-
hold Patterns and Government Policies.
(U.S. Congress, Joint Economic Commit-
tee. Studies in Public Welfare. Paper
No. 12, Part II.) Washington, D.C.:
U.S. Government Printing Office.

Kenniston, K.

1976   "Do Americans Really Like Children?"
In E. Eldridge & N. Meredity (Eds.),
Environmental Issues: Family Impact.
Minneapolis: Burgess.

Koprowski, E.J.

1973   "Business Technology and the American
Family: An Impressionistic Analysis."
The Family Coordinator, 22: 229-234.

272

Lerman, R.I.

1972   "Incentive Effects in Public Income
                Transfer Programs." (U.S. Congress,
                Joint Economic Committee. Studies in
                Public Welfare, Paper No. 4.) Wash-
                ington, D.C.: Government Printing
                Office.

McArthur, A.

1967   "Family Life Education Through Extension
                Programs." Journal of Marriage and the
                Family, 29: 607-611.

Moynihan, D.P.

1970   "Policy Versus Program in the 1970's."
                The Public Interest, Summer, pp. 90-100.

Novak, M.

1976   "The Family Out of Favor." Harper's
                Magazine, April, pp. 37-46.

Pollak, O.

1967   "The Outlook for the American Family."
                Journal of Marriage and the Family, 29:
                193-205.

Porter, S.

1977   "Government Not to List Anyone as Family
                Head." The News and Observer, Raleigh,
                N.C., July 26.

Recent Trends in Homicide

1977   "Statistical Bulletin," Metropolitan
                Life Insurance Company, 58: 3.

Report of National Conference
on Family Life

1948   Marriage and Family Living, 10: 63-66,
                78.

Roemer, M.I.

1967   "Government Health Programs Affecting
            the American Family." Journal of
            Marriage and the Family, 29: 40-61.

Rue, V.M.

1973   "A U.S. Department of Marriage and the
            Family." Journal of Marriage and the
            Family, 35: 689-699.

Schorr, A.L.

1962   "Family Policy in the United States."
            International Social Science Journal,
            13: 1.

Schottland, C.I.

1967   "Government Economics Programs and
            Family Life." Journal of Marriage and
            the Family, 29: 71-123.

Sorkin, A.L.

1971   American Indians and Federal Aid.
            Washington, D.C.: The Brookings Insti-
            tution.

Stack, C.B. &
Semmel, H.

1974   "The Concept of Family in the Poor Black
            Community." The Family, Poverty, and
            Welfare Program: Household Patterns
            and Government Policies. (Studies in
            Public Welfare, Paper No. 12, Part II.
            U.S. Congress, Joint Economic Committee,
            93rd Cong., 2nd session.) Washington,
            D.C.: Government Printing Office.

Staples, R.

1973   "Public Policy and the Changing Status
            of Black Families." The Family Coor-
            dinator, July, 22: 345-351.

Stuart, B.C.

    1972   "National Health Insurance and the
                   Poor." American Journal of Public
                   Health, LXII: 1252-1259.

The Center for Auto Safety.

    1975   Mobile Homes: The Low-Cost Housing
                   Hoax. New York: Grossman.

Thomas, L.

    1976   "Guessing and Knowing - Reflections on
                   the Science and Technology of Medicine."
                   In E. Eldridge & N. Meredith (Eds.),
                   Environmental Issues: Family Impact.
                   Minneapolis: Burgess.

Vincent, C.

    1967   "Mental Health and the Family." Journal
                   of Marriage and the Family, 29: 18-39.

Vincent, C.

    1973   Sexual and Marital Health: The
                   Physician as Consultant. New York:
                   McGraw.

*Leo Hawkins and Frances T. Wagner are extension
specialists in the area of human development at
North Carolina State University.

APPENDIX

PROJECTS IN FAMILY POLICY –

THE CONSERVATION OF FAMILY POWER

I.   Objectives

Adult programs about policy decisions and families are designed to help participants:

1.   Become aware of how public and private policy
decisions affect families.

2.   Better understand the social pressures that
weaken many families.

3.   Consider how to influence policy decisions on
a community or county level.

4.   Be aware of some recommendations that are being made by family educators to improve policies
related to families.

5.   Relate what is learned about policy decisions
to their own immediate families.

II. Teaching Suggestions

Equipment Needed

.   Chalkboard

.   Mimeographed sheets (or chalkboard or transparency) of the outline for "Background Summary Material: The Conservation of Family
Power."

.   Paper and pencils for the group.

Preparation

Enlist four members to be leaders of the four
groups. Have a meeting with these leaders and
help them become familiar with the procedure for
the program and the material in the background
summary. As many as possible should read the

background study paper, "The Impact of Policy Decisions on Families."

Procedure

1. Use a chalkboard, a transparency or mimeographed sheets to present the outline for "Background Summary Material..."

2. Separate the participants into four groups of about equal numbers. For a small number of participants pick the most interesting areas for discussion and have one, two, or three small groups.

> a. Group one will deal with Section II, "Families Are Essential." They should prepare a three minute report.
>
> b. Group two will deal with Section III, "Families Are in Trouble." They should also prepare a three minute report.
>
> c. Group three will deal with Section VII, "Some Policies that May Hurt Families." This group should name all the harmful policies, pick one to be the most harmful, and explain why they think so. Give five minutes for the report.
>
> d. Group four will deal with Section VIII, "Some Recommendations..." They should pick the "best" recommendation and tell how this policy would help families in their local area. Give ten minutes for this report.

3. Try to provide at least fifteen minutes for preparation in each separate group before having the 3, 3, 5, and 10 minute reports.

Alternative Approaches

After a group of club members are exposed to the concepts of this program and are somewhat aware of the way imporant policy decisions have impact on families the group may wish to follow up by having a local and specific approach.

1. A Local Civil Administrator

    Invite the administrative officer of your
local county or city to lead a discussion about
the policies of local government and how such
policies may affect families. Be sure to leave
time for some questions in order to make the
discussion apply to families of participants.

2. Simulated Congressional Committee

    Let the total group of participants imagine
that they are a congressional committee considering the creation of a U.S. Department of Marriage
and the Family. The major provision is that the
department will have cabinet status.

    Have a "subcommittee" of 2 to 5 members who
have already met and have prepared to defend the
law. They have about 15 minutes to present their
case.

    Have an "opposition group" of 2 to 5 "citi-
zens" from business or some organized group to
present their case in the same amount of time.

    After a question period let the group vote
whether or not to report the bill favorably or
unfavorably to the Congress.

3. Have a Debate About Minimum Family Income

    Face: In 1974, 15.4 percent of American
children lived in families with incomes below
the government-defined poverty line. Parents
of these children have a very difficult time
rearing them to adulthood.

    Activity: Organize a debate, or a panel,
or a circle discussion.

    Question: Should our country provide
every family a minimum family income?

Those in favor may say:

.   In the long run such a program would save
    money by cutting down on crime, improving
    health and reducing dependency upon society.

278

- The program would make people extremely dependent upon government and destroy incentives to
  work.

- A lot of the problem is waste and poor management. Require that they learn to manage.

- Money will not solve the problems of families.

- Anybody who wants education and some job
  training can get it at public school, community college or somewhere, then make a good
  living.

CHAPTER 15

THE DECLINE OF THE MIDDLE-CLASS FAMILY

Edward M. Levine*

During the 1970s, the state of the family became a subject of considerable discussion, commentary, and controversy. Sociological studies and journalistic statements abounded, virtually all of them suggesting or forthrightly claiming that all was well with the nuclear family, and that the other emerging family forms were admirable examples of human imagination and flexibility in adapting to the complex conditions and disruptive changes characteristic of the technological age. Modernity, it was (and is still) said, has both required and made possible changes from more traditional family forms, roles, and outlooks. Women were prominent among those advocating the need for and legitimacy of substantial modifications in marital and family roles and responsibilities, as well as often being instrumental in bringing them about. Voicing their long-held resentment at being bound by household tasks and child care, they argued that such duties denied them the fulfillment and satisfaction that men had traditionally found in work and in social and political activities.

Largely because of women's protests and mounting dissatisfaction with their roles as housewives and mothers, new issues and changes came to the fore in the past decade: equal household and childrearing responsibilities for both spouses; no-fault divorce; paternal and joint custody of children of divorce; the demand for and federal authorization of unilaterally desired abortion pre-marital contracts stipulating marital and economic rights and obligations; "open" marriages and cohabitation; communal living; the right of unmarried women (including adolescents) to bear and retain custody of their children; and the claim for the legitimacy of homosexual and transsexual "marriages." Such developments were unmistakable signs that much of the moral consensus and normative influence supporting the nuclear family were lost and that unconventional forms of marriage and family had won growing acceptance and legitimacy.

Those who found value and meaning in the nuclear family began to reaffirm their commitment to monogamous, heterosexual marriage (once implied by the term "family") that retains certain of the more traditional roles for husbands and wives (and parents and children), welcomes and cherishes children, unhesitatingly affirms marital fidelity, and holds that divorce should be avoided if at all possible. However, their efforts to stem or repulse the tide against them were thwarted by the stream of commentaries, observations, and studies flowing from academic journals and the mass media. Proponents of the nuclear family and its anchoring values found themselves to be a minority, increasingly thrust on the defensive, and depicted by some as recalcitrants clinging unreasonably to an outmoded, if not antedeluvian, understanding of marriage and family. At best, the traditional family was said to be one of several options, all of them reasonable and essentially a matter of individual preference.

These and related developments, symptomatic of the steadily weakening consensus about the value, roles, and form of the family, stirred up sufficient official concern to lead to the formation in 1979 of the White House Conference on Families. Three major regional conferences were held in the summer of 1980, providing forums for the expression of most conventional and unconventional views of what the family is or should be. They also created an arena in which a variety of determined liberal and conservative groups struggled to dominate both the numbers and views of the state delegations that were to determine the policy recommendations the Conference submitted to the president. As the 1980s began, the state of the family had become a political issue.

There is little likelihood that the government can devise policies that will revitalize and stabilize the nuclear family, a point already made by Allan Carson, if for reasons that differ somewhat from those presented here. Indeed, such policies as the government enacts, however beneficial they may prove to be in some ways, will almost surely contribute to the further deterioration of the nuclear family. Unable to offer the kinds of assistance that draw marriage partners toward each other and their children, the government is likely to enact policies that add to or intensity the centrifugal forces that have been drawing the family apart, thereby lessening its importance to parents and children. Furthermore, some of the policies likely to be advocated and enacted would further diminish parental responsibilities for certain basic needs of children that can be properly met only by parents--such as effective socialization and sound emotional development.

Confusion and disagreement abound today about what the family is and should be. A brief description of the family in earlier times can contribute to a better understanding of its contemporary state and encumbering problems.

Before industrialization fully transformed society, the family's forms and functions were shaped largely by its responses to human survival needs. Dependent chiefly on harvesting and bartering, most families knew little more than a meager, perhaps subsistence, existence. The relatively few town and city dwellers labored at equally burdensome tasks to eke out a scanty living. In such times, no one had occupational alternatives because of the common condition of scarcity. Mainly to assure that the basic needs of all family members would be met, and partly because of the traditions that governed men's attitudes toward women, the roles of the sexes were almost completely differentiated. Men attended to the most laborious work, providing for and protecting their wives and children; women assumed the household and child-care tasks. Theirs was a simple division of labor, with families producing the bulk of what they consumed and functioning largely as self-sufficient economics units. Arranged marriages were the rule and assured females their survival, men and women companionship and sexual gratification, and the continuation of the group. People were expected to fall in love after marriage.

Traditional Families

Children characteristically helped parents with their tasks as soon as they were physically able to do so. They adopted, as a matter of course, their family's culture and religion, as well as its social standing. The young could foretell their own adult life merely by observing their parents and grandparents, for change and choice were the exceptions to the rule. They leared at an early age that family roles, values, and standards were essentially consistent with those of the community, and that deviance from them could bring harsh sanctions. One easily, almost reflexively, acquired a clear sense of personal and social identity; all learned in childhood that tradition, religion, the force of circumstances, and the views of parents and adults determined the standards governing everyone's personal life and relationships.

Simple and limited as they were, individual wishes and interests were invariably subordinated to those of the family, kin, and community, however arbitrary and stifling this may have been on occasion. On the other hand, everyone had reciprocal obligations that, while automatically undertaken, assured all of companionship in times of happiness and celebration, and of help and support in times of sorrow and trouble. Elders and adults, with experience and knowledge born out of trial and error over the years, were the unquestioned guardians of the community's way of life, responsible for perpetuating its traditions and customs. In such static conditions, tightly knit kinship groups and stable, cohesive communities were eminently practical ways of adjusting to and coping with the sparse, difficult conditions of life. Where such ways of life exist today in pre-industrial societies, life is often hard, and hardened ethnocentric outlooks prevail--as in the past of industrial societies.

By creating increasing numbers of jobs and higher standards of living, and by requiring and facilitating occupational, social, and residential mobility on a vast scale, urban-industrial society wrought vast changes in the patriarchal family's values, roles, and functions. These changes, in turn, led to the emergence and dominance of the nuclear family, as well as to a society of consumers that replaced one oriented to production and saving.

Families in Transition

Work, affluence, and mobility became irresistible centrifugal forces inducing individuals and families to move from the communities in which their ethnoreligious traditions were anchored and to discard or forget these traditions. The requirement that children attend school and learn English greatly accelerated the upward mobility, acculturation, and assimilation of countless numbers of immigrants. With attenuated attachments to their ethnic traditions and identities, the offspring of immigrants began the exodus to the suburbs, a trend that took on full force after World War II.

In their new communities, these newcomers had far more in common with each other--because of similar attitudes, tastes, and aspirations--than they did with those of their ethnic background who remained in the older neighborhoods. The distinguishing characteristics of their new life style were advanced education; social status acquired through achievement, better occupations, and higher incomes; and a way of life that reflected their enjoyment of material abundance. Socially and physically isolated from kin and kind, and having largely lost or abandoned their ethno-religious traditions and values, such persons no longer had deeply internalized values or surrounding, strong social controls to guide them. Having come to depend on others for acceptance and approval, for their tastes and values, these were the "other-directed" who were first detected and described by David Riesman three decades ago. Meanwhile, as new-found affluence enabled parents to indulge themselves in life's cornucopia, their children were becoming better education, more sophisticated, and increasingly independent of parental authority.

A number of important family functions lost to them, parents' influence over their children diminished steadily, especially since the latter depended on the schools for their education and were increasingly influenced by their peers' values, behavior, and outlook on life, as well as by the mass media. With the increasing popularity and influence of youth culture in the 1960s, the historical role of cultural transmission was reversed; adolescents and youth, and even children, informed their parents of modish trends in music, dance, clothing, jargon, hair styles, and sexual attitudes, which parents gradually adopted. The influence of ethno-religious traditions declined; contemporary secular values, and the majoritarian, impulse-gratifying sentiments and behavior of youth gained ascendance.

To many, the real significance of the loss of traditions lay in the disappearance of the restraints these traditions had imposed on individual achievement and fulfillment. They were manifestly useless in helping young people determine their educational pur-

suits, select careers, and choose mates and where to
live. They were bothersome to those eager to shed
their ethnic identity and attachments in order to
assimilate and move into mainstream society. In more
recent years, such traditions have come to be regarded
as curious and colorful vestiges of a seemingly romantic past; evocative of nostalgia, but without relevance for life today. Cultural heritages live on in
remembrance and sentimentality.

From a different perspective, however, the
lessening importance of certain traditional values
appears to have been the cultural prologue to present
day anomic culture, in which values have become weak,
vacillating, and ambiguous. Then, too, the weakened
influence of moral principles rooted in religion and
tradition has led many people to consider them as
useful when the situation is appropriate, rather than
as standards with universal relevance and applicabili-
ty. This change has made possible the ascendance of
values and behavior that stress impulse gratification,
self-centeredness, and an orientation to the present,
in contrast with traditional values that emphasize
impulse regulation, regard for others, and an orientation to the future. This shift in standards and
behavior has been extremely detrimental to the well-
being of marriage and family, as well as to the
socialization and emotional development of children.

Conflict of Interests

The pervasiveness of affluence and abundance of
occupations alone might have drawn vast numbers of
women into the work force. Such changes, as well as
those which occurred in the relationship of husbands
and wives and in women's responsibilities toward their
children, would no doubt have taken place, if somewhat
less quickly, without the impetus given them by women's insistence that the democratic principle of
social equality be extended to them in work and family
life. However, the moral force of this principle did
much to hasten the changes women were seeking in their
marital roles and childrearing responsibilities.

For example, it is completely unimaginable that
any urban-industrial society could insist that girls
complete a high-school education, encourage them to
complete a college education (thereby equalizing their
individuality with that of males), and then expect

them to become housewives and mothers, rather than workers using their skills and enjoying the fruits of independence, a personal income, and, for single women, a largely self-determined way of life. The older roles are now regarded by growing numbers of women as anachronisms, unjust constraints on their aspirations for personal fulfillment. They are very much aware that laws assuring them equal work opportunities and equal pay with men have added enormous force to their wishes to become less attached to and dependent on, or singularly devoted to, marriage. For the same reason, they have become less desirous of having children. Many have achieved these objectives, and their numbers will continue to increase.

No longer wholly dependent upon men to provide for them, and contributing an important amount to family incomes, many working women have prevailed on their husbands to assume some of the responsibilities for household tasks and childrearing responsibilities. It cannot be said to what extent marital dissatisfaction, discord, and divorce result when both spouses work and pursue their social interests separately, although competitiveness and diverging social lives are responsible for breaking up some marriages. Marital difficulties caused by personality problems and incompatibility aside, the inordinate emphasis that many husbands and wives give to pursuit of their personal interests has eclipsed the needs of their marriages and distracted them from attending to these needs. This is partly evidenced by the remarkably high and unprecedented rate of divorce among first marriages during the preceding decade, a sign that many spouses were unwilling to devote the necessary efforts to resolving their marital problems and enhancing their marriages to make them at least minimally gratifying to both partners.

Despite the strains and difficulties besetting and breaking up marriage and family, there are those who believe they are as well off as ever; the more sanguine contend they are thriving. Arguing that divorce is a sensible alternative when marriage proves dissatisfying to one or both spouses, and seldom, if ever, suggesting that in such circumstances both should extend themselves to work out their problems, they usually add that since most who divorce then remarry, this is proof that marriage (if not family, whose welfare is invariably subordinated to the wishes of marriage partners) is prospering.

Those who speak so optimistically neglect to mention that the rate of divorce for second marriages is higher than for first ones. Because maximizing the individual interests of the marital partners is the implicit criterion used to evaluate the state of marriage and family, all other forms of this social institution are, therefore, said to be acceptable, sensible, and legitimate means of adjusting to the special conditions of life in which adults find themselves. For this reason, the nuclear family and the values that have historically undergirded it can no longer be regarded as morally or functionally superior. What works for or gratifies the individual adult, the narrowest kind of "utilitarianism," takes precedence over "the greatest good for the greatest number" (the family). This standard is now inferentially or openly proposed as the only appropriate standard for appraising the state of marriage and family. Chaqu' un à son gout. Solipsism is the ultimate heir of relativism, its reducio ad absurdum. From this perspective, the needs of marriage and family and mature human fulfillment, which are born of and sustained by love, attention, and complementarity, are diminished or thrust aside by those who give priority to equalizing marital and parental roles and pursuing happiness independently. Narcissistic gains, however, have increasingly diminishing returns and are empty triumphs in the longer run.

Marriage and family are less than ever regarded as normative by young people. Young adults who do not want to live along hedge against both solitude and marriage by living together (an arrangement that is often more costly to women than to men), thereby tentatively overcoming their misgivings and apprehensions about marrying. Living together is no longer uncommon among young people, since they feel free to ignore the essentially powerless moral prescriptions which not long ago effectively forbade unmarried cohabitation. This trend may be inevitable when adults viewing marriage as a matter of choice and convenience, instead of regarding it as the proper destiny of men and women.

Young people's reservations about marriage are paralleled by those of many formerly married persons who say the advantages of remaining single outweigh those of remarrying. Still, numbers of divorced people who have not found a suitable mate are dissatisfied by remaining unmarried. Yet much of what is written about divorced men and women dwells on their freedom from the constraints and compromises of marriage, and their pleasure of having so much more independence and so many fewer responsibilities for a spouse (and children). Little has been said or written about the difficulty divorced parents face in raising children alone; and few who write about divorce and its consequences discuss the trauma and unhappiness experienced by children of divorce, let alone their need for both parents to help them negotiate the awkward, occasionally tormenting, pathways of adolescence.

Nor is enough told us about the discontent many divorced persons experience living alone. The literature almost never mentions that single people, whether never married or divorced, have a significantly higher premature death rate than married persons do, although this has been well documented by James Lynch. The growing popularity of singles clubs attests more to the desire of single adults to find prospective mates than to their interest in the clubs' social events.

If, in addition to sexual gratification, companionship is the major benefit that marriage (and family) provides for men and women, it is clearly less successful in meeting this need today. However, if companionship is understood in its broadest sense as, to put it in popular parlance, the "growth" of the lives and personalities of marriage partners, then the most suitable arrangement society has devised for such a praiseworthy human goal is marriage. The equal and insistent emphasis on self-fulfillment, however, has tended to draw spouses away from each other. Personal preferences supersede the needs of keeping marriage intact and gratifying.

Costs to Children

Growing numbers of people have adopted the view that the sharply declining birthrate, which began in the mid-1960s, is a benign trend. Such persons point out that married couples should not bring more children into a world in which the present number of people already exceeds the supply of resources, particularly the unreplenishable ones. There is some merit in what they say. However, it is doubtful that Malthusian reasoning informs the decision by many married couples to forego having children. It is more likely that they (especially women) perceive children as a burden and responsibility that would interfere with their independence and drain their income.

Nevertheless, children will continue to be born, and their parents will have responsibility for rearing them. Although parents are best suited for rearing children, they have tended to shift much of the responsibility to others, such as babysitters and day-care centers. More parents will probably do so in the years ahead, and the harmful effects this has on the emotional development of children will also become more widespread.

Many, perhaps most, parents of preschool children assume it is beneficial to send them to day-care centers where they have the company of playmates, learn how to get along with other children, and are under the supervision of attentive, caring, competent adults. It is not widely known that children under three years of age who attend day-care centers part-time every day often feel deserted and unwanted; those who attend full-time every day are likely to develop intense separation anxiety. Human beings are most vulnerable to these emotionally destructive feelings during the preschool years. Unless the child's feelings of emotional security are restored during these years by a revival of the mother-child relationship, they can result in feeings of insecurity and self-worthlessness leading to serious emotional and behavioral problems (e.g., drugs, delinquency) in the years during and after adolescence.

It is understandably difficult for women (not only those with professional careers) who feel that work and self-fulfillment are necessary to their being good mothers to realize how critically important it is for them to be generally available to their children. Unaware of their children's unconscious reactions to feelings of separation anxiety, many mothers assume that they have done well by them. Some incorrectly deny that their children experience such anxiety; others conclude their children are bothered only by the feelings of uncertainty that all young children experience in day-care centers, feelings that are usually overcome with no ensuing emotional or behavioral problems.

However, as Margaret Mahler, Selma Fraiberg, and others have shown, a dependable, emotionally sound maternal presence is essential to the successful passage through the phase of separation-individuation that is so important to the development of emotional well-being. The mother's generally available support during this crucial pre-Oedipal period is needed to assure the child's attachment to her; this attachment, in turn, is the foundation of the emotional security necessary to the child's ongoing efforts to establish individuality and age-appropriate independence. Consequently, there must be one person to whom a child can turn and whom he can identify as a trusted source of emotional security. As Selma Fraiberg has insightfully said, needing one person above all others whom one can love and depend upon is a natural human trait characteristic of both very young children and adults. Those who do not have this elemental need properly met in early childhood are apt to have difficulty loving and trusting a member of the opposite sex as adults. Numbers of young adults who have experienced such parental deprivation very likely figure among those who are willing to live together but balk at getting married.

Since the infant's ability emotionally to attach itself to and identify with a needed, trustworthy, loving parent is best begun during the nursing period, mothers are best suited for caring for and meeting the needs of children during their earliest years. The continuing involvement of an emotionally present father is equally imperative in this development process. The emotional absence or lackadaisical involvement of too many fathers today is extremely detrimental to their children's healthy emotional growth. Furthermore, sons and daughters alike need both parents during their earliest (and later) years to assist them in developing a sound, heterosexual identity--a confident sense of masculinity and femininity. This psycho-social process begins in the earliest years, continues through adolescence, and is, as Warren Gadpaille has shown, the fulfillment of heterosexual feelings and behavior that are established in fetal life. Androgyny is a fiction concocted to deny the ineradicable, if vulnerable, heterosexual emotional differences between males and females, a rationalization serving those who dislike, deny, are indifferent to, or do not wish to care for their children's fundamentally different gender-identity needs.

Parents are also best able to guide the socialization of their children. This task is ill-suited to day-care center personnel, who have others, less personalized duties to perform. Moreover, the number of children they care for prevents their effective performance of such a task, aside from the fact that the responsibility is not properly theirs. Parents' secular and religious values, personal views, and idiosyncratic attitudes are not likely to be shared by most staff of day-care centers, or held as firmly and considered as important by those who do. When children spend considerable time in day-care centers because their mothers are working--as many single parents must--their socialization will suffer, inducing additional emotional costs. This is the dilemma confronting the family today, which many deny or dismiss, but for which a solution has not been found.

During preschool and school years, children need to be taught by their parents--through precept, example, reinforcement and assistance--how to adopt (internalize) and use those values and standards that will enable them to regulate their aggressive and libidinal drives. Successful (and unsuccessful) experience in using these standards is necessary for the development of the self (ego and superego) controls that enable one to become impulse-regulating, other-regarding, and future-oriented--the essential characteristics of self-reliance. When children develop inadequate self controls, as tends to occur when they are permissively, inattentively, or indifferently parented (more common than ever today), they often become dominated by their impulses. Their inability to resolve these conflicts creates further frustration which, in turn, generates anger and depression. Anxiety also builds up because of their inability to manage the pressing demands of their impulses.

Impulse-dominated persons are said to have "character defects" and "disorders," psychopathologies that many therapists and social workers say are the most common ones among today's adolescents and youth, especially those from middle-class families. Such children are the victims of parental deprivation and remain undiscussed by those who assure us that the family is as well off as ever.

Among the problems caused by impulse-domination is the exceptional difficulty in establishing sound, mutually gratifying, and enduring relationships with others--particularly with a member of the opposite sex. Thus, those who marry are more likely than not to experience marital problems deriving from their emotional troubles rather than from objective sources, with such personality problems likely to break up the marriages. Others may be unable to marry because of their personality problems. Some use drugs in an attempt to alleviate the feelings of anger, anxiety, depression, and frustration that grip them, as well as to escape from the unending pressure of their impulse life. Self-impairing or antisocial behavior (e.g., delinquency and crime) are too often the outcomes for those whose self-controls are too weak to regulate their feelings and behavior. Among the young people who suffer from character defects and disorders are those who have joined religious cults in a futile quest to resolve their troubled feelings and give meaning to their lives.

A society that encourages adults to give precedence to their personal interests inclines them to neglect or delegate responsibility for rearing their children. Yet parental surrogates cannot undertake effectively the fundamental responsibilities that are integral to the emotional development and socialization of children. Parents who are unable or unwilling to meet their tutelary responsibilities properly have also failed to show their children how to parent properly. Unless adults are willing to devote more concern and effort to the neds of marriage and family, the alternatives to the nuclear family will probably continue to gain social legitimacy--at the expense of children, the adults of the future. The social sciences, chiefly sociology and anthropology, have played an influential role in directing attention away from the needs and rights of children to the gratification of adult desires and interests.

Shortcomings of Relativism

In their studies of human behavior, social scientists have properly used a value-free, relativistic approach in order to be as objective and accurate as possible in their efforts to advance knowledge about the subjects of their research. Much valuable information about marriage and family has been gained by their adherence to this canon of scientific inquiry. This perspective has taught us to be tolerant and understanding of cultural differences, as well as more aware of our own ethnocentric biases. It has led social scientists and many laypersons properly to conclude that it is not scientifically possible to assert that one form of the family is better or superior to any other. To be scientific is to inquire and describe and learn, not to judge. Thus all forms of the family are but examples of the variety of ways in which human beings have managed to adapt or to cope with different conditions of life throughout history. In many ways this is true; various kinds of family structures, relationships, marital and parent-child roles, and values have been devised over the centuries to meet human needs in contrasting cultures.

Nevertheless, the shortcoming of the relativistic perspective is that its logic imposes the following conclusion upon those who adopt it: one can only arbitrarily or subjectively place a value on any form of the family. That is, one may value any form of the family one wishes, but this expresses no more than a personal preference which, therefore, cannot be considered appropriate or right for others—especially those who disagree (including children). Whatever is agreeable to or meets the needs or whims of the individual adult and is, therefore, valued by him, is not necessarily suitable for or congenial to other persons, whose own needs, interests, or personalities may lead them to choose differently. It is for this reason that various forms of family life are accepted by most who study marriage and family, as well as by those who, for whatever reasons, opt for some other form of family life or openly and explicitly reject the nuclear family. Thus, whatever forms of family life exist simply are; none is better or worse than any other. And when, as has been occurring during the past decade, the variations of the nuclear family become more numerous, they take on a normative character which is reinforced by their being described in academic literature merely as different forms of the family.

This nonjudgmental view of the family is not without certain trying difficulties. For example, it leaves the spouse who hopes to forestall an impending divorce with little more than his or her own preferences as the reason for attempting to repair the damage to the marriage. (The dyad, as Simmel pointed out, is the most easily disrupted group.) Marital infidelity can be regarded only as the expression of personal preference, not as a threat to the stability of marriage; adultery has been rendered meaningless. A husband who wants the child his pregnant wife is carrying is helpless to prevail against her insistence that she wants an abortion. Children's complaints that they miss their mothers' presence when they return home from school and their fathers' attention, are reduced to personal wishes with no more weight than their mothers' wishes to be elsewhere and their fathers' interest in their own affairs. Situations such as these weaken family members' concern for and identification with each other and occasionally turn them into adversaries. The values that once lent a sacral quality to the family no longer claim the support of community or society; they have succumbed to the invincible power of individuality, which is the equivalent of relativism.

An age fraught with change has coined the expression "nothing lasts forever." Given what young people have seen of the tensions and distress afflicting marriage, it is to be expected that some anticipate divorse as its outcome. But it is unlikely that they believe divorce to be emotionally beneficial to children. Some who decide to avoid marriage or approach it carefully--or opt for cohabitation as a waiting game to see if a sound, enduring marriage seems to be a realistic possibility--may very well be exercising a cautious, skeptical prudence. They have not learned that marriage, like friendship, cannot be free from plateaus of cool civility and cycles of extreme displeasure. Strains such as these are considered dangerous signs that there soon will be grounds for divorce.

Conclusions that the state of the family is sound, or that it and its variations are but social artifacts illustrating the ways in which people have adjusted to the novel and seemingly endless vicissitudes of this age, are by no means value-free. This position is obviously based on the value that it is desirable for adults to have the freedom to choose any form of family that is most congenial to them. Adult freedom of choice and personal satisfaction are the actual criteria of most who write about the family, although these criteria are not often specified. Any form of the family is "good" insofar as it is freely chosen and proves to be satisfying to the adult or adults involved. Children's needs and rights are, at best, glossed over, and often ignored, with the advantages of marital stability and continuity being subordinated to individual adult needs.

Some other criteria must be employed in attempting to ascertain the state of the family today and in the years ahead. The most appropriate standards for this purpose are those that are directly concerned with the harmony and well-being of marriage and family over time. These standards hold that contemporary variations of the nuclear family are not ordinarily in the best interest of those who opt for them; that there is, by definition, no such thing as a homosexual marriage; and that divorce should be the alternative only after all appropriate efforts have been made to resolve marital problems.

In addition, it is necessary to give primacy to standards concerned with the developmental needs of children; standards that give precedence to children's needs, not parents' wishes. Such criteria justify criticism of parental deprivation or absenteeism which, in no small measure, have been responsible for many of the problems of impulse-ridden youth--their drug culture, educational under-performance, and the skepticism with which they regard marriage and the family. The egocentric attitudes of adults toward marriage and the family have also done much to destroy the vision that necessarily and humanistically focuses the attention of adults on the welfare of children, the parents of the oncoming generation. Since society will replenish itself, it is senseless to ignore or dismiss the disintegrating and corrosive effects on the stability and quality of family life that stem from the engrossment of parents in their self-centered pursuit of happiness. Narcissism surely cannot be the ideal in terms of which we define or measure the happiness of parents and children, despite its having captured the sentiments of so many in this anomic age.

Reflecting these egocentric times, those who say that marriage and family are enjoying the best of all possible times have more accurately informed us of the transition from the nuclear to the laissez-faire family. This conception of family life pays little heed to intrinsic human needs which require satisfaction from the earliest years through adolescence and in all stages of adulthood. These bio-psychological needs are an integral part of the process of human development. Those who ignore this have either misread or misconstrued human nature, not without cost to the well-being of society. The quality of the social bond is greatly dependent upon the quality of families, the nuclei of which society is composed.

Many adults have good, satisfying marriages and family lives. Such individuals are mature enough to realize that they must make serious efforts periodically to settle the vexing problems that strain marital relationships and agitate family life. Nevertheless, it is the problem-ridden, frayed marriages that barely hold together and the substantial number of divorces that have become normative in the minds of children, adolescents, and young adults. And, far more than any preceding generation, they have experienced negligent and absentee parenting, the substitution of material gratification for their parents' love, attention, and assistance in growing up.

At present, the sociocultural and economic conditions that have done so much to improve our standard of living and enrich life by extending independence and personal fulfillment have also undercut the middle-class nuclear family's efforts to achieve stability and happiness. If such conditions persist, then the present state of marriage and family is an ill omen for the balance of this decade, and perhaps, the years beyond. Unbridled individualism will continue to trouble and disrupt marriage and family life, and children will increasingly pay the emotional and behavioral costs of negligent and inadequate parenting. However, young people may find that their quest for identity and meaning in life can be realized by turning to marriage and family and the values on which they have rested. Surely this is a more meaningful alternative than drug use, religious cults, the loneliness and aimlessness of single people. Their dissatisfactions with family life as children and adolescents may induce them to restore and revive marriage and family. At any rate, the prospects for reversing the decline of the family during the past decade depend heavily on young adults, for their decisions will largely determine the state of the family in the 1980s and the decades that follow.

REFERENCES

Fraiberg, Selma

1977   Every Child's Birthright: In Defense
            of Mothering. New York: Basic
            Books.

Gadpaille, Warren

1972   "Research Into the Psychology of
            Maleness and Femaleness." Archives of
            General Psychiatry, March, pp. 193-206.

Levine, Edward &
Shaiova, Charles

1977   "Anomie: Its Influence on Impulse-
            Ridden Youth and Their Self-Destructive
            Behavior." In Adolescent Psychiatry,
            Vol. 5, edited by S. Feinstein and
            P. Giovacchini. New York: Jason
            Aronson.

Lynch, James

1977   The Broken Heart. New York: Basic
            Books.

Mahler, Margaret, Pine, Fred &
Bergman, Anni

1975   The Psychological Birth of the Human
            Infant. New York: Basic Books.

*Edward M. Levine is professor of sociology at Loyola
University, Chicago.

Reprinted from Society, January/February, 1981: 72-78.
Copyright 1981 by Transaction, Inc. Reprinted by permission.

CHAPTER 16

SHRINKING HOUSEHOLDS

Yehudi A. Cohen*

In 1790, the average American household had 5.8 members; by 1975 this number had fallen uninterruptedly to 2.9. What caused this contraction in household membership and what does the historical trend forebode?

It is often necessary to look for the principal sources of social change outside a society; a search that can turn up some surprises. One of these unexpected findings in the evolution of the household is the role played by warfare since the First World War. The Second World War also had strong effects on the size of the household, as did the Korean and Vietnam Wars

It is not warfare as such that brings about reductions in the household's membership. It is technological advances that filter down to the household from battlefields, convoys, food processing and packaging plants turning out rations, PXs, and data processors that have slowly but steadily reduced household memberships. The household has not gotten smaller only during the twentieth century. This contraction has been going on for ten thousand years or more. Warfare does not seem to have played a role in the size of the household in tribal and peasant groups; but technology did.

These conclusions about the roles of technology in tribal and peasant groups and militarily inspired technological advances in the twentieth century in the evolution of the household are, of course, important in their own right. But they have additional significance: Technology not only provides a common denominator between tribal and modern societies, it is the bridge from which to see that the human experience from the prehistoric cultural past to the present (and probably the future) is a unified historical whole.

Reductions in household membership cannot be attributed to contraception or to ideologies of romantic love and companionate marriage. The shrinkage of household size began long before the twentieth century. Most of the contraction took place prior to 1940, before birth control became effective and reliable; notions of romantic love had developed several hundred years earlier.

Contraction in household membership is not uniquely American. In rural Japan around 1660, for example, some households had more than 20 members; in 1940, the average rural Japanese household had 5.3 individuals, reduced to 4.5 by 1965. Similar trends are observable throughout the rest of the world. Every society is but a special case of the general process of social or cultural evolution. Change in household size is an excellent example of this. The contraction of the American household from colonial times to the present echoes transformations in the household throughout social or cultural history. The analysis of the parallel leads to the singular conclusion that changes in household membership result from forces originating outside the household. These forces are principally technological and political.

Technology and Politics

The members of a household are a working unit, not necessarily a group of people sharing a common dwelling in which to eat and sleep. A household is a grouping organized to perform particular tasks: earning a living, securing materials, rearing and caring for children, and looking after the ill and indigent. The nature of the household unit is profoundly affected by the means available to it to accomplish these ends. Moreover, a household may be composed of unrelated individuals as well as kinsmen. An examination of several types of societies, beginning with the Bushmen of southern Africa, leads to an understanding of how ends and means combine to help shape the composition of the household.

In a hunting-gathering camp all the members are mobilized to secure meat and other foods in which all share equally. All are responsible for the care of all the children in the group, not only of their own offspring. All are responsible for the support of aged persons and for the care of the sick and injured. These activities are the criteria by which households in all societies are identified. By such standards, the hunting-gathering camp is really an extended-family household made up of several nuclei of married pairs and their children. Camp/households vary in size, depending on seasonal variation, availability of food and water, and other conditions. There may be as few as two or as many as ten nuclear families in a camp/household, each nucleus have an average of four or five members. These nuclei are related to each other by ties of blood or marriage; one of the rules of hunting-gathering camps is that a couple may join a camp only if one member of the pair has a sibling, parent, or child in the camp. As a result of these proliferating ties, everyone turns out to be related to everyone else.

A household's size and composition depend principally on the extent to which the resources its members rely on daily are dispersed or concentrated and the technology at their disposal. When food, water, and other resources are scattered, as among hunter-gatherers, and when productive labor entails muscular energy exclusively (as in connection with gathering wild-growing foods) or the most rudimentary tools and weapons (such as spears and bows and arrows), people must spread out over a wide terrain to get food for a balanced diet and materials for their implements. Many hunter-gatherers must fan out over a radius of about eight miles daily or every few days, the women gathering in one part of the territory while the men hunt in another. When some people disperse to gather and unt, others must remain in camp to look after children and incapacitated adults. If there are cultivated gardens, they must be tended. Dwellings as well as cildren and the indigent must be protected against animal and human predators.

There are unvarying problems. The development of an extended-family household is an excellent adaptaion to the challenge faced under hunting-gathering conditions. The large camp/household is a labor pool whose members produce and consume jointly. While some men and women are away getting food, others remain in camp looking after children, indigent adults, gardens, and so forth. It is never the same people who go out to get food or who remain in camp. There are no specialists among hunter-gathers. All adults hunt or gather or look after children, often for each other. When there are no

specialized food-getters or child-care personnel, the
need for a large household whose members share in
meeting their common and unvarying problems is accent-
uated. This, as will be shown,is an important cause
of the sharply reduced modern family, especially in
urban contexts.

The correspondence between household size and
dispersal or concentration of resources is dramatically
illustrated by settled cultivators. An example is provided by Marshall Sahlins in his study of Moala, a
Fijian atoll. Sahlins found two distinctive household
patterns in Moala. Members of one group live far from
their cultivated lands, while the others live close by
them. A three-generation household (averaging 12.8
people) predominates in the first group, while a nuclear or elementary household (averaging 9.7 people)
characterizes the second.

In examining the contrast, Sahlins showed how the
extended-family household is excellently suited to
dispersed or scattered resources. Though the garden
plots of the three-generation households are not far
from their villages as the crow flies, Fiji's hilly
terrain makes these gardens difficult to reach. As a
result, the cultivators of these plots erect huts
near their fields, where they remain several days at
a time clearing, planting, weeding, and harvesting.
Sahlins maintained that, because of its size, the
multi-generational household can release some of its
members for cultivating activities while allowing
others to remain in the village to care for local
gardens, oversee the children, and look after the
ill and indigent. In contrast, those Moalans
characterized by a nuclear or elementary family
household and living near their garden plots do
not have to be away from home more than a few hours
at a time. Their resources are far more concentrated
than those of the first group. They have no need
for a larger labor pool.

When looked at in historical perspective, two
things stand out about both Moalan household
organizations. First, the extended or three-
generation household is smaller than the hunting-
gathering camp/household. Even though the cultivated
plots of the three-generatin households are at considerable distance from their villages, these resources are nonetheless more concentrated than the

food supply of nomadic hunter-gatherers. Second, though the nuclear or elementary households of the second group are smaller than the households of the first group, these nuclear households are larger than those of modern households. (In 1930, for examle, the average American farm household had 4.6 members; in 1975, the figure stood at 3.3). The reason is to be found in the different agricultural technologies used by Moalans and modern people. Moalans, and other like them, rely on the most rudimentary hand tools in their productive activities: digging sticks, hoes, stone hand adzes, and the like. Their primitive technology forces each household to add to its labor force to get its productive work done. Where two men on even a pre-industrial American farm, for instance, could fell a tree with a large hand saw and steel axe, it takes about four or five (or more) Moalans to down a tree when preparing a plot for cultivation. Also, premechanized farmers in North America or Europe had draft animals and plows which could do the work of many people; the Moalans, who could not get beneath the topsoil, need many more people to get the household's work done. There is yet another reason the Moalan nuclear or elementary household is larger than households at higher stages of develolpment. Neither group of Moalan living under premodern conditions has schools, hospitals, old-age homes, or other institutions devoted to personal welfare. Each household has to see to the education of its own youngsters, make its own tools, look after its own sick and aged, and so forth. These activities require the constant presence of added personnel.

People like the Bushmen and Fijians tell us only why holuseholds in tribal societies are larger than ours; they do not tell us why the household has been getting progressively smaller. For this we have to look at developments that had led to greater concentrations of resources.

One of the most dramatic of these was the manufacture of commercial fertilizer. Commercial fertilizers--dried fish, oil cakes, and night soil-- were not unknown in Japan prior to the seventeenth century, but they were used in very few places. This changed around the beginning of the eighteenth century when commercial fertilizers were produced on a large scale and began to supplant manure, grass, and ashes from waste and forest lands.

    In Japan around 1700, a farm needed four or five
able-bodied adults to produce five bushels of rice,
eight or nine to produce ten bushels, and about
twelve to produce fifteen bushels. Though some households had as many as twenty family members and were
thus able to provide their own manpower, many households had only between four and seven family members.
Where did they find the additional necessary labor?
Early in the seventeenth century, if not before, the
Japanese evolved a system of hereditary servants
(fudai) who, together with their children, passed
down as a family unit from generation to generation.
They lived with their masters who, by custom, were
held responsible for the hereditary servants' food,
clothing, upbringing, pubilc behavior, and general
welfare. Though there was a uniform notation in the
population registers that they were servants and
not kin, these servants were recognized as members
of their masters' households. As a result, households were quite large.

    The effects of widespread adoption of commercial
fertilizers were dramatic. The new fertilizers--
which represented a remarkable concentration of
resources--raised crop yields with sharply reduced
household labor forces. For example, the head of
one holding who had 900 man days available annually
for work found that he needed only 185. Land could
be used more intensively and small holdings were
often found to be more efficient than large ones.
Labor on many family-size holdings thus became
wasteful. The most logical adaptation was to reduce
household size, and this is precisely what was done.
The first to be let go were hereditary servants.
Then extended families broke up into distinct
nuclear-family households. In one village, for
example, the number of households increased in the
space of a few years from 30 extended to 83 nuclear
households, and the average household membership
fell from 12.3 to 3.8.

    Taxation, too, played an important role in the
breakup of large households. Traditionally, taxes
had been assessed on the basis of crop yields. At
about the same time that commercial fertilizers made
yields more stable and the peasants more prosperous,
political authority became more firmly entrenched
and land taxes became fixed. This, too, forced many
heads of extended households to adapt by ridding

themselves of many members. Instead of relying on traditional household networks to provide needed fertilizer, firewood, labor, thatch for roofing, lumber, food, and clothing, more and more bought these services.

The American Experience

With the tribal and Japanese examples in mind, we may now understand the history of the American household. In Plymouth Colony in 1689, the average household held 5.4 individuals. About one-fourth of the households had at least one servant; but these servants were not always hired. In the words of John Demos, writing in A Little Commonwealth, "Idle and even criminal persons were 'sentenced' by the Court to live as servants in the families of more reputable citizens." The Plymouth colonists needed extra hands not only to help with agricultural work but to secure goods and services that were either dispersed or otherwise unavailable. To quote Demos again,

> The family was a "welfare institution"; in fact, it provided several different kinds of welfare service It was occasionally a "hospital"--at least insofar as certain men thought to have special medical knowledge would receive sick persons into their homes for day-to-day care and treatment. It was an "orphanage"--in that children whose parents had died were straightaway transferred into another household (often that of a relative). It was an "old people's home"--since the aged and infirm, no longer able to care for themselves, were usually incorporated into the households of their grown children. And it was a "poorhouse" too--for analogous, and obvious, reasons.

Reductions in the size of the American household were brought about by changes that were political as much as they wre technological. After the Revolutionary War, federal and local governments undertook extensive road-building programs. The new highways not only helped to weld the new nation by linking communities and regions, they made possible the establishment of new industries and markets. As a result, resources and materials started to be concentrated to a far greater extend than ever before. This concentration and the burgeoning of markets was accelerated by railroad construction before and after the Civil War. These developments were accompanied by reductions in the size of the household; the domestic unit was not able to get by with far fewer hands. Highway and railroad construction is as much a result of political initiative as it is a technological development affecting people's daily lives.

The automobile proved its worth on the battlefields of World War I. Prior to that holocaust, most banks refused to lend money to automobile manufacturers. But the war changed that. Truck manufacture erupted. In its first of many subsidizations of the automobile industry, the federal government built thousands of miles of highway to accommodate the trucks. Food, resources, and materials continued to be shipped by train, but trucks are more flexible and are able to transport goods to localities far from rail stations and depots. In consequence, markets expanded still further, concentrating food, materials, and resources even more. And household membership continued to decline in rural as well as urban areas.

It is difficult to determine precisely who inhabited households at different periods of American history. But there are several strong hints in censuss and other materials that non-relatives were commonly members of households for a long time after the days of Plymouth Colony and that reductions in household size were due, at least in part, to a growing infrequency of non-kin as household members. In 1930, when the average American household held 4.1 persons, almost 10 percent of these units had at least one non-relative. While this proportion increased to 12.3 percent in 1940 (no doubt due to the Depression) when the average size of the household fell to 3.7, only about 3 percent of American households had non-relatives in 1975.

Non-kinsmen alone do not account for the size of the domestic unit; note what happened in 1940. While there are no reliable data telling us about the presence of grandparents, spinster aunts and bachelor uncles, or other relatives in the household

at different times, we know from novels and other
accounts that they, too, used to be present in
American households more often then they are now.
Why, in any event, have households included fewer
non-members of the nuclear family in recent years?

The key to the puzzle lies in refrigerators,
freezers, preservatives, supermarkets, and shopping
malls. These, too, were as much the result of
political forces as they were technological feats.
Although there were occasional supermarkets in some
areas of the United States prior to World War II,
they were unusual and were used by relatively few
people; the same was true of frozen-food lockers.
Largely because of their novelty, commercially canned
foods were also unusual and were too expensive for
most ordinary consumers. Perhaps for the same reasons, moral judgments were often made of women who
cooked too often from cans.

In view of the technology of food packaging,
preservation, and refrigeration at the time, most
people had to shop several times a week, if not
daily, for meat, fish, dairy,vegetables, bread, and
so forth; and they had to shop for these in different stores which were often dispersed, even though
there were shopping neighborhoods in most cities.
Many people baked their own bread. Hardly anyone
owned an automobile, and women, who were responsible
for shopping, were customarily not permitted to
drive. Not least, only the affluent had enough
money to shop for more than a day or two at a time.
Financial and technological limitations often made
it impossible to prepare and refrigerate food in
quantities large enough to enable people to subsist
on nutritious leftovers several times a week.

The logistical pressures of World War II changed
this. Productivity had to be increased to maintain
adequate diets for military personnel and to replace
food and other materials lost through ship sinkings
and the destruction of farms, food processing plants,
and transportation networks in Europe and Asia. The
transformations brought about were political as well
as technological. Military requirements stimulated
the mobilization of existing knowledge about food
processing and preservation. As military pressures
mounted, governmental agencies mobilized personnel
to develop new techniques in transportation, distri-

bution, processing, and preservation. Promised contracts and profits led to the development of new
industries devoted to mass food production,marketing,
refrigeration and preservation.

Supermarkets proliferated after World War II as
as result of the techniques developed for supplying,
stocking, and managing PXs during the war. As a result of militarily stimulated advances in food processing, packaging, preservation, refrigeration,
transportation, and distribution, accompanied by mass
production of domestic refrigerators and freezers, it
was not possible for the ordinary consumer to find
every kind of food under one roof. Automobiles were
mass produced and roads built at an unprecedented
rate; the disapproval of women driving dissipated,
and this helped build the used-car market. Not only
could women's food shoping now be concentrated in one
place, they could now do their marketing less often.
As a result, households needed even fewer attached
personnel to perform the same labor that households
have always had to do. It seems, though, that the
need for attached personnel tended to remain in
working-class households where women often had to
work to supplement their husbands' income.

The need for attached kin and non-relatives decreased in many working-class households, too, as a
result of similar developments stemming from the
Korean War. Among the most notable of these were
shopping centers. With this further concentration
of marketing and services and the still greater expansion of road networks, it became increasingly
possible for one person using a car to shop for
clothing, appliances, pets' needs, and food, to visit
the dentist and optometrist, and to bank in a single
expedition once a week. This was made even easier
when, toward the end of the Vietnam War, some
shopping centers began providing child-care facilities for shopping parents; very few had done this
before 1962.

Along with increasingly onerous taxation, more
efficient contraception and declining birthrates,
greater occupational opportunities for women, and
the growth of men's participation in household roles,
these developments have contributed strongly to
reductions in the size of the household. Simultaneously, American society has witnessed a growth in

the number of women who voluntarily have children while
electing to remain unmarried; this is only beginning,
though, and it is still rare. But it is a hint of
future developments in everyday life when there will
be even greater advances in the concentration of food,
materials, and resources. When women (and some men)
say they do not need to be married to run a household
with one or two children, they are basing their judgments on physical concentrations of goods and services
and cars and are relying on efficient refrigerators,
freezers, and preservatives as well as on relatively
good incomes.

Such people, who may be harbingers of future
social developments, are not only relying on technological advances leading to greater concentrations
of goods and services. Their values and behavior
are also made possible by expanded education, of
which day-care centers are an important part. Children are now placed in day-care facilities at two or
three years of age, and sometimes earlie, thus reducing the need for a reservoir of people in the
home to oversee the youngsters. Day-care centers are
often subsidized by government agencies. These are
politically inspired influences which, together with
technological advances, have led to declining household size. What must be remembered is that neither
technological nor political influences operate alone.

Other governmental or broader social influences
have also contributed to the household's contraction.
Whereas children often used to feel obligated to take
in their aged parents (or other relatives), pensions
and retirement programs (including social security),
old-age homes, medical insurance, and expanded hospital facilities have reduced this obligation. These
programs and institutions, too, are underwritten in
one way or another by governmental agencies. They
are politically inspired.

Without trying to prophesy the nature of the
household of the future, it seems clear that technological advances in marketing and distribution
together with expanding welfare programs will reduce
the size of the household even further from its
current average size in America of 2.9. An example
of the role played by welfare policies is provided
by Israel, which has no national social security
program. Resources and services are highly concen-

trated there. The average household size for Israel is a whole has held steadily for many years at 3.8. But kibbutzim (communal settlements) have an average household size of 2.4. About half the kibbutzim have "children's houses" in which the youngsters live from shortly after birth until about the age of eighteen, visiting with their parents only a few hours a day, thus freeing both parents for full-time work without the need for back-up personnel in the household. Equally important, each kibbutz has its own built-in social security program. Even after a person retires, he or she retains full membership in the settlement and is supported by it for life. In India, by contrast, where resources and services are widely scattered, and where there is no social security, the need for back-up personnel in the household is evident. Accordingly, the average rural household in India has about six members, while the average urban household has close to five members.

Statistics often conceal more than they reveal. Reductions in household size raise many questions about the quality of life. An implication of a very small family is that its members have few people with whom to interact daily and steadily. Is this part of the problem of loneliness experienced by so many people in modern society? At the same time, smaller domestic units lead to more intense emotional interactions and this, for many, exacerbates problems about coping with intimacy and other challenges of a highly personal nature. Just as adaptations are made to dispersals or concentrations of needed goods and services, so will people have to come to terms with the realities of their family environments on the most intimate and personal levels. The frequency of emotional difficulties and rising divorce rates suggests that many people are a long way from making these adaptations.

REFERENCES

Salins, Marshall D.

1957   "Land Use and the Extended Family
                in Moala, Fiji." American Anthro
                pologist 59: 449-62.

Smith, Thomas C.

1959   The Agrarian Origins of Modern
                Japan Stanford: Stanford Univer-
                sity Press.

Stenning, Derrick J.

1958   "Household Viability among the
                Pastoral Fulani." In The Develop
                ment Cycle in Domestsic Groups,
                edited by Jack Goody. New York
                and Cambridge: Cambridge Univer-
                sity Press.

Wheaton, Robert

1975   "Family and Kinship in Western
                Europe: The Problem of the Joint
                Family Household." Journal of
                Interdisciplinary History 4
                (Spring): 601-28.

White, Lynn Jr.

1962   Medieval Technology and Social
1966   change. New York: Oxford
                University Press.

*Yehudi A. Cohen is professor in and chairman of the
Anthropology Department in Rutgers University.

Reprinted from Society, January/February 1981.
Copyright 1981 by Transaction, Inc. Reprinted by
permission.

SECTION III

ALTERNATIVE LIFE STYLES: IMPLICATIONS FOR FAMILY, SELF AND SOCIETY

I.   INTRODUCTION

Many argue that traditional marriage has failed
to keep pace with the changing cultural values of
Modern Industrial American Society. These changing
values have resulted in: (1) challenges to implicit
assumptions surrounding traditional marriage, resulting in the transformation of explicit and implicit
norms governing behavior within marital relationships;
and (2) the development of life styles which function
to meet emerging social and personal needs no longer
served by traditional marriage and family life.

II.   CHALLENGING TRADITIONAL ASSUMPTIONS

The basic assumptions of traditional marriage
have come under increasing attack. Almost all the
changes in the traditional monogamous family and in
the attitudes of people living in emerging family
forms challenge society's basic value premises regarding the family. Among these premises are the
following:

1.   Romantic love forms the basis for a successful marriage.
2.   Sex should be confined to marital relationships.
3.   A person should have only one mate, of
course, of the opposite sex.
4.   Masculine and feminine sex roles should be
clearly defined.
5.   Children should be raised in a nuclear
family setting.
6.   The nuclear family is the most effective
unit for residential living, consumption,
and social functions.

All alternatives outside the traditional marriage
pattern violate these premises; emerging changes
within the ideographic or structural form of the
nuclear family violate at least some of them. The
most consistent violations occur in the area of
confining sexual relations to a legally defined
marital relationship.

Two points should be raised regarding these basic assumptions. First, do they now or have they ever really been adhered to? Substantial evidence exists to show that they do not represent much real behavior. For example, a study carried out in the 1940's and 1950's showed that 17 percent of first born children were conceived prior to marriage. Unless we assume that every young girl who violated the sexual prohibition premise became pregnant, this is a minimum figure. It is probably safe to assume that at least a majority of the young men and women did not act according to the premise that sex should be confined to marriage.

Another myth about marriage and the family concerns monogamy (Constantine and Constantine, 1973:3). In its strictest sense, monogamy means one mate for a life time, and generally in our country this also requires lifelong sexual fidelity as well. Although traditional sexual fidelity requires sexually exclusive relationships within the context of marital bonds with one spouse, all available data in our society suggests that strict monogamy is problematic.

The Constantines report an interesting incident. They were speaking to a small suburban gathering in Minnesota about the extent of extra-marital relationships, and the suburbanites granted that such a thing might exist elsewhere but not in their community. Coincidentally, research on extra-marital relations in the community had just been published reporting that more than one-third of the couples had had at least one affair. The Constantines felt there were reasons to believe that this statistic understated the extent of extramarital relationships in the community.

The question, then, needs to be raised whether or not contemporary assumptions held by many in emerging family forms not only more adequately reflect cultural realities and values, but at the same time, result in less personal guilt and fewer mental health problems than the formerly held traditional view. In any case, there still exists in our society a value conflict between those who report that they adhere to these premises, whether they do in actual or vicarius behavior is another matter, and those who tend to ignore some or all of them. Our guess is that in the future, the variety

of emerging alternatives will probably be recognized
as a cultural reality.

III. FACTORS ACCOUNTING FOR CHANGES IN THE TRADI-
TIONAL FAMILY

There are several factors accounting for changes
in the nuclear family and the emergence and growth of
alternatives. Among these factors are at least two
primary ones: (1) the women's liberation movement,
and (2) the development of the ideas of personal
growth, open communication, and open loving relationships. Associated with these are the following basic
changes:

1. Less differentiation in family sex roles.
2. A decline in the monolithic power of the
    male.
3. More women holding jobs outside of the family.
4. The growth of equaity in sexual relations;
    females demanding and receiving the same
    sexual freedoms as the male; and of course,
    the abandonment of the double standard.
5. The remarkable changes in the legal code
    reflecting these and other factors.

We expect that the basic modal unit in our
society will continue to be the nulear family -- husband, wife, child or children. However, the changes
enumerated earlier will alter many basic values, expectations, attitudes, and behaviors in these nuclear
family units. Similarly, many who enter these
nuclear families probably will have experiences
living in an emerging alternative family pattern and
will enter the nuclear family with a clearer notion
of its advantages, disadvantages, and limitations--
which most certainly exist.

Thus, while we may lament the passing of the
traditional nuclear family as it now exists--though
this is probably in its idealized form rather than
its reality, the general dissatisfaction with
marriage may be replaced by more realistic and
workable family styles.

BIBLIOGRAPHY

Butler, Edgar W.

    1979   Traditional Marriage and Emerging
                  Alternatives, New York: Harper
                  & Row.

Constantine, Larry &
  Joan Constantine

    1973   Group Marriage: A Study of Con-
                  temporary Multilateral Marriages.
                  New York: Macmillan.

Stephens, William N.

    1963   The Family in Cross-Cultural
                  Perspective. New York: Holt,
                  Rinehart and Winston.

CHAPTER 17

THE GROWTH PERSPECTIVE OF INTERPERSONAL RELATIONSHIPS: A NEW VISTA

Herbert A. Otto*

The Growth Perspective on Relationships is an emergent concept. It is a revolutionary concept and it provides a new perspective. The growth perspective of human relationships rests squarely on the human potentiality's hypothesis. This hypothesis is very briefly that the average, well-functioning human being is functioning at from four to ten percent of capacity. William James, the well-known American psychologist, as the turn of the century made the statement that he believed we were functioning at ten percent. Margaret Med, in an article she contributed to my book, Explorations in Human Potentialites in 1966 made the statement that she believed we were functioning at six percent of capacity. Since that time, we have had so many discoveries about the human potential, including those relating to biofeedback that now the current estimate is that we are functioning at four percent of capacity. This human potentiality's hypothesis is internationally accepted.

Among the people who suscribe to this hypothesis, and some of the names may be familiar, are the following: There is the father of the human potential movement, Gardner Murphy, the famous psychologist Gordon Alport, Margaret Mead, Abraham Maslow, and others. The human potentiality's hypothesis is by no means restricted to the U.S. This hypothesis is generally accepted and one of the countries that has done a great deal of research in this area is the USSR. This is a hypothesis of hope and, unfortunately, this hypothesis of the human potential is restricted to the educated segment of our population. It is opposed by the ruling classes and it is opposed by people who are of an elitest orientation. On the other hand, the human potentiality hypothesis forms the very basis for human evolution. Why this is, I develop below.

Each person has tremendous potential and I hope, in some ways, to be able to "turn you on" to what

319

this may mean to you. So we will start out briefly to get an idea what we mean by "the human potential." What are some of the indicators of the human potential? Do you remember when you were a child and your parents stepped into the room? Sometimes you knew what they were going to say. More often you knew exactly how they felt. Remember how good things smelled?; how your vision was different? We are continually taking in sensory cues on a subliminal level, on a level of which we are not conscious. We take in a tremendous amount of cues simultaneously. Our sensory apparatus is very highly sensitive, and as children we were perhaps more sensitive than we are today. Today, as part of the human potential movement, we have training in sensory awareness that can re-awaken these sensory capacities.

Another indicator--there are Indian tribes that are able to smell almost with the acuity of a hunting dog. We all have a tremendously developed sense of smell which, of course, we stifle due to the polluted environment. All of us have tremendous reserves of strength. There are cases on record of people lifting cars under emergency conditions that have weighed thousands of pounds. There are neurological indicators that everything that has ever happened to us is stored in the human personality in some way that is not as yet fully understood. Six years ago we believed the storage area was the brain. Today we know that there is also such a thing as muscular memory. This has vast implications for psychotherapy. What I am saying is that we have stored a tremendous mass of data and, to use a computer analogy, we have not yet learned how to program ourselves to use this tremendous storage of data for problem-solving purposes.

Psychosomatic research and psychosomatic concepts are a clear indicator of human potential. Most doctors who are sophisticated and trained within the last 15 to 20 years are aware that anywhere from 70 to 80 percent of the people who walk into a general practitioner's office are suffering from functional illness. This means they have a symptomology for which no physical but an emotional basis can be found. Psychosomatic concepts are of tremendous importance because they indicate that it is not the bacteria, not the germ, not the virus that is causing the illness. It is our total outlook about ourselves, and

the well-known American psychiatrist Szaz, who is
currently a gadfly on the tail-end of the AMA and the
establishment, makes the flat statement that illness
is a symbolic way of asking for help. It is a symbolic way of saying, "I can no loner cope. I need
love and caring." Of course, we all hate to disabuse
ourselves of the myth and notion that germs, viruses,
and bacteria cause our illnesses. Yet, we know that
most of us have had tuberculosis but very few have
utilized that disease in order to say "I need caring"
to the world and perhaps to get it from the world.

Another indicator of the human potential is the
whole area of extrasensory perception, parapsychology,
psychokinesis, clairvoyance. This whole, vast area
has received a great deal of attention in the USSR.
In this country, we are still trying to prove that
the so-called "psychic phenomena" exist. In the USSR,
they no longer need the proof. They accept E.S.P.
They call mental telepathy 'radio brainwave communication.' They are trying to help people to tap into
these powers and to help the man on the street to
utilize it--a totally new approach to the subject.
We all know today that most children have extrasensory
capacities and that these capacities are trained out
of them fairly early in childhood. I want to open
this up for your consideration because many of you
here have these capacities.

We are using only a small fraction of our sexual
potential and I think we all need to know this. If
we accept that we are using a small fraction of our
total potential, then, of course, this also has
something to do with the whole area of sexual experiencing. My research has shown conclusively that if
people begin to work in this area they can have huge
increments of sexual pleasure; that the quality of
their sexual experiencing can be raised considerably,
even compounded. All this depends, of course, on the
individual's self-investment in this process. Every
person has tremendous creative capacities and powers
which lie untapped and latent.

There is a great deal of solid core research
showing that people can experience a creativity workshop (or a course) and come up with capacities that
they didn't even know or suspect they had. There is
also what I call a "Grandma Moses phenomena." The
famous primitive painter Grandma Moses discovered

that she had talents when she was in her sixties and
seventies. Most of us have talents which we will take
to our graves with us because we will never develop
them.

What I also am saying then is that every person
is the artist of his or her own creation. You are
the artist of your own creation. We determine our
own life and death--and that is hard to take, but
that is where the responsibility is. It lies totally
within each one of us.

In the light of this recognition then, I hope
that the develoment of your personal potential will
be a lifelong adventure for you. Why is this so
important? Because now we come to something that we
call the short-circuit theory. It goes something
like this: the unused human potential may go into
organismic, self-destructive paths. Athletes know
if you don't use it, you lose it. That applies to
all of us!

The human being needs to be continually pointed
in the direction of actualizing potential. We need
to be continually engaged in this process--in this
search. The actualization of human potential is the
path of human evolution. This is the road of life
affirmation. This actualization of our possibilities,
of our latent powers is life supportive and life pro-
longing. It adds quality to life; it adds vitality
to us and it gives us joie de vivre. In other words,
it gives us the tremendous sense of WOW! It's won-
derful to be alive and living!

The emphasis needs to be on the process and not
on the outcome. We must not be outcome-centered but
process-centered in this adventure of actualizing
our possibilities. The very core of the human potentiality's concept has tremendous relevance to
human relationships because the interpersonal relationship matrix is the prime matrix for actualizing
human potential. We actualize our possibilities
through relationships with people. We grew into what
we are through relations with people and we grow
into what we can be through relations with people.
If you think about that, you wil recognize that this
is where the truth lies. Ask yourself this question:
What is the purpose of human relationships? Here are
some of the answers that you will give: Companionship

is the purpose of human relationships. Human relationships help me to define myself. They give me a
self-definition. Human relationships are for pleasure, sexual and otherwise. Human relationships are
for survival. They are a necessity. We can't do
without them. Yet, all of us know about the empty
and shallow nature of most patterns of human relatedness. The game-playing; the artificiality that is
all around us in contemporary society.

Looking at this desert of stereotypes of human-
relatedness, we again ask: What is the purpose of
human relationships? And one basic answer emerges:
The actualizing of human potential is the prime
reason for the human relationships that we have.
In other words, we relate to people in order to
foster our and their personal growth; our and their
personal unfoldment; our and their personal evolution. This process needs to form the basis of our
relatedness. If you believe this, you need to undertake a fundamental reassessment of the quality, trust,
and the nature of the human relationships in which
you are engaged, because there are such things as
toxic individuals who bring out disturbance and who
create pathogenic processes in us. We need to be
aware that there are such things as psychic vampires,
people who do, indeed, suck our energies and take,
and take from us and give nothing, or very little in
return. They never change, and never grow. Conversely, we need to recognize that there are people
who stimulate us, who enhance our growth, who
challenge us, and who make us feel more creative,
more alive. We need to seek out those people. We
need to be with them. We need, in turn, to give to
them as they give to us.

Recognition of the fundamental principle that
direction determines outcome, is of the very essence
of what we call the growth concept of human relationships. The fundamental principle is, that if we
believe in this, then this indeed will be the outcome.
Namely, "my relationships exist for my and the other
person's growth. I bend my efforts in this direction." If we believe this, then the outcome is more
likely to be that.

The growth perspective of human relations operates within the framework of a number of concepts:
(1) open communication; (2) honesty (no games between

people); (3) furnishing growth opportunities and
experiences for each other. That means conscious
thought and effort expended on the question, "How am
I going to help that person to grow and how can that
person help me grow as a person and unfold my possibilities?" Risk-taking is of the very essence of
this type of growth. Openness to feelings is also.
The next principle involves recognition that human
beings are a mystery. You are a vast mystery. The
exploration of this mystery is a tremendous adventure
and the exploration the mystery of the person with
whom you co-exist and who is your companion, that is,
in part, where the excitement of life lies. We need
to recognize the human relationships are an interplay
of energy forms and that we give and receive energy.
We need to recognize that thre are masculine and
feminine components in each one of us and we need to
be sensitive and open to these components of ourselves. We need to unfold them, to celebrate and
welcome them because they represent precious assets
and precious possibilities. We need to use our intuitive capacities, our hunches, to the very hilt
when we engage in human relationships and we need to
use them, particularly, with strangers because our
growth always takes place in the context of strangers
who become intimates. There, again, lies the adventure and the challenge for each one of us. The fear
of the stranger is the greatest taboo of the bankrupt
and sterile society that it is used by such a bankrupt
and sterile society to sustain "anomie," the greatest
cancer of this culture.

What are some of the social implications of the
growth perspective of human relationships? First of
all, I think we are all aware that men and women's
roles are changing. We need to be very much aware
that contemporary research has proven conclusively
that the woman is the stronger of the specie by all
criteria that have been and can be established.
Mortality, morbidity, survival rate, number of pleasure centers, however you look at it, you find the
man is the more fragile organism of the two. This
also means that a reversal of the roles in the sense
of "interpersonal outreach" has to take place. The
responsibility for outreach to the opposite sex has
up to now, largely been the males. This has to be
reversed.

Another social implication of the growth perspective of human relationships is the importance of short term, quality relationships. That is extremely important. We need to get away from the concept of exclusively long term relationships. We need to recognize that in terms of personal growth, in terms of intimacy, in terms of openness, in terms of actualizing human possibilities, a great deal can exist between two people and can unfold in a relatively short period of time. A period of time characterizes real openness, real communication. We also need to recognize that long term relationships can turn into a matrix inimical to human growth. In other words, many long term relationships become dead and sterile. This can be reversed in some instances, but for the most part, I have a feeling it is irreversible.

We need to develop frameworks so that people can meet each other. I think Bob Rimmer's brilliant suggestions along those lines: social clubs in motels, human potential centers, this type of thing, this is where we need to move (see Chapter 19,23). We also need to move into an area that I call structured interpersonal experiences as a means of personal growth. For example, we could have such an experience by sitting down with a person with whom we want to be intimate, using our intuitive faculties and communicating to that person what we perceive as his or her strengths.

In our culture, the emphasis is always on what is "wrong" with us. How about on what is "right" with us? How about more emphasis on our strengths, our resourceds—they are indeed present! We need to confront each other in terms of our strengths and potentials. The other side, what's "wrong" with, our "weaknesses" and so on, we get that type of communication all the time. We need to share such experiences with each other as the most loving moment in our lives. That's very important. We need to share with each other the happiest sexual experience we've ever had because that may give us some indication where we may want to go. We need to share with each other what our sexual fantasies are because it also is a form of communication. We need to recognize that at the very core of the sexual experience lies an energy and affective exchange and that a lot more than we know about is taking place between two people. We need to be very aware and very much focused on the need and the importance of nourishing love and caring for each other. Love and caring for each other and for ourselves. How much love and caring do we give to ourselves? That is where growth often really starts.

I want to say then, in closing, you are faced with a tremendous challenge and that challenge is, can you make your human relations, growth experiences, a framework of growth, a framework of mutual growth, of growth for you, a means of growth for the person with whom you are intimate? That, I think, is the greatest challenge that is facing all of us.

CHAPTER 18

LONG DISTANCE MARRIAGE (LDM):
CAUSE OF MARITAL DISRUPTION OR A
SOLUTION TO UNEQUAL DUAL-CAREER DEVELOPMENT?

John Orton
and
Sharyn M. Crossman*

I.   INTRODUCTION

In recent years an optional lifestyle, sometimes
referred to as Commuter Marriage (Gerstel, 1977),
Two-Residence Marriage (Gross, 1980), or Married
Singles (Kirschner & Walum, 1978) has arisen for
those couples seeking comparable career development.
Ferris (1978) assessed the commuter lifestyle through
interviews with 10 commuting couples of varied professional and family background. Ferris found the
lifestyle to be one in which spouses lives and worked
in separate cities on weekdays and reunited on weekends.

Gerstel's (1977) study of Commuter Marriage was
based upon interviews with 74 commuting couples and
20 noncommuting, dual-career couples. She defined
Commuter Marriage as a ". . . marital form in which
members of a couple spent at least two nights a week
in separate residences and yet are still married and
intend to remain so inspite of demanding careers that
require commitments in different locations" (Gerstel,
1977:357). Therefore, in pursuing job or training
opportunities either spouse relocates, but they do so
voluntarily with the intent of maintaining the marital
relationship (Ferris, 1978; Gerstel, 1977; Gross,
1980).

Gerstel (1977) found that the greater the distance which separated couples, the more infrequently
they commuted to reunite. The distance separating
the couples in Gerstel's sample ranged from 40 to
2650 miles. However, among these commuters five
days was the mean number of days spent apart (range
3 to 60 days). Similarily, about 50 percent of
Gross' (1980) two-residence spouses spend each weekend together.

Definition of Long Distance Marriage

We propose that Long Distance Marriage (LDM) is a new variation on Commuter Marriage in that LDM participants live far enough apart that weekly re- unions to recharge the relationship are not possible for a majority of couples. But, LDM participants, like commuters, face the added expense of maintaining two separate residences while apart (see Gross, 1980).

Long Distance Marriage does not include military familes since these couples do not separate by choice, or persons who travel and their spouses because these couples do not maintain separate residences. It would include students involved in LDM to complete degrees or training. For example, an M.D. who must remain behind to complete a residency while his/her spouse moves to a position in another city/state. Further- more, completion of education or training might not mean a termination of the LDM. The LDM could be con- tinued if the newly degreed spouse has to seek employ- ment in a location other than that of his/her spouse's residence.

The problem in this study concerns whether the lower frequency of visitation among LDM participants might stress the marriage to the point of decreased satisfaction and break up. Gerstel's (1977) commuters indicated frequent reunions were essential to keeping the relationship intact.

II. REVIEW OF LITERATURE

Few investigations of the commuter lifestyle have been undertaken because such involvement is a recent phenomenon (Gross, 1980) and the participants are a hard-to-identify and highly mobile population. Thus, previous research has been limited to a few studies reporting qualitative data.

Relocation Limitations

Holstrom (1972) identified the lack of mobility of one spouse, usually the wife, due to the career commitments of the husband, as one source of conflict for dual-career couples. The husband's career inhi- bited the wife's relocation potential limiting her career opportunity choices. While the occupational mobility of husbands often has a negative effect on

328

the career development of wives, the occupational
commitments of wives were not taken into consideration
in husband's geographic mobility decisions (Duncan &
Perrucci, 1976).

Spousal immobility has resulted from two long-
standing assumptions of conventional marriage. The
first is that, while it has been acceptable for couples to pursue dual-careers (Rapoport & Rapoport,
1971), the wife's career was to be subordinate to
the husband's. The second assumption is that couples
have been expected to dwell in a single residence to
keep the marital relationship intact. The husband,
as primary breadwinner, held the career prerogative.
His choice of occupation and pursuit of career advancement determined where the family would establish
its residence. If travel or separation were necessary, it was because the husband's career required
it (Gross, 1980).

Adaptable family structure. Gerstel (1977) concluded that the best way to understand dual-residence
marriages was to combine two concepts of family
structure. One of these is coexisting plural family
forms. The other involves a conception of a family's
structure altering to fit the family's changing life
cycle. Gerstel suggested that this concept would be
brought into sharper focus if stages in career
development were specified as well. If career
sequence and complimentary family structure were
combined, an understanding of a "best fit" structural
adaptation could be gained. Thus, in the history of
one family a single residence structure is needed
when the couple is young and children are small.
This might be followed by a commuter marriage when
careers become more specialized and more income is
needed for family support. After retirement, with
income reduced and where no job requirements exist,
an extended family arrangement might be more appropriate. Thus, dual-residence structure is the "best
fit" for dual-career spouses who both have serious
commitments to uninterrupted career development.

Gerstel (1977) further indicated that most
commuters conceived of their living arrangements as
temporary. Kirschner and Walum (1978) also noted
that orientation in their respondents. When the
spouses will reunite may not be known, but as Gross
(1980) pointed out, such an outlook spared the com-

329

muters some of the stress involved in thinking that individual career development was more important than the marital relationship.

The Conventional Marriage Model

Gross (1980) investigated the rewards and strains of 43 spouses from 28 marriages that were dual-residence in nature. Data were gathered through separate interviews of spouses. The traditional marriage model was used by Gross to explain her findings on spousal viewpoints of the role differences between traditional marriage and nontraditional, Two-Residence Marriage.

Gross (1980) indicated that, while her respondents reject the traditional marital style with the wife's career subordinate to the husband's, they had no other frame of reference by which to measure their own feelings about their choice of lifestyle. Respondents perceived traditional marriage as not having the contracts within it to allow couples to conceive of dual-career development or to cope the way in which the respondents did. Consequently, they took pride in their conscious awareness of the need for each spouse's career development as well as being able to deal with the inconveniences and stresses of their living arrangement.

Potential for Disruption

This is an important point for further consideration. If such couples use the traditional model as their standard, they might also perceive their lifestyle as potentially or actually disruptive. Possible threats from the traditional standpoint include: Involvement in extramarital sex (EMS) after two residence living has begun; the likelihood of one or both spouses eventually wanting a divorce, especially if reunions are infrequent and the separation continues for a great length of time; doubt about whether the reason for involvement was for purposes of career advancement or to gain freedom from the other spouse. Gross (1980) suggested that her respondents indicated agreement on reasons for the Two-Residence Marriage was very important to a satisfactory adjustment to separation.

Societal perception. Furthermore, since two-residence couples use traditional comparisons, it is

330

likely that society would make similar judgments
while being unaware that couples commute because they
highly valued equal spousal career development. In
this connection, Kirschner and Walum (1978) found that
participants experienced considerable stress in their
social relationships when friends, relatives, and
co-workers assumed that the commuter arrangement was
actually the primary step toward a divorce. Similarly,
Gerstel (1977) found that another popular perception
of commuter couples was that, though married, these
couples were sexually free. Consequently, stress
associated with the lifestyle seems to eminate from
both intrapersonal and external or extrapersonal
sources.

    <u>Extramarital Sex (EMS)</u>. There is potential for
disruption due to participants' possible concern that
spouses could eventually become involved in EMS.
Since commuters are perceived as sexually free as
well as divorce-bound which makes socializing difficult, it is not surprising that Gross (1980) indicated
that her respondents revealed the two residence lifestyle was lonely. Thus, loneliness could be seen as
a force which might eventually push one or both members of a couple into EMS.

    Gerstel (1977) reported findings of EMS involve-
ment for her commuters which indicated that EMS activity was higher before involvement than afterward;
however, the decrease was only 7 percent, from 46 percent to 39 percent. She also found that those involved in EMS indicated that it was not as a result
of the lifestyle. This would seem to be the case
since many of those involved beforehand continued involvement after commuting began. It should be noted
that the majority of Gerstel's commuters reported no
EMS activity.

    <u>Divorce and decreased marital satisfaction</u>.
Spouses may fear that the living arrangement could
also lead to a divorce, or, at least, decreased
marital satisfaction. Gerstel (1978) found that
those who were entertaining the idea of a divorce
during commuting indicated it was not a result of
the lifestyle but that dissatisfaction with the
lifestyle caused them to rethink their marital relationships. It would seem reasonable to assume that
the consequences of less frequent spousal interaction in LDM could lead participants to question

the benefits of continuing a marriage that offered no interaction, companionship, or sharing on a frequent basis. Thus, participants might begin to consider a divorce.

It appears that the amount of potential stress would depend upon five factors. First, whether participants perceived the LDM to be temporary; second, whether couples held traditional negative sanctions against EMS; third, if couples could cope with societal misperceptions about the purpose of the LDM living arrangement as well as loneliness and other negative emotional reactions; fourth, if length of time between visitations was not too long; fifth, if total length of time to be spent living apart were to be relatively short coupled with clearly understood reasons for the LDM. Deficits in one or more of these factors could increase the likelihood that disruption might occur. Strenghs in these factors could contribute to an attitude of "sticking it out."

Furthermore, if reasons for involvement coincide with perceived advantages of the lifestyle, this could tend to reduce stress and potential for disruption. However, a perception that the reasons for involvement were not being fulfilled and that there were disadvantages to the lifestyle, could lead to distress and eventual disruption.

III. PURPOSE

The purpose of this study was to determine whether LDM is a new variant of commuter marriage in terms of distances separating couples and frequency of visitation. Also, we sought to discover whether there is potential for disruption and a decrease in marital quality or if this lifestyle is a viable, nondisruptive option for most career-committed couples.

Objectives

1. To determine, (a) the distance separating couples, and (b) the frequency of visitation.

2. To determine, (a) respondents' reasons for becoming involved and (b) to discover whether men's and women's reasons differed.

332

3. To determine whether, (a) spousal reactions to the decision to begin an LDM differed and (b) whether spouses viewed the living arrangement as temporary or permanent.

4. To determine whether LDM may be disruptive to marriage because it, (a) creates a situation with a potential for involvement in EMS, (b) whether either sex is more likely to be involved in EMS, and (c) whether or not the LDM is seen as the reason for EMS activity.

5. To determine if LDM contributes to potential marital disruption because, (a) a greater portion of the sample is contemplating a divorce after LDM began than had done so beforehand, (b) whether either sex is more likely to be considering such a move, and (c) whether or not the LDM is perceived as responsible for such consideration

6. To determine (a) if marital relations were satisfactory or unsatisfactory before as well as after LDM began, (b) if spousal appreciation changed after involvement in LDM.

7. To determine whether men and women differed regarding what they perceived as the positive and negative aspects of the LDM and to compare positive aspects to reasons for living a LDM.

IV. METHOD

Survey instrument. In 1977 a questionnaire was constructed tapping such issues as: Who initiated the idea of involvement; reactions to the decision, problems, if any, with disruptors such as EMS and divorce; evaluation of marital satisfaction and spousal appreciation; perceived advantages and disadvantages of LDM; changes in social interaction patterns; how respondents felt and responded during visitation; the effects of the LDM on children. Following two separate pilot tests, a revised 61-item, semi-structured survey instrument was prepared.

Sample. A snowball sample of LDM participants was obtained by identification of such couples through referrals by other participant-couples. In 1978 the survey was mailed out to the identified couples living

333

across the United States. Each spouse was contacted separately. Of these, 114 questionnaires were returned. Since we were not utilizing a population created from couples known to match the criteria for inclusion, it cannot be said that we had a population or that our sample is such in the true sense of the word. Therefore, findings cannot be generalized beyond these 114 respondents.

Objective #1 was formulated to test our notion that LDM participants differ from commuters on distance separating couples and frequency of visitation.

Forty-nine percent of the men were separated from their spouses by 500 or fewer miles and 51 percent of this group were over 500 miles apart. (One respondent's spouse was out of the country.) Of the female respondents, 54 percent were separated from their spouses by 500 or fewer miles and 46 percent were separated by greater distances. (One respondent's spouse was out of the country.) In many cases distances separating couples were considerable: More than 2,000 miles for 11 percent of respondents, more than 800 miles for 31 percent. The mean distance of separation for males was 1996 miles. The mean distance for females was 1942 miles (spouses out of the country not included). The range was from 100 to 3,300 miles.

Originally, 35 percent of the males and 35 percent of the females reported that they visited each weekend. Twenty-five percent of the males and 22 percent of the females visited every two or three weeks. Forty percent of the males and 43 percent of the females visited once per month or less often. Taken together, 65 percent of the males and 65 percent of the females visited twice per month or less frequently. After some time had passed in the LDM, respondents indicated there were almost no changes in their visiting frequencies.

Objective #2 was deseigned to test the premise that LDM participants became involved for reasons of career or professional growth and goal attainment. Secondly, we sought to determine whether spouses differed in their reasons for participating to discover whether there was clear understanding of reasons for involvement.

When respondents were asked why they had chosen to enter the LDM lifestyle, respondent-created categories were: (a) Job location at marriage, 6 percent males, 9 percent females; (b) transferred, 4 percent males, 2 percent females; (c) professional advancement, 44 percent males, 44 percent females; (d) could not find a suitable position in present location, 20 percent males, 20 percent females; (e) desired to be separated from spouse, 2 percent males, 2 percent females; (f) desired different location/climate, 4 percent males, 4 percent females; (g) to increase or maintain present income, 14 percent males, 12 percent females; (h) other, which included training/graduate program location, loss or reduction in employment benefits if relocate, to complete education/training, 6 percednt males, 7 percent females.

Objective #3 was to determine whether spousal reactions to their decision differed and if spouses viewed the move as temporary or permanent.

We asked what respondents' reactions were to their decision. Responses were collapsed into four categories: 1) Positive feelings toward involvement which included opportunity, challenge, enthusiasm, and excitement, 20 percent males, 38 percent females; 2) mid-level feelings which included ambivalence, only mutually acceptable choice, 60 percent males, 41 percednt females; 3) negative feelings (specific) which included resentment and distrust, 9 percent males, 4 percent females; 4) negative feelings (general) which included fear, anxiety, and envy, 11 percent males, 17 percent females. (Envy was mentioned with regard to spouses who were remaining in the couple's primary residence. They reported they envied their spouse's opportunity to experience a new, challenging situation.) Men were significantly different from women in that men reported more feelings of ambivalence.

The perception of the temporary or nontemporary nature of the lifestyle is an important aspect of the adjustment process. 1 The three categories included were: 1) Yes, the LDM is temporary, males 88 percent, females 89 percent; 2) No, the LDM is not temporary, 8 percent males, 8 percent females; 3) UnSure, 4 percent males, 3 percent females. No significant differences were found between the sexes

on this perception. Both sexes indicated that they
considered the LDM to be temporary.

Objective #4 was to determine whether the LDM
lifestyle might be disruptive because of potential
for involvement in EMS.

To fully determine the incidence of EMS and
related situational dynamics, several aspects of EMS
activity were investigated. These included: number
of participants involved in EMS before as well as
after the LDM began; whether either sex was more
likely to become involved; and whether those participating in EMS saw it as a result of the LDM. (Frequencies will be shown since this objective addresses
only the subgroup of respondents who gave affirmative
responses.)

When spouses were asked if they were engaging in
EMS before the LDM, only 6 males and 5 females indicated they were involved (n=11). After the LDM had
begun, however, 10 males and 20 females reported
engaging in EMS (n=30). Comparisons of these 30 men
and women revealed a nonsignificant trend with females
more likely than males to be active in EMS. As to
whether or not LDM was perceived as a contributing
factor to EMS: yes, 5 males, 6 females; no, 5 males,
14 females. Thus both males and females denied
causality and no significant differences were found
on this perception. This may be a response made to
protect the perceived positive aspects of the lifestyle and is reported here with caution.

Objective #5 was to determine whether a substantial number of participants were contemplating a
divorce before as well as after the LDM began, whether
either sex was more likely to be considering divorce,
and whether or not the LDM was seen as a contributing
factor.

A minority of the participants were thinking
about a divorce both before and after the LDM began.
Of these, before the LDM, 15 were males and 30 were
females, (n=45). After the LDM began, 18 were males
and 33 were females (n=51). A comparison of men and
women in the latter subgroup revealed a significant
difference between the sexes. Females were more
likely than males to be considering seeking a divorce
after the LDM occurred.

We asked those contemplating divorce if they believed it was a result of the LDM. Three response
categories were used: (a) yes, males 3, females 8;
(b) no, males 13, females 23; and (c) uncertain, s
males 2, females 2. Comparisons of men's and women's
responses revealed no significant differences. Respondents did not believe that the lifestyle was
causal.

Objective #6 was to determine if marital relations had been satisfying or unsatisfying before as
well as after the LDM began; secondly, to determine
whether spousal appreciation had increased, decreased,
or remained the same after involvement began.

There were five degrees of choice ranging from
very satisfied to very unsatisfied. Degrees of satisfaction for males before the LDM, 67 percent were very
satisfied, 4 percent satisfied, 8 percent neither
satisfied nor dissatisfied, 17 percent dissatisfied,
2 percent very dissatisfied. Of the females, 58 percent were very satisfied, 1 percent satisfied, 16
percent neither satisfied nor dissatisfied, 17 percent
dissatisfied, 8 percent very dissatisfied. Both males
and females were very satisfied with the marriages
before the LDM. After beginning the lifestyle, 73
percent of the males were very satisfied, 0 percent
satisfied, 10 percent neither satisfied nor dissatisfied, 16 percent dissatisfied, 2 percent very dissatisfied. Of the females, 67 percent very satisfied, 6
percent satisfied, 10 percent neither satisfied nor
dissatisfied, 11 percent were dissatisfied, and 6
percent were very dissatisfied. The majority of
respondents indicated they were still very satisfied.
No significant differences were found.

We asked respondents to indicate whether they
had experienced a change in spousal appreciation
since living apart. Three response categories were
used: 1) appreciate spouse less, 19 percent males,
12 percent females; 2) no change in appreciation,
22 percent males, 5 percent females; 3) appreciate
spouse more than before, 59 percent males, 83 percent
females. A significant difference was found between
the sexes. Females were more likely than males to
have become more appreciative of their spouses after
experiencing the LDM while males experienced no change
in appreciation.

337

Objective #7 was to determine whether males and females differed regarding what they saw as the positive and negative aspects of the LDM and to compare these to reasons for having become involved. Participants indicate all positive aspects of their LDM. Responses were categorized as follows: 1) Professional growth and goal attainment, 31 percent males, 22 percent females; 2) freedom and independence, 27 percent males, 25 percent females; 3) personal growth, 21 percent males, 31 percent females; 4) financial gain, 6 percent males, 8 percent females; 5) other benefits, which included health, retained employment benefits, best of both worlds (career and family), 15 percent males, 14 percent females.

No significant differences were noted between the groups on advantages of the lifestyle. Both sexes cited professional goal attainment most frequently, but many respondents indicated freedom and independence to be an important advantage. Thus, we analyzed a question which isolated this issue. This question asked if respondents had experienced a feeling of freedom and independence since living in an LDM. Respondents were given three response categories: (a) Yes, 45 percent males, 70 percent females; (b) No, 47 percent males, 21 percent females; and (c) sometimes, 8 percent males, 9 percent females. Analysis of the responses of the total sample revealed a significant difference between the sexes. Women were more likely than men to have experienced such feelings.

Participants indicated that the greatest disadvantages were: (a) loneliness, males 23 percent, females 13 percent; (b) separation and distance, males 19 percent, females 10 percent; (c) missed communication on a face-to-face basis, males 8 percent, females 18 percent; (d) missed sex, intimacy, 6 percent males, 10 percent females; (e) missed companionship, 17 percent males, 13 percent females; (f) expense of maintaining two residences, 17 percent males, 10 percent females; and (g) negative emotional reactions which included tension, frustration, despression, limited social life, 10 percent males, 26 percent females. No significant differences were noted on these perceptions.

When reviewing reasons for becoming involved in
the LDM, both males and females indicated they do so
for professional advancement. Since they saw their
greatest advantage as obtaining the desired advancement, it would seem they would have suffered little
disappointment in terms of career development.

VI. DISCUSSION

Long Distance Marriage participants do differ
from commuters in that the majority only reunited
twice per month or less frequently land these patterns
were not found to change appreciably once involvement
had begun. Furthermore, the vast majority of our
respondents indicated that they only spent two to
three days together when they did visit. The infrequent and short visits could be the case because
slightly less than half of the respondents would
have to make a costly 1000 mile or greater round trip
with each visit.

Since couples were engaged in LDM on a temporary
as well as a voluntary basis, the investigators did
not find it surprising that a large proportion of the
respondents were employed in university positions,
especially that of faculty member. Both Gerstel and
Gross had many academics in their samples. As Gerstel
(1977) pointed out, due to the greater autonomy of
academician as well as mid-year vacations, these professionals' careers may be very adaptable to the
commuting lifestyle. Furthermore, the academic job
market is tight and tenured position are not typically given up easily. Also, finding two faculty ap-
pointments at the same university, if both spouses are
professors, is quite difficult. Therefore, this lifestyle seems as if it would be particularly attractive
to the career-growth-oriented academic.

Costs and Benefits

When reporting reasons for beginning a LDM,
professional advancement was most often given by both
sexes. However, women also selected the lifestyle to
overcome problems of career inhibition. Women showed
slightly greater percentages in job location at
marriage, to complete education or training. Furthermore, respondents indicated it was more likely to be
the wife than the husband who left the primary residence and established the second residence in another

339

city/state. This is perhaps one reason why women were more positive about the decision to live in a LDM while men were significantly more likely to have mixed feelings about it. That is, women saw the LDM as a way to move impediments out of their career development path. Men, on the other hand, who were older on average than were women and perhaps more often had their careers established, saw it as only allowing them to accrue more career achievements. Thus, husbands, who had no career development constraints, were understandably less excited or positive about involvement than were wives.

This idea can be further substantiated by the fact that the respondents indicated wives were more likely to initiate the idea of LDM than were husbands. Therefore, while wives stood to gain much through improvement in career and opportunity via LDM, husbands would lose a valuable asset to their own career advancement. The loss of the emotional support and the comfort of the wife's companionship is just such an asset. Furthermore, men's ambivalent feelings could, to some extent, support Gross' (1980) findings that even among men who fully believe in equal spousal career development there was still an underlying notion that the wife's career should be subordinate to the husband's. While these husbands experienced guilt over such feelings, they could not deny them. These findings are especially thought provoking in light of what spouses indicated were advantages of LDM.

Goal attainment and freedom and independence. Men found their greatest advantage to be career advancement. On the other hand, women, who also found career advancement as a major advantage were significantly more likely than men to have also experienced feelings of freedom and independence. This finding is in direct contradiction to what Gerstel (1977) reported. She noted that both men and women discovered greater feelings of independence during commuting and that such feelings were seen by both sexes as an advantage.

While couples probably had fairly equalitarian relationships before LDM, men did not find freedom and independence to be a very important advantage because men already felt freedom and independence within their marriages while women did not. The

340

notion of women's careers being subordinate to those
of men may have contributed. Most women entered the
LDM for purposes of career advancement just as men
did; however, not until after the marital relationship was no longer a central aspect of their lives,
did women discover the degree to which the marriage
had constrained a true sense of independence and
feelings of freedom. Thus, professional growth and
goal attainment coupled with independence and freedom could only be attained by women when complete
career-development equality with men came about.
Such equality occurred through deemphasizing the
marriage and making career primary. Furthermore,
it seems likely that once marriage and, indirectly,
husbands were no longer seen as a stumbling block
to progress, spousal appreciation increased in women.
By the same token, the marriage had not been seen as
a stumbling block to men so spousal appreciation
showed no change for them.

Spousal Solidarity in Coping with Potential Disruptors

Most spouses seemed to be united in their perceptions of and reactions to several of the identified
potential disruptors. This unity may have aimed them
in their ability to cope.

The fact that both spouses identified with LDM
living arrangement as temporary is an example of
this spousal solidarity. Also, our respondents reported an overwhelming willingness to terminate the
LDM and rejoin their spouses if a career opportunity
presented itself. This supports Gerstel's (1977)
conjecture about family structure flexibility.
Furthermore, if spouses used the traditional marriage
model for comparison to their living arrangement, it
could be that adherence to traditional values could
explain why most of the participants were not involved in EMS or contemplating divorce. Spouses
experienced many of the same stresses or disadvantages
of the lifestyle; therefore, they could empathize with
each other. This empathy, plus traditional values for
stability, could actually have resulted in spouses acting as a mutual support system even though separated.
Our respondents indicated that they communicated by
telephone at least once per week or more frequently
and no decrease was noted over time. (Typical calls
lasted at least fifteen to twenty minutes for the
majority of respondents.) Couples' consistent com-

341

munication, agreement on the temporary nature of the
LDM, a willingness to rejoin spouses if possible, a
determination by most to remain faithful and stable,
a history of having had a happy marriage as well as
still perceiving the marriage as happy, and increases
in spousal appreciation among the women as a function of the LDM all may have provided the connective
links which enabled many participants to remain a
mutual support system while separated.

It must be noted, however, that all spouses were
not presenting a united front. A minority of both
sexes were active in EMS and contemplating a divorce.
Women were more likely than men to be involved in
EMS and considering a divorce after the LDM began.

Gerstel's commuters reported that considering
divorce was not a result of the new lifestyle. Long
Distance Marriage respondents also indicated that no
connection existed between LDM and divorce consideration. Since our respondents showed almost no change
in the number of those considering a divorce before
(n=45) as compared to during (n=51), it seems that
dual-residence living does not lead to considering
a divorce.

The implications of EMS activity seem less clear.
The number involved in EMS before LDM was 11 participants, but after LDM began this group size increased
to 30. Yet, these respondents indicated that involvement did not come about as a result of the LDM.
One possible argument to explain this finding is that
perhaps among those involved in EMS, fidelity was not
an important aspect of their marital relationship.
But, if this were the case, why did involvement commence for so many only after the LDM was in progress?
Further research is needed to find the answer to this
and other questions. For example, why were women more
likely than men to have become involved in EMS and
why was divorce considered before the LDM began? Is
it a case of considering a divorce and then opting
to become involved in LDM instead? If so, that does
not explain why couples claimed that their marriages
were happy before and after LDM began. Or is it that
some participants contemplated sacrificing a happy
marriage to pursue their careers?

342

VII. CONCLUSIONS

The results of this study suggest we can tenatively conclude that for this sample: Commuter Marriage and LDM do differ because of less frequent visitation among the majority of LDM participants. This conclusion results from the fact that almost half of the spouses would have to travel 1,000 or more miles round trip each time a visit was undertaken. Also, males and females were separated from their spouses, on the average, over 1900 miles. Thus, LDM can be seen as a new variant of Commuter Marriage.

Men and women become involved in LDM for purposes of career advancement on a temporary, not a permanent, basis. The women became involved for career advancement as well as to overcome obstacles to career development while the men did so to continue career advancement. Once involved in the LDM, women were significantly more likely to experience feelings of freedom and independence than men were.

Involvement in EMS and divorce contemplation were not issues for a majority of either men or women in this sample. Those who were engaging in EMS or contemplating getting a divorce indicated the lifestyle was not causal.

Respondents' marriages were satisfying to them. Also, spousal appreciation improved significantly for women, plus the indirect implication that spouses who were contemplating divorce did not report that they had become divorced. Both sexes were able to meet career goals. Respondents did not find LDM to be disruptive to their marital relationships.

VIII. IMPLICATIONS

Responses from this sample bear implications for marriage and family therapists who might advise dual-career couples on the viability of LDM for career development. The findings imply that LDM in itself is not a threat to marital stability or satisfaction for most couples who become involved. In fact, this living arrangement may improve some aspects of the marriage, particularly for women, and make career development more equal for both spouses. Thus, LDM may be a stepping stone to greater career opportunities for both sexes as well as enabling women to

develop a greater sense of independence. It may also
lead to a deeper appreciation of the marital relationship for both spouses, but especially for women.
This is perhaps the case because the lifestyle enables
women to remove impediments to career development.

It also should be noted that the median length
of marriage was ten years and respondents' median
ages indicated they were middle-aged. Thus, it may
be that successful involvement is more likely for
mature couples with well established relationships
where mutual trust and open communication are more
likely to have been developed. Both Gerstel (1977)
and Gross (1980) reached this same conclusion.

BIBLIOGRAPHY

Duncan, R.P. &
Perruci, C.

1976   "Dual occupation families and migra-
               tion." American Sociological Review,
               41, pp. 252-261.
Ferris, A.

1978   "Commuting." In R. & R.N. Rapoport
               (Eds.), Working Couples. New York:
               Harper & Row, pp. 100-107.

Gerstel, N.

1977   "The feasibility of commuter marriage."
               In P. Stein, J. Richman & N. Hannon
               (eds.), The Family: Functions, Con-
               flicts, ,and Symbols. Reading,
               Massachusetts: Addison-Wesley, pp.
               357-367.

Gross, H.E.

1980   "Dual-career couples who live apart:
               Two Types." Journal of Marriage and
               the Family, 42, pp. 567-576.

Holmstrom, L.

1972   The Two-Career Family. Cambridge:
               Schenkman.

Kirschner, B.F. &
Walum, L.R.

1978   "Two-location families: Married
               singles." Alternative Lifestyles, 1,
               pp. 513-525.

Rapoport, R. &
Rapoport, R.N.

1971   Dual Career Families. Hammondsworths,
               England: Penguin Books.

345

*John Orton is Assistant Professor of Family Relations
in the Department of Home and Family Life, College
of Home Economics at The Florida State University,
Tallahassee, Florida 32306.

*Sharyn M. Crossman is an Assistant Professor of
Family and Human Development in the Department of
Family and Human Development, College of Family
Life at Utah State University, Logan, Utah 84322.

CHAPTER 19

OPEN VERSUS CORE MARRIAGE

Jerry Meints*

This paper explicates and explores the distinctions between open and core marriage. The
functions and dysfunctions of open marriage are
discussed, and the core-marriage model is offered
as an advancement on the open marriage model.
Findings from a 2-year content analysis of
"swinger type" advertisements are discussed.

The bisexual aspects of open and core marriage
are discussed. Research findings on homophobia
are reviewed. It is suggested that a higher propensity of "failure" exists among open marriages
than core marriages. In spite of this propensity,
open marriages have become more frequent, due to
American acceptance of the extra-marital-rela-
tionship model and the homophobia associated with
the core marriage model.

I. INTRODUCTION

Researchers in traditional and alternative family
patterns have long cited the problems inherent in the
traditional marriage model. The Roys (1975) wondered;
"is monogamy outdated?" David Cooper (1971) apocalyp-
tically predicted "the death of the family." Alvin
Toffler (1970), spoke of the "fractured family."

Meanwhile, other researchers have suggested
possible cures for the ills that infect the family.
Marcia Lasswell (1976) suggests "no-fault marriage"
as an alternative to the usual destructive trends
involved in crumbling relationships. Gordon Clanton
(1977) suggested more mature and humanistic means for
understanding and coping with jealousy. The Deloras
(1975) indicated the need to move from a "product-
oriented" to a "person-oriented" society. Orleans
and Wolfson (1975) predicted more variety and diversity in family systems and relationship models.
Butler (1978), the Constantines (1975), Morton Hunt
(1975), and others, have predicted similar trends
towards increased participation and experimentation
in alternatives to traditional monogamy.

The purpose of the present work is to examine more closely 2 specific alternative family patterns. This paper explicates and explores the distinctions between open and core marriage. The relative merits of each are discussed, and core marriage is suggested as an advancement on the open-marriage model. Basically, both models deviate from the traditional monogamous "closed" marriage. Both open and core marriage share a number of features which challenge the basic assumptions of traditional marriage.

Butler (1979) has delineated the basic cultural assumptions which underlie traditional marriage. Most alternative family patterns challenge, or call into question 1 or more of these beliefs: (1) romantic love is the basis for traditional marriage; (2) Sex "should" be confined to the marital relationship; (3) Persons "should" have only one mate of the opposite sex, for life; (4) Sex roles "should be rigidly differentiated; (5) Children are "best" raised within the nuclear family; and (6) The nuclear family is the best unit for economic consumption and social action.

In spite of these beliefs, and despite the fact that often the marriage and family literature treats both models as if they were inseparably similar, a sufficient amount of difference does exist to warrant systematic elaboration and analysis.

II. DEFINITIONS

Open Marriage was defined by the O'Neills (1973) as a "relationship in which the partners are committed to their own and to each other's growth." Open marriage, defined as "permissive monogamy" (Crosby, 1976), may be seen as an innovative attempt to reconcile the expanding desire for multilateral intimacy and the restricting need for security, predictability, and commitment.

Open marriage entails open communication, open companionship, and optional open sexuality. As Butler (1979) suggests, open marriage includes "undependent living, personal growth, individual freedom, flexible roles, mutual trust, and expansion through openness."

Open marriage has a number of normative features, some of which are portrayed in Figure 1-A. These features include: (1) a primary pair-bonded relationship

348

which emphasizes individuality as the cohesive impetus;
(2) secondary or "satellite" (Francoeurs, 1972) "Type
A" relationships outside the pair bond which encompass
primarily companionship; and (3) Type B secondary relationships which sanction sexual intimacy outside the
pair bond.

Both platonic and sexual relationship activities
usually occur outside the primary pair-bond residence
and independent of the primary mate. Secondary "Type
B" relationships are generally with members of the
opposite sex and are reported to involved only infrequent bisexual sharing with the primary mate (Knapp
and Whitehurst, 1977). Sexually open marriage most
generally involves proscribed heterosexual promiscuity.

Core Marriage has undergone a process of redefinition transformation that reflects the changes in
significant authors' personal lives. The transformation of Peter and Susan Heck, for example, has been
obscured and confused by recent publication dates of
antiquated material abstracted and quoted from earlier
publications.

The Hecks (1974, 1975, 1976, 1977) have been
credited with pioneering the model of core marriage.
Originally, the Hecks' core marriage tended to resemble
open marriage on a number of dimensions: (1) Sex outside the pair-bond was described as permissible and
"inevitable." (2) Mutual consent of the pair-bonded
couple regarding auxilliary or satellite relationships
was not required. (3) Secrecy concerning satellite
affairs was interpreted as permissible.

A videotaped interview with the Hecks (1975) by
Butler and Meints revealed the changing norm structure
of the core-marriage model. According to this most
recent interpolation (see Figure 1-B), core marriage
entails the folowing features: (1) A pair-bonded
couple who emphasize the primacy of their core relationship over and above any considerations of individual growth or satellite relationships. (2) Type "A"
internal secondary relationships, involving a platonic
companionship which is shared within the primary pair
bond. (3) Type "B" internal secondary relationships,
which include sexual intimacy and also are shared by
the core couple.

According to the core-marriage model, both types of satellite relationships must be shared and mutually sanctioned by the core couple. For example, if Carol is somehow bothered by Alice's intimacy with Bob, this satellite relationship would be abandoned for the sake of maintaining the prominence of the primary pair-bond.

III. FUNCTIONS AND DYSFUNCTIONS

Open Marriage: The positive and negative aspects of open marriage are highly variable, and depend on how each couple interprets and implements the model. The following aspects are merely general guidelines based on the literature and various research studies.

Functions: While making it very clear that open marriage is not for everyone, nor is it a panacea, the O'Neill's (1973) cite many potentially positive consequencies of a successful open marriage. These include: (1) emotional maturity; (2) confident self-identity; (3) the assuming of personal responsibility; (4) synergy (in which the combined energies of an open relationship produce more total energy than the sum of its constituent parts); (5) greater problem-solving and decision-making skills; (6) the development of supportive (vis-a-vis dependent) love and caring; (7) personal growth; (8) equality; and (9) more open communication and honesty.

Butler (1979) suggested several additional potentially positive consequences of open marriage: (1) transcendence of jealousy; (2) "undependent" living; and (3) role flexibility. Knapp and Whitehurst (1977) based their contribution to the list of potential benefits on a study of 104 respondents living in open relationships. These included: (1) excitement of new experiences; (2) increased vitality and enjoyment of sex with spouse; (3) the lessening of possessiveness; and (4) fewer feelings of isolation.

Dysfunctions: While open marriage has many positive features, several potential risks or drawbacks must be taken into account. In an article entitled "Why Open Marriage Doesn't Work," Robert Rimmer (1978) argued that sexually open marriages (Type B open relationships) do not work because: (1) "...they are sabotaged by the pressure of a million mundane problems and demands..." which multiply geometrically as the number of relationships increase; (2) such relationships create "insecurity" and "subtle rejection;" (3) they foster the "romantic illusion" that greater intimacy is possible with a relatively uninvolved stranger via a satellite relationship, than with one's longtime spouse. Rimmer believes the impetus behind the quest for sexually open marriages is the driving human need to be confirmed by another person (other than one's spouse) as a total human being.

Ramey (1978) listed several problems related to maintaining open marriage satellite relationships, or what he calls "intimate friendships." These include: (1) scheduling problems (coordinating spouses, satellite relationships, babysitters, private rendezvous, etc.); (2) becoming involved in a satellite relationship with someone who wants the affair to become a primary relationship, a situation which threatens the primary pair bond; and (3) becoming involved with someone who is in a closed relationship.

Butler (1979) cited an economic problem: job loss resulting from societal reaction to the public discussion of an open or core marriage lifestyle. Finally, by interpreting "intimacy" as a zero sum phenomenon, Greenwald (1975) argues that an open relationship threatens an "intimacy of two."

Core Marriage: Given the similarities of open and core marriage, many of the functions and dysfunctions associated with open marriage also apply to core marriage. In this section, I explicate the consequencies which distinguish core from the open marriage model.

Functions: A major dimension differentiating open and core marriage is growth emphasis. Growth emphasis may be plotted along a continuum ranging from personal (individual) growth to couple growth. While theoretically, open marriage as espoused by the O'Neill's (1973) implies an emphasis on both individual and couple growth, divorce rates suggest a greater degree of emphasis, is placed on individual growth (Meints, 1977).

In contrast, the core marriage model emphasizes primarily the growth and maintenance of the couple. Core marriage avoids several drawbacks usually associated with open marriage: (1) fewer mundane scheduling problems are encountered, given the core-

351

marriage emphasis on "sharing" extramarital rendezvous vis-a-vis separate affair management; (2) sharing limits the degree of "insecurity" and "subtle rejection;" (3) sharing also minimizes the "romantic illusion" of instant intimacy usually associated with independent outside satellite relationships; (4) sharing further lessens the threat that the satellite partner may have primary-relationship designs on one or the other partners in the core relationship; and (5) since both partners relate socially, and in some cases, sexually to the newly-included satellite partner or partners, a personal veto may be exercised by either core partner simply for the sake of maintaining the integrity of the core relationship. This built-in dual evaluation and veto option can greatly minimize the threat of jealousy.

Dysfunctions: Like open marriage, core marriage may suffer from problems relating to involvement with persons who are in closed relationships. Additionally, job loss may result from the stigma of public labeling associated with this alternative lifestyle.

Open marriage is generally considered to merely license heterosexual extramarital affairs, although Knapp's study (1976) has shown that sexually open marriages sometimes involve a bisexual sharing of a satellite partner. Core marriage, in contrast, generally entails either: (1) bringing another couple into the pair bond for either swinging or group sex behavior; or (2) bringing a single person into the pair bond for a shared bi-sexual experience.

The Hecks (1975) reported that such bi-sexual sharing often entails group sex, yet is primarily among two women and one man. It is interesting to note, however, that group sex patterns did not reflect this prdominantly female bi-sexual trend. Basically, as Butler (1979) suggested, bisexual behavior is more predominant and acceptable among women than among men. This sexist male homophobic double standard, the fear of the potential male bisexual emphasis of the core marriage model, is probably the most salient dysfunction of the core marriage model.

Homophobia: George Weinberg (1973) has defined homophobia as the "irrational fear of homosexuality." He considered homophobia to be more acute among Americans and more predominant among men than women.

Experimental research by Morin, Taylor, and Kielman (1975) demonstrated that men create significantly more social distance between themselves and "known homosexuals" than do women. Levitt and Klassen (1974) found negative attitudes toward homosexuality more prevalent among rural white men. Weinberg attributed homophobia to: (1) a general fear of deviance; (2) religious prejudice; (3) the secret fear of actually being homosexual; and (4) a reaction to the fear of being incorrectly labeled homosexual.

Homophobia, of course, perpetuates macho stories about (among others) "rolling queers" and "faggots who pick up and make advances towards unsuspecting hitchikers." Homophobia also precludes serious, intelligent discussion or questioning, since the discussant himself might be "suspect." Thus, homosexuality is relegated to perennial ignorance.

Research by McConaghy (1967) offered physiologic correlates which substantiate the homophobic response among men. McConaghy found the lumescent response of heterosexual men, to pictures of nude men, significantly less than that of the homosexual control group. Heterosexual men's penises actually shrank, due to "fear." Other primate research and studies on penile structure have supported the idea that the penis is a fairly reliable "fear meter" (Pengally, 1978).

Sherrill (1977), in surveying attitudes toward homosexuality, found that those who viewed homosexuality as "always wrong" showed a broad base of intolerance and reflected the following attitudes: (1) deep racism and sexism; (2) abhorrence of all non-conformity (particularly atheism and socialism); (3) rejection of all manifestations of the "sexual revolution" (e.g., feminism, abortion, etc.); and (4) incessant patriotism.

Many journalistic and impressionistic discussions of bisexuality predict its increasing appeal among Americans. Alex Comfort (1975) has predicted that within the next decade, bi-sexuality will become a normative sexual-lifestyle preference. Duberman (1977) asserted that bi-sexuality is definitely on the rise. Libby (1977), however, suggested that actual research on bi-sexuality is inconclusive and few, if any, conclusions may be drawn.

353

We may conclude, however, with respect to core marriage, that bisexuality elicits a homophobic response in many men unless it pertains to a one male-two female configuration. Some women report this to be unfair and sexist.

This dual standard is, however, reinforced in the male erotic media by their frequent presentation of glossy centerfolds depicting two or more women relating sexually. The connotation is, however, bi- rather than homosexual.

Men find such depiction erotic since they may vicariously project themselves into the role of either participant without leaving the fantasy realm of male heterosexuality. Consequently, such "glossies" have rarely shown 2 men and 1 woman interacting sexually.

Not all couples living in core marriages are homophobic. Many report bisexual sharing experiences to be an acceptable advancement over non-shared independent satellite relationships.

Freud was profoundly convinced that we are born into this world as bisexuals, our heterosexual or homosexual orientation being conditioned later by socio-psychologic variables (Whitten, 1974).

When a small sample of bisexuals were interviewed and videotaped by Meints and Butler, bisexuality was misunderstood along a number of dimensions: (1) Gays incorrectly viewed bisexuality as a "closet cop-out." Libby's (1977) literature review supports the widespread nature of this misconception. (2) Straights also dismissed bisexuals as being homosexuals. (3) An emerging "bisexual community" does indeed exist (see Blumstein and Schwartz, 1974).

The respondents in my sample reported the belief that bisexuality was the most "natural form" of sexual expression; and by its making available only 2 rigid, diametrically opposed sexual-preference categories, society is, in effect, asking them to perform "unnatural acts."

X-Rated Want Ads: A 2-year content analysis of X-rated want ads in the Los Angeles Free Press has generated some interesting conclusions pertaining to

354

the bisexual aspects of core marriage. A total of 3,354 separate ads were analyzed. Ads range in content from the simple "straight swinging couple seeks same" to the bizarre "dominant female with foot fetish, seeks couple. He: passive, into panties. She: dominant, into leather and chains."

Of those ads which pertained to sexually open relationships (i.e., where either couples seek other couples, couples seek singles, or singles seek couples) 58% were considered to be bisexually oriented. Only 42% were considered straight (heterosexual couple seeks same). Based on this somewhat surprising preponderance of bisexual activity among sexual libertarians, we might conclude that for the majority, homophobia does not significantly impede adoption of the core marriage model.

Figure 1-C explicates some sexual-preference options available to couples involved in core marriages. The type of sexual option is determined by the existence and intensity of homophobia among the members of the primary pair bond.

IV. CONCLUSION

Further, more systematic research is needed to substantiate the tentative conclusions suggested in this article. In general, viable alternatives are emerging which, rather than replacing traditional marriage, are attempts to modify its normative structure.

As has been suggested, open marriage is a much more well known alternative mode, and fits the long-term American acceptance of extramarital relationships. Open marriage, however, due to its very "openness" and subsequent lack of sharing within the pair bond, seems likely to perpetuate the trend toward serial monogamy and divorce.

Core marriage, while somewhat complicated by homophobia, seems to promise the continued and increased potential for survival of the core relationship. Core marriage seems to be an advance on the open marriage model in that it basically results in fewer dysfunctions for the couple.

Finally, data suggest that homophobia is much less prevalent among sexual libertarians than it is estimated to be among the general population.

FIGURE 1-A: Open Marriage Model of Relational Structures

FIGURE 1-B: Core Marriage Model of Relational Structures

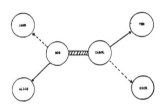

FIGURE 1-C: The Core Marriage Model of Sexual Preference.

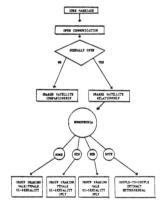

BIBLIOGRAPHY

Butler, E.W.

1979   Traditional Marriage and Emerging
               Alternatives. New York: Harper and
               Row.

Clanton, G., &
Smith, L.G.

1977   "The Self-Inflicted Pain of Jealousy."
               Psychology Today 10, (March).

Constantine, L., &
Constantine, J.

1975   "Where is Marriage Going?" In Delora &
               Delora (eds.) Intimate Life Styles.
               Pacific Palisades, California: Good-
               year Publishing Company (Paperback).

Cooper, D.

1971   The Death of the Family. New York:
               Vintage Books.

Crosby, J.F.

1976   Illusion and Disillusion: The Self in
               Love and Marriage. Belmont, California:
               Wadsworth Publishing Company, Inc.
               (Paperback).

Delora, J.R. &
Delora, J.S.
(editors)

1975   Intimate Life Styles. Pacific
               Palisades, California: Goodyear
               Publishing Company (Paperback).

Duberman, L.

1974   Marriage and Its Alternatives. New
               York: Praeger Publishers, Inc.
               (Paperback).

Francoeur, R.T. &
Francoeur, A.K.

1973   Hot and Cool Sex: Fidelity in Marriage.
              In Marriage and Alternatives (Libby &
              Whitehurst, eds.) Palo Alto, California:
              Scott, Foresman and Company.

Greenwald, J.

1977   Creative Intimacy. New York: Pyramid
              Books (Paperback).

Heck, P., &
Heck, S.

1975   Open and Core Marriage. Video Documen-
              tary by Meints and Butler, University
              of California, Riverside.

Heck, P., &
Heck, S.

1976   "Core Marriage Part I: A New Kind of
              Relationship." Emerge, pp. 7-9, 30.
              Reprinted from a 1974 edition of Swing.
              Heck and Heck (eds.).

Hunt, P., &
Heck S.

1975   "The Future of Marriage." In Intimate
              Life Styles, Delora & Delora (eds.).
              Pacific Palisades, California: Good-
              year Publishing Company.

Knapp, J.J.

1976   "An Exploratory Study of Seventeen
              Sexually Open Marriage." Sex Res. 12
              (3):206-219 (August).

Lasswell, M.E., &
Lasswell, T.E.

1973   Love, Marriage, Family: A Develop-
              mental Approach. Glenview, Ill.:
              Scott, Foresman Company (Paperback).

Levitt, E., &
Klassen, A.

   1974   "Public Attitudes Towards Homosexuality:
                 Part of the 1970 National Survey by the
                 Institute for Sex Research." Journal of
                 Homosexuality, 1(1), pp. 29-43.

Libby, R.W., &
Whitehurst, R.N.

   1977   Marriage and Alternatives: Exploring
                 Intimate Relationships. Glenview, Ill:
                 Scott, Foresman and Company (Paperback).

McConaghy, N.

   1967   "Penile Volume Change to Moving Pictures
                 of Male and Female Nudes in Hetero-
                 sexual and Homosexual Males." Behavior
                 Research and Therapy, 5, pp. 43-48.

Meints, J.

   1977   Unpublished interview with respondents
                 living in core marriages.

Morin. S.F., Taylor, K., &
Kielman, S.

   1975   "Gay is Beautiful at A Distance." Pre-
                 sented at the 83rd Annual Meeting of
                 the American Psychological Association,
                 Chicago.

O'Neill, N., &
O'Neill, G.

   1975   Shifting Gears. New York: Avon Books
                 (Paperback).

Orleans, M., &
Wolfson, F.

   1975   "Future of the Family." In Intimate
                 Life Styles, Delora & Delora (eds.).
                 Pacific Palisades, California: Good-
                 year Publishing Company.

Pengally, E.

1978   Sex and the Human Life, ed. 2.
                 Redding, Mass.: Addi on Wessley.

Ramey, J.

1978   "Are You Ready to Open Your Marriage?"
                 Forum.

Rimmer, R.

1978   "Why Open Marriage Doesn't Work."
                 Forum (February).

Roy, R., & Roy D.

1970   "Is Monogamy Outdated?" The Humanist,
                 March/April.

Sherrill, K. &
Duberman, M.

1977   Quoted in "The Anita Bryant Brigade."
                 Skeptic (November/December).

Toffler, A.

1970   Future Shock. New York: Random House.

Weinburg, G.

1973   Society and the Healthy Homosexual.
                 Garden City, New York: Anchor Press
                 (Paperback).

Reprinted from the Society for the Study of Alternative
Lifestyles, Vol. 1, No. 1, October 1979 Newsletter.

CHAPTER 20

NOTES ON NONTEMPORARY SINGLES

Edgar W. Butler*
and
Jerry Meints*

I.   INTRODUCTION

America is primarily a marriage oriented culture.
Hence nontemporary singles are often perceived as
deviants.   Even Ben Franklin referred to single men
as "the oldd half of a pair of scissors."   Yet in 1975
there were 47 million people in America classified as
single.   This included people who were not married,
or were separated, divorced and widowed.   Approximately 20 million of these single people were males and
27 million females.   This large amorphous aggregate
may be divided into two categories: those who are
nontemporary singles and those temporarily single who
plan to marry or remarry.

II.   AMERICAN MARRIAGE

Historically, the American fascination with
marriage is relatively unique.   In both medieval
society and during the middle ages marriage was the
exception rather than the rule, reserved for only
those few with sufficient economic security.   Even
today European patterns reflect less of an emphasis
upon marriage: i.e., late marriages predominate and
no marriages occur at all for many.   For example, in
France 28% of the women remain unmarried (Melville,
1977).

In spite of the relative arbitrariness of "Marriage" as a cultural value, singles continue to experience social pressure and differential treatment, in
work, credit, tax, and housing, etc.   Parents continue
to be the major source of pressure towards marriage.

III.   THE RISE OF SINGLES

Several social factors account for the increasing proportion of singles.   First is divorce; a national divorce rate which often reaches 50% adds significant numbers to the population of single people.

363

Second, the United States Census Bureau reported a trend toward later marriages, when compared to figures a decade ago. For men the mean age increased from 22.8 to 23.3, for women from 20 to 21.

Third, deals with changes in values. Tom Wolf characterizes the 1970's as the "I, me, me, my decade," where an emphasis on personal growth and novel experience has overshadowed the earlier emphasis on marriage, family, and community stability.

Fourth, we seem to expect much more from marriage today, perhaps too much, for everyone to deliver. We expect a healthy partner, fulfillment, and personal growth (Melville, 1977). Unfulfilled expectations often lead to a search for another, more satisfying relationship.

IV. ADVANTAGES AND DISADVANTAGES

One of the worst and most common problems of being single is feeling that it is a "problem." Many singles are treated as if they are in trouble or are unwanted by other people or cannot pair off with another person in a satisfactory manner. Although in the future singles may have equal status with married couples, this is probably an optimistic view since there is little demonstration of such equality in contemporary America. Nevertheless, there are some indications that single people, like other minorities, are pushing for rights and societal attitudes that make it unnecessary for them to have to be alone or be considered abnormal; to make people consciously aware of their strengths, weaknesses, and so on.

Many laws discriminate against single people, especially in regard to taxes, rent, promotions, child adoption, and so forth. Most media, advertisements, and family courses in colleges and universities stress the nuclear family and "couple front." Thus, there is a constant reminder to the single person that marriage is the primary socially acceptable status in our society. Some single people find they are rejected by married people because they are seen as a threat to marriage.

While singles report that they can become extremely lonely at times, that one must be a self-starter, take the initiative, and get involved with other people or otherwise become a social isolate, there are some substantial advantages to being single. Singles are able to shift for themselves; no one can force singles to do things, go places, and so on, and they can establish their own priorities. They can live where they want, consult with whom they please, travel, try out different life styles, and make decisions without consultation, coercion, or consensus (Seal, 1974:18). Generally, they report that being single makes the self stronger.

Bird (1975) argues that women should stay single on the basis of data suggesting that while the health of married people is generally better than that of single people, the difference is nowhere near as great for women as for men. She believes that single women are better off than married women insofar as health is concerned. Contrary to popular belief, single women aren't as nervous as they are made out to be, and they report fewer mental disorder symptoms than married women do. Data from a variety of mental disorder surveys show that marriage is harder on women's nerves than on men's and that housewives report more psychological symptoms than wives who have jobs. While both single and married women can be unhappy, marriage makes a bigger difference for men than for women.

Generally, single women are more stable, less anxious, and happier than married women. Also, happiness in marriage is experienced more by men than by women. For women to control their own economic resources, they have to remain single (Bird, 1975). For example, while 49 percent of the shareholders listed on the New York Stock Exchange are females, they own less than 20 percent of the shares. Many women are unable to make decisions on buying and selling their holdings, let alone make decisions affecting corporation policies. Also, while marriage was once regarded as insurance against loneliness, this is no longer true.

V. SWINGING SINGLES

There is a popular image of the "swinging" life style of singles, their clubs, bars, and so on. Many cities appear to have an abundance of single bars and apartment houses for coed singles. Ads for singles' weekends and excursions appear in the travel sections of newspapers in large cities. Starr and Carns (1972)

ask whether this is an unprecedented institutionalization of this new life style in cities and whether the
swinging singles' life style is a reality. They suggest that relatively little is known about singles in
the city.

Most singles prefer not to live in singles' complexes that "fabricates and formalizes the meeting
and dating process." In contrast to many reports
about swinging singles, singles cherish their houses
or apartments as a haven of privacy in a large city
environment. They typically prefer privacy and solitude. Only very rarely do meaningful encounters
develop between a single person and others in their
apartment house or neighborhood. Few relationships
evidently evolve from casual neighborhood meetings
and those that do "are reviewed as eventful because
they are so atypical." This is an interesting contrast to the "proximity" factor in mate selection.

Starr and Carns (1972) categorized single females
as follows: (1) those who aspire to develop work
roles into careers; (2) those who view work only as
an "experience" - not as an end in itself or a lifetime career, but merely as a temporary status until
they get married and becomes wives and mothers; (3)
single working girls who do not like either being
single or working and would prefer to be wives and
mothers. Males were categorized as being: (1) those
who are conventional and career oriented, who strive
for success in the corporate world, and who subscribe
to the traditional definition of success as prestige
and financial gain; (2) those who consciously reject
traditional work options and values and who are working in temporary jobs that provide for the minimal
necessities; (3) those straddling both work worlds
but belonging to neither, who typically crave material
success but lack talent, skill, or motivation and are
probably going to become frustrated at not finding a
job that will satisfy their material cravings.

Most single visit singles bars only one or two
nights a week, if that often (Starr and Carns, 1972).
These bars are generally noisy, and sitting is discouraged by the arrangement of narrow counters and
lack of seats; interaction tends to be primarily non-
verbal. Attendance appears to vary inversely with
the amount of time a person has lived in the city.
The longer they live there, the less likely they are

to visit singles bars. Males typically use swinging singles bars for a longer period of time than females. Males use singles bars as a hunting ground for sex partners whereas females are using the bars as a scene for husband hunting, with a very low chance of success.

For most singles in the city, social organizations are not significant sources for dating partners. Also, interestingly, singles report that parties are seldom a useful setting for meeting dates, and many "singles only parties" advertised in the newspapers end up being old folks' meetings. Most young singles avoid them like the plague. Since virtually all possible ways to meet dates are eliminated, there is only one major alternative in life--work. "Work was the most frequently cited institutional setting for making friends and meeting persons of the opposite sex." This is quite a problem, of course, if the single works in a company where coworkers are older and most of them are married and, thus, the single person once more is precluded from establishing close friendships and perhaps meeting dating partners. This is one of the primary reasons that stewardesses, as an example, patronize singles bars. Most singles do not like to date people that work within their own office milieu but tend to have dates arranged through office friends and utilize a "friend-of-a-friend" pattern.

A predominant theme emerges from singles research. The popular image of swinging singles is patently false. Most singles do not lead lives of wild, sensual abandonment. Generally, they are people coping with the same problems that everyone else faces, which include finding a place to live, searching for job satisfaction, and seeking friends, dates, and ultimately mates. The climate and the environment in which singles are attempting to do all of this is not a conducive one. Most singles are ill-prepared for establishing stable human relationships (Starr and Carns, 1972)

VI.   PREPARING FOR STABLE RELATIONSHIPS

Although not all singles are interested in committed relationships, statistics suggest that most singles are temporarily in that role and moving towards relationships. Singles often find themselves lacking important interpersonal skills necessary for the building of stable relationships.

The most important skill singles need is in "making contact," i.e., where to go and what to do. Meints (1979) reporting from his experience with singles' workshops suggests that singles avoid the standard disco, bars, night clubs, etc., but visit places not having the "making it" expectation structure built into them. For example, he suggests going shopping, to college, concerts, skiing, sports events, favorite restaurants, traveling, etc.

Secondly, singles often preclude making contact by the assumptions they implicitly hold. Beliefs like "I'm not attractive enough;" "I'm a loser;" "I'm transparent, everyone can see right through me;" "People will think I am, or am only interested in, a sex object;" or "I am the only person who is self conscious." Such assumptions often prevent single persons from risking the opportunity for making contact and expressing themselves.

Next is the problem of intimate communication. Often communication is sabbotaged by contradictions between words and body language which may result in double messages. Getting the body in sinc with words help clear the path for intimate stable commitment.

Fourth, is the issue of sexual fulfillment. Often singles, in spite of popular stereotypes to the contrary, are not skilled in sexual awareness. Basic issues of sexual functioning, body awareness, sensitivity training, erogeneous techniques, sexual centering, etc., are helpful in promoting successful relationships.

Finally, it is helpful when singles see themselves as a "process of becoming" rather than a fixed character type. A focus upon Maslow's model of self actualization helps people to recognize a hierarchy of needs which progress (when met) towards fulfilling one's own unique potential.

BIBLIOGRAPHY

Bird, Caroline

    1975   "Women Should Stay Single," in J. Gipson Wells (ed.), Current Issues on Marriage and the Family, New York: Macmillan, pp. 32-40.

Maslow, Ebraham

                     "Some Basic Propositions of a Growth and Self-Actualization Psychology," in Ard (ed.) Counseling and Psychotherapy. Palo Alto: Science and Behavior Books.

Meints, Jerry

    1979   "Sex, Singles, and the Relationship Addict." Presented at the 1979 annual Society for the Study of Lifestyles, Culver City, California.

Melville, Keith

    1977   "Marriage and Family Today." New York: Random House.

Seal, Herb

    1974   Alternative Life Styles. Singapore: FEP International.

Starr, Joyce R. &
Donald E. Carns

    1972   "Singles in the City." Society, 4 (February):43-48.

Wolf, Tom

    1975   "The '70's." New York, July.

*Edgar W. Butler, University of California, Riverside, Jerry Meints, Chapman College, Orange, California.

CHAPTER 21

THE ONE-CHILD FAMILY: A NEW LIFE-STYLE

Sharryl Hawke
and
David Knox*

Only children and their parents are victims
of stereotyping and criticism. As a result,
potential parents and parents of one child
have questioned whether having a single child
is a desirable alternative. The authors
examine positive and negative consequences
of the one-child family for the child and
his/her parents.

"How many children do we want?" is a question
most married couples ask. Current concerns about inflation, population, and the wife's career are causing
young couples to reevaluate commonly held beliefs
about which family size is best (Peck, 1971; Whelan,
1976). While most couples decide to have two children,
a small but growing number remain childfree. About
10% choose the third alternative--to have one child
(General Social Science Survey, Note 1; Redding,
1974).

When most couples are asked why they don't consider having an only child, they often reply that
only children are spoiled and lonely and that it takes
at least two children to make a real family. One
parent of two children declared, "Being an only child
is almost like having a disease--it's not fair to the
child and his/her parents."

Are these beliefs justified? Does the one-child
family have negative consequences for children and
parents? As parents who have one child, we sought
answers to these questions. We surveyed 102 parents
of only children (54 were interviewed; 48 completed a
questionnaire) and 105 only children (53 were interviewed; 52 completed a questionnaire). These data and
the available literature (mostly dated) revealed a
stark contrast to what is commonly believed about only
children and their parents (Hawke & Knox, 1977).

Advantages of the One-Child Family

The life-style of the one-child family is significantly different from that of the multi-child family. But most members of one-child families regard the differences in positive terms. The benefits occur for the child, his/her parents, and the family as a unit.

Advantages for the Child

Ninety-eight percent of the only children surveyed believed that being an only child has its advantages. "I was never compared to a brother or sister," "My life was more private than if I had siblings--I had my own room," and "I got most of the things I wanted like band instruments and my folks took me with them to Europe" were frequent comments made by only children.

But in addition to avoiding sibling rivalry, having more privacy, and enjoying greater affluence, what kind of person is the only child? Several studies have compared the intelligence, school performance, and self-confidence of only children with children who have siblings. In an IQ study involving over seventy thousand children, only children were found to have the highest IQ of any group measured (Thompson, 1950). Regarding language development, only children have larger vocabularies and better verbal skills than children with siblings (Davis, 1937). "Only children use bigger words," recalled an adult only, "because they spend more time around adults."

These early intellectual abilities help throughout the school years. The grades of only children are as good or better than students who have brothers and sisters (Lee & Stewart, 1957). And, more only children who go to college have performance records equal to or superior to children with siblings (Bayer, 1966).

In addition to being bright children and successful students, only children are generally self-confident and resourceful. They are not the "shrinking violets" so often assumed. In general, from preschool through adulthood only children display more self-reliance and self-confidence than their peers with siblings (Guilford & Worchester, 1930; Dyer, 1949; Rosenberg, 1965). "My only will never need a book on assertion," expressed one parent.

And although only children are often thought of as friendless, one researcher found that they are consistently the most popular group among elementary students (Bonney, 1944). "Because I didn't have readymade companions at home," remarked one adult only, "I had to seek out friends. I learned to enjoy meeting new people and to work hard at maintaining friendships."

Although less is known about only children as adults, in general, they are as likely to have successful careers, happy marriages, and good parenting experiences as people who grow up with brothers and sisters (Cutts & Moseley, 1954).

All in all, being an only child seems to provide the climate and experiences which produce successful, self-confident human beings. "I've never considered being an only child a handicap," remarked a young mother. "Only non-onlies think it's a disadvantage." However, it should be kept in mind that in many of the studies on only children, social class is uncontrolled and because a disproportionate number of only children are found in middle and upper class families, their positive attributes are not surprising. Whether or not these positive attributes are characteristic of lower class only children is an issue for subsequent research.

Advantages of Parents

Parents of only children are quick to point out the advantages of the one-child family for themselves. "Being the parent of one child is having the best of two worlds" in the view of one parent. "I can experience the joys and frustrations of being a parent without getting so tied down by parenting responsibilities that I haven't time to pursue my own interests."

In naming more specific advantages of the one-child family for themselves, parents in our survey most often spoke of time. "Kids take a lot of time--but one kid takes far less than two," reflected the mothers of a four-year-old. To further evaluate the time issue, we asked 245 mothers of two children about the differences between having one and two children. Over 60% said that they had less time to themselves since their second child was born. And, only 5% agreed that "two are as easy as one."

Having one child is also related to increased personal and marital happiness when compared to having several. Rossi (1972) concluded that adjustment becomes more difficult with each additional child. And reported marital satisfaction drops with each subsequent child (Feldman, 1971; Knox & Wilson, 1978). "By having an only child you've got some time left for yourself and your spouse," remarked one parent.

In general, the parents in our study were very different from the over-anxious, unfulfilled image so often painted of single-child parents. One-half of the mothers worked outside the home, and often expressed a belief that having one child and working were compatible. One of the mothers said, "Having one child meets my maternal need without 'over-satisfying' it and I've got the time to pursue a meaningful career." Fathers suggested that having one child put less financial pressure on them. "My closest friend is putting three daughters through college and it's about to kill him," expressed the father of an only child. "The advantages to parents to stop with one are obvious," continued this father. "The only hurdle is getting over the fear that something awful will happen to your child if you don't provide a brother or sister."

Advantages for the Family Unit

"The one-child family is a small deck which makes it hard to get lost in the shuffle," observed a teenage only. Since family members continually look to each other for acceptance, fulfillment, and counsel, what kind of family-style is produced by the intense one-child family?

The most noticeable characteristic is the close times among family members. Only children--young and old--believe they have a closer relationship with their parents than people with siblings have with their parents. Parents express the same belief. In a recent study of college students, 40% of the only children reported that their parents were the strongest influence in "making me the person I am today." But only 3% of those students having siblings gave this reply (Falbo, 1976).

In addition to closeness, decision making in a one-child family tends to be more democratic than that in a multi-child family. "When there are several kids, parents often feel they must make the family decisions so that the children will be treated fairly," remarked the parent of one. "In our family we don't have to worry about playing favorites, so we let Marshall participate almost equally in making family decisions." The lines of authority are less clearly drawn in the one-child family and parents seem to relax more in their role (Bossard & Boll, 1956).

Another important one-child family advantage is affluence--spending power. The three-person family simply has more money to spend than larger families at the same income level. While money does not buy happiness, it does provide recognized benefits. "Having more money" was an advantage often referred to by both children and parents when describing the one-child family.

"Since children are small and don't eat much," expressed one parent, "it's easy to believe that raising two children isn't much more costly than raising one." The U.S. Commission on Population Growth and the American Future disagrees. A second child cost almost as much as the first. The only savings are in reference to hand-me-down clothes and toys--a small part of the total childrearing expense. In 1972, rearing one child through age eighteen cost about $53,000, while rearing two cost at least $100,000 (Population and the American Future, 1972, p. 81). The words "we can't afford it" are spoken less often in the one-child than in the multi-child family.

The image presented by one-child parents of a close, democratic, affluent family-style is considerably different from the long-admired American portrait of the "Walton" family-style with its tangle of relationships and clear lines of authority. One mother in a one-child family observed that the end results are different. "Parents with several children often seem to view parenting as an all-consuming job. For my husband, daughter, and me, life is more like a three-way adventure."

Disadvantages of the One-Child Family

"The one-child family is just like everything else--the bad comes along with the good," remarked

the father of an adult daughter. Most parents and
their only children agree. Let's examine the negative
consequences.

Disadvantages for the Child

From the only child's point of view, the major
disadvantage in being a single child is "not getting
to experience a brother or sister relationship."
Only children speak of missing "a confidant," "someone
to help me face the world," "someone to help care for
aging parents," or "someone to 'fight' with." In such
statements only children are obviously considering
only the good side of sibling relationships and are
not acknowledging the possibility that a sibling relationship might be apathetic, competitive, or even
hostile. "Some of my closest friends have siblings,"
observed an adult only, "and they have little in
common with them and never see them. Having a brother
or sister does not guarantee a companion."

In addition to wanting a companion, only children
also feel extra pressure on them to succeed. "I'm
glad my parents are interested in what I do," said
one twelve-year-old, "but I often wish they had
another kid to think about so they would get off my
back once in a while. I think about my folks as
Mama and Papa Bird--each perched on one of my
shoulders." But the disadvantage of undivided attention lies not in the attention itself but in the concentrated "dose" received by the only child.

A third disadvantage only children express is
a feeling that they have no help in caring for their
aging parents. "I know that brothers and sisters
seldom contribute equally to the care of their
parents," said one daughter of invalid parents, "but
I'd give anything to share a little of this load."

Disadvantages for the Parents

One-child parents also recognize disadvantages.
"The most difficult concern for me is the thought of
my child dying. I can't face being left childless,"
acknowledged one mother. Another parent believes the
biggest drawback is having only one chance to "make
good" as a parent. "If you have two kids and the
first bombs out, you can always hope the second will
redeem the family name," suggests this parent. A

third parent adds, "Constant criticism that you are selfish is a disadvantage. You've got to have thick skin or the criticism of your family size will get to you."

But the disadvantage most plaguing to parents of only children is the tightrope they must walk between healthy attention and overindulgence. As suggested earlier, most parents believe it an advantage to have more time, money, and energy for their child, but those resources must be provided in a manner which enriches rather than indulges. "I firmly believe it's not how much you give your child, but how you give it," said one mother. "The problem is knowng when your giving helps and when it hurts."

Disadvantages for the Family Unit

Just as there are disadvantages to the only child and his/her parents, there are disadvantages for the family unit. While most one-child family members enjoy an unusually close parent/child relationship, the three-person group can result in a two-against-one situation. In some instances, one parent and the child align against the other parent. In other instances, at least from the child's perspective, the deck is always stacked two parents against one child.

Finally, there are families in which having only one child leaves members unfulfilled—one child is simply not enough. The risk seems especially high for the mother who has no outside interests; one child is not sufficient to meet her emotional or mothering needs. Similarly, a father strongly wishing for a son may not find contentment in a single daughter. And a child unable to fulfill companionship needs outside the family may feel "wronged" by not having a sibling.

The disadvantages for the only child, his/her parents, and the family unit can result in regret, disappointment, and even guilt about a decision to have one child. A family fearing these outcomes stands little chance of having a healthy, happy experience.

Can the Disadvantages be Overcome?

How important are the disadvantages of the one-

child family? Should they prevent a couple from having an only child? "No" was the answer given by 62%
of the one-child parents we surveyed. "Certainly
there are disadvantages," says one mother, "But I
know of no family size that doesn't have its problems.
The trick is to resolve them."

And the parents of only children have some
solutions. For example, to overcome an only child's
discontent about not having a sibling, parents suggest
that the child be encouraged to place more value on
friendships. One adult remarked about her experience,
"I don't know what having a sister would be like, but
I can't imagine having a blood sister more than I do
the woman who has been my dear friend for fifteen
years."

To combat the problem of excessive attention and
indulgence, two remedies were suggested. One was for
parents to observe other children their child's age
to develop a realistic basis for judging their son's
or daughter's behavior and progress. It was also
suggested that parents develop personal interests to
avoid expecting their child to fulfill their own
achievement needs.

The question of an only child's death is difficult, but parents believe it must be put into perspective. The death of any child is tragic, but
another child can never replace the dead child. "To
believe that one child can substitute for another is
not to value individual life very highly," believes
one mother. Similarly, concerns about being criticized and having only "one shot at parenting" need
perspective. "Once you stop thinking of parenting
as a competitive sport, these worries subside,"
according to a young father.

All parents and children need to be realistic
about and plan for the parents' advancing years.
For the one-child family it is crucial. Planning
that is done before a crisis arises spares both child
and parent undue anguish. "We have been saving for
over twenty years so that our child wil not be financially burdened with us," shared one parent. "And
we've already decided that we will use the money to
go into a nursing home if necessary before we will
intrude in our only's marriage.

378

As for the possible two-against-one situation, many parents believe just recognizing the potential problem helps. "If you're aware the problem can exist and take steps to prevent it, there is no reason for it to torment the family," expressed one father. "When I saw my daughter and wife began to pair off, I knew that I had to improve my relationship with each of them. That meant not going back to the office at night and listening to rock music with my daughter. It's now the three of us rather than 'them and me.'"

In general, one-child parents suggest that disadvantages of the one-child family can be overcome by positive attitudes and actions. One couple said, "If you believe the one-child family is healthy and stimulating, you will make it so. If you are guilty or doubtful about your decision to have one child, chances are you will let an unhealthy situation develop." Happy relationships depend on how people deal with each other--not on how many people there are.

Conclusion

A reconsideration of the one-child family alternative may result in fewer babies being born for the wrong reasons. One study shows that many parents have a second child not because they really want it but because they believe they "must have a second to save the first" (Solomon, Clare & Westoff, 1956). Other couples have a second child to satisfy grandparents' wishes, to try for a child of the opposite sex, or to conform to the two-child family model so attractively portrayed by media.

Increasingly, family life specialists are noting that our world can no longer afford children who are born for these reasons: The only legitimate reason for having a second--or a first--child today is wanting that child for himself/herself.

REFERENCE NOTE

1. General Social Science Survey, July 1975. Conducted by the National Opinion Research Center, Chicago.

B I B L I O G R A P H Y

Bayer, A.E.

    1966   "Birth order and college attendance." *Journal of Marriage and the Family*, 23, 484.

Bonney, M.E.

    1944   "Relationships betwen social success, family size, socio-economic home background, and intelligence among school children in grades 3 to 5." *Sociometry*, 7, 26-39.

Bossard, J.H.S., & Boll, E.S.

    1956   *The large family system: An original study in the sociology of family behavior*. Philadelphia: University of Pennsylvania Press.

Cutts, N.E., & Moseley, N.

    1954   *The only child*. New York: Putnam.

Davis, E.

    1937   "The mental and linguistic superiority of only girls." *Child Development*, 8, 139-143.

Dyer, D.T.

    1949   "Are only children different?" *Journal of Educational Psychology*, 36, 297-302.

Falbo, T.

    1976   "Does the only child grow up miserable?"
                  Psychology Today, 9, 65.

Feldman, H.

    1971   "The effects of children on the family."
                  In Michel (Ed.), Family issues of em-
                  ployed women in Europe and America.
                  Lieden, The Netherlands: Brill.

Guilford, R.B., &
Worchester, D.A.

    1930   "A comparative study of the only and
                  non-only child." Journal of Genetic
                  Psychology, 38, 411-426.

Hawke, S., &
Knox, D.

    1977   One child by choice. Englewood Cliffs,
                  New Jersey: Prentice-Hall.

Knox, D., &
Wilson, K.

    1978   "The differences between having one and
                  two children." The Family Coordinator,
                  27, 23-25.

Lee, J.P., &
Stewart, A.H.

    1957   "Family or sibship position and scholas-
                  tic ability." Sociological Review, 5,
                  94.

Peck, E.

    1971   The baby trap. New York: Bernard Geis.

Population and the American Future

    1972   Report of the Commission on Population
                  and the American Future, Vol. 28, No.
                  2. Washington, D.C.: U.S. Government
                  Printing Office.

Redding, E.

1974   Parents' attitudes and behavior con-
            cerning fertility during postpartum.
            Unpublished doctoral dissertation,
            Oklahoma State University.

Rosenberg, M.

1965   Society and the adolescent self-image.
            Princeton, New Jersey: Princeton
            University Press.

Rossi, A.S.

1972   "Family development in a changing
            world." American Journal of Psychiatry,
            128, 106.

Solomon, E.S., Clare, J.E., &
Westoff, C.F.

1956   "Social and psychological factors
            affecting fertility." Milbank Memorial
            Fund Quarterly, 34, 160-177.

Thompson, G.

1950   "Intelligence and fertility: The
            Scottish 1947 survey." Eugenics Review,
            41, 163-170.

Wheland, E.

1976   A baby. . . maybe? New York: Bobbs-
            Merrill.

*Sharryl Hawke is Staff Associate, Social Science
Education Consortium, 855 Broadway, Boulder,
Colorado 80302. David Knox is Associate Professor
of Sociology, East Carolina University, Greenville,
North Carolina 27834.

Reprinted from The Family Coordinator, Vol. 27
(July, 1978):215-219. Copyrighted 1978 by the
National Council on Family Relations. Reprinted by
permission.

CHAPTER 22

PROCESSES SURROUNDING THE DECISION TO REMAIN
PERMANENTLY VOLUNTARILY CHILDLESS

Patricia Thomas Crane*

I. INTRODUCTION

In the traditional view the family is conceived
as an institution existing in part for the purpose
of fulfilling the essential social function of reproduction (Veevers, 1975:483) - reproduction is a
basic and universal function of the family. A
marriage wherein the couple deliberately chooses not
to have children is, in this society, considered
contranormative, perhaps immoral, and at the very
least, atypical. Individuals in a marriage are expected to subordinate selfish desires to the vital
social imperative that requires it's members "to be
fruitful and multiply, and replenish the earth."
According to the functionalist view, so important is
the reproductive function to society that deliberately childless marriages are considered to be in conflict with the dominant cultural expectations (Blake,
1974:302-303).

Values which encourage having children are held
by the vast majority of Americans, in fact, the
majority of childless couples are not that way by
choice (Williamson, 1966:41). Specifically, only
about 5 percent of married couples voluntarily forego
parenthood (Veevers, 1972b), a figure which does not
appear to be increasing.

Until very recently, the phenomena of childlessness has been virtually ignored as a field of study.
Research concerning childlessness is limited whereas
historically, the literature on the family has been
characteristically devoted to inquiry into other
facets of parenthood. Thus, voluntary childlessness
represents a structural variation of the traditional
family form about which little is known specifically
with regard to the dynamics involved in the process
of making the contranormative decision.

II. THE ANALYTICAL FRAMEWORK - DECISION AS SOCIAL PROCESS

The following analysis constitutes a partial look at several of the contingencies involved in the process leading to a decision to remain childless. Such a process is conceived to have began in childhood (i.e., early socialization experiences) and continues after one identifies oneself as voluntarily childless. This paper, however, shall be confined to the process leading to the decision.

A process perspective, then, will be utilized to trace the development of the respondent's attitudes toward motherhood and children, as well as the significance of role models which may have contributed to an awareness of such an alternative. Then, issues relevant to this process during courtship and marriage shall be examined.

III. SAMPLE

Because voluntarily childless couples constitute only an estimated 5 percent of the population, and because they possess deviant attitudes with regard to parenthood - they are difficult to locate for research purposes. Thus, because there is no defined population of childless wives, large, representative samples are very difficult to obtain. Eleven in-depth interviews of voluntarily childless wives have been obtained and analyzed to date.

IV. PROCESS ISSUES TEMPORALLY PRIOR TO COURTSHIP AND MARRIAGE

Initially I assumed that the forthcoming issues discussed in this section were part of the process of becoming deliberately childless, and had temporally preceeded the actual identification of ones' self as deliberately childless. However, the questions in the interview did not specificaly ask for temporal placement with regard to the development of one's image of motherhood or attitudes toward children. Doubless, however, one's attitudes toward children and motherhood constantly undergo renegotiation over time - in the true sense of a process - as opposed to their being specifically temporally identifiable and then not changing.

A. Images of Motherhood

The issue of what motherhood means to those who
deliberately choose to remain childless is an important one. On the outset of conducting my research, I
assumed that motherhood would not likely be described
favorably by the wives because such a favorable attitude toward motherhood would be inconsistent with
refusal to enact it as a role. Respondents were
asked to discuss their conception of how "motherhood"
was generally conceived. What I found impressive
about their comments was a rather condescending
recognition that "society" has a "vested interest"
in presenting motherhood as appealing such that conventional couples would be attracted to it. However,
when queried about their own views of motherhood, it
was apparent that they perceived the two views as
being quite discrepant. What was particularly striking about the wives' characterization of motherhood
was their implicit suggestion that they held a more
"realistic" view of motherhood. Such negative char-
acterizations may reflect a defense used to protect
themselves against pro-natalist arguments (Veevers,
1975.[1] At the very least, however, the data from
my sample suggests that the voluntarily childless
conceive of themselves as mavericks within their
own culture.

B. Attitudes Toward Children

One's attitude toward children is certainly of
relevance in trying to understand why women voluntarily forego motherhood. Initially I expected the
deliberately childless to view children unfavorably.
This general lack of appeal on the part of children,
I assumed, led one to discover new priorities that
would suplant the traditional career of motherhood
for women. However, five of the eleven wives interviewed contend they either don't care for children
or feel uncomfortable being around them, yet six
respondents either expressed no opinion or noted that
they liked children. Thus, on the basis of my sample,
liking or disliking children does not seem to account
for whether or not one will choose to remain childless.
The simple explanation that a woman just doesn't like
children and that is why she is not having them is not
borne out by this data, which suggests that other considerations are taken into account when one makes a
decision to remain childless.

C. Role Models for Childlessness

Sociologists often explain behavior that runs
counter to the norms of the group in which they are
socialized by taking into account the likelihood that
the individual may have identified with and assumed
the values of another group or reference individual.
With regard to this issue, I speculated that childlessness, as an alternative family form, is partly
a function of having early contact with others who
for one reason or another never had children.

Eight of the eleven wives interviewed reported
that they had known someone, or usually some couple
(usually during childhood or adolescence) who, for
some reason, never had children. I suggest that these
people served as role models, or at least played some
part in introducing the possibility of childlessness
as an alternative to conventional marriage.

One striking characteristic of the wives'
descriptions of the couples they had known who were
childless was a description of the "glamourous" lifestyle that the wives were noticeably impressed with.
Their glamourous lifestyle was commonly attributed to
their not having children. Of relevance here is the
concern among the wives of achieving for themselves
a glamourous lifestyle expected as a result of foregoing procreation (Crane, 1978:23).

V.   PROCESS ISSUES OCCURRING DURING COURTSHIP AND MARRIAGE

Not surprisingly, there was no single path to a
decision to remain childless. Rather, there were
multiple paths leading to a decision from which certain patterns could be delineated. The following
represents aspects of this process.

A. Assuming They Would have a Conventional Marriage

Although the data suggests that the process leading to the decision to remain childless begins prior
to courtship, it appears that most of the respondents
I interviewed identified courtship as the first stage
of the process (at least it was the first time the
issue had relevance for them). Nine of the eleven
wives interviewed reported they had assumed during
courtship, and even several years following marriage

that they would eventually have children.[2]

One interesting feature of the data was that more than just assuming they "would go the way of every other girl they had ever known" eight of the wives reported that they had never discussed the prospect of eventually having children with their husbands while they were dating or engaged. This important conversation never occurred between those eight wives and their fiancees. Thus, the dual aspects of assuming, on the one hand, that they would eventually procreate and then never discussing plans for parenthood prior to marriage with their fiancees was characteristic of the wives interviewed.

Most of the wives reported that there was no apparent point in time when a decision was actually made not to have children.[3] When the interview guide was constructed, I assumed (albeit naively) that respondents could tell me exactly when it was that they and their husbands sat down and decided not to have children. I also expected many wives to relate tales of how difficult it was to find a potential spouse that would be willing to go along with such an unusual decision.[4] Rather, what I did discover was that when asked "when did you decide to remain childless?" six wives were unable to pinpoint an exact time and instead spoke of evolved "tacit" understandings (implicit agreements) between herself and her spouse which only sometimes led to an explicit, formalized agreement.

B. A Series of Postponements - "Putting Off"

The typical process of coming to a decision involved a prolonged postponement of childbearing until such time that it was no longer considered desireable at all. Rather than explicitly rejecting motherhood, they described themselves as repeatedly deferring procreation until a more convenient time. Because most wives assumed they would eventualy have children, essentialy what transpired in the interim between marriage and actualy identifying oneself as deliberately childless was a slow process of rationalizing why it wasn't yet convenient to have a family. After a sufficient period of "putting it off" had transpired these wives evidently came to the awareness that there never was going to be a "right time."

C. Precipitating Events

Some wives identified a particular precipitating event that resulted in a formalized agreement with their spouse that they forego having children. Evident in their descriptions of various precipitating events (e.g., goals that had caused them to put off having children had come to fruition, health, advancing age, etc.) was the notion that indeed they had been putting off making a commitment to a decision, and had the particular event not occurred, the decision may have been continued to be postponed (at least not in a formalized sense).

D. A Search for Specificity

Noticeable in the reports of how a decision was reached is a lack of clarity as to how or what actually happened. The vagueness surrounding the decision was also apparent to the wives as they tried to relate what led them to their decision. It appeared in their discussions that as a result of their discomfort with such a mystifying lack of insight into that actual events leading to their decisions, they were attempting to fit a linear, organized explanation to a process which had apparently not been reflected on prior to the interview.

Thus, wives were uncomfortable with the vagueness and lack of insight (which they themselves perceived) regarding events leading to their decision. Consequently, their attempts to ameliorate this ambiguity consisted of attempts to outline specific insights or awarenesses they had which played a role in the process leading to the decision. The following represents the generic elements reputedly involved in that process: seductiveness of the lifestyle, observation of the effect of children on their friends' marriages and a recognition that there are no guarantees that should they have children, they would "turn out right."

1. _Seductiveness of the life style_. Although conventional couples may also postpone starting a family until a more convenient time, they eventually reproduce, whereas for many of the wives I interviewed, the postponement period experienced was sufficient enough such that when the opportunity to start a family presented itself, the benefits accruing to the childless lifestyle was perceived as outweighing the

perceived benefits which could be derived from having a family. Therefore, in the process of coming to define oneself as voluntarily childless, all wives were in agreement that a major component of the process was the seductive effect of a lifestyle without children. For couples who elect to have children after a substantial postponement, it would appear that any change in their lifestyle should be carefully planned for and its effects anticipated in order that as smooth a transition as possible be implemented.

2. <u>Observing the effect of children on their friends' marriages</u>. Another theme commonly discussed with regard to a decision process is a witnessing of the impact that children have on their friends' marriages. While childless wives are still in the process of "putting off" having children, many of their friends and relatives had become parents. In many cases their children were seen as having a disruptive effect on the marriage, which served to reinforce the advantages accruing to the lifestyle the childless were engaged in.

In addition to children being seen as hampering the quality of the relationships between the parents, five wives described instances where their friends' children, in contrast to the "little bundles of joy" their parents purported them to be, were seen by the childless wives as constantly burdensome.[5] These experiences made having children appear even more undesireable, when coupled with the reinforcing experiences they were having as a function of their "childfree" lifestyle.

3. <u>A recognition that there is no guarantee that their children would "turn out right."</u> In addition to observing (perhaps selectively) that children are a hindrence to the maintenance of a satisfying marriage and that they are "alot of trouble," what I found interesting about several of the discussions of the events that led to identifying oneself as voluntarily childless, were reports of having witnessed children who "turned out screwed up." It appears that the childless wives I interviewed were very aware of the possibility that if they had children, they could just as easily turn into a disappointment as anything else. The notion here is that these women were concerned that despite earnest efforts at good parenting, there could be no guarantee that one's efforts would be

389

successful. This tendency leads me to speculate
whether or not parents, prior to having children, were
as concerned with this same possibility. In other
words, perhaps childless wives were overly concerned
with the possibility that their children may prove
disappointing.

4. <u>Disassociation from childed couples</u>. As
children came to be seen as creating "hassles" and
disruptive of social occasions, seven of the wives
reported they began to disassociate themselves from
their childed friends in an effort to maintain or
"protect" their lifestyle which was by now becoming
increasingly more attractive rlative to their childed
friends. Many wives reported that they gradually lost
touch with their friends who had children. Other
childless couples (or single friends) serve as a support group to which these wives may turn for understanding and validation of their decision, as well as
being free to share the same lifestyle. However, the
above does not represent the experience of all the
wives interviewed. Four of the respondents reported
no such tendency to "abandon" friends who became
parents. Rather, they reported experiencing no difficulty in accommodating these couples into their social
network.

VI. SUMMARY

The decision to remain childless is seen as the
outcome of a gradual process, usualy characterized by
prolonged postponement. General themes of this process included: wives' assumption prior to marriage,
that she and her husband would eventually have children; the absence of a discussion with their fiancees
prior to marriage concerning future plans for childbearing; precipitating events that forced an explicit
choice; postponement until a more convenient time
(usually unspecified) until finally an implicit understanding was evolved that there was never going to be
a more convenient time; a seductive childfree lifestyle which reinforced their postponements; observing
(albeit selectively) that children often disrupt
marriages; and finally, an awareness or a concern that
any children they might have would not necessarily
"turn out right."

VII. CONCLUSION

This paper has presented a partial look at the process of events leading to a decision to remain childless. No attempt has been made to imply that this is a complete nor representative analysis of that process, rather, the research presented herein was exploratory in nature and there are many more questions which remain to be asked. Certainly any complete analysis of the process of the leading to the decision to parent or not would want to contrast the experiences of childed wives with those who have elected to forego parenthood. Also - such an analysis would probably wish to include husbands - as it is most likely that their own unique perspective would add much to an analysis of such a process.

In conclusion, then, much still can be learned about the process leading to a decision to remain childless.

FOOTNOTES

1. Veevers (1975:475) corroborates my finding that the voluntarily childless tend to hold a number of "unusual" beliefs concerning the attributes of the kinds of persons who become parents.

2. Veevers (1973a:359) also reports that like conventional couples the women in her sample also assumed that they would have one or two children eventually.

3. Veevers (1973a:360) also reports that couples in her sample were at a loss to explain exactly how or when the transition came about, but that they agreed that it was an implicit decision.

4. It is recognized that the lack of such a tendency (on the basis of my sample) may not represent the experience of many deliberately childless women, but rather, may be an artifact of such a small sample.

5. Veevers (1975:477) also observed that when the childless observe parents being hostile toward their children or expressing anger or resentment which they inevitably feel occasionally, they conclude that just as they suspected all along, "they are making the best of a bad situation."

BIBLIOGRAPHY

Blake, J.

    1974   "Coercive pronatalism and American population policy." Pp. 276-317 in Rose Laub Coser (Ed.), The Family: Its Structures and Functions. New York: St. Martin's Press.

Crane, P.T.

    1978   "Processes surrounding a decision to remain childless." Unpublished manuscript presented at the annual Pacific Sociological Association meetings in Spokane, Washington (April).

Veevers, J.E.

    1972   "Factors in the incidence of childlessness: an analysis of the census data." Social Biology 19:266-274.

    1973a   "Voluntarily child-free wives: an exploratory study." Sociology and Social Research, 57:356-366.

    1973b   "The child-free alternative: rejection of the motherhood mystique." Pp. 183-199 in Marylee Stephenson (Ed.), Women in Canada. Toronto: New Press.

    1975   "The moral careers of voluntarily childless wives: notes on the defense of a variant world view." The Family Coordinator (October):473-487.

Williamson, R.

    1966   Marriage and Family Relations. New York: Wiley.

*Department of Behavioral Sciences, California State Polytechnic University, Pomona, Pomona, California.

CHAPTER 23

AN ALTERNATIVE FAMILY FORM FOR OLDER PERSONS:
NEED AND SOCIAL CONTEXT

Gordon F. Streib*

Open societies provide opportunities
for persons to create new and innovative
family and community alternatives which
may lie outside the mainstream. This
paper examines the need and the context for
alternative living arrangements for older
persons, and describes some recent attempts
to devise new family arrangements for the
elderly. Particular attention is focused
upon Share-A-Home in Florida, a "family" of
non-related senior adults who share their
own household, employ a manager, and share
expenses. This pragmatic amalgam group is
placed in sociological perspective through
the theory of shared functions.

One of the important and intriguing aspects of an
open society is the opportunities it affords small
groups of individuals to create new and innovate family and community arrangements outside the mainstream
of the culture. This has been true in the United
States since its founding. One can get a glimpse of
the historical roots of communal families by reading
Nordhoff (1875) and more recent studies by Kanter
(1972, 1973) which report the development, viability,
and problematics of these alternative forms of the
family in contemporary America.

The increase in formation of intentional communities and communes for young people has stimulated
suggestions in the gerontological field that such
arrangements would be idealy suited to the needs of
the elderly. They could pool resources and live more
economically; they could share tasks such as housework,
meal preparation, and shopping; they would provide
companionship for each other; they could care for
each other in case of emergencies.

Need and Context for Alternative Living Arrangements

In order to understand the context for alterna-

393

tive living arrangements for the elderly, we should
have an awareness of the modal patern of living
arrangements for the period beyond age 65. Census
data show a marked decline in the percentage of persons living as a couple in a single household. There
is an increasing differential in longevity of men and
women so that at age 75 and over, around 40% of all
men are still living with a spouse in their own household in contrast to less than 15% of the women.

There is an increasing number of elderly people
who encounter problems living independently in their
own homes, due to a number of conditions: (a) they
are often widows, and have difficulty in coping with
the problems of upkeep of the house and yard; (b)
they often live in areas away from children or relatives, who might offer services and assistance; (c)
they are often left in declining neighborhoods, and
are sometimes the victims of criminals; (d) the increasing number of women in the labor force means
that daughters are not available to take care of an
elderly parent or relative; (e) it is increasingly
common for older people who live to their 80's or
90's to find that their adult children, aged 60 and
older have their own health and retirement problems,
and cannot be counted on for care; (f) older siblings
rarely live together, except for single or never-
married persons. Even widows do not ordinarly move
in with siblings; (g) the longer life expectancy of
females, coupled with the lower income of widows and
the effects of inflation combine to give urgent reasons for finding more economical ways of maintenance
than living alone in a single house.

When a disability occurs among the elderly,
housing changes are considered in about half the
cases, according to a nationwide survey reported by
Newman (1976). The two major alternatives are moving
into the household of relatives, or entering a nursing
home. Changes are very likely to be considered when
the person is over 75, or is female.

In earlier and more traditional times, the first
alternatives to be considered were for the elderly
person to move in with children, or for children to
move in with parents. These solutions are increasingly rejected in urban America, both by the adult
children and the elderly themselves. Both generations
prize their freedom and independence; the older genera-

394

tion frequently does not want to endanger the affectional ties with their children by living with them.

Another recent solution for the moderately dependent elderly person is the initiation of home care which has as its purpose maintaining the older person in his/her own residence as long as possible. His needs are met by supplying housekeeping services, Meals-on-Wheels, visiting nurses, therapists, transportation services, and CETA workers to make home repairs. When there is a multiplicity of services required, the coordination of activities becomes complicated and the costs escalate.

The Continuum of Living Arrangements

Alternative family and living arrangements can be understood in relation to the continuum of housing in which older persons live, ranging from living independently and autonomously in a private house or apartment to a full care institution where twenty-four hour a day skilled nursing care is provided. Understanding the continuum enables one to see where the various alternatives lie. Among the several crucial theoretical and policy issues, perhaps the most significant is that of age segregation versus age integration.

The classic study of Rosow (1967) of different degrees of age segregation in Cleveland, Ohio neighborhoods pointed to the social benefits of a residential environment which has a large number of age peers. Hochschild's (1973) detailed case study of one small apartment building offers important confirmatory qualitative data on how age integrated housing may have positive outcomes for older persons. Congruent findings are reported in Johnson's (1971) study of a mobile home community in the San Francisco Bay area.

Carp's (1966) study of Victoria Plaza in San Antonio, the first low income older person facility, is a landmark of before-after research on the housing of the elderly. Its main finding is that improved housing enhances the morale of older people. This was shown by increased activity, more informal social contacts and a decrease in disengagement.

395

There are other studies which have reported high
satisfaction in age-integrated living arrangements.
In recent years, there has been the development of retirement communities which, according to the research
findings (Jacobs, 1974; Bultena & Wood, 1969) are
highly preferred by residents. One implication of
these studies is that there is no one desirable form
of retirement environment that is endorsed by <u>all</u>
older persons, or can be recommended for all elderly
people.

Another variant living arrangement, retirement
hotels, was studied by Albrecht (1969). She found
these were a preferred and accepted type of housing
for a small segment of the elderly. Albrecht states
that the hotels serve a good purpose as they presently operate, especialy if they limit their clientele
to the active, the independent, and the "young"
retirees. However, there are potential problems and
difficulties for persons living in these retirement
hotels, particulary when a person's physical or mental condition deteriorates. Stevens' (1976) study
of elderly tenants in a slum hotel in a large middle
western city emphasizes some of the difficulties as
well as the advantages from the standpoint of the
residents who choose this kind of housing arrangement.
This type of housing seemed to be preferred by male
"loners," who are wary of too much social involvement.

There is little information in the literature on
cooperative living arrangements, which could fill an
important gap on the continuum. However, there is a
great deal of information on the final step, nursing
homes--the last refuge for many older persons. Often
the elderly will make many compromises and alternative
arrangements to avoid institutionalization because of
the negative stereotypes held about nursing homes by
both young and old. There is a vast and growing
literature on this subject. Some reports are written
from the advocacy point of view, in order to expose
the conditions, such as <u>Tender Loving Greed</u> (Mendelson,
1974); <u>Old Age: The Last Segregation</u> (Townsend, 1971);
and <u>Why Survive: Growing Old in America</u> (Butler, 1975).
There are other investigations written from a more
scholarly and dispassionate stance, such as the works
of Tobin and Lieberman (1976), and Gubrium (1975).
These gerontologists attempt to analyze how long-term
care settings operate and how they affect the older
people who reside in them.

All of this rich literature briefly reviewed here points to the need for studying and understanding the need for alternative living arrangements which lie somewhere on the continuum between living independently and autonomously in a private house or apartment, and entering a nursing home, either proprietary or non-profit, with the possibility of total dependency.

Communal Living and Alternative Family Forms

Students of the family concerned with living arrangements for the elderly must be aware that the study of housing is highly related to family and kinship concerns. The variety of family structures of the elderly (Sussman, 1976) can be rich and varied.

The communal literature offers some guidance as to the problems and issues which are involved in alternative living arrangements (Kanter, 1973). Suggestions on day to day operations are found in Gorman (1975). The problem of timing and the formation of communes--which can be very crucial--has been discussed by Kinkade (1977), the founder of two successful groups. However, Streib and Streib (1975) have pointed out it is unlikely that there will be a widespread development of truly communal living for the elderly. Three factors form the basis for this prediction: (a) the structural constraints of contemporary society; (b) the conditions and attitudes of the elderly themselves; and (c) the attitudes of the young communards towards including older people in their communities. Furthermore, communal living usually involves a sharing of work and household tasks. If the elderly suffer from varying degrees of physical impairment, it is a difficult problem to decide on an equitable division of duties. Communal sharing of property and income would also pose a thorny problem for many of the elderly.

New Cooperative Family Arrangements for the Elderly

In recent years there have been a number of attempts to devise new family arrangements for the elderly as a means of solving many of their problems of economic security, dependency and loneliness. Like earlier forms of communal living, these new arrangements are predicated on the notion that unrelated adults can live together as a family.

One approach, attempted in Miami, Florida (United Home Care, Note 1) involved the matching of people who had a home to share with isolated elder people who were seeking housing and companionship. However, the matching process proved to be difficult, and the project was disbanded. The major problem was that people offering their homes wanted household chores performed, while the elderly people seeking homes were unable to perform these tasks.

A second example of a cooperative housing arrangement for people over 50 is just being initiated by the Back Bay Aging Concerns Committee and the Grey Panthers of Greater Boston. This is a non-profit neighborhood project in which houses or apartments will be owned or rented and the residents will share responsibility for housekeeping, cooking, and household management.

A third example reported by Wax (1976) has been developed by the Jewish Federation of Metropolitan Chicago. It has a strong back-up of social services including a resident case worker who is present five days a week, and a psychiatrist who is on call. There is also the use of a rich array of volunteers organized by the social agency. The ecology of the Chicago alternative involves a complex of town houses, rather than a single building.

Share-A-Home -- A Pragmatic Amalgam

In this paper, we will focus upon Share-A-Home, a new and ingenious concept which has proved to be successful in Florida in providing a solution to the problems of housing and family life for ambulatory elderly people. The idea was started in 1969 by James Gillies with an original unit of twenty elderly persons who jointly owned a 27 room house and facilities. Once the first family was successfully established, there appeared to be a need for other units, and others were formed in the Winter Park and Orlando area. As the number of families grew, there was also a need to set up an association to assist in the formation of new families.

In 1972, Gillies founded the Share-A-Homes Association, Inc., a non-profit tax exempt organization chartered under the laws of the State of Florida. It has a board of eleven directors chosen from the community. While the Association does not control or

supervise the daily life of the families in an institutional sense, it does provide information and assistance when new families are formed, and while they are
in operation. For example, it loans funds to families
for basic repairs, or for furnishings which might be
necessary to get a family started or to provide more
comfortable surroundings. Share-A-Home has a coordinating function in relation to the families. One might
conceive of this organization as performing a kind of
surrogate parent role for the ten families now in
operation.

The units are in a variety of housing: two are
in former Rolins College residential buildings, one is
in a former Catholic convent, another in a spacious
mansion, another in a six bedroom ranch house, and
others are in various kinds of dwellings in residential neighborhoods that can accommodate from eight to
twenty persons. The utilization of a variety of
building structures is indicative of the overall prag-
matism and adaptability of the Share-A-Home idea.

The concept is a "family" of non-related senior
adults who share their own household and divide up
the expenses of running it. The cost averages from
$325 to $400 a month, depending on the costs of each
unit and whether or not the person shares a room.
This makes it a far less expensive solution than
nursing homes for the isolated elderly person who
cannot afford to keep his own household, or who does
not want to live alone. A salaried manager and staff
take care of finances, housekeeping, and are responsible for providing food, transportation, laundry services, and the like. The family retains the privilege
of retaining or dismissing the management.

Gillies organized Share-A-Home from a different
premise than other cooperative living arrangements
in that he stipulated that a paid staff perform the
necessary tasks. He recognized that it was unrealistic to expect older people with varying degrees of
ability and disability to cooperate harmoniously in
cooking, shopping, meal planning, housekeeping, over-
seeing special diets, monitoring medication, providing
transportation, arranging for medical attention when
members are sick, etc.

The monthly share of expenses covers all household costs including rent, food, maintenance, and

staff salaries. Only personal items as clothing and medicine are excluded. The management staff is responsible for providing transportation to members for medical service to the physician of their choice, or to church, shopping, club activities, and the like. Each family owns or leases a car.

New members have a 30 day trial period before being accepted or withdrawing. There are no age limitations. The requirements to be accepted for membership in a family are: to be ambulatory, to be able to take care of their person, to have had a recent physical examination, and to have appointed someone of their choice as their power of attorney. No admission fees are charged; no contract is signed, and members may withdraw from the family at any time.

In the words of Gillies, "These elderly people live together as a family. They eat together, work together, and play together, thereby eliminating loneliness. They have formed an association together for their economic and social benefit. All members share birthdays, outings, expenses, fun and joys that only a loving family can know. These are the necessary ingredients to retain their self-respect and to live a life with dignity. They have the security of a normal home life and the feeling that they are part of something worthwhile."

Thus, the Share-A-Home families meet three important social-psychological needs which have been stressed in many studies of aging: (a) free choice, (b) association with others who give affection and concern, and (c) feelings of dignity and autonomy.

The Share-A-Home Association has received inquiries from groups all over the United States seeking information about the concept. At present, family units are being formed in Cleveland, Ohio; Greensboro, North Carolina; and Norfolk, Virginia.

Sociological Perspectives on the Share-A-Home Model

Share-A-Home, as one model of alternative family arrangement, can be analyzed from several sociological and gerontological perspectives. A primary set of ideas is found in the theory of shared functions developed by Eugene Litwak and his colleagues (Litwak, 1965; Litwak & Figueira, 1968). These sociologists assert that in complex modern societies, families and formal organizations must coordinate their efforts if they are to reach their goals. The way in which bureaucratic structures and family groups are articulated is a crucial matter in an urban-industrialized society.

Streib has made the distinction (Streib, 1972, p. 6) "Bureaucracies are social structures which have instrumental bases for operation, emphasize impersonality, are organized on the basis of formal rules, and stress professional expertise. On the other hand, a family as a prototype of primary groups is characterized by face-to-face contacts, employs affective bases for judgments, and stresses diffuse demands and expectations."

The Share-A-Home model (developed quite independently of the work of Litwak and others) provides a new kind of social group in American society which blends in one location both familial and bureaucratic functions. Litwak's theory conceives of these functions as being carried out in different locales with the activities being coordinated for a common purpose. In a sense, Litwak saw the need for networks which inform, coordinate, and refer persons who are trying to cope with problems which fall in that gray zone between the formal structures of our society and the traditional family groups.

Share-A-Home is not a traditional family, but it does have many family characteristics and it has been considered as family on some legal grounds (Sussman, 1976). At the same time, the organizational structure of the Association (such as having a board of directors) shows its formal characteristics which are typical of a bureaucratic organization. As an amalgam group (primary and bureaucratic) a Share-A-Home family tries to deal with both uniform tasks and non-uniform tasks, and its social structure and function suggest the need for a sharper understanding of how it might provide important services for some older Americans.

The analysis of Share-A-Home as a mixed social structure forming a unique amalgam indicates that it combines the need for trained experts in certain areas and also the need for flexibility, sensitivity and concern in interpersonal relations. We do not wish to argue that all bureaucratic personnel are insensitive

401

and inflexible, or that all families are composed of sensitive, compassionate, caring persons. The realities of everyday life belie this notion. However, the point we are stressing is that the goals, the recruitment process, the training of personnel, the development and invoking of rules, the modes and types of reward and punishment are fundamentally different in bureaucratic structures and primary groups. It is this unique amalgam structure that makes Share-A-Home of interest to both theorists and practitioners in the family field.

Forecasts Regarding Share-A-Home

Share-A-Home is an intriguing natural experiment which has been developed as an alternate form of the family. We have shown that such arrangements fulfill an important need in the continuum between independent living and total dependence. The questions which arise are: Can it remain a viable alternative arrangement in the years ahead? What are the major factors which seem to enhance its viability and what are the considerations which would impede its acceptance in other areas?

The analysis of the future of Share-A-Home can be viewed at three levels: the individual, the community, and the societal. At all levels, there are enhancing and inhibiting factors which are operative and which will determine its future prospects.

At the individual and family level there are convincing reasons for families to support Share-A-Home and to consider having an older relative join a family group. Our present knowledge indicates that such an alternate family form helps persons to cope with loneliness, enables them to live economically in a safe, healthful environment, and also reduces the fear of crime. Furthermore, the adult children feel assurance that their parents are in a setting where someone is aware of the elderly person's needs and condition, and would get help immediately in an emergency--yet the living arrangement does not have the stigma of being an institution. There is much more freedom to come and go, pursue hobbies and interests, and express their individuality. Because of its structure and the relationships which are fostered, this kind of living arrangement offers many social benefits.

On the other hand, there are strong motives to maintain one's own home or apartment with the freedom, autonomy and privacy one has always known. The personal resistance to change which is characteristic of some elderly persons is definitely an inhibiting factor.

When we turn to community factors which are operative, we find there are strong interests in having alternatives available for the slightly dependent elderly. Most families dread to send a relative to a nursing home unless absolutely necessary. Moreover, from the standpoint of the community, the Share-A-Home approach is more economical than other forms because taxes are paid on the properties and to date, the families have operated without subsidy from any public source.

Other factors at the community level may impede the establishment of Share-A-Home families. One issue which was faced successfully in a Florida court test was whether the families were in violation of a local zoning ordinance. In Orlando the judge ruled that unrelated adults did constitute a family. However, this issue may have to be faced in other communities. In some neighborhoods, persons are reluctant to see any exception to nuclear family residences. While they might not object to a cooperative of quiet elderly persons, they fear that any "unconventional" family might set a precedent for other cooperative groups which they would consider undesirable. In these cases, anxiety about property values becomes a prime consideration.

Another possible source of negativism might originate from owners of proprietary nursing homes or boarding homes who may consider alternatives like Share-A-Home as a threat to their business.

At the broader level of the society, there are also moltivating and impeding factors at work. At the societal level there are segments of the public who will view family alternatives positively because they are self-sustaining and are helping to deal with an important problem in the care of the elderly. Share-A-Home is also an opportunity for religious organizations to fulfill religious and ethical concerns by sponsoring local family units.

403

On the negative side of the ledger, one source of impeding factors may come from the complicated skein of rules, regulations, and laws which have been developed at the national and state level to deal with the exploitation of the elderly in institutions and residential arrangements. Cooperative family arrangements like Share-A-Home for the elderly are not formalized bureaucratic structures. If they are treated as such and have to fill out endless forms, hire recreation directors, social workers, dietitians, and meet other formal bureaucratic regulations, their essence as a family will be destroyed, and their financial advantage will be lost. This may constitute one of the more challenging dilemmas facing persons interested in organizing new family groups and those who become new family members.

Conclusion

In contemporary America there is an awareness and a concern for the needs of older persons. However, there is a gap in the continuum of family and living arrangements ranging from an independent household to a nursing home. A variety of experiments and models have been suggested and attempted to meet this need. One such model is Share-A-Home in Florida, a pragmatic amalgam which provides cooperative family living for non-related senior adults who live in a home, employ a manager, and share expenses. A board of directors of community citizens provides leadership and guidance.

When we consider the future of Share-A-Home, it is difficult to predict whether the concept will flourish and spread, or whether the present families will die out and become a tiny thread in the tapestry of American experimental communities and family forms. The community is concerned that the elderly be well taken care of, but there is an uneasy feeling among some groups about communal groups or any "unnatural" family forms which might diminish property values. On the one hand, our society wants people to provide for their own financial needs with a minimum of support from the public treasury. On the other hand, governmental bureaucracies may set up rules and regulations that hamstring the development and operation of innovative family arrangements such as Share-A-Home.

Persons working in the policy and family practice fields, as well as researchers and theorists of Ameri-

404

can family life, will have to face a basic question:
How can government bureaucracies, concerned with the
welfare of the elderly, be made responsive and flexible to such innovations as Share-A-Home? They should
be supportive of them without smothering them in
paper work, job specifications, and unnecessary regulations. It becomes increasingly clear that bureaucracy structures are usually incapable of dealing
satisfactorily with non-uniform tasks of the kind
which are part of family life. Yet the care of the
slightly dependent elderly is characterized by an
abundance of non-uniform tasks. It is in this area
that thoughtful and innovative solutions are required
and it is hoped that students of the family will pro-
vde some workable answers.

REFERENCE NOTE

1. United Home Care Services, Inc., Miami, Florida.
    Share-A-Home pilot project: Summary, evaluation,
    findings. Report to the Administration on Aging,
    Department of Health, Education and Welfare,
    July, 1977.

B I B L I O G R A P H Y

Albrecht, R.

    1969   "Retirement hotels in Florida." In C. C.
                Osterbind (Ed.), Feasible planning for
                social change in the field of aging.
                Gainsville: University of Florida
                Press.

Bultena, G. L., &
Wood, V.

    1969   "The American retirement community:
                Bane or blessing?" The Journal of
                Gerontology, 24, 209-217.

Butler, R.

    1975   Why Suvive? Being old in America.
                New York: Harper & Row.

Carp, F. M.

    1966   A future for the aged. Austin, Univer-
                sity of Texas Press.
Gorman, C.

    1975   People together: A guide to communal
                living. St. Albane, Herts, England:
                Paladin.

Gubrium, J.

    1975   Living and dying at Murray Manor.
                New York: St. Martin's Press.

406

Hochschild, A R.

    1973   The unexpected community. Englewood
                    Cliffs: Prentice Hall.

Jacobs, J.

    1974   Fun city: An ethnographic study of a
                    retirement community. New York: Holt.

Johnson, S. K.

    1971   Idle Haven: Community building among
                    the working-class retired. Berkeley:
                    University of California Press.

Kantner, R. M.

    1972   Commitment and community: Communes and
                    utopias in sociological perspective.
                    Cambridge: Harvard University Press.

Kantner, R. M.

    1973   Communes: Creating and managing the
                    collective life. New York: Harper &
                    Row.

Kinkade, K.

    1977   "Please don't start a commune in 1977."
                    Communities: Journal of Cooperative
                    Living, 25, 2-7.

Litwak, E.

    1965   "Extended kin relations in an industrial
                    society." In E. Shanas & G. F. Streib
                    (Eds.), Social structure and the family.
                    Englewood Cliffs: Prentice-Hall.

Litwak, E., &
Figueira, J.

    1968   "Technological innovations and theoreti-
                    cal functions of primary groups and
                    bureaucratic structures." American
                    Journal of Sociology, 73, 466-481.

Mendelson, M.A.

1974   Tender loving greed. New York: Random.

Newman, S. J.

1976   "Housing adjustment of the disabled el-
            derly." The Gerontologist, 16, 312-317.

Nordhoff, C.

1967   The communistic societies of the United
            States. New York: Schocken (first
            published 1875).

Rosow, I.

1967   Social integration of the aged. New
            York: Free Press.

Stephens, J.

1976   Loners, losers and lovers: Elderly
            tenants in a slum hotel. Seattle:
            University of Washington Press.

Streib, G. F.

1972   "Older families and their troubles:
            Familial and social responses." The
            Family Coordinator, 21, 5-19.

Streib, G. F., &
Streib, R. B.

1975   "Communes and the aging: Utopian dream
            and gerontological reality." American
            Behavioral Scientist, 19, 176-189.

Sussman, M. B.

1976   "The family life of old people." In
            R. H. Binstock & E. Shanas (Eds.),
            Handbook of aging and the social
            sciences. New York: Van Nostrand.

Tobin, S. S., &
Lieberman, R. A.

1976   <u>Last home for the aged</u>. San Francisco:
          Jossey-Bass.

Townsend, C. <u>et</u> <u>al</u>.

1971   <u>Old age: The last segregation</u>. New
          York: Bantam.

Wax, J.

1976   "It's like your own home here." <u>New</u>
          <u>York Times Magazine</u>, November 21,
          38+.

*Gordon F. Streib is Graduate Professor in the Depart-
ment of Sociology and Faculty Associate of the Center
for Gerontological Studies, University of Florida,
Gainsville, Florida 32611.

Reprinted from <u>The Family Coordinator</u>, Vol. 27
(October 1978):413-420. Copyrighted 1978 by the
National Council on Family Relations. Reprinted by
permission.

CHAPTER 24

EDUCATION FOR CHOICE: IMPLICATIONS OF ALTERNATIVES IN LIFESTYLES FOR FAMILY LIFE EDUCATION

Eleanor D. Macklin*

Given the increasing range of lifestyle alternatives available in contemporary society, it is important that family life educators prepare individuals to make wise lifestyle choices. The article reviews the contemporary alternatives to the traditional family, notes some of the skills and knowledge required by these alternatives, and suggests a format for preparing students to make appropriate lifestyle choices. The following lifestyle options and their implications for family life education are reviewed: to marry or not to marry, to parent or not to parent, to co-parent or single-parent, to make a lifelong or open-ended commitment, degree of androgyny, to be sexually exclusive or non-exclusive, gender of partner, and to live alone or with others. An educational approach is proposed, based on a humanistic perspective and designed to foster knowledge about available alternatives, increased awareness of individual values, and the development of decision-making and conflict-negotiation skills.

One of the major trends in recent years has been the growing range of available lifestyle options from which to choose and the increasing freedom with which to make that choice (Macklin, 1980). This has important implications for the youth in our society and for those seeking to prepare them to deal realistically with their futures.

Traditionally, our dominant culture has assumed that its adult members would select a mate of the opposite sex, marry, have children, be sexually exclusive, live together till death did them part, and acknowledge the male as primary provider and ultimate authority. Although it is clear that many did not, in fact, live this way, the majority did so and little

411

support was given to those who did not. Given such a world, it was appropriate that family life education would focus primarily on such topics as mate selection, parenting, home management skills, and the developmental phases of the nuclear family.

But the above is no longer the case, for increasingly the traditional pattern is neither the reality nor the ideal for many. In 1978, fewer than one-third of the U.S. households consisted of a married couple with children under 18 (compared to 40% in 1970), and in over half of these the mother was in the labor force (U.S. Bureau of the Census, 1979a, Table A; U.S. Department of Labor, 1979). Almost one-quarter of the households consisted of persons living alone, and increasing numbers were living as single parents or as partners of persons to whom they were not married. By 1990, close to one-third of all children will experience the divorce of their parents (Glick, 1979a), and large numbers of these will, in turn, become members of stepfamilies.

The field is alive with new terminology as researchers seek to identify the seemingly endless variations currently evolving. Dual-career families, commuter marriage, the binuclear family, blended families, group marriage, sexually-open marriage, gay fathers, lesbian mothers, the open family, and the urban commune are only a few of the many present forms. Preparing persons to deal constructively with the complexity of the new pluralism and to make informed choices for themselves with regard to lifestyle is the challenge of family life education in the '80s. The question becomes how best to meet the challenge. This article will review the available lifestyle options, suggest some of the skills and understandings required to deal with them effectively, and propose a format for introducing students to these.

Contemporary Lifestyle Options

What are the lifestyle choices which persons must be prepared to make today? It is not easy to organize the multitude of alternatives into some logical and meaningful series of options. A helpful approach is to view the alternatives as variations on the traditional nuclear family. One is then led to the following list (see Table 1):

412

Table 1
Contemporary Lifestyle Options

The "Nontraditional" Alternative	The "Traditional" Alternative	The Choice Which Students Must Be Prepared to Make
Never-married singlehood; non-marital cohabitation	Legally married	To marry or not to marry
Voluntary childlessness	With children	To parent or not to parent
Single-parent (never-married once-married); joint custody and the binuclear family; the stepfamily	Two-parent	To co-parent or single-parent
Renewable contract; divorce and remarriage	Permanent	To make life-long or open-ended commitment; to stay married or to divorce; to remain single or to remarry
Androgynous marriage (e.g., O'Neill's "open marriage," dual-career marriage, commuter marriage	Male as primary provider and ultimate authority	Degree of androgyny
Extramarital relationships sexually open marriage, swinging, Ramey's "intimate friendship"	Sexually exclusive	To be sexually exclusive or non-exclusive

413

Table 1

Contemporary Lifestyle Options (continued)

The "Nontraditional" Alternative	The "Traditional" Alternative	The Choice Which Students Must Be Prepared to Make
Same-sex intimate relation-ships	Heterosexual	Gender of partner
Multi-adult households (e.g., multilateral marriage, communal living, affiliated families)	Two-adult household	To live alone or with others, and with how many others

To Marry or Not to Marry

Although once viewed as a sign of abnormality in men and undesirability in women, singlehood is increasingly seen as an acceptable option today (Libby, 1977; Stein, 1978). The average age at marriage is gradually advancing (of women aged 20-24, 29% were still single in 1960, 36% in 1970, and 49% in 1979--U.S. Bureau of the Census, 1980: Tables A and B). Thus, people are single longer, and although the vast majority will still choose to eventually marry, it is predicted that 8 to 9% of those presently in their twenties will experience a lifetime of singlehood (Glick, 1979b). In addition, large numbers of adults experience being single as a result of divorce or widowhood (e.g., in 1976, 30% of the adult males and 37% of the adult females were either never-married, divorced, or widowed--U.S. Bureau of the Census, 1977).

There are also increasing numbers who choose to live with a partner without being married (Macklin, 1978; Yllo, 1978; Jacques & Chason, 1979; Newcomb, 1979). The great majority of these persons will eventually marry, although not necessarily each other, but some will choose for a variety of reasons to cohabit as a permanent alternative to marriage, particularly those who have experienced a previous marriage and divorce. It is estimated that at the present time, unmarried-cohabiting couples represent only about 3% of all "couple households" in the U.S. (U.S. Bureau of the Census, 1980, p. 3-5), but almost 50% of a recent sample of marriage license applicants in Los Angeles had lived for some time with their current partner before marriage (Newcomb & Bentler, 1980).

The above realities have a number of obvious implications. For instance, students need guidelines for assessing their own readiness for marriage and the extent to which a committed partnership with another is currently or potentially an appropriate life choice for them. If the decision to cohabit and/or to marry is to be a thoughtful one, individuals must have a realistic understanding of the relative costs and benefits, both socio-emotional and legal/financial, of these lifestyles. In addition, both males and females must plan their lives with the anticipation that at some point in their adult years

they may be voluntarily or involuntarily single, and
be encouraged to develop the skills and resources
needed for a successful independent life.

To Parent or Not to Parent

Although it was traditionally assumed that
marriage would inevitably lead to parenthood, and
couples who were without children were either to be
pitied or criticized, voluntary childlessness is
becoming a more common phenomenon, at least among
urban educated professionals (Veevers, 1979). The
'70s witnessed a definite trend toward postponement
of childbearing (among ever-married women aged 25-29,
the percentage remaining childless increased from 16%
in 1970 to 25% in 1978--U.S. Bureau of the Census,
1979b: Table 7). It is currently estimated that
about 10% of all couples will remain voluntarily
childless (Veevers, 1979). However, because of
the strong pronatalist orientation of our society
(Calhoun & Selby, 1980), research uniformly reports
that voluntary childless couplex experience some
degree of disapproval from others (e.g., Ory, 1978).
If one accepts that parenthood is not equally appropriate for all, education must foster an atmosphere
which supports childlessness as an acceptable option,
and so do what it can to help individuals determine
whether parenthood is, in fact, the best option for
them.

To Co-parent or Single-Parent

There has been a dramatic increase in the number
and proportion of single-parent families during the
past decade, due to an increase in separation and
divorce and in the number of families headed by
never-married mothers. In 1979, 19% of all households with children under 18 were maintained by
single parents (17% by mothers, 2% by fathers), and
it is predicted that 45% of all children born in 1977
will spend some time as a member of a single-parent
family (Glick, 1979a). The most pressing problems
experienced by such families are economic, coupled
with the struggle of fulfilling parental roles while
living in a society which still maintains negative
attitudes toward single parents and their children
(Parks, Note 1). Students need to be prepared for
the increasing prevalence of this family form, understand its commonly experienced problems, realize that

416

it can be a viable lifestyle for both fathers and mothers, and be aware of sources of community support for such families.

It should be noted that many so-called single-parents are, in fact, functioning as co-parents, although the other parent is not an official member of the household. An example would be those divorced couples who elect joint custody (where the court assigns divorcing parents equal rights to, and responsibility for, the minor child--Milne, 1979) and who are living as a "binuclear family" (where the child is part of a family system composed of two nuclear households with varying degrees of cooperation between and time spent in each--Ahrons, 1979). Students should be challenged to think creatively about ways of maintaining family when the spousal unit dissolves, realize that co-parenting is an option in the event of divorce, and recognize the factors which predict the success of such an option.

In this context it should be noted that step-families (where one or both of the married adults have children from a previous union with primary residence in the household) now comprise about 10 to 15% of all households in the U.S. (Glick, 1979a), and this number increases greatly when one includes all remarriages in which one of the two adults was a parent in a previous marriage. Clinical experience suggests that the stepfamily is structurally and psychologically different from the traditional nuclear family and that an understanding of its special complexities is necessary for its success (Visher & Visher, 1979), yet few persons are prepared for this reality. With so many presently involved in stepfamilies, it is crucial that persons be helped to understand the special characteristics of this unit, that teachers be aware that many members of their classes may be actively involved in such households, and that persons be prepared to cope effectively with the stresses predictable for that unit.

To Make Lifelong or Open-ended Commitment

The idea of renewable couple-written contracts is not new (e.g., Weitzman, 1974), but is not yet fully recognized within our legal system. The State still holds that when persons marry, it is for life (unless the State decrees otherwise) and with certain universally designated obligations to one another. However, increasingly, couples are being encouraged informally to develop for themselves clearly specified contracts, spelling out their expectations and promises to one another, in a wide range of areas such as economic, task-sharing, child-rearing, social life, and career development, including specified periods for renegotiation and evaluation and techniques for dealing with any conflicts which may arise (Whitehurst, Note 2).

Classroom exercises which give the student the experience of thrashing out such a contract serve to alert the individual to the range of potential problem areas, give practice in negotiation, and elicit discussion about the possible criteria for termination of a relationship. Since unexpressed and often unconscious expectations brought into a relationship are a common source of problems in relationships (Sager, 1976), it is crucial that students be taught the importance of being in touch with their own needs and expectations, learn to verbalize these, and be open to hearing the needs and expectations of the other. One might also argue that given the short-lived nature of many relationships in present society, and the prevalence of divorce, time should be spent exploring the concept of commitment and the dynamics of termination.

Degree of Androgyny

Our society has made significant strides toward removing sex-role stereotyping and achieving more sharing of child-rearing and household responsibilities, although there has been more change in attitude than in practice (Scanzone & Fox, 1980). In 1979, nearly half of all wives 16 years old and over (with and without children) were working or looking for work, and slightly over half of all children under 18 living in two-parent families (60% in one-parent families) had mothers who were in the labor force (U.S. Department of Labor, 1979). As women come to espouse the same career goals as men, and as parental and professional roles are seen as equally appropriate for both sexes, increasing numbers of families will be confronted by the conflicting priorities of home vs. work, and of wife's career development vs. husband's (Gross, 1980; Skinner, 1980).

418

Akin to the concept of the androgynous, or non-gender-roled, relationship is the widely discussed "open marriage," a relationship characterized by functioning in the "here and now" with realistic expectations, respect for personal privacy, role flexibility, open and honest communication, open companionship, pursuit of identity, mutual trust, and equality of power and responsibility (O'Neill & O'Neill, 1972). It is interesting to find that, although the past decade has witnessed much support for many of the values inherent in open marriage, research suggests that few college-educated couples actually evidence these characteristics (Wachowiak & Bragg, 1980).

Similar to open marriage is the concept of "open family," with its emphasis on flexible role prescriptions across both age and gender, clear communication with extensive negotiation and decision by consensus, open expression of emotion, and mutual respect (McGinnis & Flannegan, 1976; Constantine, 1977). But, once again, in spite of increasing lip service given to these values, there is little evidence that American families reflect them in actual practice.

It seems clear that education must continue to sensitize students to the issues of gender equality and prepare them to deal realistically with the conflicts they are likely to experience if they seek to live more androgynous lives. It also seems clear that if more egalitarian relationships are to be a reality of our society, there must be a more conscious fostering of this ideal and training for such relationships.

Whether to be Sexually Exclusive

Among the well-documented realities of modern life are the increases in reported sexual interaction with someone other than one's spouse or primary partner (particularly for women), the fact that the first incident is occurring at a younger age, and the finding that rates for women are becoming similar to those for men (Athanasiou, Shaver, & Tavris, 1970; Hunt, 1974; Bell, Turner, & Rosen, 1975; Levin, 1975; Maykovich, 1976). Moreover, research has made it clear that extramarital sex is not necessarily indicative of or contributive to a poor primary or marital relationship (Johnson, 1970; Hunt, 1974; Bell et al., 1975; Levin, 1975; Glass & Wright, 1977; Atwater, 1979). There are, in fact, couples who have made a mutual decision to allow one or both to have openly acknowledged non-competing sexual relationships with satellite partners (Ramey, 1976), believing that such a relationship maximizes the opportunity for both personal growth and emotional security. It is also clear that for many persons such a lifestyle is not functional. The viability of non-exclusivity as a lifestyle appears to depend on such variables as the quality of the primary relationship, the demands of the outside relationship, and the personalities of the individuals involved (Knapp & Whitehurst, 1977).

Given the above, it follows that persons need to be prepared for the reality that, at some point in their lives, they or their loved ones may violate the traditional norms of sexual exclusivity, and to be given the skills and perspective necessary to deal constructively with such an eventuality. Students need to be taught that there are, in fact, viable alternatives to traditional exclusivity, but that these do not work well for many. In order that they can better determine whether a nonexclusive lifestyle is likely to be appropriate for them and/or their partner, they must gain a knowledge of the kinds of problems which can be anticipated, an understanding of the personal characteristics associated with success, and a realistic appraisal of their own needs and limits.

Bernard (1977) has suggested that since in to-day's society it is difficult to achieve both sexual exclusivity and permanence, and since to insist on sexual exclusivity seems to lead to a pattern of serial monogamy, we would be wise to redefine marital fidelity to mean "living up to one's vows." If one were to follow this suggestion, it appears that one function of family life education is to help students think clearly about what promises they can realistic-ally make to their partners. It is possible, for instance, that instead of promising a lifetime of exclusivity, a couple might agree to the process by which they will deal with any desires for extramarital intimacy. Thus, it becomes necessary for the curricu-lum to include the teaching of communication and conflict-negotiation skills (e.g., Gordon, 1970; Guerney, 1977; Mace & Mace, 1977; Miler, Nunnally, &

Wackman, 1979) and that some consideration be given to constructive approaches to the problems of jealousy and possessiveness (Mazur, 1977).

Gender of Partner

Until recently, gender of partner would not have been considered a choice which persons voluntarily made, nor would the selection of a same-sex partner have been viewed as an acceptable alternative. But the '70s ushered in important changes with regard to the viability of gay relationships and the social acceptability of homosexuality as a personal lifestyle (Bell & Weinberg, 1978; Harry & Lovely, 1979; Masters & Johnson, 1979). It is anticipated that there will be an increasing number of individuals who experience intimate relationships with persons of the same sex at some point in their lives, who choose to live as acknowledged homosexuals, and who challenge the laws which discriminate against them. Family life education can do much to increase society's understanding of such persons and help to eliminate the myths and prejudices surrounding this lifestyle.

Given the above goal, it follows that family life curricula should ideally include activities geared to help young persons understand those who differ in choice of sexual partner, appreciate the similarities between homosexual and heterosexual relationships, and accept themselves should their choice be atypical. Students need to realize that there are many, often as yet poorly understood, reasons for sexual preference, and that sexual preference is not necessarily consistent throughout a lifetime. They need to make the necessary distinctions between gender identity, sex-role identity, and gender of preferred sexual partner, and to recognize that one's sexual preference is distinct from one's degree of masculinity or femininity. And, so that they may participate as informed citizens, they need to understand the issues related to the legal rights of gay persons, particularly those concerning marriage and parenthood.

To Live Alone or With Others

The relative strength of one's needs for emotional closeness and for personal space is basic to the decision of whether to live alone or with others, and, if with others, with how much obligation to the others. Multiadult households, such as communes and multilateral marriage, are instances of living patterns based on an expectation of high degrees of sharing and togetherness. For many, the communes associated with the late '60s and early '70s resulted from a desire for community, and those few which survived usually evidenced a high degree of social organization and subordination of the individual to the group (Kanter, 1972, 1973; Mowery, 1978; Ruth, 1978). Multilateral or group marriage (Constantine & Constantine, 1973; Constantine, 1978), a lifestyle characterized by three or more partners each of whom considers him or herself personally committed to more than one of the other partners, necessitates a high energy investment in consensual decision-making.

It is important to note that most of these more complex living ventures have not continued for long. While much of their demise can be traced to poor organizational and interpersonal skills, even more basic may be the fact that persons came into them with little awareness of the demands of these living arrangements and with high hopes for a sense of togetherness coupled with a firm personal commitment to individual freedom--mutually exclusive needs which will inevitably clash if not consciously reconciled. Helping persons recognize the importance of assessing their own needs and limits, in particular their relative needs for intimacy and autonomy, as they make a choice of living pattern, can be an important function of family life education.

A Suggested Approach

The challenge of preparing persons to deal constructively with contemporary alternative lifestyles is a difficult one. The issues are controversial, the requisite skills and understandings are many, and resources are limited. There are many who will argue that even to acknowledge the existence of alternatives is to legitimize them, and that such legitimation works only to further erode the stability of an already over-stressed society. They suggest that to present the student with a smorgasbord of choice will serve merely to further confuse and to foster a climate of normlessness and anomie. There are others who will say that the purpose of education is to inform, and that to deny students an opportunity to explore and discuss the realities of contemporary society is to ill-prepare them to move intelligently within that society. The question is: How can we help students examine the available alternatives in a way which will simultaneously enhance both their awareness and understanding and their sense of personal competence and direction?

The approach to be presented here is based on a humanistic perspective operating within a Kohlberg framework (see Englund, 1980). Thus, the intention is to maximize the opportunity for personal growth and individual choice while pressing for an awareness of the values underlying one's choices and the effect of these choices on the larger social system. The proposed format seeks to stimulate both cognitive and affective learning (Olson & Moss, 1980), and equal emphasis is devoted to the development of values, skills, and knowledge. The goal is for students to become sufficiently aware of their own values, of the decision-making process, and of the available alternatives that they can make mature, informed, functional lifestyle choices for themselves and understand those who make choices different from their own.

The proposal is envisioned as a first course in family life education, thereby laying a foundation for later courses which would focus in more depth on such topics as parent education and couple relationships. Having developed in their first course an appreciation for the wide range of current family forms, students in the advanced courses would be less likely to fall into the present trap of discussing parenting only within the traditional nuclear family, or viewing couple relationships as only premarital or first-marriage.

Establishing a Supportive Environment

In order that students may grow in self-awareness and experience an unbiassed exposure to the various options, staff must create a classroom atmosphere of mutual acceptance, conducive to self-disclosure and mutual sharing. It must be clearly understood that no one lifestyle is necessarily correct for all and that each lifestyle has its own particular set of costs and benefits, both for the individuals involved and for society. It is often helpful to begin such a

423

course with a discussion of the guidelines to be
followed during the course, and to have these posted
in a conspicuous spot. The list should be generated
with the students and include those procedures which
they think are necessary if they are to feel safe
sharing their ideas and experience with one another.
Students should be encouraged to speak for themselves
rather than for others (e.g., "It is difficult for me
to imagine myself ever feeling comfortable living with
a guy if I wasn't married to him" rather than "I can't
imagine anyone ever feeling comfortable..."), and
judgmental comments should focus on process rather
than content (e.g., "You have not told us why you
would prefer to have a wife who didn't work" rather
than "You are really old-fashioned if you don't want
your wife to work"). It is important that the teacher
model the agreed-upon principles and help students to
act upon them.

Getting in Touch with Values

Just as the instructor makes decisions regarding
classroom procedures based on his/her value system,
so students must come to realize that they will make
their lifestyle choices based upon a particular system
of values. For them to make conscious and consistent
choices, it will be necessary that they have some conception of the value system from which they are operating.

Because so much of an individual's value system
and role expectations are influenced by the family in
which s/he grew up, it seems reasonable to begin such
a course with an analysis of one's family of origin.
Assignments can include such activities as: construction of a family genogram, depicting the members of
the family and their structural relationship to one
another; observation of one's family in interaction,
with particular attention to communication patterns,
roles, power, rules, cohesion, and how family members
deal with conflict (Carnes, 1981); interviews of
significant family members regarding importance
attached to marriage and family and their views of
the family's roles, rules, and traditions.

As students share the structure and roles within
their family system, the wide variation in family
patterns in modern society should become vividly obvious. The teacher can take the opportunity to dia-

424

gram in detail some of the described patterns, noting, for instance, the complexities of the stepfamily with its frequent role ambiguities and loyalty conflicts. Students can learn the basic concepts used to analyze family functioning and those components of healthy family process which appear to operate irrespective of family structure (e.g., Lewis, Beavers, Gussett, & Philips; 1976; Olson, Sprenkle, & Russell, 1979). Most importantly, they can begin to articulate the value patterns which have been modeled by their family and which are likely to play a significant role in their own life choices. Values clarification and moral development will be fostered throughout the course as the teacher seeks to elicit a diversity of opinion, explores a variety of lifestyles, and raises questions designed to encourage students to consider the possible reasons for, and personal and societal consequences of, the various lifestyle options.

Decision-Making and Conflict-Negotiation Skills

The ability to make decisions, both for one's self and with others, is a crucial skill in a society which espouses freedom of choice and respect for the needs of others. It is, therefore, necessary that students learn the basic skills associated with decision-making and conflict-negotiation: the ability to send complete, congruent "I" messages, the ability to listen to a message and to confirm that it has been received accurately, and the ability to identify and evaluate alternatives (Miller et al., 1979). Taught relatively early in the term, these skills can be practiced in the course of later class discussion. Journals in which students keep a record and analysis of their own communications with significant others, and of their observations of the communications of others, will serve to keep these skills in focus and allow an opportunity to monitor student progress.

Knowledge of Alternative Family Forms

If students are to make informed decisions for themselves, they must have knowledge of the various options open to them. It is suggested that class time be given to consideration of each of the eight life-style choices listed in Table 1. Discussion should seek to place each lifestyle option in historical perspective, noting the societal and psychosocial factors that led to the development of the tradition-

al way and its alternatives, identify the personal
and social costs and benefits typically associated
with each, and review the available research. The
extent of such coverage will vary with the nature of
the student body.

It is important during the above discussion to
note that the various options are not theoretically
mutually exclusive. Thus, it would be possible to
"mix and match" the alternatives in any number of
different combinations. One can, for instance, choose
to stay single, have children, co-parent, make a permanent commitment, be sexually non-exclusive, have a
same-sex partner, and live communally. It is possible,
therefore, given the increased acceptance of pluralism
in modern society and a careful choice of associates,
to write one's lifestyle script in any of a number of
ways. One must also realize that the particular lifestyle one ends up living is not always a matter of
choice, and may be thrust upon one by circumstances or
the wishes of others--some lifestyles results from
ideology and personal choice, while some are borne of
necessity. Students should also understand that lifestyle choices are not necessarily made "once and for
all." Given the rapid social change and inevitable
personal developmental changes, choices made at one
point in life may not be the choice and/or the reality
at another point in life.

In addition to the above cognitive focus, it is
suggested that students be provided some first-hand
experience with persons living these various alternatives. This can be provided in several ways: persons
living a given lifestyle can be asked to come to class
to share with the students their own particular experience, or students can interview persons living in
various lifestyles and then share their observations
with the class. One class period might include, for
instance, reports from students who have interviewed
single-parent fathers, in which they describe the
nature of the living arrangement, the history of that
arrangement, and the problems and satisfactions experienced. Given such information, the class could
speculate about the viability and the prevalence of
the particular lifestyle in the future.

There are numerous assignments which could be
given near the end of the course to help students
articulate and summarize what they had learned about

their own lifestyle preferences. A role play in which
they are asked to develop a premarital or precohabita-
tion contract with another class member would encourage them to review those lifestyle issues which couples should discuss and negotiate prior to a long-term
commitment. This would require that each individual
take a position on such questions as whether and when
to have children, child care and house maintenance
roles, use of leisure time, and the nature of acceptable outside relationships, thus establishing their
current view on these matters. The act of negotiating
with their "partner" would also provide a good indicator of their current skill at constructive communication. In addition, students might be asked to write a
summary paper, indicating their anticipated choice for
each of the lifestyles options, with reasons for that
choice.

Conclusions

Although the dominant family pattern in our
society continues to appear very traditional (with
the majority choosing to marry, remain married, have
children, live in single-family households, and be
sexually exclusive and heterosexual), there have been
significant changes which must be reflected in education for contemporary family life. First, there have
been dramatic increases in the proportion of working
wives, single-person households, divorce and remarriage rates, stepfamilies and binuclear families, and
persons living together unmarried, each with its own
set of complexities and personal and social implications. Second, there has been an increased emphasis
on quality of interpersonal relationships within
marriage and the family, with little preparation in
how to achieve this. Third, and most important, there
has been a continued evolutionary movement toward individual freedom of choice, with a growing awareness
of lifestyle options and acknowledgement that lifestyle choices made at one point in life may not be
appropriate at another point. This means that,
irrespective of one's preferred lifestyle, individuals
today are faced with greater expectations of family
life but little knowledge of how to meet these, the
stress of continual decision-making and negotiation,
the uncertainty that comes from having few available
role models for many of the newer lifestyles, and the
insecurity that comes from venturing in new directions
with little societal support.

If we are to equip students to deal effectively with these realities, it is important that family life educators:

1. foster an awareness of the range of family living patterns within our society and of the personal and societal implications of this growing pluralism;

2. provide as much information as possible about the available alternatives, so that students can make informed decisions for themselves and react intelligently and supportively to the lifestyle decisions of others;

3. help students become aware of the values, needs, and expectations which grow out of their own socialization, and understand the impact which these will have on their own choice of lifestyle and family pattern;

4. focus on building those basic decision-making and communication skills needed to constructively negotiate familial conflict and generate creative lifestyle solutions; and

5. provide some understanding of the basic components of healthy family functioning which appear to operate irrespective of lifestyle and family form.

If will not be easy for educators to do the kind of educating which has been indicated, and much of it cannot be accomplished solely within the secondary or college curriculum. Many of the lifestyle issues which confront persons today do not become a reality until adulthood, and although it is important that they be introduced earlier, instruction will be most relevant when the individual is actively involved in decision-making. Many constituencies will be uncomfortable with the open approach which is espoused here, and hence, modifications will frequently be necessary. What is suggested is an ideal based on the assumption that individuals have a right to make decisions about how they will live, that it is only through personal and societal exploration of new ways that necessary adaptation and evolution occurs, and that given sufficient factual information, opportunity for experience, and skills with which to process that experience,

persons will, in general, make wise, functional lifestyle choices. It is hoped that family life educators
can gradually move to implement this ideal.

REFERENCE NOTES

1. Parks, A. <u>Single parent families: Meeting the challenge of the 1980's.</u> Unpublished paper presented at The Groves Conference on Marriage and the Family, 1981. (Available from the author, Parents Without Partners, 7910 Woodmont Ave., Bethesda, MD).

2. Whitehurst, R. N. <u>Relationship contracts: Making, keeping, and breaking them.</u> Unpublished paper presented at The Groves Conference on Marriage and the Family, 1981. (Available from the author, Dept. of Sociology, University of Windsor, Windsor, Ontario, Canada N98 3P4).

B I B L I O G R A P H Y

Ahrons, C. R.

1979   "The binuclear family: Two households, one family." <u>Alternative Lifestyles,</u> 2, 499-515.

Athanasiou, R., Shaver, P., & Tavris, C.

1970   "Sex." <u>Psychology Today,</u> 4, 39-52.

Atwater, L.

1979   "Getting involved: Women's transition to first extramarital sex." <u>Alternative Lifestyles,</u> 2, 38-68.

Bell, A. P., & Weinberg, M. S.

1978   <u>Homosexualities: A study of diversity among men and women.</u> New York: Simon & Schuster.

Bell, R. R., Turner, S., & Rosen, L.

1975   "A multi-variate analysis of female extramarital coitus." <u>Journal of Marriage and the Family,</u> 37, 375-384.

Bernard, J.

1977   "Some moral and social issues." In R.
                W. Libby and R. N. Whitehurst (Eds.),
                Marriage and alternatives: Exploring
                intimate relationships. Glenview, IL:
                Scott, Foresman.

Calhoun, L. G. &
Selby, J. W.

1980   "Voluntary childlessness, involuntary
                childlessness, and having children: A
                study of social perceptions." Family
                Relations, 29, 181-183.

Carnes, P. J.

1981   Family development I: Understanding
                us. Interpersonal Communication Pro-
                grams.

Constantine, L. L.

1977   "Open family: A lifestyle for kids and
                other people." The Family Coordinator,
                26, 113-121.

Constantine, L. L.

1978   "Multilateral relations revisited: Group
                marriage in extended perspective." In
                B. I. Murstein (Ed.), Exploring intimate
                life styles. New York: Springer.

Constantine, L. L., &
Constantine, J. M.

1973   Group marriage: A study of contemporary
                multilateral marriage. New York:
                Macmillan.

Englund, C. L.

1980   "Using Kohlberg's moral developmental
                framework in family life education."
                Family Relations, 23, 7-13.

431

Glass, S. P., &
Wright, T. L.

    1977   "The relationship of extramarital sex,
length of marriage, and sex differences
on marital satisfaction and romanticism:
Athanasiou's data reanalyzed." Journal
of Marriage and the Family, 39, 691-703.

Glick, P. G.

    1979   "Children of divorced parents in demo-
graphic perspective." Journal of Social
Issues, 35, 170-182.

Glick, P. C.

    1979   "Future American families." The Washing-
ton COFO Memo, 2, 2-5. (b)

Gordon, T.

    1970   Parent effectiveness training: The
"no-lose" program for raising respon-
sible children. New York: Peter H.
Wyden.

Gross, H. E.

    1980   "Dual-career couples who live apart:
Two types." Journal of Marriage and
the Family, 42, 567-576.

Guerney, B. G., Jr.

    1977   Relationship enhancement; Skilling
training programs for therapy, problem
prevention, and enrichment. San
Francisco: Jossey-Bass.

Harry, J., &
Lovely, R.

    1979   "Gay marriages and communities of sexual
orientation." Alternative Lifestyles,
2, 177-200.

Hunt, M.

    1974   "Sexual behavior in the 1970's."
                 Chicago: Playboy.

Jacques, J. M., &
Chason, K. J.

    1979   "Cohabitation: Its impact on marital
                 success." The Family Coordinator, 28,
                 35-39.

Johnson, R. E.

    1970   "Some correlates of extramarital
                 coitus." Journal of Marriage and the
                 Family, 32, 449-456.

Kanter, R. M.

    1972   Commitment and community: Communes and
                 utopias in sociological perspective.
                 Cambridge, MA: Harvard University Press.

Kanter, R. M. (Ed.)

    1973   Creating and managing the collective
                 life style. New York: Harper & Row.

Knapp, J. J., &
Whitehurst (Eds.)

    1977   "Sexually open marriage and relation-
                 ships: Issues and prospects." In R. W.
                 Libby and R. N. Whitehurst (Eds.),
                 Marriage and alternatives: Exploring
                 intimate relationships. Glenview, IL:
                 Scott, Foresman.

Levin, R. J.

    1975   "The Redbook report on premarital and
                 extramarital sex: The end of the double
                 standard?" Redbook, October, 38-44,
                 190-192.

Lewis, J., Beavers, W. R. Gussett, J. T., &
Philips, V. A.

1976   No single thread: Psychological health
        in family systems. New York: Brunner/
        Mazel.

Libby, R. W.

1977   "Creative singlehood as a sexual life-
        style: Beyond marriage as a rite of
        passage." In R. W. Libby and R. N.
        Whitehurst (Eds.), Marriage and alter-
        natives: Exploring intimate relation-
        ships. Glenview, IL: Scott, Foresman.

Mace, D., &
Mace, V.

1977   How to have a happy marriage: A step by
        step guide to enriched relationships.
        Nashville: Abington.

Macklin, E.D.

1978   "Non-marital heterosexual cohabitation:
        A review of research." Marriage and
        Family Review, 1, March/April, 1-12.

Macklin, E. D.

1980   "Nontraditional family forms: A decade
        of research." Journal of Marriage and
        the Family, 42, 905-922.

Masters, W. H., &
Johnson, V E.

1979   Homosexuality in perspective. Boston:
        Little, Brown.

Maykovich, M. K.

1976   "Attitudes vs. behavior in extramarital
        sexual relations." Journal of Marriage
        and the Family, 38, 693-699.

Mazur, R.

1977   "Beyond jealousy and possessiveness."
              In R. W. Libby and R. N. Whitehurst
              (Eds.), Marriage and alternatives:
              Exploring intimate relationships.
              Glenview, IL: Scott, Foresman.

McGinnis, T. C., &
Finnegan, D. G.

1976   Open family and marriage: A guide to
              personal growth. St. Louis: C. V.
              Mosby.

Miller, S., Nunnally, E. W., &
Wackman, D. B.

1979   Couple communication I: Talking together.
              Interpersonal communication Programs.

Milne, A. L. (Ed.)

1979   Joint custody: A handbook for judges,
              lawyers, and counselors. Portland:
              Association of Family Reconciliation
              Courts.

Mowery, J.

1978   "Systemic requisits of communal groups."
              Alternative Lifestyles, 1, 235-261.

Newcomb, M.D., &
Bentler, P.M.

1980   "Cohabitation before marriage: A com-
              parison of married couples who did
              and did not cohabit." Alternative
              Lifestyles, 3, 65-85.

Newcomb, P. R.

1979   "Cohabitation in America: An assessment
              of consequences." Journal of Marriage
              and the Family, 41, 597-603.

Olson, D. H., Sprenkle, D.H., &
Russell, C. S.

1979   "Circumplex model of marital and family
            systems I: Cohesion and adaptability
            dimensions, family types, and clinical
            applications." Family Process, 18, 3-28

Olson, T. D., &
Moss, J.J.

1980   "Creating supportive atmospheres in
            family life education." Family Rela-
            tions, 29, 391-395.

O'Neill, N., &
O'Neill, G.

1972   Open marriage: A new life style for
            couples. New York: M. Evans.

Ory, M. G.

1978   "The decision to parent or not:
            Normative and structural components."
            Journal of Marriage and the Family,
            40, 531-539.

Ramey, J. W.

1976   Intimate friendships. Englewood Cliffs
            NJ: Prentice Hall.

Ruth, D. J.

1978   "The commune movement in the middle
            1970s." In B. I. Murstein (Ed.),
            Exploring intimate life styles. New
            York: Springer.

Sager, C. J.

1976   Marriage contracts and couple therapy.
            New York: Brunner/Mazel.

Scanzoni, J., &
Fox, G. L.

1980   "Sex roles, family and society: The
       seventies and beyond." Journal of
       Marriage and the Family, 42, 743-756.

Skinner, D. A.

1980   "Dual-career family stress and coping:
       A literature review." Family Relations,
       29, 473-481.

Stein, P. J.

1978   "The lifestyles and life chances of the
       never-married." Marriage and Family
       Review, 1, July/August, 1-11.

U.S. Bureau of the Census

1977   "Marital status and living arrangements:
       March 1976." Current Population Reports,
       Series P-20, No. 306. Washington, D.C.:
       U.S. Government Printing Office.

U.S. Bureau of the Census

1979(a) "Household and family characteristics:
       March 1978." Current Population Reports,
       Series P-20, No. 340. Washington, D.C.:
       U.S. Government Printing Office. (a)

U.S. Bureau of the Census

1979(b) "Fertility of American women: June 1978."
       Current Population Reports, Series P-20,
       No. 341. Washington, D.C.: U.S.
       Government Printing Office.

U.S. Bureau of the Census

1980   "Marital status and living arrangements:
       March, 1979." Current Population Re-
       ports, Series P-20, No. 349. Washing-
       ton, D.C.: U.S. Government Printing
       Office.

U.S. Department of Labor

1979   "Multi-earner families increase." <u>News</u>,
       October 31. Washington, D.C.: Office
       of Information.

Veevers, J.E.

1979   "Voluntary childlessness: A review of
       issues and evidence." <u>Marriage and</u>
       <u>Family Review</u>, 2, Summer 1-26.

Visher, E. B., &
Visher, J. S.

1979   <u>Stepfamilies: A guide to working with</u>
       <u>stepparents and stepchildren.</u> New
       York: Brunner/Mazel.

Wachowiak, D., &
Bragg, H.

1980   "Open marriage and marital adjustment."
       <u>Journal of Marriage and the Family</u>,
       42, 57-82.

Weitzman, L. J.

1974   "Legal regulation of marriage: Tradi-
       tion and change." <u>California Law Re-</u>
       <u>view</u>, 62, 1169-1288.

Yllo, K. A.

1978   "Non-marital cohabitation: Beyond the
       college campus." <u>Alternative Life-</u>
       <u>styles</u>, 1, 37-54.

*Eleanor D. Macklin is an Assistant Professor, Depart-
ment of Family and Community Development, University
of Maryland, College Park, MD 20742.

Reprinted from <u>Family Relations</u>, Vol. 30 (October,
1981):567-577. Copyrighted 1981 by the National
Council on Family Relations. Reprinted by permission.

CHAPTER 25

ALTERNATIVE SCRIPTS WITHIN THE GAY WORLD

Wayne S. Wooden*

I. INTRODUCTION

To be homosexual in America has historically
meant to be labeled as different. But until recently such differences have implied being "deviant"
and have generated such negative institutional sanctions as being "sinful" or "immoral" (religious),
"sick" or "mentally disturbed" (medical), and/or
"criminal" (legal). In the decade of the 1970's,
however, being gay or lesbian came to be viewed as
a "variant" rather than a "deviant" form of sexual/
social expression, and thereby viewed as a legitimate alternative to traditional family patterns. The
gay lifestyle has now emerged as one of but many forms
of lifestyles and living arrangements that are being
defined under the heading of the "contemporary family."
The nature of this shift in societal labeling and gay
self-esteem; and the impact this shift has generated
for lesbians, gay men, and the contemporary family,
are the focuses of this chapter.

II. REVIEW OF THE LITERATURE

Much of the scholarly literature in the past
dealing with homosexuality has focused on either the
etiology or cause of homosexuality, or on the process of "coming out" and assuming a gay or lesbian
identity. Recently, however, scientific inquiries
into all aspects of the gay lifestyle have materialized. Homosexuality is an included topic for sessions
at professional meetings, and numerous articles and
research findings have been published in a variety of
academic journals including the Journal of Homosexuality, the Journal of Social Issues, and the Journal of
Alternative Lifestyles. These studies have broadened
our understanding of homosexuality in both its historical and contemporary context. Furthermore, the subject of homosexuality is discussed more freely in the
mass media--press, television, and cinema in particular. Popular publications aimed specifically at the
gay market have proliferated with many (e.g., Christopher Street, The Advocate) offering insightful

articles pertinent to the gay and lesbian community.

III. EVOLUTION OF THE GAY MOVEMENT

Like all oppressed minorities, the modern American gay movement cites a certain reference point--the so-called "Stonewall Riots" of June, 1969--as the incident which sparked the beginning of a collective outcry against policy harassment and public discrimination. Like the social movements of the 1960's (which proceeded the gay movement), the push for gay rights has had striking similarities. Perhaps the most fundamental similarity between, for example, the black movement and the gay movement, is the shift in self-labeling and self-esteem. The shift from "Negro" to "Black" reflected an increasing emphasis upon an ethnic and cultural identity (rather than purely a racial identity) with the larger society becoming more sensitized to the black experience and that of other ethnic minorities. Likewise, the shift from "homosexual" to "gay" (or "gay men" and "lesbians") has meant a concurrent emphasis upon pride, a sense of community, and social solidarity as a minority group. In fact, increasing public attention has been directed towards these new minorities. The "sociology of minority communities" now includes both the gender minorities (women) and the behavioral or sexual minorities (gays) alongside the more traditional ethnic and racial minorities (Blacks, Chicanos) in its analysis of minority group relations.

Questions inevitably arise as to the extent of this minority group. The Kinsey report published in 1948 indicated roughly 10 percent of the male population had experienced continual same-sex encounters leading to orgasm with roughly 4 percent of the male population being exclusively homosexual. The figure of 10 percent is commonly used as one indicator of the extent of the gay community. If this figure is correct, it means that the gay minority is nearly as large as two other, more visible, minority groups-- namely Blacks (over 11 percent) and the aged (10 percent). It appears that the gays are a sizeable minority group; in some urban communities, furthermore, they wield significant political and economic clout.

440

IV. THE GAY IDENTITY

A recent typology (Cass, 1979) has noted six stages in the formation of a gay identity: identity confusion, identity comparison, identity tolerance, identity acceptance, identity pride, and identity synthesis. In general terms, the first four stages can be viewed as maintaining a more restricted identity ("in the closet") with the later stages indicative of a more open, integrated gay (rather than homosexual) identity. The author contends that the final stage is the ideal although most homosexuals do not reach this goal due to societal pressure and social disapproval of the gay lifestyle.

Other research has also examined the social process of gay identity formation. One study (Dank, 1971) noted that there was on the average a six-year interval between time of first sexual feelings and the decision one is a homosexual. Another study (Riddle & Morin, 1971) found that gay men first acted on their homosexual feelings an average of five years earlier than lesbians. Other research (Saghir & Robins, 1973) found that gay men and lesbians were more heterosexually active at an earlier age than were heterosexuals. In yet another study (Riddle, 1977) it was found that at least a fifth of all lesbians and a tenth of all gay men have children which indicated that they had assumed their homosexual identity later in life; this study also showed that parent's sexual orientation appeared to have no effect on the sexual orientation of their children. Another study (Peplau, 1979) of 127 lesbians found that the group preferred "autonomy and independence" compared to a similarly matched group of heterosexual women.

Undoubtedly one of the major accomplishments in the gay movement in the past decade is the image of the gay as being as equally a positive image as that as being straight. One heterosexual psychologist has even argued that gays may be healthier than straights (Freedman, 1975), and the recent Masters and Johnson research has indicated that heterosexuals can learn much about sexuality from the mutually supportive types of relationships that have developed among some gay male and lesbian couples. The gay community has thrived in numerous urban cities, and a recent account (Shilts, 1982) has shown how influential the gay com-

munity has been in civic affairs (in San Francisco).
Added to the contemporary urban landscape is the
presence of defineable gay neighborhoods or gay
ghettos (Levine, 1979). Gay men and lesbians are also
emerging as viable political candicates, political
appointees, entertainers, and professionals in all
walks of life and occupational pursuits. Gays, of
course, have consistently held positions in all
facets of society; what is strikingly different,
however, is that not until recently have they done
so without having to "cover-up" their affectional
orientation lifestyle.

V. SEXUAL/SOCIAL PATTERNS

With, on the whole, a more positive identity
emerging within the gay community, it should be of
no surprise that the image of the gay identity and
the nature of long-term relationships should also
change. As the gay lifestyle has become more open,
gays are finding it easier to be up-front with
heterosexual friends, siblings, and parents. Likewise, gays, through their community, social, and
political organizations, have been able to interact
in supportive and platonic ways.

What increasingly distinguishes the newer relationships from homosexual relationships in the past
is the markedly lower amount of "role playing" in
that one partner assumed a more traditionally feminine
sexual/social role and the other assumed a more traditionally masculine role. Such extremes have been
replaced by more "equalitarian" (and androgynous)
roles with both partners negating traditional sexual/
social role stereotyping and assuming a more contemporary, all encompassing and varied role. In this
regard, the gay movement has joined the women's and
men's movement in challenging and loosening the rigid
sex role expectations. Quite likely this shift in
emphasis has assisted in increasing the authenticity
and acceptance of the gay lifestyle scripts by the
larger heterosexual society.

At the same time, extremes in gay imagery are
still noted within the male community with the entire
gay men's subculture assuming a more "masculine"
identity. Perhaps as the movement has become more
open, a concern for presenting a less stigmatized
image to the straight community has lessened the

support and presence within the gay community for the more stereotypical "feminine" aspect with its "sissy" image and "camp" humor. The modern gay male is more likely to go to western style bars which present a more "macho" image; dance bars and bars that offer nightclub entertainment for both gay men and lesbians as well as for straights (such as Studio One in Los Angeles) are proliferating.

Finally, the strength of the gay community in the past years has materialized due to the increase in the range of activities that gays can enjoy together which are apart from the bar and bath scene (with its sexually charged atmosphere). Besides the proliferation of gay political organizations, gay community centers are opening up which provides rap sessions and social, medical, and legal services. There are now gay student organizations on university campuses and courses on the gay lifestyle taught in various academic disciplines. There are gay athletic clubs, gay outdoors clubs, gay religious organizations (i.e., Metropolitan Community Church, Dignity, etc.), and organizations for parents and friends of gays. Likewise, there are gay subgroups in many professional organizations (gay doctors, gay dentists, gay engineers, etc.).

What these developments indicate is that being gay in today's society is more than just a sexual orientation. Increasingly it is meaning a social orientation that offers one the opportunity to increase one's support group in a less sexually-emphasized manner. And in this way, the supportive non-gay person is also included. The modern gay individual is just that--gay, proud, and attempting to build a more humanistic community with other gays and straight alike. This is comparable to the sixth stage in the gay identity model: gay synthesis.

Of great importance, then, to the new emerging gay community is the support of concerned heterosexuals. Organizations such as "Parents and Friends of Gays" have formed across the country to assist families in understanding their gay relative and in sharing in their gay lifestyle. Much more needs to be done in this area of counseling and educating the heterosexual community. The homophobic nature of our society has perpetuated "negative" stereotypes of gays which affects both gays and their family members.

With the growth of the public gay movement, and with the national exposure generated by those in opposition to the public gay, our society can come to discuss this issue in a more objective and scientific way. There is a great need to "demystify" the gay lifestyle. Ignorance and misconceptions about homosexuals has long plagued our society. Sound academic research, public forums, and open explorations of the subject are to be encouraged.

What does gay life mean to society? The gay lifestyle can be viewed as a "variant" form of life-style that is <u>not</u> out to "destroy" civilization or the "family." Being gay does not mean being anti-family; in fact, for most gays there is wide inter-action in all realms of family life. Not only are many gays themselves parents, they are viable in all realms of family life. Contemporary family patterns would include, therefore, gay couples (some gay couples have been together for over forty years). Recent research on the older gay male (Kelly, 1977) has indicated a healthier life adaptation to old age among gays since these men have cultivated strong networks of social groups and dealt with the psycho-logical problems of independence earlier in life than married heterosexual men. Gays, therefore, can be examples for the non-gay community with respect to life "passages" and adaptive strategies.

In conclusion, heterosexual society has much to gain by freeing, rather than repressing, the gay life-style. Helping the gay person to become a full-fledged participant in society can only add to the rich cultural diversity that has made our society so unique. The "gay world" indeed offers an alternative script. A person's sexual orientation should not be used to deny that person his or her rightful place in our society--particularly when that person has so much to offer.

BIBLIOGRAPHY

Bird, Caroline

    1975   "Women Should Stay Single," in J.
                      Gipson Wells (ed.), Current Issues in
                      Marriage and the Family. New York:
                      Macmillan, pp. 32-40.

Maslow, Ebraham

    n.d.   "Some Basic Propositions of a Growth
                      and Self-Actualization Psychology,"
                      in Ard (ed.) Counseling and Psycho-
                      therapy. Palo Alto: Science and
                      Behavior Books.

Meints, Jerry

    1979   "Sex, Singles, and the Relationship
                      Addict." Presented at the 1979 annual
                      Society for the Study of Lifestyles,
                      Culver City, California.

Melville, Keith

    1977   "Marriage and Family Today." New York:
                      Random House.

Seal, Herb

    1974   Alternative Life Styles. Singapore:
                      FEP International.

Starr, Joyce R., &
Carns, Donald E.

    1972   "Singles in the City." Society, 4,
                      (February):43-48.

Wolf, Tom

    1975   "The '70's." New York (July).

*Department of Behavioral Sciences, California State
Polytechnic University, Pomona, California 91768

CHAPTER 26

QUESTIONING THE PRIMACY OF THE PRIMARY: AN ANALYSIS OF HUMAN BONDING

Lyn H. Lofland*

I. INTRODUCTION

A recently published book, Return to Main Street (Eberle, 1982), describes the experiences of a family who moved from Chicago to the small town-less than 4,000--of Galena, Illinois. In a review of the book, the reviewer summarizes some of the author's comparisons between "city" and "country" living.

> She makes some telling points as she trots out comparison after comprison between life in the city and life in the country...The city person lives among strangers; the country person among friends...She makes an excellent point when she talks about city dwellers neutering people. We neuter people when we don't look at them as they serve us, the clerks in groceries, tellers in banks, waitresses in restaurants, etc. In the country, you not only know the grocery clerk, your children go to school and play together (Seglund, 1982).

This brief extract surely "plays" a refrain familiar to anyone who has read anything about western societies written in the past 200 years. From Tönnies to Eberele, the plot is the same: contrast strangers with friends and come down on the side of "friend"

Editors Note: The following article was prepared by Professor Lyn Lofland as part of an informal presentation to a special session at the Pacific Sociological Association meetings in San Diego, 1982. Thus, this paper was not written with publication in mind but served instead as a "think through" exercise for sociologists sharing Dr. Lofland's ongoing reflections on the nature of social bonding loss, public and private life. We believe students will greatly benefit from reflecting and "thinking through" with Dr. Lofland the ideas presented in this informal piece.

447

relationships. Contrast the segmental role relationship of occupational knowing combined with extensive
personal knowing and "vote" in favor of the latter.
Contrast the "fleeting relationship" with permanent,
stable interactions and "of course" stability is to
be preferred. And so on through the litany of invi-
dious comparison in which the primary group and the
primary relationship always win.

In this paper, I want to explore in tentative
and preliminary manner, some ideas about the <u>primacy</u>
of the primary groups and relationships in Western
scholarly[1] thought and about consequences of that
primacy.

I will begin by outlining only a bit of the
evidence for the primacy that primary groups/rela-
tionships enjoy in Western thought. This I do
briefly as I suspect that few will find the assertion
anything other than "obvious." I want then to ask
the questions: But are primary groups/relationships
truly preeminent? And even if they are, are they as
singularly so as we seem to think? Finally, I will
ask and hazard an answer to the question: regardless
of the "true" situation, what does our belief in this
primacy do to our thinking about other segments or
realms of social life.

A word of caution. I will be utilizing familiar
materials, but I will be making unfamiliar distinctions among them. I will, for example, be distinguishing between the "public" and "private" realms,
but I include in the private realm all those entities
which are nominally "public" but "primary" in character (e.g., stable, cohesive neighborhoods, tribes,
entire small communities [hamlets, villages], etc.)
as well as the more traditionally included family
and friendship groupings. I hope these unfamiliar
distinctions will not prove confusing.

II. THE PRIMACY OF THE PRIMARY: THE FAMILY AS
     IDEAL TYPE

The "primacy of the primary" in Western thought
seems to be composed of two interrelated postulates.
<u>First</u>, primary relationships and the social organiza-
tional forms of these relationships (i.e., primary
<u>groups</u>: families, friendship groups, neighborhoods,
tribes, communities, etc.) are the <u>best</u> human rela-

tionships and organizational patterns--the sine qua non, as it were, of the creation of "healthy" children and "healthy adults.[2] Second, other than primary, relationships must be understood as lesser and inferior relational forms rather than as equally valuable alternatives or viable substitutes.[3] Two hundred years of scholarly literature devoted to the loss of community, the continuity of community; the loss of personal relationships, the continuation of personal relationships; the destruction of the family, the survival of the family; the presence of alienation, the absence of alienation; the dehumanizing character of modern life, the humanizing potential of modern life, and so forth, has taken as its "of course" assumptions the two postulates suggested above.[4]

Consider, for example, how thoroughly discussions and debates about the character and quality of relationships in Western societies focus on the realm of the "primary"--what I will later call the "private realm." Those who argue, for example, that modern urban society is alienating, do so on the grounds that the family has been weakened or destroyed (e.g., Lasch, 1977 discussed in Cancian, 1980), that neighborhoods are merely enclaves of strangers (Merry, 1980), or that the well beloved "community" of the nostalgically evoked past (usually defined, by implication, if not directly, as the overlap of cultural, acquaintance, and geographic space) has disappeared under the onslaught of (the choice of combinations of choices depending on the preferences of the critic): industrialization, modernization, urbanization, capitalism, technology, the decline of religion, etc.[5] Conversely, writers who counter this dismal view do so on the grounds that varying primary groups are alive and well. In many neighborhoods, local sentiment abounds (Hunter, 1978, 1975, 1974). Families thrive as never before, perhaps are stronger than in the past (Cancian, 1980 is a useful review of the critics of the family critics; see also Hutter, 1981). Spatially contiguous communities may have disappeared, but they have been replaced by "networks" of kin and friends (Fischer, 1982, 1977; Hutter, 1982; Wellman, 1979, 1976)--"community without propinquity" to borrow Webber's (1963) felicitous phrase.

In sum, if we use the "family" as the symbol of the primary group and its relationships, the family stands, in modern Western thought, as the quintessential human arrangement.

III. QUESTIONING THE PRIMACY OF THE PRIMARY: IS
      INTIMACY ALL THERE IS?

But what is the "symbolic" family isn't the
quintessential human arrangement? Or, at least, what
if it isn't quite as quintessential as we think? Let
me grant, momentarily at least, that the primary group
is necessary for childhood socialization; that multi-
faceted and relatively stable connections between
helpless infant/child and responsible older human are
required for the development of a relatively satisfactory "self." But having achieved that "selfhood"--
how requisite is the continued tie of the primal apron
string?

This, what I suppose one might call, rather
apostate question began to occur to me as the consequence of some work I did on human loss and connection.
I was interested in exploring the building blocks of
the social bond, the various linkages (or, as I came
to conceive them, threads) that humans use to attach
themselves to one another. I chose to pursue this
interest by investigating the "loss" experience--
through intensive interviewing, reviewing first person
accounts of grief and case materials from scholarly
works among other data sources. My analysis of these
materials led me to postulate that humans "connect"
to one another in seven different ways--what I called
the "threads of connectedness" (Lofland, 1982). We
are linked to others by the roles we play, by the help
we receive, by the wider network of others made available to us, by the selves others create and sustain,
by the comforting myths they allow us, by the reality
they validate for us and by the futures they make
possible. I did not claim, and do not do so now,
that this listing is exhaustive nor even that it is
the most felicitous one could conceive. I did, however, find it useful in thinking about varying patterns of connectedness and how such patterns might be
related to grief.

Now in thinking about the possibility of variance
in connectedness, as it were, I began to generate some
hypothetical (but, I thought, plausible) patterns.
Figure 1 illustrates four different ways that a person
(A) might distribute his or her "connections"--each of
the seven variations in linking symbols between Person

450

PATTERNS OF CONNECTEDNESS

1. Full range of connections, spread among multiple others.

    ------------   ============
    A++++++++++++B   A::::::::::::C A...........D

                        A#############E
                        ****

2. Limited connections, spread among multiple others.

    A------------B   A::::::::::::C A...........D
                        #############

3. All connections to a single other, multiples of such others.

    ************   ************   ************
    ------------   ------------   ------------
    ::::::::::::   ::::::::::::   ::::::::::::
    A++++++++++++B   A++++++++++++C   A++++++++++++D
    ============   ============   ============
    ....
    ############   ############   ############

4. All connections linked to a single other.

                    ****

                    ::::::::::::
                    A++++++++++++B
                    ============   ----- role partner
                    ....   +++++ mundane assistance
                    ############   ::::: linkages to others
                                     ##### creation & main-
                                           tenance of self
                                     ***** support for com-
                                           forting myths
                                     ===== reality maintenance
                    Figure 1   ..... maintenance of
                                           possible futures

From Lyn H. Lofland, "Loss and Connection: An Exploration into
    the Nature of the Social Bond," in W. Ickes & E. Knowles (eds.),
    Personality, Roles and Social Behavior, Springer-Verlag, 1982.

451

A and Person B, Person A and Person C, and so forth, standing for one of the seven links or threads. Thus, in the first pattern, we conceive of a person who, in a network of others, manages to encompass all seven ties, but with a minimum of multiple bonding to any one person. That is, Person A in this pattern is tied to Person B as a role partner and for mundane assistance, to Person C as a ine to others, to Person D through reality and future maintenance and to Person E as a creator and maintainer of self and as a supporter of comforting myths. Pattern 2 imagines a person, also with a minimum of multiple bonding, but in this instance, lacking the full range of possible linkages. Here Person A is tied to B as a role partner, to C as a link to others and as a creator and maintainer of self, and to D through future maintenance; the other possible connections are simply missing. Pattern 3 postulates someone who is maximally multiply bonded to multiple others, while Pattern 4 illustrates maximal multiple bonding, but to a single other. One can imagine many other possible patterns and can complicate the picture enormously simply by varying, more than has been done here, the number of others to whom any given actor is linked.

Now as I ruminated about these hypothetical patterns, it struck me that patterns 3 and 4, respectively, might be seen as graphic representations of those cynosures of all Western eyes: the primary group and the primary relationship. Pattern 4 is a picture of a primary relationship: multi-faceted and relatively stable, but since it involves only one other person, it is not, of course, the ideal. The Western ideal is Pattern 3: multi-faceted, relatively stable relationships to multiples of others. Here, one is close to, has "intimacy" with[7] a number of other people. One is cozily encased in the embrace of family, of neighborhood, of friendship network, of community.

Appreciating, of course, that I was looking not at empirical reality but at my own hypothetical creations, it nonetheless occurred to me that these patterns 3 and 4 were only two patterns among others. It certainly seemed plausible, for example, that if one looked very closely at the relational patterns of 100 individuals, one would find some individuals who matched pattern 3 and some who matched pattern 4, but others who matched patterns 1 or 2 or others not yet generated. And granting the possibility of individual variation while holding time and space constant, it occurred to me that it was at least thinkable that one might find social/cultural variation by letting time and space vary. One might wonder, that is, whether there is historical and cultural variation in the range, dominance, and/or idealization of extant patterns. In short, might quite viable and fully satisfactory alternatives to the primary group and relationship exist empirically as well as in terms of preferences and idealizations.

Obviously, such speculation does not emerge out of isolation. In being "struck" by these possibilities, I was merely bringing into my own focus what others, in varying contexts, have been suggesting. Simmel's discussoin of "sociability" certainly provides some hints (1950). Richard Sennett goes further than hints. In The Fall of Public Man, he describes the well developed public culture of 18th Century London and Paris with its appreciation of impersonal (read, non-primary) but urbane relationships (Sennett, 1977; see also, 1980). There is Claude Fischer's recent differentiation between the "public and private world of city life" (1981). Jacqueline Wiseman's articulation of the "quasi-primary relationship" that occurs between customers in second hand clothing stores (1979) is suggestive. As is Peggy Wireman's development of the concept of the "intimate secondary relationship" (1978). And if we can get beyond viewing the empirical materials as indicative of "pathology," so are such works as Michael Lieber's Street Life: Afro-American Culture in Urban Trinidad (1981); Elliot Liebow's Tally's Corner (1967) and Elijah Anderson's A Place on the Corner (1978)--all of which describe "rounds of relationships" that are by no means primary, but no less real or significant for that.

But it if is possible that other relational forms not only exist in other times and places or in little noted and little remarked places here and now, but exist as dominant or alternate or even preferred patterns, then possibly the primacy of the primary in our thinking is distorting our vision. Let me, finally, consider the consequences of such possible misperception relative to a single sphere of social life--what I shall call "the public realm."

IV. CONSEQUENCES OF THE PRIMACY OF THE PRIMARY: MISUNDERSTANDING THE PUBLIC REALM

The "city" as a particular settlement form generates a new realm of social life, what I will call "the public realm." Speaking "ideal typically" rather than purely empirically, one can argue that in pre- or non-urban settlement forms--the tribe, the village, the small town--public life and private life conjoin. The characteristic form of social organization in these settlement forms is the "community"-- again defined as the overlap of geographical, cultural, and acquaintance space. That is, pre- or non-urban settlement forms are primary groups containing other primary groups. In such settlement forms when one leaves one's persoal or private space (if the group even makes such a distinction), one moves into a world of acquaintances, kin, friends, enemies, etc. with shome one shares a culture and a history. All relationships, that is, are primary. What is defined as appropriate behavior among primary groups is as appropriate in "private" as in so-called public space.[6]

But in the city, this "conjoining" of realms disappears. As the city emerges, so does the separate and quite discrete public realm. In the city, when one leaves private space, one moves into a world of many unknown others, large numbers of whom do not share one's values, history, or perspective. The public realm, I'm suggesting, is a different world from the private realm and its existence is what differentiates, essentially, the city as a settlement from other settlement types.

We know something about this realm, about its normative structure, its characteristic relations, its aesthetics, and so forth, but we know a great deal less about it than we do about the realm of the private or primary, a direct consequence of the primacy of the latter. work in urban sociology, for example, is dominated by an obsession with the primary group: with the face and future of families, neighborhoods, friendship groups, and so forth in the city.

And when we view the public realm, because we view it through the lens of the primary and evaluate it by the standards of the primary--a consequence of its primacy--we distort what we see. Research suggests, for example, that the public realm is characterized by norms quite different from those which characterize the private (Karp, Stone, & Yoels, 1977 is a good review of the empirical materials on the public realm). Civil inattention contrasts with focused attention; a preference for the "audience" role (viewing the spectacle rather than interfering with it) contrasts with the expectation of participation and involvement. Civility and tolerance in the face of diversity contrasts with a high valuation on, and expectation of, similarity and sharing. Looked at in its own terms as a separate sphere of social life, the public realm is merely different. Looked at through the lens and judged by the standards of the private, it appears unfeeling, sadistically unhelpful, disintersted, unconcerned.

Similarly, research suggests that the public realm is characterized by relations which are fleeting, segmental, and impersonal (although not exclusively so), contrasting with the intimate, multi-faceted, pesonal relations that characterize the private.[7] Looked at in its own terms as a separate sphere of social life, the characteristic relations of the public realm are merely different. Looked at through the lens and judged by the standards of the private, it appears cold, inauthentic, dehumanizing, alienating.

In sum, there is a social realm "out there" different from the realm of the primary. It is one that may provide pleasure, meaning, significance, liberating anonymity, for many people; one that may, in fact, provide an alternative--a satisfactory alternative to the dominating world of primary groups and relationships. That we know so little about it that we cannot say whether it does or could do or ever really has done these things is strong testimony to the primacy of the primary. What else may be similarly obscured.

REFERENCE NOTES

1. The primacy of the primary can be located in popular thought as well but I shall not here consider
that fact.

2. I am here using "healthy" to stand for all the varying attributes assigned by diverse writers to their
preferred sorts of human beings.

3. Even scholars who have begun moving toward a more
"appreciative" stance relative to relational alternatives in the modern world are still likely to
evaluate these alternatives as inferior substitutes
to "genuine" (read, primary) relationships. See,
for example, Stone, 1954; Karp, Stone, & Yoels,
1977:Chapter 4. For a rare exception, see J. Wiseman, 1979.

4. The exact origin of this primacy is unclear. Perhaps it can be traced to the nostalgic dichotomous
thinking of the 19th & early 20th Century writers
like Tönnies and Durkheim and others who were
concerned with the wrenching shifts that the industrial revolution perpetrated on the human fabric;
perhaps to early and later 20th Century thinkers
like Cooley, Mead, and Peaget who identified the
primary group as essential to early socialization;
perhaps to the small town bias of those C. Wright
Mills identified as the "social pathologists"
(1942); perhaps to the small community models which
dominate in anthropological description; perhaps to
some combination of the above along with factors
not even conceived. For similar musings about the
origin of the dominance of the "community" model
in urban sociology, see L. Lofland, 1975:145.
(This paper is, in fact, a continuation of concerns
initially expressed in that publication.)

5. Gusfield, 1975 is a nice review of this chorus.

6. Some family scholars have argued that during the
16th through the 18th Centuries, family life was
less internally absorbing than it is or is expected to be today because individual family members were integrally involved in the "public"
sphere (Aries, 1962; Hutter, 1981; Shorter, 1975).
What these scholars mean by public sphere, however,

is simply the traditional community. One primary group (the immediate family) is viewed as having been overshadowed by another primary group (the community of kin and acquaintances). In my terms, the conversation is still focused on the private realm.

7. I am defining "intimate relations" as those which are multi-bonded. In some portions of the literature, the term takes on a more specific meaning, suggesting a merging of selves, a profound sharing of "deep" feelings and experiences, and so forth. This is a perfectly legitimate usage, but it is not the one I am employing. In my usage, persons who have lived in one another's co-presence for many years, for example, sharing biography and history (inhabitants of a stable village or tribe, say) are intimates, even if they have never had a single "soul searching" conversation.

B I B L I O G R A P H Y

Anderson, Elijah

    1978   A Place on the Corner. Chicago: The University of Chicago Press.

Ariès, Phillipe

    1962   Centuries of Childhood: A Social History of Family Life, Robert Baldick (trans.). New Hork: Knopf.

Cancian, Francesca

    1980   "Social Critics on Recent Changes in Close Relationships and an Alternative View." Unpublished ms.

Delph, Edward

    1978   The Silent Community: Public Homosexual Encounters. Beverly Hills: Sage.

Eberle, Nancy

    1982   Return to Main Street. New York: Norton.

457

Fischer, Claude

1982   Two Dwell Among Friends: Personal Net-
      works in Town and City. Chicago: The
      University of Chicago Press.

1981   "The Public and Private Worlds of City
      Life." American Sociological Review,
      June:306-316.

1977   Networks and Places: Social Relations
      in the Urban Setting. New York: The
      Free Press.

Gusfield, Joseph R.

1975   Community: A Critical Response. New
      York: Harper & Row.

Hunter, Albert

1978   "Persistence of Local Sentiments in
      Mass Society." In David Street and
      Associates (eds.), Handbook of Contem-
      porary Urban Life. San Francisco:
      Jossey-Bass.

1975   "The Loss of Community: An Empirical
      Test Through Replication." American
      Sociological Review, October:537-552.

1974   Symbolic Communities: The Persistence
      and Change of Chicago's Local Communi-
      ties. Chicago: The University of
      Chicago Press.

Hutter, Mark

1981   The Changing Family: Comparative Per-
      spectives. New York: Wiley.

Karp, David, Gregory Stone, &
William Yoels

1977   Being Urban: A Social Psychological
      View of City Life. Lexington, Massa-
      chusetts: D.C. Heath.

Lasch, Christopher

1977   *Haven in a Heartless World*. New York:
            Basic Books.

Latané, Bibb, &
John M. Darley

1973   "Bystander 'Apathy.'" In John Helmer &
            Neil A. Eddington (eds.), *Urbanman:*
            The Psychology of Urban Survival.
            New York: The Free Press.

Lieber, Michael

1981   *Street Life: Afro-American Culture in*
            Urban Trinidad. Boston: G.K. Hall &
            Co. & Cambridge, Massachusetts:
            Schenkman.

Liebow, Elliot

1967   *Tally's Corner: A Study of Negro Street-*
            corner Men. Boston: Little, Brown.

Lofland, Lyn H.

1982   "Loss and Human Connection: An Explora-
            tion into the Nature of the Social
            Bond." In William Ickes & Eric Knowles
            (eds.), *Personality, Roles and Social*
            Behavior. New York: Springer-Verlag.

1975   "The 'Thereness' of Women: A Selective
            Review of Urban Sociology." In Marcia
            Millman & Rosabeth Kanter (eds.),
            Another Voice: Feminist Perspectives on
            Social Life and Social Science. Garden
            City, New York: Doubleday Anchor.

Merry, Sally E.

1980   *Urban Danger: Life in a Neighborhood*
            of Strangers. Philadelphia: Temple
            University Press.

459

Mills, C. Wright

    1942   "The Professional Ideology of Social
                Pathologists." American Journal of
                Sociology, 49:165-180 (September).

Seglund, Wanda

    1982   "The American Dream Lives." Sacramento
                Bee, March 28.

Sennett, Richard

    1980   Review of Jacques Donzelot, The Polic-
                ing of Families. The New York Times
                Book Review, February 24.

    1977   The Fall of Public Man. New York: Knopf.

Shorter, Edward

    1975   The Making of the Modern Family. New
                York: Basic Books.

Simmel, Georg

    1950   The Sociology of Georg Simmel (ed. by
                Kurt H. Wolff), Glencoe, Illinois:
                The Free Press.

Stone, Gregory P.

    1954   "City Shoppers and Urban Identification:
                Observations on the Social Psychology
                of City Life." American Journal of
                Sociology, July:36-45.

Webber, M.

    1963   "Order in Diversity: Community Without
                Propinquity." In L. Wingo (ed.),
                Cities and Space. Baltimore, MD: The
                Johns Hopkins University Press.

Wellman, Barry

    1979   "The community Question: The Intimate
                Networks of East Yorkers." American
                Journal of Sociology, March:1201-1231.

Wireman, Peggy

    1978   "Intimate Secondary Relationships."
                        Paper presented at the Meetings of the
                        American Sociological Association.

Wiseman, Jacqueline

    1979   "Close Encounters of the Quasi-Primary
                        Kind: Sociability in Urban Second-Hand
                        Clothing Stores." _Urban Life_, April:
                        23-51.

*Lyn H. Lofland, Department of Sociology, University of California, Davis, California.

THE TRANSITION OF AMERICAN FAMILIES
MAJOR RAMIFICATIONS FOR CLINICAL WORK

Larry W. Criswell*
and
Alec Robbie**

I. INTRODUCTION

The extended family with a strong dependency between two, and often three, generations existed in
traditional America as a support for individual needs.
Today it appears that individuals must often turn to
other avenues for support.

The family has been the primary unit of our
society and has served as the social environment
through which we were first socialized to our environment. The traditional structure, which consisted of a
homemaker mother, breadwinner father, children, and
grandparents, is now in the minority (Goldenberg and
Goldenberg, 1980). The modern family takes on different structural characteristics, diverse living
arrangements, and diverse organizational patterns.
A number of important causal factors created by
societal shifts in conditions are bringing about these
major effects on the family. Goldenberg and Goldenberg describe some of these changes:

> Even the nuclear family is undergoing dramatic
> change. American women working at paying jobs,
> even when young children are in the home, al-
> ready outnumber those who stay at home, two-
> income families are becoming more commonplace,
> resulting in many changes in role-sharing,
> child rearing, use of day care facilities and
> domestic help, and relationship changes between
> husband and wife. A "career woman" in the past
> was likely to be defensive about not devoting
> her time and energies to her home, husband,
> and children. Today she probably is either a
> working wife trying to attend to her job and
> home (with assistance from her husband and
> others), a single woman who may or may not
> marry, a married woman who has chosen to delay
> or forego having children, or the head of a

single-parent household (Goldenberg and Goldenberg, 1980).

Major studies have suggested that the family is the central group to the large majority of the populace, and that most people depend upon the family for personal happiness and satisfaction. The problem now is that of meeting the needs of individuals and of the new kinds of family unit (i.e., blended families, single-parent families, communal, etc. (Glasser, 1980)).

The problem appears to be that the family is in transition in response to the influences of major social conditions. The actual size of families today are smaller in size than in the past, and an increasingly larger number of adults are remaining single. In fact, there has been mention of a new-found push and celebration for individual freedom and independence from the traditional extended family responsibilities which had been accepted as part of an individual's social responsibility.

II. SOCIETAL CHANGE AFFECTING FAMILIES

Diversity in living arrangements, both in experience of men and women over their life courses and in the make-up of households at given points in time, will continue to mark the next decade. The once typical household--two parent, and children, with a husband-breadwinner and wife-homemaker--has faded in prominence. Although most Americans still live in conventional nuclear families sometime during their lives, traditional families are a small minority of all households at any given time. Other types of households--two worker families, families whose children have moved away, retired couples, single-parent families, and men and women living alone--are proliferating and are becoming an increasing proportion of households overall (Masnick and Bane, 1980).

The phenomenon of more and more individuals spending less and less time in transitional family living arrangement, has provoked a good deal of anxiety on several counts (Halleck, 1976). First, families and family relationships in our society have long been considered major elements of a meaningful life. If fewer and fewer people live in families, this source of meaning and satisfaction may be lost, leaving many people disoriented and alienated. Second, families have long sheltered and cared for society's dependent members: children, the elderly, the sick, the disabled, and the poor. Changes in the family lead to question about who will take care of these dependents (Masnick and Bane, 1980).

But what may lead to the change in the nuclear or extended family? A list of changes can readily be developed and some items on this list would probably include female role change, financial conditions of the family, the nation's recession, politics, the E.R.A., new sexual mores, people living longer, effects of mass media on the family, and an overall fragmentation of roles within the family. Within the last 12-15 years the U.S. has been changing awareness in the roles women play in contemporary society. Today's women know that they can enter the business world, compete, and have their own careers. With this realization, a woman can now choose to be a mother and housewife, a career woman, or a mother and career woman. With these options comes the affects on the family. If a woman decides to pursue a career, she then puts off having a family until later. A woman may now live alone, with a roommate, or not move out of her original nuclear family. All of these options affect the traditional nuclear family. Tying together the nation's recession and financial problem, in the contemporary family, one readily sees the need for a two-income household. With these added financial pressures, children may be postponed to a later date due to economic uncertainties. As the couple gains financial security, children may not seem as important due to the age of the couple or new priorities. All of these events impact whether or not a nuclear family is established.

Emerging now is a sexual revolution like none other in history. The mass media promotes casual sex, sexual exploration, and less serious partner bonding. This may have a devastating effect on the family due to the fact that stability in relationships is being tested. The media may tell one that is is OK to "play-around," to explore one's own limits, and not worry about a hard line commitment. Because of this attitude, the family may come under fire for its old-fashioned conservatism and attitudes. Basically, what is being said here is that the traditional nuclear family has not found a way of incorporating liberal thinking of today's society.

A family member's role, based on that person's age and sex, defines certain expected, permitted, as well as forbidden patterns of behavior. As was mentioned before, American society has undergone both a sexual evolution and a sex-role revolution. The former has liberalized attitudes toward erotic behavior and its expression. The latter has changed the roles and spouses of both men and women, in the direction of greater equality. Due to this equality and other factors previously mentioned, both spouses are usually employed. In what Rapoport and Rapoport (1969) call role overload in a dual-career family, various stressors are likely to appear when two people try to play too many roles at work and at home for the time and energy they have available. Children in such situations are often given increased responsibilities which may cause disengagement in the family and may lead to that child not selecting to pursue a nuclear family situation in her/her later life.

With all these factors affecting the family and its future, we are already seeing the end results. Fewer marriages, people waiting longer to marry and thereby possibly negating the possibility of children, higher divorce rates, and society as a whole having to accommodate a variety of family structures. The birth rate now is the lowest in our history; the divorce rate's the highest ever and the highest of any industrialized country (Olson, Russell, and Sprenke, 1980). Parenting without marriage has risen sharply in recent years: 15% of all births are now illegitimate (Masnick and Bane, 1980). All of these factors are leading to people now waiting to marry, and, again, children may be postponed or not considered. Our society is likely to continue to experiment with unconventional family patterns and nonfamilial living arrangements. There are now many compositions of the family unit: the nuclear family, extended family, blended family, common law family, single-parent family, commune family, serial family, composite family, and cohabitation (Butler, 1979; Goldenberg and Goldenberg, 1980).

The individual feelings resulting from family disruption are critical. Alienation from others can be very detrimental. When alienated, one may feel depressed and senses a low level of selfworth. This is made worse when no family ties are there to help one who feels alone or unwanted. The "Who Am I" statement and "What is life all about" statement tend to mount up and there seems to be no way out except to become more depressed. With no family ties it is also hard to have one's needs met from others if no socialization skills have been learned or nurtured from the family environment. People need ties to get a portion of their needs met. When one can't get satisfaction from the family, one may turn to his/her peer group for these need satisfactions. If one has a positive peer group to elicit these needs from, then nurturing exists, but not all needs can be met from this type of group and a faulty sense of security may be established. Also, as mentioned before, the family has traditionally been the place where dependent members of society have been maintained. But because families are now not fulfilling this role, the city, state, or federal government may be called in to help. Here again one sees that vital needs and concerns met by the family may now be superficially met by institutions or programs. Either way, the individual is losing out of the nurturance which can be instilled by the family unit (Kemper, 1976).

III.   WHAT CAN BE DONE TO HELP CONQUER THESE NEEDS?

Problems may arise when the traditional nuclear family is altered or put aside totally for another family lifestyle. Alienation, identity crises, rebellion, and overview of the bureaucratic resources are but a few (Kempler, 1976). So, what can be done to help an individual who is having any of the aforementioned problems?

One logical area is the professional resources of mental health experts. A client may often attempt to utilize a "friend." A professional should be viewed as one who can help or re-educate a person to look at life in a different light. Skills can be learned so that a person can reenter the main stream of life and have adaptive qualities that did not come from the family environment. The professional can help a person become his/her own best resource, whereupon the client can decide for him/herself as to what is important in life. After a person is more emotionally suited to have a life on her/her own, independent of a traditional family environment, he/she can then explore different or alternative life-styles.

Many overviews raise questions here about whether the increasing numbers of one- and two-persons households will lead to a society in which large numbers of people are essentialy alone and cut off from others (Halleck, 1976). This answer, along with the previously mentioned alternatives, depends on the extent and quality of relationships outside the household with friends, neighbors, and others. These relationships are not well understood, at least partly because most statistical sources focus only on relationships within households (Masnick and Bane, 1980). For most people during the next decade there will be more opportunities for cross-household family relationships. People can be taught to crease new types of families. As previously mentioned, persons may want roommates, platonic or otherwise, or explore any variety of new and satisfying living environments. Whether cross-household family ties actually are maintained depends on several things, including geography, available time, and personal preference (Nye, 1976). The important point is that despite changing household patterns, almost everyone lives in a family during childhood and most people live in a family household at other times in their lives as well. They establish family relationship guidelines that can persist despite changes in households. These guidelines can help the person in the future establish or maintain a family group he/she has incorporated into his/her life.

The decreased size of families and the difficulties in many cases of maintaining family ties may, however, increase the importance of friendship, neighborhoods, and organizations as sources of social support and of personal ties (Uzokia, 1979). Roommates and partners already provide young unrelated individuals with a substitute for familial relationships. These friendships often resemble family relationships in their intensity and intimacy and in the needs that are met (economic, sexual, social, emotional), but they differ in the breadth and commitment endurance. Because such ties are not embedded in a large and relatively stable kinship, they are more easily suspended for other endeavors. In addition, people who live alone may seek out places to live and work where they expect others to share their interests and circumstances. Retirement communities,

"singles," apartment complexes, and urban neighborhoods may be the basis of social life for groups of
relatively homogeneous households.

Self-disclosure is a prerequisite for the formation of meaningful interpersonal relationships in a
dyadic or in a group situation (Yalom, 1975). One
must be aware of one's wants and wishes for achievement of satisfaction. From deciding what to eat for
dinner to familiar wants, one must disclose to truly
begin to be understood. Self-disclosure is related
to optimal psychological and social adjustment in a
curvilinear fashion: too much or too little self-
disclosure signify maladaptive interpersonal behavior.
Too little self-disclosure usually results in severely
limited opportunity for reality testing (Yalom, 1975).
If an individual fails to disclose himself in a relationship, he/she generally forfeits an opportunity to
obtain valid feedback. Furthermore, he/she prevents
the relationship from developing further; without
reciprocation, the other party will either withdraw
from further self-disclosure or else rupture the
relationship entirely. Too much self-disclosure can
be as maladaptive as too little (Yalom, 1979). In-
discriminate self-disclosure is not a goal of mental
health nor a pathway to it. Urban life would become
unbearably sticky if every contact between two individuals entailed a sharing of personal concerns and
secrets. Furthermore, a great deal of self-disclosure may frighten off an unprepared recipient. In
a rhythmic, flowing relationship, one party leads the
other in self-disclosures, but never by too great a
gap. So, with adaptive self-disclosure techniques,
assimilated throughout life or taught by a mental
health professional, one can begin to reach out and
establish a positive alternate family environment.

IV. CLINICAL RAMIFICATIONS

In viewing the shortcomings of current knowledge
in regards to the fabric of American life, attention
needs to be devoted to five major areas:

    1 - The lack of understanding of the nature
        of lifestyle choices.
    2 - Inadequate information about reconstituted
        families.
    3 - Incomplete knowledge of the single-parent
        family experience.

4 - Confusion about how the family compares with other group experiences.
5 - Inadequate knowledge of the place of the family in aiding individuals to function within society (Rice, 1977).

Increasing knowledge in these areas requires more than casual awareness of family issues, but rather for the clinician to develop and focus on the knowledge base, skills, base, and values base of clinical practice.

The preparation of today's clinicians will need to provide for the expansion of the clinician's knowledge base in certain key ways:

1 - The expansion of one's understanding of the dynamics of lifestyle choice. What are the major variables which go into the decision making process of selecting one's style of life?
2 - A better understanding of the dynamics that exist in alternative families.
3 - The familiarity of the broad group of professional and nonprofessional human resources which would be applicable to the diversity of individual and family needs.
4 - A continual updating of different approaches with the diverse alternative family structures.

The teaching and learning of new skills for working with diverse human problems will also need to be a part of today's clinical preparation. The skill of working with clients in the discovery of alternative and new sources of support will be a focus of training. To mention a few, the skills recommended for preparation for clinical work are:

1 - Ability to apply theories of family therapy to restructured family groups.
2 - Ability to help clients develop and discover their own individual self-worth and interests.
3 - Ability to assist client in locating support social groups (i.e., Parents Without Partners, Political groups, sororities, people samplers, Sierra Club, and other special interest groups).

470

4 - Ability to help clients develop and create a
    substitute surrogate extended family.
5 - Ability to facilitate the establishment of a
    situation where disclosure is possible at
    depth for client with one or more other
    persons.
6 - Assist client in developing social supports.

To do all of these things, the clinician will
need to take a look at his/her own value system in
hopes of understanding his/her own feeling of diverse
lifestyles and to develop an acceptance of where the
client is at in today's environment. If this is impossible with a particular client, at least being able
to be aware of this may result in making a positive
referral:

> "Anyone who works with families must eventually
> develop opinions as to the optimum distribution
> of values such as equality, freedom, and power
> in social units" (Halleck, 1976).

Robert Morris indicates that a fundamental question for human service work today given the manpower
squeeze and limited resources is: how can we, as
social service providers with limited resources, tap
into the vast reservoir of family and unpaid informal
resources which are still in existence? (Morris, 1980).

BIBLIOGRAPHY

Glasser, Paul

    1980   "Dean's Viewpoint." Catalyst, Arling-
ton, Texas: Human Resources Center,
Graduate School of Social Work,
University of Texas at Arlington,
Summer.

Goldenberg, Irene, &
Goldenberg, Herbert

    1980   Family Therapy: An Overview. Monterey,
CA: Brooks Cole Publishing Co.

Halleck, Seymour L.

    1976   "Family Therapy and Social Change."
Social Casework, October.

Kempler, Atman L.

    1976   "Extended Kinship Ties and Some Modern
Alternatives." The Family Coordinator,
April.

Masnick, George, &
Bane, Mary Jo

    1980   The Nation's Families: 1960-1990.
Boston, MA: Auburn House Publishing.

Morris, Robert

    1980   "American Families in Changing Times:
Some Uncomfortable Issues for Social
Workers." Catalyst, Arlington, Texas:
Human Resources Center, Graduate School
of Social Work, Univerity of Texas at
Arlington, Summer.

Nye, Ivan F.

    1976   "Ambivalence in the Family: Rewards
and Costs in Group Membership."
Family Coordinator, January.

Olson, David H.

1980   "Marriage and Family Therapy: A Decade
                Review." Journal of Marriage and the
                Family, November.

Rapoport, R.N., &
Rapoport, R.

1969   "The Dual-Career Family: A Variant
                Pattern and Social Change." Human
                Relations.

Rice, Robert M.

1977   American Family Policy: Content and
                Context. New York: Family Service
                Association of America.

Uzokia, Azubike F.

1979   "The Myth of the Nuclear Family:
                Historical Background and Clinical
                Implications." American Psychologist,
                November.

Yalom, Irvin D.

1975   The Theory and Practice of Group
                Psychotherapy. Basic Books, Inc.

*Director, Social Work Program, Chapman College, Orange,
California.

**Received his M.F.C.C. Masters Degree from Chapman
College, Orange, California.

CHAPTER 27

REBUILDING THE FAMILY

Clifford Alexander*

I. THE NEED TO REBUILD THE FAMILY

Before one can decide how to rebuild the family,
it is necessary to understand what the family is and
why it needs to be rebuilt.

Technically, the term "family" includes a unit
of two or more single adults or a childless married
couple as well as a unit of at least one child and one
adult with moral and emotional claims on each other.
However, for our purposes, the word "family" will
refer to a unit composed of at least one adult and
one child. It could be two employed parents and their
children (18.5 percent of all American households),
a father who is the full-time breadwinner and a mother
who is a full-time homemaker with their children (16.6
percent of all households), a single mother and her
children (6.1 percent of all households), or a single
father and his children (.6 percent of all American
households, and rising rapidly). Other groups, which
will be discussed later, are a family with stepparents (there are over 25 million stepparents in
America with one of every eight children being a
stepchild) (Pogrebin, 1980:177).

Few sociologists, psychologists, or educators
would deny that the American family needs assistance.
They all agree there are sad deficiencies in many
American families and that new thinking and experimenting are called for, but they do not see the traditional family as being "dead."

In pointing out the problems in the family, many
people overlook the strengths and positive gratifications in relationships found in many homes, and they
tend to exaggerate tensions, antagonisms, absurdi-
ties, and banalities. Nevertheless, enough concern
among those involved with families suggests that
there is a definite need to propose concrete solutions which can be used to rebuild and strengthen the
family.

Inasmuch as many people believe one of the major factors of the decline of the family as a socially acceptable and viable structure is the tension and hostility in the family among adults, this may well be the best place to begin our examination of family problems.

II. UNDERSTANDING FAMILY PROBLEMS

Many critics of marriage and the family imply through their criticism that they expected to have a glorious marriage bestowed upon them as if it were a gift from God. They were disappointed with what they got. However, people who have good marriages also say (along with their spouses) they had to work to make the marriage successful, and they continue to work hard at succeeding. To work in this sense does not mean employment, but it means being sensitive to spouses, listening to spouses, trying to understand one another's feelings, not taking immovable stances, and being generous of spirit (Spock, 1974:1-10).

Today, the various lifestyles found within those American families present an interesting study (Feldman and Thielbar, 1972:1-18). A person's lifestyle and that of his family is not an individual pattern of behavior. It is influenced by participation in social groups and the interpersonal relationships of the other members of the family with other individuals and groups. Family lifestyles enter into many aspects of a family member's life. The way a person behaves in his family and the way the family operates will influence how he/she will behave in many other areas. The very lifestyle of the family within the member's economic strata implies their lives' central interests. In America a variety of influences can play upon a person's central interests, creating a situation in which lifestyles differ according to sociologically relevant variables such as religion, age, sex, economic status, and ethnic background.

To understand family problems and conditions, the inquirer has to ask, which family are you addressing? Is the family upper, middle, or lower class, or is it one which defies categorization? It is difficult to generalize problems across class lines. Methods formulated for helping families depend upon the social and economic status of the family.

With the influx of Asian families into the American society, there has been a growth in the number of extended family units. Extended families are households made up of the nuclear family plus other relatives (such as grandparents and unmarried, but older, brothers and sisters of the mother and father). Additionally, this extended family is especially significant in Mexican/Latin families. The extended family is sometimes called the con-sanguine family because the members are tied to-gether by birth. The composite family is common among Vietnamese people living in California. This unit is formed when two separate nuclear families live together. Other countries have polygamous and polyandrous families, but these are illegal and rarely encountered in the United States.

Each type of family structure generates dif-ferent types of problems. Before one can accurately define, or understand, a family's problems, one must first know the actual class level and the perceived class level the family envisions for itself, what the parental arrangement of the family is, what the child population consists of, and where the family is living, and parenting styles.

III. PARENTING STYLES

Diana Baumrind (1975:12-37) made a major in-vestigation into how various types of parenting/ family lifestyles control and effect children's behavior and consequently family life. Her investi-gation found three main types of parents, each of which has a different effect upon children and thus the average family's life: (1) authoritative, (2) permissive and (3) modified authoritative.

The first type of parent, the authoritative, directs his/her children firmly, consistently, and rationally. Issues rather than personalities are focused upon. The parent uses power when necessary. This type of parent brings about children who are independent and self-reliant, because the parent uses reason, power, and reinforcement to achieve acceptable behavior. This, then, becomes the child's pattern of behavior.

477

The more permissive parent (second type) behaves in an affirmative, accepting, and benign manner toward a child's impulses, actions, and aims. In the long run, this "freedom" which the child or children take as being permission to do whatever they want, makes the child dependent on the parent. In this parenting situation, the family structure is likely to be unguided and chaotic as every family member does as he/she wants at any given moment.

The third type of parent, modified authoritative, who has learned to modify his/her role in response to the child's needs and expressed wishes creates an atmosphere in which the child's growth pattern is most facilitated. This type of parent is more of an expert in the general needs of growing children. These parents believe they should be receptive to, and aware of, the child's needs and views before making any attempt to alter the child's actions. These parents see the child maturing through different stages with different features in each state.

The latter style of parents tend to have a better family lifestyle with their children because each child and each parent follow the golden rule with one another. In most cases families with this type of communication between the leadership and the followers will have less conflict and more understanding.

IV. DEVELOPING AND MAINTAINING COMMUNICATION WITH FAMILY MEMBERS

In general, there are four motifs which characterize the education process: (1) training, (2) data feedback, (3) confrontation, and (4) process observation and feedback. Each is a separate vehicle for uncovering and specifying problems. For example, during training, participants learn skills which allow them to share previously unshared data and to pinpoint problems not previously identified. In data feedback, the counselor collects and reports previously unshared data to the family, thereby indicating the sorts of problems the members find in the group without identifying the member who is concerned about a particular problem. In confrontation, one member of the family reports his/her dislikes to another and vice versa. In process observation and feedback, the

478

counselor reports his or her impressions about the
ways the family members are working together, speci-
fies problems the family seems to be having and urges
the family to work on these specific problems. All
of these design motifs are followed by individual
counseling, problem-solving learning, action, ongoing open-ended discussions, and group evaluation
of the progress.

Areas on which the family probably needs to work
include: clarifying and improving communication
skills, establishing individual and collective goals,
uncovering conflicts, and improving group interaction
procedures. Counseling is rarely satisfying or productive for all group members, and can, initially be
frustrating to some. In this case additional work
must be done with these individuals so they can work
within the family structure. Other areas which may
need to be learned are productive and positive
methods of solving problems, making decisions and
ways of assessing changes.

Self-renewal is one of the primary objectives of
family counseling. In fact, self-esteem is probably
the core value of counseling. Attendant values involve expanding all of the family's consciousness of
how the others think and feel, and of finding more
and diverse choices for handling difficulties and
decisions. Very important to famiy counseling and
individual self-renewal are the valuing of I-Thou
interactions, a collaborative, democratic conception
of freedom with major emphasis on participation and
interpersonal caring. The value of internal, group
commitments is important so new directions and system
may be psychologically owned by and participated in
by all the family members (Schumuch, 1979:24-25).

V.   DEFINING THE FAMILY COUNSELING PROCESS

Many people still feel that if they seek counseling either for themselves or for another family
member, the family has somehow "failed." Others,
perhaps less informed, feel that to ask for assistance through counseling means the individual is
"sick" or "nuts." Sophisticated adults know that
this is not true. Most, if not all, adults have a
period in life when counseling services from a professional can add depth to their understanding of a
problem and assist them through a traumatic period of

their life which has been caused by their inability to erase an old childhood fear (or "message") which is now inappropriate in their adult life.

Additionally, in today's uncertain world filled with tension and conflict as well as violence, many children need the extra support that a counselor or psychologist can provide in the formative years. Family counseling for one or two members, or for all members, of a family has proven to be effective for many families who have reached a stalemate in their efforts to solve their own internal problems—whether those problems be family problems or problems with a child/family member who has ceased functioning in his/her most effective manner.

There are certain characteristics of an emotionally mature adult which indicate this person is able to function effectively at home and at work. An adult who is cheerful and serene, alert and alive to new experiences, and courageous in attempts to handle difficulties without being discouraged. The mature adult is also tolerant and understanding of others (Baumrind, 1975:12-37).

Conversely, the immature adult becomes less effective when faced with criticism or disapproval, they lack tolerance (patience), and they lack feelings for others. They have undue pride and obsession with possessions. When discouraged, they tend to "blow up." Typically, the immature adult always feels his/her position is "right" and finds it difficult to compromise, as they are unusually taking themselves and their personal needs too seriously.

Family counseling has, as its goals, the uniting of the family so that it can work together in harmony and understanding, and solving problems and conflicts in a manner which gives solutions which all members are comfortable with. The objectives which the family counselor attempts to meet are training the family to make decisions, accepting responsibility, "carrying" on in spite of immediate difficulties, and to make plans for the future which would appreciate the potential and contributions of all members of the family unit. Counseling sessions are geared to assist members in bringing out their fears and facing them. Also they assist them in making friends with not only family members but others outside the family.

A family in counseling learns that human beings become emotionally mature and self-satisfied by having certain psychological needs met. These needs include affection, praise, and appreciation. They need to come to grips with their sex role in life and they need to appreciate the adventure that role can bring them. They need to meet each new experience with a background of stability. And they need to develop an outlook which looks forward to each new experience accompanying each new age bracket.

Another sign of an emotionally mature adult is a sense of humor. The sense of humor can be used as an escape mechanism and a way to relieve tension. All individuals need the ability to accept and be accepted for one's self; the ability to laugh at life's predicaments and to generally enjoy life.

Finally, a mature person will have a strong set of values on which they focus for a healthful, happy life. Counseling can give individual family members the tools to work toward these goals.

Psychologists identify five ways to work toward attaining mental health and relieving tensions. These methods encourage people to attain emotional stability by:

(1) Involving each family member in some type of activity (a hobby, recreational activity, or creative sport) in which the individual can feel accomplishment and pride.

(2) Each member would have time to explore and establish strong convictions of what is valuable in human life and to have a faith or philosophy to sustain their needs in time of stress and strive to provide emotional security for daily living.

(3) Each member of the family needs to learn how to face facts about anxiety -- what produces it and how to handle it.

(4) Each family member needs to be encouraged to belong to a group or organization which participates in socially useful activities in the community, in order to broaden the

individual's base outside that of the
nuclear family unit.

(5)   Finally, each family member needs to be
      loved and to love. Given love, any human
      more fully enjoys life and is basically
      secure.

Effective family counseling will work toward
these goals and will utilize the methods or techniques of counseling which will be most effective and
productive for the individual family or family members involved in the counseling process.

The selection of counseling methods or techniques to be used for any individual or family unit
depends upon the situation and the system under which
the particular counselor works. An effective counselor or psychologist will have several techniques
within his/her personal skills which can be used in
different situations and to solve different types of
problems.

VI.   CONTRACTING AS A COUNSELING PROCESS

The goal of family counseling is to provide a
framework within which each individual family member
can function adequately, work toward mature adulthood, and work toward personal fulfillment.

In reaching for this goal, contracting is an
excellent method by which to positively reward various family members for good behavior and punish them
for unacceptable behavior.

In contracting, a mutual agreement between the
parent(s) and child(ren) is formed as a result of a
negotiation process. The negotiation process results
in a commitment on both sides. The party on one side
agrees to do something, and the party on the other
side promises something in return. Then the commitment is written down. While a contract between a
parent and child can be purely verbal, there are
several benefits for writing down the contract. A
written agreement prevents subsequent misunderstandings and arguments. It is also specific and
concrete if the actions (or non-actions) specified
in the agreement are observable/countable/measurable.

The contract should be positive in tone, so that the child (for instance) promises to do something, rather than promising not to do something or to stop doing something. The contract must be fair so that both parties feel they have negotiated a good deal.

As in business with contracts, the contract should be designed to be successful. All parties to the agreement should realize that the art of negotiation is something that improves with practice. Neither the child or parent is born knowning how to negotiate agreements. Since the parent possesses a preponderance of the power, he/she must learn to give up some of that power in the spirit of compromise. The child learns she/he can be trusted with some of the parental authority. This develops the sense of responsibility.

The advantage of beginning this type of family negotiation and problem-solving when the children are younger is most evident when the child enters his/her teenage years. At that time the power of negotiation begins to shift and the adolescent values the adult nature of the contract and the opportunity to deal with his/her parents on a mature, adult level.

VII.   DEVELOPING COMMUNICATION AND UNDERSTANDING
       WITHIN FAMILIES

> "The saddest teenager I ever knew was
> Stuart Stark, whose parents bridged the
> generation gap. I was so sorry for the
> kid I could have cried. His mom and
> dad would go around saying things like,
> 'Groovy,' 'Wow,' 'Uptight,' and 'Hey
> man.' They dug their son's records, ate
> the same breakfast food, grew sideburns
> (not his mother), and protested every-
> thing their son protested. Not only
> were they a drag to both generations,
> but they took away Stuart's inalienable
> right to play Parental Squares with the
> rest of the guys" (Bombeck and Keane,
> 1977:121).

Humor may be Erma Bombeck's forte, but lurking near the surface is always the truth, coupled with her unique method of bringing the poignant home to

483

her reader. She is able to bring the everyday events
of family ordeals into some sort of acceptable perspective, something parents and children are not
always able to do in the heat of the battle.

One way to put an end to the war between parents
and children, and between children and children, so
that various family members can communicate with each
other, is to consciously work toward improved family
communications. This is not achieved by parents
attempting to behave like teenagers. It is most
often acceptable when parents allow their children
to reach for adulthood.

VIII. THE ECLECTIC APPROACH

Typically, books concerned with topics on the
family, rebuilding the family, or family discipline
advocate a single system or approach to problems,
such as "active listening," "behavior modification,"
or "value setting." In most instances, the authors
of the system or method say, "This is the way to...."
Once you understand the nature of child rearing and
child psychology, you can quickly see the inadequa-
cies of a single system. For what is effective in
child rearing and family planning? It is a desire
to help the child (and the parents) become the most
effective citizen(s) they can be and to produce productive people, for themselves and the community in
which they live. Regardless of the system advocated
for effective interaction among adults and children,
desirable behavior must be developd, and undesirable
behaviors avoided.

Whatever the family structure, the approach
taken to child discipline and child rearing must in-
corporate a number of different systems in order to
be effective.

In discussing any approach it is important to
take individual factors into account: the age of
the person involved, training, background, and social
differences. This applies to adults, too. Many
theories of child and family training simply state,
"This is how to handle the situation...." This
approach, following a single, rigid set of rules,
does not take into account the personalities of the
individuals involved, their education, or personal
differences. There are many strategies which can be

used to gain an effective, loving family which works together toward common goals. There is more than one way to do anything, including raising children.

It is especially important to remember that each individual is unique, both with a combination of genes and a biological temperament different from those of any other child in the family, or any other adult, anywhere.

Probably the most effective way to work toward an effective family development plan is to take a developmental approach to it. Every day family members are teaching and reacting to people around them. Additionally, the development of a human being from birth through adulthood dictates that varying strategies are more appropriate at different stages of development.

Each person needs to find methods of solving problems, teaching family values, and developing good discipline methods with which he is comfortable and which are effective in a particular family setting. The most effective family member (adult) will not try to use a system for parenting or being an effective spouse which does not feel comfortable and which is not giving that individual positive reinforcement.

IX.   THE SYSTEMS APPROACH TO A DYNAMIC RELATIONSHIP

The family system is defined as a....

> set of dynamic general relationships
> which together process stimuli (input)
> through a subsystem of closer relation-
> ships, thereby producing responses
> (outputs) (Baumrind, 1975:12).

Some troubled families, for a variety of reaons, turn inward on exploiting, damaging, and destroying each other, while others turn outward inflicting violence on the world. Either action may be a symptom of stress within the family. Other families, despite their circumstances, are maturing, sustaining forces of strength to their members. Other families do badly by one member and beautifully by another. Some familiies are gradually overwhelmed by the burden of genetic heritage or environmental conditions. These are families in distress.

485

To understand family problems there must be investigations into ways distress occurs, why it occurs, and what can be done about it. Sometimes the pattern of relations between members go awry when the family has not developed avenues for negotiation of conflicts, and these, left unresolved, threaten to repeat. Skewed family relations can be a factor of physical diseases, and in turn, the disease can become a part of the pattern, the excuse for avoiding threatening conflict. Another manifestation of the family in distress is abuse of one family member by another family member.

One of the concerns of many parents is the problem of drugs in the family. It is a fact that drugs are a part of today's culture. The drugs young people take may, often times, be introduced into the youth's life by the parent.

Young and old drug users come from every walk of life. Estimates very as to what percentage of America's youth is involved in some aspect of the illegal drug world, but authorities in high schools and colleges often put the figure well above fifty percent. That number, however, doesn't differentiate between the one-time experimenter and the everyday user (Stevens and Freeman, 1977:6-8). How many adults are involved, in an on-going way, with drugs, has not been determined, but police and medical authorities are quick to point out it is a very high percentage among certain subcultures and socio-economic groups.

X. THE WEEKLY FAMILY MEETING APPROACH

The Dreikurs Technique is a process of establishing, implementing, and maintaining a weekly family meeting, an approach referred to as the Family Council. Rudolf Dreikurs and Associates (1974) developed and tested a system which accords to each family member his/her rights as well as the insistence that each family member perform his/her duties. It is the contention of the book that this system can dramatically improve the emotional well-being of every member of the family.

The key to the system is the Family Council, which is based on the idea that not only are people equal, but they should be treated as equals. The

Council is used for both problem-solving and communication building. If practiced and utilized according to the system, and maintained faithfully, Dreikurs feels it will strengthen family relations. The system was expressly designed to show families how to bring order to our chaos, to solve conflicts in the home in a supportive, ego-building manner, and to arrive at decisions in a democratic environment.

It's a given truth that most people want to be happy, and they want to be happy within their family setting. But it is also true that many parents are unhappy with their children, even though they love them. Usually it isn't only the physical work in raising children that bothers parents, it's the irritations and frustrations the parents feel when they can't control their children's lives, behaviors, and thoughts. Too often a lack of mutual respect exists in families where the parents are unhappy with the children's behavior. Parents expect children to respect them and other adults, but often do not realize the children are worthy of and need the same type of respect.

This respect can be effected through the processes found in the weekly family meeting. In order for a weekly council to be successful, eight basic elements must be included:

> (1) equality of all members,
>
> (2) mutual respect,
>
> (3) open communication,
>
> (4) regularity,
>
> (5) agreed-upon rules,
>
> (6) joint deliberation,
>
> (7) reciprocal responsibility
>
> (8) mutual decision-making.

If these basic facets are contained in the meeting, family members will learn to express themselves, to listen and be listened to, and to think independently about concerns of the larger group.

Another benefit of the weekly meeting is that the business of the family can be handled more efficiently, quickly, and simply. One of the functions of the family meeting should be to explore the extent of the workload at home and to distribute that work so there is an exchange of tasks and no one is stuck with the worst or easiest job, all the time.

Additionally, since it would be foolish to expect a group of people living together to function smoothly as a unit all the time, there needs to be a conflict resolving mechanism in the family meeting which will respect the individual while respecting the freedom of the other family members. Through a concentrated effort to keep the family meetings functioning, the family will grow and strengthen. The goal of the meetings is not to avoid conflicts, for there will always be conflict, but to provide a method of solving conflicts. The ultimate goal is to reach agreements which will allow all participants a feeling of success in the decisions made. The four actions necessary to solve conflicts democratically are: creation of mutual respect, pinpointing of the issues, seeking out areas of agreement, and the sharing of responsibilities.

One of the ways to assist the family as it attempts to work together as a unit is to work toward equality. Even in the process of using family meetings it's difficult to attain. The constraints of living together as a family make it advisable for each family member to consider the rights and feelings of others. The weekly family council assists the self-centered person in acknowledging the existence and needs of others.

All in all, there is much to be gained through the process of using a family meeting on a regular basis. Parents are able to achieve a better relationship with their children, to communicate more effectively with them, and to solve mutual problems in a way which makes each member of the family feel important. Additionally, all members of the family learn how to listen to other people and to other people's problems and how to cooperate in finding solutions to those problems. Parents learn how to look beyond the expressed conflict and find out what is really going on with their children. Family members learn how to make plans work because everyone is sharing in the responsibilities rather than separating into order-takers and command-givers.

In short, in the family meetings a person can learn to be a socially responsible, cooperative human being.

XI. HOW TO REACH THE VULNERABLE PERSON

One of the attributes which all successful individuals need is self-esteem, a favorable attitude toward one's self. Margaret Mead said, "People who have high self-esteem have had key people in their lives who have treated them with concern and respect" (Block, 1982:15). Rosenberg agreed, "The amount of parental concern and attention one receives are significantly related to self-esteem" (Block, 1982:16).

This concept is explored in two important books written on the subject of self-esteem: The Antecedents of Self-Esteem by Stanley Cooperfield and Your Child's Self-Esteem by Dorothy Briggs. These two authors have established four sources of self-esteem: power (which is the ability to influence and control others), virtue (which is the adherence to ethical standards), significance (which comes from affection, attention, and acceptance of others), and competence (which is the successful performance in meeting demands for achievement). It is possible to achieve feelings of self-esteem if only one of these sources is present, but not easy.

When a child or adult has a high sense of self-esteem he/she is less likely to feel threatened when approaching a new situation. When there is a failure, it can be put in perspective and some of the fault attributed to conditions over which the person has no control. A person with high self-esteem can retain his/her values and personal opinions even if they are not held by the majority, he/she can publically express his/her opinions even if they are not widely held. Self-esteem is one of the attributes teenagers need in order to avoid being led by peer group pressure into activities contrary to family and personal values.

It is important for all members of a family to have appropriate self-esteem if they are to function well in the family or in the world. High respect and emphasis should be placed on developing good self-esteem in all family members. With children, well-defined limits seem to help establish self-esteem. Children with good self-esteem are permitted to participate and plan in decisions which affect their lives. Parents whose children have high self-esteem use significantly less physical force and far more reasoning when disciplining their children. Children know what is expected of them and they react to those expectations.

Children with self-esteem have parents who are almost totally accepting of them, who set clearly-defined and consistently enforced limits, and who respect individual actions which are permitted, within defined limits, and which help the family as a unit.

If the forces at work throughout the world today threaten to wreck the family as we know it, there exists several methods to save the family. Adults should be provided with education about parenting, children about the changing world around them, and their role in shaping the future, and both adults and children must work together to keep the lines of communication open between them.

Together parents and children can save the family.

B I B L I O G R A P H Y

Baumrind, Diane

    1975   "The Contribution of the Family to the Development of Children." <u>Schizo-phrenia Bulletin</u>, 14, 12-37.

Birchler, Gary

    1975   Marriage and Divorce. <u>Journal of Personality and Social Psychology</u>, 31, 349-350.

Block, Joel

    1982   Is Your Spouse Also Your Friend? <u>Newsday Magazine</u>, February 28.

Bombeck, Erma &
Dean, Bill

    1977   <u>Just Wait Until You Have Kids of Your Own</u>. New York: Faucett Crest Books.

Dreikus, Rudolf, Gould, Shirley, &
Corsin, Raymond J.

    1974   <u>Family Council</u>. Chicago: Henry Regency Company.

Feldman, Saul D., &
Thielbar, Gerald W.

    1972   <u>Diversity in American Society</u>. Canada: Little Brown and Company.

Pogrebin, Letty Cartin

    1980   <u>Growing Up Free</u>. New York: McGraw Hill Book Company.

Schumuch, Richard A.

    1979   "Family Revival Through the Process of Family Counseling." <u>The Psychological Digest</u>, 45, (3), 24-25.

Spock, Benjamin

    1974   <u>Raising Children in a Difficult Time</u>.
                 New York: W. W. Norton and Company,
                 Inc.

Stevens, Anita, &
Freeman, Lucy

    1977   <u>I Hate My Parents</u>. New York: Cowles
                 Book Company.

*Department of Social Work, University of Nevada,
Las Vegas, Nevada.

CHAPTER 28

COGNITIVE RESTRUCTURING AND SYSTEMS:
A STRESS REDUCTION TECHNIQUE
IN FAMILY COUNSELING

Elaine S. Karr*

I. INTRODUCTION

When a family member contacts a family counselor
for help because the family is experiencing stress,
most of the time the contractor, typically one
parent, labels another family member, usually a
child, as the one who is causing all the problems
and throwing the family into crisis. The "misbehaving" child becomes known as the "identified
patient" who is blamed for the others feeling emotionally upset.

Consequently the goal may be to change the
child's behavior (the stressor or source) in order
to restore the family's equilibrium. When the therapeutic intervention is aimed at the individual, i.e.,
the child or some other family member, then the
counselor is communicating that other people and
specific events in the life of the family cause the
family to feel the way they do. Thus, we often blame
people or things within the family but not the family
itself, as a "whole", for the feelings of emotional
and physical stress. In doing this, an important
factor not only in the cause of stress, but in the
management of stress, is often overlooked. The
factor is how the "family thinks" and not just how
individual members think. Irrational family thinking
or irrational familial beliefs can be the primary
underlying source of the stress. To reduce the
stress, then the counselor or therapist needs to address the irrational family beliefs that are manifest
in the patient's behavior. Thus, the identified
patient actually is a symptom of the unresolved conflict stemming from the faulty familial beliefs that
may be hidden from the various members' awareness.

Cognitive restructuring, based on rational-
emotive therapy, within a systems orientation can be
a stress reduction technique in family counseling or
therapy (Ellis, 1978:15-19). The model for examining

the relationship between thoughts, feelings and behaviors is not new to the field of family therapy. The rational-emotive approach utilizes predominantly a phenomenological perspective (Ellis, 1978:15-19). The thesis is that disturbed mental and family relationships primarily stem from the perceptions that family members have and the views they take of events within the system. Although the system may contribute to the distrubances in major ways, the kind of family system that exists for family members is not the primary cause, i.e., the individual irrational beliefs were at the "root of the problem" and not the family beliefs adhered to by the family as a whole. This is contrary to what many practitioners in family counseling believe. A popular approach is the systems perspective which contends that the family members become dysfunctional within the framework of the complete family system wherein they live and interact. Hence, the family counselor needs to focus on the whole family to see how they affect each other. A covert basis for how they relate to each other in order to keep the family in harmony, pathologically or non-pathologically can be the family myths entwined with the irrational family beliefs. Thus,

> "....the individual's behavior and family myth go hand in hand...the role that the individual plays is meaningless until and unless viewed in the framework of the relationship...and both points of view, the individual and the relationship must be kept together..." (Ferreira, 1963:55-61).

To apply Cognitive Restructuring (the RET Model) through systems theory is rather new. To approach a dysfunctional family via a systems orientation is to view the family as an organic unit with the members functioning interdependently. Being interdependent, a change in one member affects the other members. All members strive to maintain homeostatis or status quo. Therefore, there will be a resistance to change. To understand Cognitive Restructuring with Systems, it is necessary to discuss the concepts of system and the A-B-C model of rational-emotive therapy separately.

II. THE CONCEPT OF SYSTEM

The system orientation in family therapy has its roots in the early 1950's. During that period, the primary emphasis was on the individual patient and his/her symptoms. The dominant theory and technique was psychoanalytic and the therapeutic model was designed to help the patient achieve insight into the unconscious defenses and conflicts. Formerly, the emphasis in treatment was on the family of orientation or early familial rearing, and its relationship to the psychopathology in the analysis. However, family systems theorists, e.g., Bateson, etc., observed that even in analytic therapy, the present family played a crucial role in the maintenance of a successful treatment. Specifically, family members seemed able to potentiate or to prevent efforts of the client to change even after a very comprehensive analysis, and individual clients often made dramatic changes after major shifts in the structure of the family, and that these modifications frequently could not be linked to the results of individual psychotherapy (Fox, 1976).

Another significant area in the history of family therapy was schizophrenia research conducted during the 1950s. During the study of the families of schizophrenia, it became evident that in almost every case there were long-standing marital conflicts and the psychotic episodes of the "patient" appeared to be related to cycles of the parental marital conflict (Napier and Whitaker, 1978).

As the battle intensified, the child would have to be hospitalized. Once that occurred, the parents would call a truce so that they could parent their hospitalized child. In a real sense, the child's psychosis helped to stabilize the family by providing the parents with a way to avoid their confrontation. The family's very stability seemed to be maintained by the periodic "illness" (Napier and Whitaker, 1978).

As a result, the family began to be viewed in a very different way. The family began to be thought of as a whole rather than as a genetic assembly of individuals. As a whole, the family assumes the characteristics of a system.

495

The systems concept is not entirely new. In the 19th century, a French sociologist, August Comte, strived to comprehend why and how society was possible. For Comte, society was conceptualized as a type of organism and was to be viewed through the prism of biological conceptions of structure and function. Another theorist, Herbert Spencer, specified in a systematic list the ways in which society could be viewed as analogous to an organism:

1. Both society and organisms can be distinguished from inorganic matter, for both grow and develop;

2. In both society and organisms an increase in size means an increase in complexity and differentiation;

3. In both, a progressive differentiation in structure is accomplished by a differentiation in function;

4. In both, parts of the whole are interdependent with a change in one part affecting other parts (Turner, 1974).

As one can see, there are marked similarities in the properties of society, family and living organisms, especially in the areas of interdependence of the parts and specialization of functions.

The family is a microcosm of society. It is a type of social organization with its unique rules, values, beliefs and goals. A change in one part (family member) can offset the entire balance. Societal change functions similarly. An example might be the youth counter culture of the 1960's. Traditional values were challenged and there was conflict between the establishment and the younger generation. Solidly entrenched values and norms gave way to new ones, which eventually were acceptable to both groups and equilibrium was restored. What is important to remember is that the whole is greater than the sum of the parts, i.e., the family is created by the union of the individuals who eventually become parents. They started their family with beliefs from their own families and often past experiences but their own family takes on a new character of its own apart from their past and present individual thinking.

496

III. FAMILY MYTHS

An important homeostatic mechanism of the family relationship is the family myth. Myths are:

> "... a series of fairly well-integrated beliefs shared by all family members, concerning each other and their mutual position in the family, beliefs that go unchallenged by everyone involved in spite of the reality distortions which they may conspicuously imply" (Ferreira, 1962).

Family members struggle to maintain these beliefs in order to keep relationships in balance. It's as if they (the beliefs) are the family defense mechanisms. Ewing and Fox (Fox, 1976) reported a three-generation myth that centered on the idealization of the mother and how it was forbidden to dispute her perceptions. Another reported irrational belief behind the myth of "one for all and all for one" was "the survival, safety and dignity of its members depend on the family. Who ever separates him/herself from the family is lost" (Palazzoli, et al., 1973). This irrational belief may be related to "blood is thicker than water". How a family translates this into self-talk is, "I can hardly exist without my family and find it awful to be without my family." The consequence is that a feeling of despair and complete inadequacy will be felt and the person will never be able to cut the "family umbilical cord."

IV. THE A-B-C's MODEL

A common assumption is that thoughts and feelings are unrelated. If this assumption is held to be true then people feel powerless to change the way they feel. According to Ellis (1977), people have innate and acquired tendencies. Therefore, we can to a large extent, control how we feel and behave by our basic values and beliefs; by the way we interpret an event and by the actions that we choose to do as a consequence of what we experienced. This can be put into A-B-C framework and can be used in family counseling if the members are mature and old enough to take part. For example, they are shown that it is not an activating event (A), an event that occurs,

497

that has caused their emotional consequence (C), the way they feel, but rather the innately predisposed and learned belief (B), what they are telling themselves about (A). Usually this selftalk is based on long-held beliefs that supposedly have been handed down from families and society. Cognitive restructuring focuses on part (B), i.e., the internal thought processes which are often irrational.

Clinically, the A-B-C model works this way: (A) is the event that occurred. For example, in terms of the family, a young child in the third grade is misbehaving in school and the mother is called in. (C) represents the prevailing feeling of the parents and the child and also the behavior. The parents and child are upset and both parents and child can become defensive. Did (A) actually cause the bad feelings? There was something internally happening between (A) and (C) and is the source of the feelings (C). That is (B), the belief which shapes what we say to ourselves about the event. What probably is being said is "children shouldn't misbehave because then we're not a good family" - good parents have well trained children. What will people think of our family? It's as if the parents are the ones being criticized for poor performance. In order for them to preserve their self-esteem and reputation of the family, their child has to be a model child. The misbehavior in school started the process, but the irrational beliefs produced the despair and feelings of inadequacy. The family myth that evolves is "children in our family are perfect". Of course, no child is able to live up to the implied expectation and some kind of acting out is inevitable. As can be seen, often it is the irrational family belief that is behind the stress that is being felt. If the internal self-talk (B) is centered on the evaluation of "how awful it is," then feelings such as depression and anxiety can follow. Similarly, anger and hostility usually develop following an evaluation of "there is absolutely no excuse for unfairness."

Families do have the capacity to change their myths or irrational beliefs. This can occur through cognitive restructuring which can reduce family stress. The family can learn new coping skills to change their family's way of thinking. Homework assignments are effective as practice techniques.

498

The following excerpt illustrates this technique. I will call the family the Jackson family.

The family consisted of two elderly parents in their seventy's and a middle-aged single daughter. The daughter lived with her parents while she went to college and finally moved out at the age of twenty-five when she decided to live together with a man. The relationship ended after several years after he "wanted out." Depressed, and in despair, she moved back into her parents house for a year. She then moved and began a series of live-in relationships with different men. Within the past year, she has been engaged in sexual relationships with older teenage girls. Despite the daughter's apparent satisfaction with this lifestyle, the parents are convinced that her behavior is pathological and have sought help from numerous counselors to change their daughter's behavior and have their anxiety relieved. The daughter, even though she likes her life, has agreed to go along with her parents for counseling but is angry that her parents aren't accepting of her and think that she is "diseased."

The first task that the counselor has is to uncover the family myth and irrational beliefs (B). In this case, the myth is that "parents always know what is best for their children even when the child is an adult." Along with the myth is the irrational belief (B) that the dignity and esteem of the family depends on its members. Whoever deviates brings shame and embarrassment to the family. Of course, parents, being older and wiser, set the standards. If these expectations are not met, then both parents and child view themselves as failures (C).

Once the counselor shows the various family members that their upset (C) did not stem from the activating event (A), their daughter's lesbian relationships but, on the contrary, the set of irrational beliefs (B) - the counselor then can help them dispute the beliefs by having them ask themselves: "In what way would it prove awful if this situation continued and people were critical of our family? Where is the evidence that our family has to be like other families? Why must the family come first, and if it doesn't then I am a rotten person for letting the family down." When the family confronts the irrational beliefs, then it is possible for a new effect to take place. Even though they might feel it would be desirable for their family to be like most other families, still it isn't the "end of the world" if it doesn't work out that way.

If the dynamics are broken down into A-B-C, then the family can construct their own diagram at home and learn to apply cognitive restructuring on their own, thereby reducing their family stress. A good home exercise is the Steinmetz et al. (1980) model which can be adapted to a systems format. It is illustrated as follows:

(A) Activating Event

_____
_____
_____
_____

(B) Family Belief

_____
_____
_____
_____

(C) Feelings and Behavior

_____
_____
_____
_____

The family members think of a strong, unpleasant emotion that they are feeling and write that emotion under (C). Then, under (A), they write in the event that happened before the emotion occurred. Finally, under (B) they attempt to pinpoint the family belief or myth that links the feelings to what occurred. Is the belief rational or irrational? How is it causing family distress?

V. SUMMARY

Reducing family stress through the utilization of combining cognitive restructuring (based on RET) and a systems orientation is a relatively new approach. Historically, RET has been used extensively in marital counseling with dyads. Ellis (1978) reported a phenomenological perspective versus a systems point of view. Hauck (1977) discussed three patterns of child-rearing grounded on irrational beliefs. A structured approach to group marriage counseling in implementing systems theory as a part of a multiple approach was introduced by McClellan and Stieper (1977). There is an enormous amount of research that solidly supports the central hypothesis of RET and cognitive behavior therapy (Ellis and Geiger, 1977) and as well as systems therapy (Fox, 1976). What is apparent is the minimal reference to a combination of cognitive restructuring, based on RET and systems orientation as a stress reduction technique in family therapy. This is not a simple approach, even though it may appear to be as easy as the A-B-C's. A common occurrence is for the counselor to slip back into focusing on the individual's irrational beliefs (which is part but <u>not</u> all of the stressor) rather than sticking with <u>the</u> family as a unit and therefore the family's irrational belief system. Another pitfall is to work on changing the behavior of the identified patient (usually the child) versus the irrational family beliefs and myths that give rise to the problematic behavior which spurred the family into seeking counseling.

BIBLIOGRAPHY

Ellis, A.

1978   "A Rational-Emotive Approach to Family
       Therapy Part I: Cognitive Therapy."
       <u>Rational Living</u>, 13, 15-19.

Ellis, A.

1977   <u>Handbook for Rational Emotive Therapy</u>.
       New York: Springer.

Ferreira, A. J.

1963   "Family Myth and Homeostasis." <u>Archives</u>
       <u>of General Psychiatry</u>, 9, 55-61.

Fox, R.

1976   "Family Therapy." In I. Weiner (ed),
       <u>Clinical Methods in Psychology</u>. New
       York: Wiley.

Hauck, P.

1977   "Irrational Parenting Styles." In
       A. Ellis and R. Grieger (eds.),
       <u>Handbook of Rational-Emotive Therapy</u>.
       New York: Springer.

McClellan, T., and
Steiper, D.

1977   "A Structured Approach to Group
       Marriage Counseling." In A. Ellis
       and R. Grieger (eds), <u>Handbook of</u>
       <u>Rational-Emotive Therapy</u>. New York:
       Springer.

Napier A., and
Whitaker, C.

1978   <u>Family Crucible</u>. New York: Harper
       and Row.

Palazzoli, M. S., et al.

1973   "Family Rituals - A Powerful Tool in
              Family Therapy." Family Process, 12,
              445-453.

Steinmetz, J., et al.

1980   Managing Stress - Before it Manages
              You. Palo Alto, California: Bull
              Publishing Company.

Turner, J. H.

1974   The Structure of Sociological Theory.
              Homewood, Illinois: Daisey Press.

*Private Practice, Los Angeles, California.

503

CHAPTER 29

A FAMILY INTERVENTION: THREE PERSPECTIVES

James Buchholz*
and
Richard Nyberg**

I.   INTRODUCTION

Family therapy as a distinct therapeutic model
found its genesis in the 1950's.   Since then, however, no single comprehensive theory of family
therapy has emerged.   Rather what we find today is
a plethora of therapy techniques for the family, each
presuming a certain conceptual framework.   Certainly
implicit theories provide the presuppositions for the
varied technical orientations, but as one commentator
noted, often, "...a therapist's theory was just a
rationale for his or her own clinical style" (Guerin,
1976:16).   Consequently, as yet no one has been successful in unifying the many "schools", or "styles",
which the major clinicians practice; and which we
therapists emulate.

The purpose of this chapter is to comment on
three orientations to family therapy.   To facilitate
this goal we will offer a case presentation.   This
will provide the material for a discussion, and
eventually a comparison, of how the three family
therapists might proceed.   The three selected are
Salvador Minuchin, Virginia Satir, and Murray Bowen.
They were done so because of the fact that all offer
creative and innovative insights to family therapy.
In addition, these particular ones were selected
because their intervention approaches to the family
clearly differ in emphasis--in what the process of
family therapy is.   Specifically, Minuchin places
importance on individual, here and now, functioning
within a family structure; Satir because of her
very practical approach to facilitating family communication patterns; and Bowen because of the importance he places on individual differentiation
from one's family through insight.   Therefore, it
is to the task of tracing Minuchin's participant-
observer style, Satir's empathetic-artistic style,
and Bowen's didactic-coach style, in the intervention
with a family that the following is dedicated.

II. A CASE STUDY EXAMPLE

The case study to be presented here will serve as the concrete foundation upon which all subsequent speculations will be founded. It concerns a family that one of the authors had seen in therapy. This is a white, upper-middle class, professional family, who live in a suburban community in New Jersey. The family consists of Mr. and Mrs. C., who have been married ten years, their nine year old son Michael, and their seven year old daughter Laura. This family came for counseling upon the recommendation of Michael's third grade teacher, who had subsequently referred Michael to the school's Child Study Team for a complete evaluation.

Michael, the identified patient, is a nine year old boy with a cherub-like face and blond hair. He wears heavy glasses and is of average height/weight for his age. When seen by the therapist he appeared neat and well cared for, and while his manner was somewhat abstracted, his appearance was not remarkable. Michael is an intelligent child, evidencing this through a WISC-R score of 121. This places him in the superior range of mental functioning. He also has an active and creative capacity for fantasy, which emerges in his prolific fabrications of comic strips, stories, drawings and the likes which he produces in spare moments.

Laura is a seven year old girl, currently in the second grade. She also, is an attractive child, with dishwater blond hair and a graceful, confident demeanor. She is a serious student who has always performed at the top of her class, even as early as kindergarten. She is Mrs. C's favorite child, as she characterizes Laura as "perfect", and Michael as "terrible". The worker sensed that behind Laura's school success and pseudo-adult style lies an anxious young girl; so driven by her need to gain approval through achievement that she finds it difficult to relax enough to simply be the child she is.

Both Mr. and Mrs. C are intelligent professional people. Mr. C is thirty-seven years old, and holds a Ph.D. in biochemistry. He is employed by a large chemical corporation, and functions at the executive/professional level. Mrs. C., also thrity-seven, has earned a masters degree in biochemistry. Although she currently functions as a full-time homemaker, she is seeking a position as a university laboratory assistant. Both Mr. and Mrs. C appear to lack affective spontaneity, and outwardly disparage anything that is frivolous or non-scientific. Life, for them, is pursued with calculated logic and scientific objectivity.

The referral sent to the Child Study Team by Michael's teacher suggested that, although Mike is an intelligent boy who possesses the capacity to do work that is above grade level, he regularly gives the impression that he is a poor student. He forgets assignments, fails to do homework, etc., often claiming that he didn't understand the instructions given to the class. Hence, he gives the appearance of being "disorganized" and "irresponsible", unable to do classwork without intense personal instructions. Michael's teacher also noted that he sometimes seems oblivious to his surroundings, hiding underneath his desk or in the clothes closet. When confronted with his behavior Michael typically remains silent, or opens his mouth wide and bobs his head around. He has also been known to sing "nonsense songs" when asked questions concerning material being discussed with the rest of the class.

It was suggested that Michael doesn't relate well to other children in school. He appears socially inept, not knowing how to approach or play with others. He can usually be found reading or playing alone, but if he does interact with other children he often becomes excited and acts inappropriately. He might do this by leaving a game early, hitting his peers for reasons which aren't always obvious to the others, or change rules arbitrarily in games.

In the process of follow-up on the referral, the therapist observed Michael in his classroom setting and on the playground. These observations were in general agreement with the views presented by the teacher. Some of Michael's former teachers were contacted as well, and their statements concerning Michael's school behavior in the past were congruent with those presented in the referral. Some additional information gathered from these discussions suggested that Michael became easily frustrated when not immediately able to grasp concepts. He was said to have displayed a tendency to withdraw from reality into the fantasy world of his daydreams, and lacked any interest in forming relationships with peers; prefering instead to play with machines like the tape recorder and other teaching devices.

Having received several different perspectives on Michael's behavior within the school setting, the therapist proceeded to arrange a meeting with the C. family; this in the hope of establishing a contact for some sort of counseling in the event that the pending medical examinations, and learning consultant's reports, proved negative. By the time that contact was made with Mr. and Mrs. C. they had already met with Michael's teacher. While Mrs. C. was anxious to speak with the worker, and hoped to get some recommendations on what might be done to help her son, Mr. C. expressed the feeling that Michael's problems were not so severe as to warrant counseling. He also deemed psychology worthless and unscientific, but agreed to meet with the worker once if it would serve to get his wife off his back. He made it clear, however, that he would not participate in or contribute to our discussion concerning Michael's behavior; and that he was certain that Michael would outgrow this "immaturity" as he grows older. The father further contended that he was much like Michael when he was a child, and, as anyone could readily see, he had obviously adjusted well, becoming a highly respected professional.

The initial meeting with the C. family was a tense affair. All members of the family appeared nervous and apprehensive. The chairs in the office were arranged in a circular manner with the worker flanked on either side by Mr. and Mrs. C., and Michael and Laura wedged between the parents. Laura sat near the mother, Michael next to the father. The following diagram illustrates the seating of the initial interview.

M

Mr. C.

L

Therapist

Mrs. C.

After some perfunctory opening remarks and a few comments designed to put the family at ease, the

worker asked the general question of why each felt
they were in to see him. The question was directed
toward Mr. C. who remained aloof and silent. Mrs. C.
acted as though the question was meant for her and
answered immediately. She said that they had come to
discuss Michael's problem with school, and to see if
anything could be done to help the situation.

Recognizing that Mrs. C. was presently acting
as the spokesperson for the family, the worker made
an attempt to elicit a response from Mr. C.. He
asked Mr. C. what his opinion of the situation was.
The father replied that he did not feel that Michael
had any problems which the family couldn't work out
themselves. These remarks made Mrs. C. agitated, and
she proceeded to defend her point that indeed Michael
did have problems. She began to relate these by
noting that Michael was a "difficult" child. She
claimed that as a baby he didn't seem "cuddly" like
other babies she had held, but rather became stiff and
tense when picked up. She also said that he always
appeared overly sensitive to any sort of moderate
stimulation, crying when brought into department
stores because of the lights, music, and crowds, or
screaming when he simply had an itch. She further
spoke of his need to routinize activities, being
obsessed with the desire to have his day run on a
strict schedule, and of the pleasure that he finds in
repetitive activities such as listening to the same
records over and over again.

While Mrs. C. related the history of Michael's
"problem," the worker asked others for their perceptions of what was being said. Mr. C. noted that he
couldn't understand why everyone was making such a
fuss over Michael, since, in his opinion, these
activities were not at all strange; and that certainly
Michael would outgrow them. Michael appeared detached
throughout most of the discussion. He either remained silent or else suggested he didn't know the
answers to queries directed to him. Laura said little
when addressed by the worker, but responded actively
when enlisted by her mother to share her perceptions
of her brother. Here Laura noted that Michael was
"odd" and that he remained as an outcast with most of
their neighborhood peers. She agreed with Mrs. C.'s
reports that Michael interprets other children's loud
play as yelling at him, and either responds to it by
withdrawal or fighting. Laura further related that

the other children simply don't like Michael because he acts so strange.

At this point Mr. C. became angry and shouted at Laura for acting as though she was such a "goody-goody." He suggested that all this talk was "foolish and illogical," and that he couldn't see where it could possibly lead. He moved to end the session at this point.

Subsequent sessions with Mrs. C. revealed certain information about her relationship with her husband, as well as some background information pertinent to our future discussion. Mrs. C. noted that her relationship with her husband had always been a "cool" one. She suggested that she decided to marry him because they were in the same field of study in graduate school, and that she felt that it was about time for her to get married. She claimed that there was never much emotional investment in their marriage, but rather that it was a bond of convenience more than anything else.

She noted that her pregnancy with Michael was unpleasant, and that when she learned that she was pregnant she felt angry and trapped; knowing that she would have to forego her career pursuits. She harborded feelings of resentment, also, throughout most of her pregnancy, finding herself jealous of her husband's career and depressed at the prospects of herself being simply a housewife. Mrs. C. claimed that near the end of her pregnancy she had "warmed up" considerably to the idea of having a child, but that once Michael was born these feelings quickly dissipated. This was largely due to the fact that Michael was a "fussy" and "troublesome" child, and that she felt inadequate at mothering him; often fearing that others would interpret Michael's behavior as an indication of her ineptness in being a mother.

Mrs. C. further related that beyond her general anger and anxiety at being a mother that she could expect little support from her husband in efforts to socialize and discipline the children. She views Mr. C. as an ineffectual husband and father; one who has saddled her with the entire responsibility for raising the children. She reports that Mr. C.'s contact with the children is only at his convenience.

These conversations with Mrs. C. also revealed
that throughout the eight years since Laura's conception she and Mr. C. have had no sexual intercourse;
and that Mr. C. has, on occasion, had extra marital
affairs.

Finally, Mrs. C. spoke briefly of her own and
her husband's family situations before their marriage.
She noted that she had only one sibling, an older
brother, who was not very intelligent and who was
easily dominated by others--especially her parents.
She characterized herself as the "smart responsible
child" in the family. Her father, she said, was a
"wild and angry man." He was prone to fits of violence, especially when drunk. Further, he had no
respect for Mrs. C.'s mother, and evidenced this
openly with his numerous extra-marital affairs.
Mrs. C.'s mother enlisted her as a confidant, telling
her what a poor husband she had and how lonely and
upset she was. Mrs. C.'s father was very protective
of his daughter, finding fault with all of her boyfriends. She claims that he would wrestle with the
boyfriends to assert his own masculinity, and to
show them that he was a better man than anyone his
daughter would bring home. Once when he was drunk
he became openly seductive towards Mrs. C. She
was an early adolescent at the time, and was extremely
frightened by his actions.

The picture that she presented of Mrs. C.'s
family situation was quite different. He was the
eldest child in a very large family. He has four
younger brothers and three sisters. Mrs. C. claims
that her husband's family was quite poor and lived
in a rundown rural area. She noted that her husband
was always ashamed of his family and had feelings of
resentment at having to grow up in poverty. Reportedly, Mr. C. has always been a loner because of the
embarrassment he felt at his family's economical
situation; and to this day finds it hard to relate
to people on a casual, friendly basis. She suggested
that Mr. C. has come to face the world with a "chip
on his shoulder" and maintains the attitude that he
has to "get others before they get him." He reportedly
has been able to channel this aggression into his
career in becoming a "superprofessional," but has
made many "enemies" along the way.

With this case material in mind, we can now turn our central task of speculating on how Salvador Minuchin, Virginia Satir, and Murry Bowen might intervene with the C. family.

III. THE MINUCHIN APPROACH

"I am myself plus my circumstances" (Minuchin, 1974:6) is a quote of Ortyga y Gasset which is of key importance to Salvador Minuchin. He believes that indeed "no man is an island." Rather that we all are what we are, and who we are, in a psycho-social-bio ecosystem. Further, it is one's immediate family that provides the individual with a basis sense of self, an identity. Consequently, since the family is the "..matrix of identity.." (Minuchin, 1974:47) it is to the family that Minuchin focuses his attention in serving those in psychological, and often physical, pain.

Structurally the family is viewed as a functional, hydrolic system. This structure is "..an invisible set of functional demands that organize the ways in which the family members interact" (Minuchin, 1974:47). The family is composed of "transactional patterns," the relatively stable ways in which members relate to one another, as well as how they adapt to internal and external forces which impinge on the system. According to Minuchin, each member within a family functions some role in the task of maintaining the system; and that the vicissitudes of life, and the stages of individual and family growth, require of the family constantly new adaptive postures.

Within the nuclear family system are sub-systems. Typically this would include the parental, spouse, and sibling sub-systems. The role of each of these is, hopefully, to coordinate their efforts in maintaining the whole system's functional integrity. Problems, both corporate and individual, arise when one of the substysems fails to contribute adaptively to the whole; when it abdicates on its functional responsibility. When this occurs, the entire family system is thrown into disequilibrium, and consequently loses its capacity to facilitate individual growth, and to make adaptive responses to its internal and external environments. It is at this point in Minuchin's view that individual pathology--symptomatic of familial dysfunction--emerges.

In viewing the C. family from Minuchin's perspective, we would see a family clearly in functional distress. While Michael certainly is in pain, and in need of corrective intervention, the pathological seed is not to be found in his personality. Rather, since "..children function as conflict-detouring mechanisms" (Minuchin, 1974:8), Michael's are but an expression of a system in distress--a system of family pathology. Consequently, according to Minuchin, the goal of intervention with this family would be to relieve Michael's symptomatic behavior by first assessing where it fits into the family system--how it functions in the family--and secondly, by conceiving of a plan to correct the system. The goal then is to promote a more adaptive family, one without the need for Michael's symptoms.

In pursuing this end, Minuchin finds it incumbent on the therapist to "join" the family: to "... become an actor in the family drama" (Minuchin, 1974: 60). By joining the family the therapist psychologically enters the family so as to experience firsthand its dynamics. From this vantage point Minuchin would make his assessment, and, as a functional member, (albeit more objective than the others) would seek to restructure the family so that it will be more corporately and individually adaptive.

In this process a family map is of paramount importance. "A family map is an organizational scheme" (Minuchin, 1974:90) which charts the family's predominant transactional patterns, as well as their sub-systems. In turning to the C. family, a family map would appear as follows:

FATHER   MOTHER

                        LAURA

        MICHAEL

Minuchin's (1974:53)
  key:
Clear Boundaries------
Diffused   "   ......
  (emmeshed)
Rigid Boundaries_____
  (disengaged)
Affiliation ========
Overinvolvement ========
Conflict
Coalition
Detouring

Here we find graphic expression of the family dynamics.
The father is psychologically seen as outside the
family. This is depicted by a rigid boundary. The
mother and sister are in an alliance; one which not
only short-circuits the functional parent, spouse and
sibling sub-systems, but also undercuts each's individual autonomy through the overinvolved enmeshed
relationship between mother and her responsible
"tattle-tale" daughter. The map further portrays
Michael's place as the symptom bearer of the family
system. He is seen to function not only as to divert
the spouse system from their own conflicts, but also
provides a focus to justify mother's overinvolvement
with the daughter; an alliance which serves to satisfy
emotional needs of the mother left frustrated through
her marriage.

According to Minuchin, Michael's symptomatic role
in this family is critical. Since the entire system
proved unable to respond creatively to the internal
requirements of the executive function, it became
rigid in the transactional pattern illustrated above.
It is therefore crucial for its current homeostatis,
albeit a maladaptive homeostais, that Michael remains
symptomatic. For without Michael's problems the
parents would no longer be diverted from the family's
fundamental problem, viz, a malfunctioning executive/
spouse sub-system. In short, the parents, so as to
rigidly maintain the sad status quo, need a troubled
child.

The family map is the product of the therapist's
assessment of the family. To Minuchin it results from
the therapist's skillful joining with each member of
the family, and with each sub-system. This is a
critical point. The therapist must join with all
aspects of the family so as to: 1) arrive at an
accurate diagnosis/assessment; 2) broaden the problem
focus to the entire family; and 3) lay the ground-plan
for the task of restructuring the family system--all
without provoking unyielding family resistances.

In Minuchin's view, the ideal resolution to the
C. family's problem would look something like this:

514

```
HUSBAND        WIFE
-----------------------

FATHER         MOTHER
-----------------------

CHILD          CHILD
```

Here the spouse, parent, and sibling sub-systems would
be free to function adaptively and homeostatically;
flexible to internal and external contingencies, with
a clear operational hierarchy, and a functional distribution of tasks. However, Minuchin believes that
no system can tolerate too great a disruption at one
time. Consequently, his intervention would aim at
maintaining the system to a degree, while gradually
restructuring it towards the goal; this "...in such
a way that they are not threatened by major dislocation" (Minuchin, 1974:119).

In hazarding successive approximations, eventually transforming the family into acting in functional
transactional patterns, Minuchin first joins the
family. With the C. family this would require the
immediate enlistment of the father, the one most
resistant to change. Given this man's technical
propensity Minuchin might appeal to Mr. C.'s scientific penchant by claiming that "...as a therapist I am
at times more artistic than scientific, and I'll need
your scientific skills in helping me make your son
happier." This might enlist the "outside" father by:
1) placing him in the appropriate, socially accepted,
executive function in the family; 2) defuse the
father's defensive negative attitudes towards psychotherapy; and 3) manipulate him publicly into active
and cooperative participation in the therapeutic
process.

In effect, in joining with the family members
Minuchin believes that "I turn other family members
into my co-therapists" (Minuchin, 1974:121). Once
the most resistant member is enlisted into the process, by hook or crook obviously. Minuchin would
then turn to the subtle task of restructuring.

Rather than attacking the marital dysfunction
head on, it seems likely that Minuchin would work
towards disengaging the mother-daughter coalition.
By pointing out that the daughter works too hard at

515

being responsible (all the while affirming how fortunate the parents are to have such a responsible child), as well as entering into more playful activities, Minuchin would begin to open a back door to the central family problem. If the girl is encouraged by the parents to spend less time in the system, the system will begin to lose its homeostasis. Presumably, the mother will then begin to feel her pain more; which, in turn, might make her more amenable to dealing with her husband. In essence, Minuchin's maneuver to place himself between the mother and daughter, promoting each's autonomy, is aimed at having repercussions throughout the entire system. And, to Minuchin, it is as the system loses its balance that it is most vulnerable to therapeutic change.

In restructuring the family Minuchin might employ a variety of techniques. With the aim of restructuring the mother--daughter boundary, we saw hom Minuchin might have intervened. This intervention might, in turn, begin to re-form appropriate boundaries throughout the system.

Secondly, because action precedes insight in Minuchin's view, the therapist would want to manipulate the physical space in the sessions. This would be aimed as having the family act out boundaries which the therapist wants them to move towards. One way this could be achieved with the C. family would be to change the seating arrangement. As noted in the previous seating arrangement diagram, during the initial interview the family's dynamic boundaries, their transactional patterns, were embodied in their selection of seats. By trading seats with the mother to the folowing:

$$M$$
Mr. C.   L
Mrs. C.   T

the therapist would be actualizing boundaries during the session which he hopes to eventually see in the new family structure.

In addition to the in-session tasks which stimulate the formation of new boundaries (e.g., asking the parents to decide on ways that Laura might be encouraged to play more), Minuchin utilizes homework assign-

ments. In this way he holds that the clients are
"...in effect taking the therapist home with them"
(Munichin, 1974:6). With the C. family Minuchin
might have the parents agree to get together at a
certain time, and for a specified period, each
evening to discuss how they might encourage their
daughter to be more playful/spontaneous (each quality,
of course, precisely what the spouse sub-system
needs). In addition, the father might be assigned
the task of spending forty-five minutes each night
alone with Michael for the explicit purpose of
reading his science fiction comics to his son. (Mr.
C. has an exhaustive collection of comics which serve
as a refuge from family interaction.) To facilitate
this, (actually to paint the father into a corner)
Minuchin might explain that, since the child has such
a good and creative ability to entertain fantasies
(the paradoxical view of one of the presenting symptoms), and since the father is both a respected
scientist and lover of good comics, that each would
really enjoy the task.

In this final regard Minuchin would be utilizing
the symptom in service to the restructuring process.
This would be achieved by: 1) capitalizing on both
the father's and son's defensive adaptive maneuvers;
that is to say, employing the existing systemic resources, maladaptive as they are, in service to the
restructuring tasks; 2) return the father to the
father--son relationship; and 3) begin the process of
redefining the child's symptoms, i.e., from the
family's perception of fantasy as part of Michael's
pathology to one of his strenghs.

According to Minuchin, the role of the family
therapist is to "...manipulate the family system
towards planned change" (Minuchin, 1974:140). To
accomplish this he has to firstly know the family
structure, their boundaries, and their transactional
patterns. In addition, the family therapist must
know how the presenting problem serves the family
system. With this in mind the therapist then "...
becomes an actor in the family play" (Minuchin,
1974:138), joining sub-systems, entering alliances,
with individuals, disrupting transactional patterns,
and manipulating the entire system. In short, just
about anything which promotes the system's movement
towards greater adaptability and functionality. All
of this, of course, must proceed while satisfying

the "first rule" of family therapy, i.e., "...to
leave the family willing to come again for the next
session" (Minuchin, 1974:212).

IV. THE SATIR APPROACH

     At this point, the family presented in our case
study will be examined from the perspective offered
by Virginia Satir in her theory of family therapy.
In order to better understand how this particular mode
of family treatment would apply to the case at hand,
a brief overview of several of Satir's most basic concepts will be offered, as they appear embodied in her
goals for treatment. Secondly, in assessing the case
study, our focus will be upon pertinent issues from
Satir's theory of family interaction. Specifically,
this will include: 1) the notion of self-esteem and
how this plays an important role in the selection of
a spouse; 2) environmental or societal stresses
affecting the family that seeks out therapeutic help;
and 3) the process of triangling that often causes
children to be pulled into their parent's distressed
marital relationship.

     It has been suggested that the most basic element
in Satir's theory, and hence, the major treatment
goal, is that of "maturation" (Foley, 1974:94). Satir
writes that maturation is the most important concept
in therapy, because it is the touchstone for all the
rest (Satir, 1967:91). What she means when speaking
of maturation, is that state of functioning when one
is fully in charge of oneself and one's actions, and
is able to make choices and decisions based on an
accurate perception of oneself, others, and the context in which one finds oneself. The mature person
can acknowledge the choices and decisions that they
make as their own, and accepts responsibility for
their outcome (Satir, 1967:91).

     Although this might appear to be a rather broad
and idealistic treatment goal, one must remember that
it remains the hub around which all secondary treatment goals are constructed. That is, there are
several intermediate steps which must be implemented
and fit together in order to arrive at the over-
arching goal of maturation. One of these secondary
goals is that of developing the ability to manifest
oneself clearly through communication. Satir suggests
that people must be able to communicate clearly if

they care to give and receive information that accurately conveys what is being thought or felt (Satir, 1967:64). She claims that the meaning of words is often unclear, hence it is important for open dialogue to take place between people in order that they might clarify and qualify what they mean. Satir is quick to note, however, that communication is more than simply a verbal process. One communicates on at least two levels: 1) the denotative level, and 2) the metacommunative or non-verbal level (Satir, 1967:76). Unless one is sending clear messages on both levels, misunderstandings resulting in stress may occur.

Implicit within the concept of communication for Satir is her emphasis on expression of feelings. Foley suggests that the focal point on which Satir's communication theory revolves is the emotional or feeling level of this process (Foley, 1974:93). He notes that Satir attempts, from the beginning of treatment, to engage the family in therapy by responding to their "pain." Faulty patterns of communication can evolve from many sources, but ultimately one must get beyond the pain and anger that one feels at not being understood before one can deal with any of the other issues. Hence, expression of feelings is a necessary correlate to open communication.

Another important component necessary for helping a person toward mature functioning is a sense of differentiation of self from significant others, and an acceptance of differences in those who are important to us. This concept of differentiation is intimately related to Satir's notion of self-esteem. That is, if a person has a low sense of self-esteem he will be crippled in the areas of individuality and autonomy (Satir, 1967:8). Satir believes that people with low self-esteem attract one another in the world of social and sexual relationships. Each entertains the fantasy that the other will take care of them and provide them with that which is lacking in their life. Once these such persons become married, however, this illusion is quickly dispelled. The spouses soon realize that they are called upon to give as well as to receive in this relationship (Satir, 1967:11). Each partner experiences the other as being "different" from what they had expected and needed in a marital relationship, and any hope of somehow merging with their mate and having all of their deficiencies eliminated is shattered. Hence, work toward differentiation of self, as outlined by Satir, must necessarily entail work toward developing greater self-esteem.

As Satir proceeds with her elucidations on the couples' sense of frustration, and their unrealistic expectations in terms of marital needs, i.e., they gradually awaken to the fact that he/she does not exist primarily to meet the needs of the other, the logical outcome points toward a stress situation. Each member of the marital dyad, upon finding that their needs will not be met automatically, finds it difficult or impossible to negotiate clearly for what they desire or to effect any sort of compromise. They will often move, at this point, to "triangle" one of their children into their relationship. This is done by the parents, in an attempt to have their needs met through this child, and also to express their aggression indirectly toward one another as well (Satir, 1972:58-59). This development brings us full circle, back to the need for effective patterns of communication, a means to adequately express one's feelings and a persistence in working toward becoming a mature and fully functioning person.

Having outlined some of the major theoretical foundations of Satir's concept of family therapy, we can now turn to our case study to explore how this mode of treatment could be implemented in practice. When attempting to encapsulate Satir's style of initiating treatment with families in distress, two variables stand out immediately. These are: 1) her attempt to "join" the family in a relaxed, non-threatening manner, and 2) her willingness to direct questions to all members of the family in a low-keyed, probing way, geared toward allowing everyone to express where the "pain" in their family resides for them. Using these guidelines from the beginning, Satir might have made her first contact with Mr. and Mrs. C. by telephone. Here she would attempt to present herself as a warm and understanding person, one who is interested in what they have to say. To Mr. C.'s initial resistance, Satir might have replied that she could understand how he might feel confused over many of the issues that both the school and Mrs. C. were raising, and that she would hope that he might come to the first session to express his bewilderment.

The initial interview with the family would involve an assessment of what each member hopes or
expects to get from treatment. During the first
interview, it is also imperative that the therapist
bring the family to the point of recognizing how
they experience the pain of their dysfunctional family
system. This can be done by merely asking each family
member to discuss when they first noticed the symptom
or what has been done to relieve it (Satir, 1967:110).
In the case of the C. family, this direct tack might
not be effective. In this situation Satir might observe the family interaction surrounding the question
of Michael's symptom. She might point up that this
whole question must be a very painful one for everyone. She would suggest that Mr. and Mrs. C. must
feel the tension that comes between them as a result
of this situation. She could also note that Laura
must feel torn as well, since she receives mixed
messages from both parents concerning how she should
react toward Michael's behavior. Finally, Satir might
note that Michael must feel very confused about this
whole matter, wondering if, in the end, he is alright
or not.

If Satir can get all members of the family to
feel the pain that the "family symptom" causes each
of .them individually, she can key into their probable
puzzlement over why the symptom exists and what they
can do about it (Satir, 1967:110-111). Here she would
suggest that everyone finds it hard to understand why
their family hurts so badly. She would point out that
often we do everything that we know, and yet things
remain the same. Satir makes these sort of comments
in an effort to decrease the threat of blame and to
accentuate the idea of good intensions exercise to
no avail (Satir, 1967:110). If she senses that the
family is actively experiencing the pain and confusion
that is a result of their collective dysfunctioning,
Satir moves to gain information by means of the family
chronology.

The taking of the family chronology serves a
myriad of purposes. First, it provides the therapist
with a wealth of information concerning the family
process and its evolution from the time when Mr. and
Mrs. C. were first dating to its present status.
Secondly, it serves to take the focus off Michael as
the "identified patient," and shows everyone that the
family has a history where they all experienced hap-

pier moments (Satir, 1967:113). Finally, the family
chronology will serve to point up the "different-ness"
in each member of the family. Satir writes that,
"Different-ness is a loaded idea in dysfunciontal
families" (Satir, 1967:123). She would want to continually note how Mr. and Mrs. C. are, indeed, different from one another in many ways, just as their
parents were different, and that the ways in which
they have been handling their different-ness may be
unsuitable for them.

Hence, through taking this family chronology,
Satir would quickly learn that both Mr. and Mrs. C.
entered their marriage with a low sense of self-
esteem. Mr. C. may have hoped that his wife would
provide the nurturance and acceptance that he had
never received as a child. Mrs. C. may have felt
that her husband would be a strong figure upon whom
she could depend for support and approval. Once
married, their illusions were shattered and the sense
of disappointment set in. To complicate matters,
Michael was conceived early in their marriage. This
put added stress on their relationship, in that they
now had to carry what Satir characterizes as, "the
extra load" of parenting (Satir, 1967:26). Hence, a
disillusioned Mrs. C. was left with no opportunity
to gain the approval she required through the outlet
of a career. A frightened Mr. C. faced the prospect
of becoming a father, and being required to give his
child love and support, while he, himself, remained
frustrated in his attempt to secure the reassurance
he needed.

It would soon become apparent to Satir that this
family is showing the signs indicated in the postulate
that, "a pained marital relationship tends to produce
dysfunctional parenting (Satir, 1967:2). Mr. and Mrs.
C. undoubtedly learned to communicate their feelings
of anger and disappointment toward one another through
their first child. Mrs. C. covertly communicates the
message that if Michael has problems, it is because
Mr. C. is an ineffectual father, unable to lend their
son the support and approval he requires to be a
"normal" child. Mr. C., in his denial of Michael's
"problems," is suggesting that Mrs. C. is an over-
demanding mother, unable to love her child for what
he is. Both parents need to have Michael exhibit problem behavior in order that this subtle power struggle
might continue. Hence, the "rules" that this family

operates within are uncovered by means of the family chronology and observation of family interaction.

Satir would then want to intervene in this faulty network of communication by attempting to have the family clarify what they mean when they communicate and verbalize how they feel about the messages being sent. She would do this first, by creating a setting in which all could take the risk of looking clearly and objectively at themselves and their actions (Satir, 1967:160). This is facilitated by the active participation and direction offered by the therapist in the counseling sessions. Satir would undoubtedly ask family members to continually repeat or restate their messages if they are unclear so that nothing is left to the imagination. She would also want to ask for continual feedback regarding how family members feel about issues being discussed, and to point up non-verbal inconsistencies that go with verbal messages. Finally, she might use some direct confrontation when she felt that the family was ready for it.

Direct confrontation might come in the form of suggestions that Mrs. C. is acting very much like her own mother when she shuts Mr. C. out of her life and aligns herself with her daughter. It might also be noted that Mr. C. has never really learned to trust his wife enough to ask for the affection that he so desperately desires. The consequences of these actions are a storing up of hatred and resentment that ultimately emerges through their child's symptomatic behavior.

It would be of great importance to the therapeutic process that the C. family actively practice clear and direct patterns of communication both in therapy sessions and at home. To enable this to take place, Satir might assign homework tasks in the form of games that the family could play together. Several of these games, outlined in her book, Peoplemaking, are designed specifically for this sort of task. If the C. family would pursue at a more open stance on communication and expression of feelings, they would be taking their first steps toward the ultimate goal of family maturation.

V. THE BOWEN APPROACH

The final portion of this paper will deal with
Murray Bowen's view of family therapy as it applies
to our case study. For Bowen, the family is an emotional system made up from a variety of emotional
subsystems. Bowen would suggest that the "nuclear
family" is really non-existent. Rather, what is
generally referred to as the nuclear family is but a
tip expression of a multigenerational entity. However alienated the nuclear family is from its family
of origin, be it geographical, psychological, or
cultural, Bowen holds that individuals within any
particular family system are influenced significantly
by their ancestry.

As Bowen translates this into family assessments,
he seeks to investigate as far back into its antece-
dent history as possible. To Bowen, there is a "...
remarkable consistency of family functioning through
the generations" (Bowen, 1976:86). Since he believes
that family members are "replicas of the past," Bowen
explores emotional systems and styles of family relations, which were valued, taught, and passed on
through the generations, and the current family style
of relating serving as its legacy.

In scrutinizing the influence which the family
of origin has on any family problem, Bowen is particularly interested in the "levels of differentiation"
of the various members. For both past and present
family members, Bowen attempts to answer the query,
"How successful was each individual in differentiation
from their family of origin?" For while Bowen believes that the family is essential in providing the
nurturing context for developing individuals, that is
the matrix of pre-adult development, the family can
also impede this process of individuation. To best
grasp this we must briefly explore Bowen's notion of
"differentiation and indifferentiation."

In Bowen's view, every individual functions at
some level of differentiation from his or her family
of origin. In a somewhat arbitrary fashion, Bowen
postulates a differentiation scale from 0 through 100,
with the least differentiated the former, the greatest
the latter. Within this scheme the average adult
functions somewhere around the 45-55 range, the
superior in the 60's. What this means is that the

greater one's differentiation rating, the greater one's emotional and physical independence from one's family. The less one's differentiation, the greater one's immersion in the family. In short, the more differentiated, the greater the individual's ability to function autonomously, discover self, and respond to the environment. The less one's differentiation from their family, the less one's autonomy and the greater one's bondage to feelings -- reacting to the environment. Hence, "a poorly differentiated person ..." to Bowen "...is trapped within a feeling world" (Bowen, 1976:67).

With these assumptions, Bowen concludes that it is from the family that individuals receive their basic differentiation rating -- the "real self." To Bowen the "real" or "solid" self says, "This is who I am, and what I believe, what I stand for, and I will do or will not do in a given situation" (Bowen, 1976:68). The basic differentiation rating is the legacy of one's family system. Furthermore, Bowen goes on to suggest that certain offspring will tend to be less differentiated than their parents; and so on until, as "...we follow the most impaired child through successive generations, we will see one line of descendants producing individuals with lower and lower differentiation" (Bowen, 1976:86). To Bowen, it is the schizophrenic that is the natural outcome of this downward spiral.

Certain individuals tend to be less differentiated than their parents because they are "triangled" into the emotion system. Triangles are the cornerstone to Bowen's theory. They are the, "basic building blocks of any emotional system" (Bowen, 1976:76). A triangle exists when a dyadic relationship, faced with stress, enlists a third to provide it stability; the price of which is some form of family symptom. In short, when a marital couple is in conflict and seems unable to cope with it, they will "triangle" a child to discharge the anxiety generated by their seemingly unresolvable discord. It will be this triangled person who will tend to bear the family symptom, and be a less differentiated self than the parents.

Just why a certain child is selected by the parents to be triangled is a complex matter in Bowen's writings. It may have to do with the parental sibling positions, triangled emotional systems brought into the marriage which predate the birth of children or outside stress factors. Whatever the reason, it is certain that triangles will appear in any emotional system, and that they have the capacity to interlock and draw in others again, when stress becomes unbearable.

Finally, as we found with the family therapists previously noted, Bowen views the family as the locus of treatment. It is the family unit which precipitates most of the psychological complaints that bring people into treatment. Even though one member may come with a particular symptom, the dynamic roots of this problem are to be located in the family's emotional system. In short, a symptom is conceived by Bowen as the negative side of a family triangle. Consequently, it is the therapist's task to analyze the family's emotional system, perceive its triangles and initiate the process of "de-triangling" individuals from their enmeshed family system. Hence the goal is, "to restore love and togetherness in the family" (Bowen, 1972:161), and to "...help individual family members to a higher level of differentiation" (Foley, 1974:116).

With these comments in mind we will now turn to the C. family in an attempt to examine Murray Bowen's approach to family treatment as it pertains to this particular case. Although it is certain that Bowen recognizes the family as the locus of treatment, unlike the previous theorists we have discussed, he does not always require that all family members participate in the therapy process. He notes that, "My optimum approach to any family problem, whether marital conflict, dysfunction in a spouse, or dysfunction in a child, is to start with the husband and wife together ...but this optimum is not always possible..., hence some 30 to 40 percent of family hours are spent with one family member, mostly for situations in which one spouse is antagonistsic or poorly motivated" (Bowen, 1976:185). Keeping in mind Bowen's adage that, "a theoretical system that thinks in terms of family and works toward improving the family system is family psychotherapy" (Bowen, 1976:169). We can recognize that this is a valid position in the realm of family treatment.

526

Concurrent with Bowen's view of family psychotherapy is the fact that nowhere in his published
literature does he openly discuss dealing with resistant clients. Rather, he appears to presuppose a
highly intelligent, motivated, and wealthy clientele;
for his therapeutic intervention process is often
quite time consuming and rigorous. In this sense,
Bowen would undoubtedly have dealth exclusively with
Mrs. C. in this particular case, keeping the emphasis
and focus clearly on family patterns of interaction.
Since Bowen believes that, "The mechanisms that operate outside the nuclear family ego mass are important
in determining the course and process within the
nuclear family" (Bowsen, 1976:178), he might engage
Mrs. C. in treatment by suggesting that before Michael
can begin to be understood and changed, she herself
would need to assess how the patterns of relating
which she has learned from her family of origin contribute to Michael's behavioral symptoms.

If Mrs. C. would agree to pursue treatment with
Bowen, her first task would be to compile a detailed,
"chronological review of symptom development, with
specific dates and circumstances at the time of each
symptom eruption, because many symptomatic eruptions
can be timed exactly with other events in the nuclear
and extended family fields" (Bowen, 1976:181). For
this she would have to go back to her family of origin
and do some interviewing to secure the required information. Once she had completed this task, which
could take from three weeks to several months, Bowen
would take on his "coach" role. Here, he would
examine the material, pointing out triangles and enmeshed relationships, and ask for feedback from Mrs.
C. in order to establish the validity of his assumptions. The intent at this point is to afford some
insight into the process that holds Mrs. C. captive
to her current manner of relating to others.

Once insight is established, Mrs. C. would be
further "coached" in the task of "detriangling" herself from her family of origin. Bowen would undoubtedly point up the fact that Mrs. C. was triangled
into a relationship with her mother and father which
served to dissipate the stress that occurred between
them in their marriage. He might suggest that this
very same process is mirrored in her own nuclear family. There, Laura serves as her confidant and source
of gratification, while her husband, like her own

father, remains detached, only to be reached through their mutual involvement with Michael, who like her brother, needs to be taken care of. In order to break up this insidious network of interlocking triangles, Mrs. C. would need to go back to her parents to work toward getting them to relate to her on an individual level, rather than as a means of reducing anxiety between themselves.

Hence, under the guise of friendly visits home, Mrs. C. would be put to the task of: 1) meeting alone with each of her parents in the hope of getting them to recognize and relate to her as an individual rather than a stopgap for their own marital stress, and 2) attempting to facilitate direct discussion between her mother and father, while she, herself, remains detriangled. Although this appears to be a fairly straight-forward task, it will be no mean feat to accomplish a breakthrough in well established coping patterns. Mrs. C. will undoubtedly need to visit her parents numerous times over the course of at least one or two years, writing countless letters and visiting her equally triangled brother. If after all of this work and constant coaching from Bowen, Mrs. C. is able to detriangle herself from her parents, a radical change should be seen in her extended and nuclear families.

The most obvious result of this process would be a freer, more differentiated Mrs. C. She would have the capacity now to "respond" to her parents and brother rather than "reacting" at the smallest indication of stress. Secondly, Mrs. C.'s parents would become more capable of dealing directly with one another, and perhaps would no longer require Mrs. C.'s brother to act as the oaf who constantly requires direction. Finally, Mrs. C. should be prepared, at this point, to enter her own nuclear family with renewed freedom and flexibility. She has acquired a myriad of detriangling techniques that she should now to able to use with her husband and children.

If this is beginning to sound like a smooth and predictable process, a false image is being perpetrated. Bowen will be quick to point out that in this work toward differentiation, some family members may become worse off for the process. That is, if Mrs. C., while becoming increasingly independent,

528

begins to be perceived as threatening by her husband, he might cause a stress situation in their marriage which could occasion Michael's symptoms to become exaggerated. The ultimate goal, of course, is to, "help family members become systems experts who know the family system so well that the family could re-adjust itself without the help of an outside expert, if an when the family is stressed again" (Bowen, 1971:168). This could only become possible if Mrs. C. would ultimately detriangle herself from her dysfunctional marital and family relationships, and allow everyone to experience the benefits of this freedom.

Naturally, it is hoped that somewhere along the way Mr. C. will feel the need to be "coached" toward differentiation himself. If this could happen, then ultimately, the C. family would be relating on a healthy, detriangled level of functioning. Hence, Michael would no longer be required to exhibit pathological seeming behavior and Laura would be free to act like the child that she is. It is, however, a long process that requires much hard work, motiva-tion, and financial resources.

VI. INTEGRATION OF THE THREE APPROACHES

In light of the foregoing, it is clear that there is a basic theoretical unanimity among the three theorists surveyeds, including the assumptions that: 1) individual maladaptation is causally related to family dynamics, and 2) the family is the locus of treatment. However, as evidenced by the above dis-cussion, techniques or styles of intervention based on these premises are somewhat disparate. To date we are aware of no empirical evaluative studies endors-ing one style above the other, consequently, when selecting a treatment of choice, one must take into consideration the idiosyncratic nature of the family dynamics as well as the idiosyncratic disposition of the therapist.

With this in mind, in attempting to select the ideal treatment of choice for the C. family, we would suspect that each of the three reviewed modes of family intervention would have their own shortcomings. With regard to Satir's interventive style, we feel that, given Mr. C.'s proclivity toward one-dimensional communication, and ostensible denial of the illogical or feeling level of communication, that his resistance would be massive against any change on this level. His style of communication is simply too entrenched in his personality and emotional needs, hence it seems highly improbable that this person would agree to participate in any form of communication exercises. Consequently, unless the Satirian therapist is inordinately skilled at evoking more effective levels of communication from this family, then this approach would appear to be contraindicated.

Bowen's interventive approach, on the other hand, might prove fruitful if: 1) Mrs. C. is willing to invest the time required for this form of family therapy, 2) financial and emotional resources are readily available, and 3) Mrs. C. could place a moratorium on her current marital unhappiness and the immediate family dysfunction so as to pursue the multigenerational insight oriented requirements for Bowen's intervention. However, recognizing that Mrs. C.'s general level of differentiation and ego functioning to be at the lower end of Bowen's scales, it is doubtful that she would be equiped to maintain the rigorous investment required here.

Although there are also shortcomings involved with Minuchin's approach, including the important question as to whether he could, indeed, enlist Mr. C. as a "co-therapist," these authors find his approach to be the treatment of choice with this case. Reasons for this decision would include: 1) the use of the current family system, including symptoms as a fulcrum for change, 2) Minuchin's willingness to appear "foolish" so as to enlist the father in the therapeutic effort, 3) his use of hidden agendas to subtly manipulate (restructure) the family system, 4) his emphasis on problem solving and immediate reduction of "pain" in the family, and 5) his ability to "join" a less than functional family system to act himself as the needed executive function until the parents can actively accept the role themselves.

Family therapy, as a unified theoretical system, is yet to be realized. Movement in this direction will entail intense and long term empirical evaluation. Until that time, however, the authors feel comfortable with the fact of varying, ununified treatment styles, as these allow for an individualized approach to particular family dysfunctions. To this point, there is enough diversity in styles to encompass most family and therapist idiosyncracies.

BIBLIOGRAPHY

Bowen, M.

1972   "Toward the differentiation of a self
             in one's own family." In Framo, J.
             (ed.), Family Interaction: A Dialogue
             Between Family Researchers and Family
             Therapists. New York: Springer Press.

1971   "The use of family theory in clinical
             practice." In Haley, J. (ed.),
             Changing Families. New York: Greene
             and Stratton.

1976   "Theory and practice of psychotherapy."
             In Guerin, P. (ed.), Family Therapy,
             Theory and Practice. New York: Garden
             Press Inc.

Foley, V.

1974   An Introduction to Family Therapy.
             New York: Greene and Stratton.

Guerin, P. (ed.)

1976   Family Therapy, Theory and Practice.
             New York: Garden Press Inc.

Minuchin, S.

1974   Families and Family Therapy. Cam-
             bridge Massachusetts: Harvard Uni-
             versity Press.

Satir, V.

1967   Conjoint Family Therapy. Palo Alto,
             California: Science and Behavior
             Books.

1972   Peoplemaking. Palo Alto, California:
             Science and Behavior Books.

*James Buchholz, 410 N. Dryden, Arlington Heights,
    Illinois.
**Richard Nyberg, 15 Sheridan, Irvine, California.

CHAPTER 30

SEEKING FAMILY THERAPY: THE PROCESS
OF ASKING FOR HELP

Jane Totman*

I.   INTRODUCTION

People purportedly seek out counselors of whatever persuasion because they are faced with a problem
they want help with or they wish to change themselves
and/or at least to explore their options to change.
Many counselors make these assumptions except in some
very obvious situations.   It is the purpose of this
chapter to examine the notion that clients or patients
wish help to change and to suggest what other purposes
and motivations might be involved in one or more contacts with a counselor.

II.   INTAKES

The first phenomenon worth noting is the failure
rate of first appointments--"intakes"--of most counseling agencies.   The nationwide estimate is over 30%.
This event is commonly attributed to various factors:
fear that getting counseling or therapy means the
person is crazy, ambivalent about seeking help, the
refusal of one of the parties involved to cooperate,
a wish to take care of one's own problems, the perceived negative attitudes of the person answering the
agency phone, the resolution or elimination of the
presenting problem, etc.   Perhaps it would be useful
to add another dimension--the fact that the person
calling has taken some specific action designed to
add another alternative to his/her repetoire of
problem-solving behaviors.   It is easy to underestimate the power of the simple act of a phone call to
arrange a vent to a profssional person whose role it
is to make things better or at least more understandable.   Consider the impact on a marital partner
or a recalcitrant child of the statement, "I've made
an appointment to see a counselor."   The entire
troublesome situation may take on new dimensions,
behaviors and attitudes of family members may change,
the problem may be upgraded to crisis status, or
downgraded.   Even an individual wrestling with
personal dilemmas may, with one phone call, feel less

alone and have a sense of some one out there who is
willing to help--if it becomes _really_ necessary.

III.   ONE CONDITION OF PROBATION IS . . .

Many therapists and counselors are cynical about
the interest and motivation of those clients who have
been ordered by a judge and probation officer to obtain psychological aid or go to jail. Most proba-
tioners (parolees or persons on "dimension" programs)
will choose counseling over incarceration. This is
one obvious group of clients whose purpose in re-
questing assistance for alleged emotional disorders
may be problematic. Interestingly, some of these
customers do get involved in the therapeutic endeavor,
particularly when other family members are also included. It is frequently the spouse or the children,
along with the probation officer, of course, who
support a real effort on the part of the offender
to be different--meaning mostly less difficult and
burdensome to the family and the community. If the
law violator is able to go beyond the initial goal
and become a positive and contributory member of
society, all the more cause for celebration. It is
still prudent, however, to wonder about the incentive
of the sentenced counselor.

IV.   MARITAL COUNSELING

Many couples seek professional help with marriage
or living together problems. Everyone tells them to
go see a clergyman, lawyer, physician, their parents,
or to use newspaper or T.V. advice-givers. Any
experienced marriage counselor will tell you that in
the majority of cases, appearing in their offices,
the ball game is already over. Typically, one of
the partners has already made the decision to leave
and the remaining member doesn't want him/her to go.
Why come in at all if, in fact, in one person's mind
the end is at hand and there is no turning back. The
reasons are familiar--guilt over leaving a not-so-bad
person with whom one has shared part of his/her life
(often parenting children together) for another one,
internal and external pressure to try to resolve
problems by submitting to this one last ministration--
the "I-tried-everything-but-nothing--not even coun-
seling--helped" rationalization, fear that the deserted or about-to-be deserted partner will make good
on self-destructive threats which will tend to make

534

one's life very complicated and unpleasant and will spoil the new relationship, the state has a law that says reconciliation efforts must be made before a divorce can be granted, etc. The major purpose, then, for appearing at the counselors office is not to resolve or lessen the difficulties of the marital situation so it can continue in a better, happier fashion--or even to resign oneself to an unhappy but more palatable home life. A typical example are Harry and Sophie, married 20 plus years, who are purportedly seeking counseling because Sophie wants a "trial separation." Harry doesn't. When asked why, Sophie, with Harry present, complains that he has always been mean with the children (all but one are adults now), he takes her for granted, he drinks too much, is not very clean and neat, is careless about his appearance, and she needs a rest from him after all these years. When Harry becomes more thoughtful of her and the children, cuts down on his drinking, and improves his appearance, interestingly, Sophie still wants a separation. Her family tells her she's crazy. Harry is bewildered and depressed and wants to stay married. He doesn't feel life would be much without Sophie. Sophie, of course, has a boyfriend she would like to get to know better.

The reasons on the leaver's part are to obtain the official sanction to depart more or less gracefully and in a socially acceptable way, and to leave the partner behind (also any offspring) in sympathetic and, hopefully, competent hands. The leavee (left), on the other hand, wishes to enlist the counselor as an ally at the outset in his/her fight to maintain an unbroken married (or otherwise committed) state. If the counselor does not come down clearly on the non-separation side of the issue, it is common for the leavee client to either question the capability and morality of the therapist or to switch to another one. If the leavee finds him or herself without a companion after a few weeks, he/she may stay with the counselor because he/she feels lost, scared, depressed, and crazy--and this non-family trained person at least is familiar with the situation and seems to care. Besides, who wants to try to deal with the sympathetic and unsympathetic relatives and childrens' questions and usually disruptive behavior alone?

V. PARENT-CHILD CONFLICT

In contrast to the marital scenario, parents and
minor children come to the counselor's office not
just because of internal discomfort but because someone else is complaining about the kid's behavior or
attitude. These someone elses may include the police,
the school, the probation department, neighbors, relatives, or a combination of the above. Parents usually
feel their expectations for their children are relatively fair and just and are angry, dismayed, and
embarrassed when the kid doesn't do what they're
supposed to. Most parents have been sufficiently
exposed to mental health doctrine (dogma?) to believe
they are to blame, at least in part, for whatever
sorry state of affairs exists. Johnnie won't go to
school, Julie uses drugs, George is rude, defiant,
and impossible to live with, Helen is promiscuous,
Billy fights with other kids on the playground,
Allen peeped up a little girl's dress, Mary refuses
to talk to her teacher or any member of her family,
Harold's only friends are hoods, etc.

Parents really do want some relief from whatever
the painful script is--but how they want it done is
for the therapist to tell them that they are right
and the kid is wrong. Then the counselor is supposed
to fix up the kid. The son or daughter from his/her
perspective would like some affirmation from a powerful adult that his behavior and attitude are acceptable or at least understandable because there is
actually nothing very wrong with them or because his
inept parents caused him to act that way due to their
almost complete incompetence or meanness. The youth
then wishes the professional to see the rightness of
his ways and then to set his parents straight. In
the child's view, these usually should take the forms
on the parents' part of increased permissiveness,
fewer rules, more freedom, little disapproval, and
absolutely no threats of further drastic action.

Again, the counselor may well find the true
intention of the call at the office door is not a
call for validation by each of the waning factions.
Other motives may also be discerned. Some parents
want approval to be very angry and to do something
awful to their errant son or daughter--like hit them,
send them to reform school, farm them out to relatives or strangers, etc. Some parents have given up

and want the authorization (formal o.k.) to throw in the towel.

Some kids enjoy talking and being with their counselors in order to underline their ability to get along well with most adults, especially those who do not have characteristics similar to their parents. "You're the problem, Mom and Dad!"

It is an error to assume that these motives for entering family counseling are to be regarded only as therapeutic puzzles to be solved by the counselor. They certainly may be--but they may also be phenomena in and of themselves, serving their own purposes within the family group.

VI.   RESEARCH AND IMPLICATIONS

Researchers in outcome studies of individuals, couples, and families who have received professional counseling are sometimes perplexed by the honorable ratings given by "drop-outs" clients or the unfavor-able assessments of persons perceived by their therapists as having benefitted from their experience. One possible partial answer might be that the client/patient and the counselor are not really pursuing the same objectives. The next obvious question might be--Is that o.k. or is it bad? Should counselors close their doors to applicants who really don't have problem resolution clearly in mind? Should we be about trying to identify more carefully what is really going on in this special kind of encounter between human beings? Have our research instruments reflected only our own wishful perspective without attending to the other realities of the therapeutic process? Counselors have their set of institutional expectations, behaviors, goals, projected outcomes, etc. for their therapeutic organizations. Our clients may have quite another set--and it may be as utili-tarian and meaningful as the professionals think theirs is.

BIBLIOGRAPHY

Allen, George

   1977   Understanding Psychotherapy.
                Champaign, Illinois, Research Press.

Cross, James

   1979   "Can Casework Be Rational." Points
                & Viewpoints Section, Social Work,
                Vol. 24, No. 3, May, pp. 245-249.

Fischer, Joel

   1973   "Is Casework Effective?, A Review."
                Social Work, Vol. 18, No. 1, January,
                pp. 5-20.

   1976   The Effectiveness of Social Casework.
                C. C. Thomas.

Reid, William &
Ann Skyne

   1969   Brief and Extended Casework. New York:
                Columbia University Press.

Wood, Katherine

   1978   "Casework Effectiveness: A New Look
                at the Research Evidence." Social Work
                Vol. 23, No. 6, November, pp. 437-458.

*Associate Professor of Social Work, Department of
Social Science, California State Polytechnic University, Pomona.

CHAPTER 31

ANOTHER VIEW OF FAMILY CONFLICT AND FAMILY WHOLENESS*

C. Terry Warner and Terrance D. Olson**

A family life educator's suggested solutions of family problems will spring from his beliefs about the sources of human conflict. This chapter sketches a theory of conflict that is rooted in the individual's betrayal of his/her own fundamental values. Hypocrisy and self-deception ensue, and individuals insidiously provoke each other to do the very things for which they blame one another. This means that people can desist from the attitudes that throw them into conflict and live harmoniously. But because of their self-deception, seeing how to do this is not easy. Ultimately, the solution lies in moral responsibility. Implications for family life educators are explored.

Whatever we do in teaching people to live together productively and lovingly in families will depend upon our beliefs about why things go wrong in family situations. A family life educator's practice is tied to his or her theory, even though that theory may not have been explicitly formulated. Does he/she think that people whose families are in conflict can be victims of one another and the situation, or do they collaborate in the problems from which they suffer, even when they seem to be victims? This is the root question because its answer determines whether such people can in fact do anything to¹ eliminate the problems, and, therefore, determines what educators should teach about how a healthy family life can be achieved. We think the next decade will witness revolutions in traditional thinking about this issue, and these revolutions will dictate new practices in all the so-called helping services, including education.

A basis for this hope is a new theory of human behavior that appears in a forthcoming book and includes a new way of accounting for conflict. According to the theory, participants in conflict situations systematically deceive themselves about the sources of their difficulties. The book explains how, in our era, we have tended to import these self-deceptions into our theories about human conduct; our prevailing

conceptions of humanity tend to partake of our self-
deceptions. To these culturally dominant conceptions
of humanity there is an alternative that is shown to
be conceptually more powerful than any of them and
that unifies in a single point of view the manifold
observations of social behavior that have led many to
regard human beings as hopelessly complex.[1]

This presentation does not set forth the alternative theory of which we speak, for doing so would
require a careful dismantling of some of our fundamental presuppositions about people. Instead, we will
provide a simple sketch of the outlook on human conflict that the new theory suggests. Our purpose will
have been achieved if the reader acquires a sense of
how this outlook differs from the ways in which we
usually perceive people.

Because its theoretical underpinnings are not
included here, the sketch may appear deceptively
simple; its implications may not be readily apparent
to everyone. However, the theory from which the sketch
is drawn accounts for much of what Freud called the
"psychopathology of everyday life," including the
difficult problems of modern family life, and it sets
forth the conditions that must be satisfied in order
for families to be healthy and whole.

There are two axes along which the theory inter-
sects the theme of this issue. One concerns what we
teach about the nature of family life and the other
concerns how we teach it. We have chosen to concentrate on the first of these axes and to defer to
another context a discussion of new directions in
learning that are implied by our theory.

Values and Conflict

First, conflict among people is related to their
values; we can act either in accordance with, or
contrary to, those values. In particular situations
we can feel morally summoned to do a particular thing,
or constrained not to do something; it is in such
situations that our values make contact with our
conduct. These feelings to do or to desist may be
called "moral imperatives."

Such felt moral imperatives do not necessarily
express what others expect of us, or even the general
morality of our community, but embody values that are

personal and perhaps unique to us. We are not saying
that there are universal moral imperatives, but only
that people do, from time to time, feel morally constrained to do or not to do particular things.
Examples: a father feels that it is right to spend
time, this evening, helping his daughter with her
mathematics assignment. An uncle senses that he is
called upon by his conscience to apologize to a nephew
whom he has treated demeaningly. A teacher understands
that she is obligated to do the best she can to help
her students learn and grow. There is nothing
inherently immoral about refusing to help one's
daughter or failing to apologize or even teaching
moderately but not superbly well, but for these individuals, in these particular situations, the actions
we've described would constitute actively going
against their own commitments; for them, the actions
would be immoral. We call this strictly personal
immorality "self-betrayal," in order to convey the
idea implicit in it of being untrue to oneself.

Not surprisingly, this inauthenticity shows up in
whatever one does in carrying out one's self-betrayal.
One will conduct oneself hypocritically--will live in
a lie--in an effort to make the personal wrong that is
being done seem right. This inauthenticity can take
such forms as depression, low self-esteem, bitterness,
irritability, jealousy, and many other maladaptive
attitudes. We have chosen to illustrate it initially
with a very ordinary instance of family selfishness:

Sara: Daddy, I can't figure this math problem
          out.

Howard: (her father, watching Monday night foot-
          ball, and feeling that he should help
          Sara) Sure you can. You've just got to
          struggle with it.

Sara: But I've tried, and I'm getting nowhere.
          If you could ... (Sara begins to cry,
          her head on her book)

Howard: You're trying to take the easy way. They
          wouldn't give you the problem if they
          hadn't taught you all you have to know to
          solve it. (his voice rising) Why do you
          wait until I'm right in the middle of
          watching my game? In fact, you should be in
          bed, young lady. Why do you leave your
          homework 'til the last minute, anyway?

Sara: I didn't think it would take me very
         long...

Howard: Well, ask your sister upstairs. She had
         the same math last year. She's going to
         know it better than I am.

Sara: But I've just got one question.

Howard: (his anger blossoming) Sara, I'm tired
         of you trying to get me to do your work
         for you. Now I've told you what you need
         to do to get that done and you're just
         avoiding doing it.

Sara: (pouting) When Danny asks for help you
         help him...

Howard: Oh boy ... Look, if you would do what you
         are supposed to do, I would be glad to
         help you. There is a difference between
         helping Danny after he's struggled with
         something and helping you when the only
         struggle you've had is to ask me to do
         your work for you.

Sara: But Danny's smart. He doesn't have to
         struggle...

Howard feels that he ought to help Sara, but is
refusing to do so. His encouragement of her to
struggle with the problem until she can figure it out
might in other circumstances be good advice, but in
this case he is giving it as part of an effort to mask
and justify his own moral failure--to make it seem
right. He also accuses her of procrastinating, complains that she is intruding unfairly on his time, and
gets angry and impatient over her inconsiderateness of
his own needs and desires.

Howard is not pretending; he is not acting a lie.
He is, as we sometimes say, living a lie. The very way
he sees Sara, as inconsiderate and intrusive, is part
of the lie, and so is the anger he feels about her
inconsiderateness. In this particular case the value
he is placing on watching the football game, which
makes her request of him insensitive and unreasonable,
is part of the lie. These are all interconnected
aspects of the lie he is living--the self-deception he
is in. The way he sees and feels about the situation

is part of his effort to justify himself in not doing what he himself feels is right.[2]

From Howard's point of view, Sara's inconsiderateness and procrastination is the problem; or else the pressure he felt at work, or else his strong desire to watch the game. Now in our tradition of human behavior studies, as in our daily life, we tend to take Howard at his word. In his view, circumstances, either in his own make-up or in the environment, are responsible for his conduct; he has become angry <u>because</u> Sara has been pestering him, or <u>because</u> he wanted to watch the game, or <u>because</u> of his <u>hard day</u>. As observers, our assumption is that we understand Howard when we can explain, by reference to factors outside his control, why he acted as he did and that those factors make his irritability and impatience understandable. In the last analysis--so this traditional doctrine would have us believe--Howard is not an <u>agent</u> so much as a <u>patient</u>. He does not act but is acted upon. He is not responsible for his behavior toward his daughter, for there are extenuating circumstances which excuse him for his conduct.

Against this standard view of the situation, we are suggesting that the way Howard sees and feels about Sara is part of his endeavor to justify himself. He is actively insisting that he is Sara's victim. For if in this altercation with her he is seen as a patient rather than as an agent--if his perceptions and feelings are seen as caused by her or the circumstances rather than produced by him--then he cannot be held responsible. He is exonerated. Thus his upset feelings are part of the lie he lives; they are evidence that something outside himself--his work, Sara's inconsiderateness, etc.--is responsible for the trouble that he is, in fact, stirring up. "See how inconsiderate you are," is the message he is conveying to her, "to produce this much anger in me?"

Does this mean, then, that Howard "really knows" what he's doing?--that he's just playing a part?--that he doesn't actually feel angry? No, he is not merely pretending; he is not harboring a secret knowledge that he is living a lie. His emotions are aroused and could be measured by a galvanic skin indicator. But there is, nevertheless, a sense in which his emotion is not genuine; for, contrary to what <u>he</u> thinks, nothing external is making him angry. Howard's anger is genuine in than it is felt, but inauthentic in that it is not caused by anything that is happening to him. He becomes angry as a non-verbal means of proving that circumstances are making him angry.

Of course we wonder about Howard's authenticity when we hear his sudden pleasantness on the telephone with Fred (especially since Fred's call comes as Howard's team gets the ball, first and goal, on the opponent's eight yard line). If we have just entered the room we will not guess that a moment earlier he was angry. But we do not need to observe how chameleon-like Howard is in order to see that he is inauthentic. He is giving off clues constantly. We can see this by comparing him to another father, whom we may call "Howard II," who simply helps his daughter when he feels he should. Howard II will have no occasion to carry on defensively, to blame Sara II, or to value the televised game inordinately. He will simply help. The same is true of yet another Howard, Howard III, who, when asked by Sara III for help, feels, for her sake, he should not help. So he says simply, "You need to work that out for yourself." Again, no defensiveness, no accusation, no inordinate lust for television. Proving themselves justified is not an issue for these other fathers, because their justification is not put in question by what they are doing. The telltale clues that Howard gives off are his protestations and accusa- tions--his stylizing of himself as being wronged. This would be true even if Sara _were_ lazy and inconsiderate, as he says, and even if the game _were_ the greatest superbowl contest of all time. Self-justification of the sort we are studying is a sign that, by the indi- vidual's own values, something is not right.

Another point about Howard's self-deception needs to be understood. The features of conduct that we have described do not occur in sequence; they are not mental steps he goes through in order to blame someone for what he himself is doing. He does not first feel he ought to help Sara, then betray himself, than cast about for a lie to live as a cover for this self- betrayal, and then work up an emotion to show that he is Sara's victim. Rather, his self-betrayal _is_ the living of such a lie, the working up of such an emotion. It takes neither planning nor particular intelligence to do it; Archie Bunker, for example, is as adept as anyone you could meet.

So one can't "catch oneself" in the process of producing the sort of encompassing, behavioral lie we are describing. To betray oneself is already to be living it. Self-betrayal, in this sense, is a resistant perceptual style freely chosen by the individual.

There is more to say about the trouble that Howard creates and his method of creating it to make himself seem innocent. By seeing Sara as inconsiderate and by feeling inconvenienced, irritated and, finally, angry about her inconsiderateness, he makes himself out to be her victim. By this means he makes it clear that he bears no responsibility for the trouble he is helping create. But of course if he is her victim then she is his victimizer. Howard is accusing his daughter—letting the family think she is insensitive, lazy, and disorganized—as part of exonerating himself in his own failure to act responsibly.

What about Sara's feelings in the scene we have presented? How would you feel if you were Sara—fairly dealt with or put down? Would you want to take responsibility to do your homework? Whether or not Sara started out acting responsibly and unself-consciously in seeking her father's help, she did not do so once he attacked her. She began to sob softly. She made excuses. She followed the very pattern of her father's self-betrayal: she was defensive and accusing. From her point of view her father and the circumstances were responsible for the trouble. She is not the agent that he accuses her of being. She is a patient.

This brings us to a surprising and important principle: the responsibility-evading, accusing attitude of the self-betrayer—Howard in this case—tends to <u>provoke in those he accuses the very behavior of which he accuses them</u>. If they accept the provocation, as Sara did, then the self-betrayer has his proof that they are to blame and that he is innocent. Clearly Howard can say that he is not simply imagining that Sara is irresponsible. Her behavior even now proves that she is—she whimpers, she makes excuses, she tries to say that he is being unfair.[3]

The variations upon this theme are many. For example, the style of self-betrayal that we have described for both Howard and Sara we call "childish." But Howard might act self-righteously instead of childishly. In such a case he might ceremoniously switch off the television—his team still has first and goal on the opponent's eight—and, with a feeling of self-sacrifice and moral nobility, work out the problems with Sara. He would condescendingly answer her questions. His explanations would be attended by a strained patience. Inwardly, he would be congratulating himself on his self-control. In 15 minutes the homework would be done, and Howard would have a sense of having risen above the selfish level on which most fathers operate and, in spite of his daughter's irritating irresponsibility, done his duty. But he would have given Sara everything except himself. His would have been a refusal to help her in the guise of "doing all he could."

Moreover, Sara would not have felt helped. The attitude of her father would have put her down, just as, in the actual case, his anger did. She would not have responded well--would not have tried hard to solve the problem for herself. In the future she would probably be less inclined to ask for help when she needed it. And this would have given Howard more justification for feeling that his daughter was irresponsible and that he was, without losing his temper or even uttering a harsh word, rising above adversity.

So whether Howard is childish or self-righteous, he provokes Sara to do what he blames her for, and thus validates in his mind his self-justification. In both of these cases she is reciprocally provoking him by the way she evades her responsibility and accuses him in her heart. Whatever their styles of self-betrayal, they are both provoking the other and by this means extorting validation for the lie being lived.

We can represent this situation in the following diagram:

Collusion

We call this kind of destructive cooperation collusion. When people collude--when each provokes or entices the other to do the very thing he says he hates--each is making himself out to be the other's victim. Each is constantly ready to take offense at what the other does. Without their collusive self-betrayal, there would be no occasion for enmity between them.

Lest it appear that the simple model we have been developing is simplistic, let us consider a more

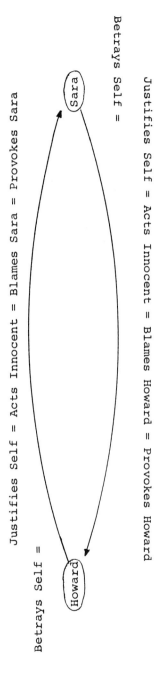

FIGURE 1. Collusion.

involved and convoluted instance. The marriage of
Robert and Marcia was on the verge of ending. Marcia
was at the end of her tether because Robert was
insensitive, thoughtless, and unwilling to "communicate." She was obsessed with the idea that he was
philandering, or at least flirting; she was sure that
he wanted to abandon her in favor of someone less
dowdy and more exciting. She blamed him for her
claustrophobic feelings in the confined world populated
only by herself and her children.

For a long time neither family nor friends had
observed evidence of what she accused Robert of; on the
contrary, he seemed to them to love her genuinely. In
fact, she herself never cited evidence of his supposed
infidelity; she simply "knew" that it was so: "A woman
knows," she often said. When he protested his innocence, she accused him of compounding his unfaithful-
ness with dishonesty. When friends or family defended
him, she accused them of collaboration. She sobbed on
her pillow at night until she thought her heart would
break. Her contention was that she grieved more than
other women who were similarly situated because of her
idealism about marriage and because she had "given my
heart totally to my husband." She told her troubles to
anyone that would listen, asking them how she could
possibly have the marriage she had longed for--how she
could possibly cherish, honor, and be intimate with a
man who was as self-interested and callous as Robert.

In fact, despite her endless protestations, Marcia
never lovingly gave Robert her heart. Many times she
felt that she ought to; "giving oneself" in marriage
was an obsession with her. But she did not. The moral
imperative that she felt, or placed upon herself, did
not come to her in the form of a general requirement to
love Robert: instead it was specific to situations.
Sometimes she would feel that she ought to prepare a
favorite dish for him; other times to touch him, to
look into his eyes, to make him a gift, or to thank him
for something he had done. On these occasions when she
felt a particular action morally required of her, she
violated her moral sensibility and did not act as she
felt. The result was that she saw him through accusing
eyes. From her point of view, even the expressions on
his face were irritating. It wasn't simply in her
manner that she insisted that Robert was preventing her
from loving him, it was in the very way she saw him
that she carried out this insistence.

No one will be surprised to learn that this

continuous hostile behavior of Marcia's provoked
Robert's retaliation. Feeling wounded and unfairly
dealt with, he viewed coming home as a trial by fire,
and stayed away as often as he could. The more he
stayed away, the more Marcia had her proof that he
didn't love her and the more reason she had to com-
plain, to withhold her favors, and to feel depressed.
For his part, the more Marcia attacked him, the more
reason Robert had to feel abused, and the more
justified he felt in not wanting to come home. So
Robert and Marcia helped each other create the forces
that separated them from each other.

     To each of them it looked like the other was at
fault, and an outside observer might well have said
that they were incompatible. But our view is that each
engaged in a series of free acts of self-betrayal that
not only took the other's behavior as an excuse but
actually provoked the other to that behavior.

     What we have been exploring here is a way of
understanding human conflict that differs from traditional explanations. We are suggesting that, at least
in many cases, human beings are not the victims of
provocations; situations do not overcome them. Their
provoked responses--whether of impatience, resentment,
anger, irritation, self-pity, or fear--are not effects
of causes that lie beyond their control but are instead
means of justifying themselves. "See how irresponsibly
you have been acting," Howard seems to say, "in order
to irritate me to this extent!" Their responses to one
another are not passive, but purposeful. In an
enormous variety of ways people make themselves unhappy
in order to justify themselves in the compromises they
are making of their own values.

The Self-Betrayer is Self-Deceived

     In considering this possibility that we conspire
with others to produce the unhappiness that afflicts
us, we encounter a peculiar problem. The problem is
that this conspiratorial behavior does not look like
what it is. From an observer's point of view it
appears that either Howard is sincerely put out by the
unreasonable request of an irresponsible daughter or
else that he is producing his irritated behavior "on
purpose." If he is producing it on purpose, he is
merely pretending--play-acting, if you will--and is not
really unhappy at all. If he is sincere, then the
explanation we are giving of his behavior is far off

the mark. Thus, it appears that our explanation can't be right; Howard's irritation is either intentional, and he's not _really_ irritated, or else he's really irritated and not acting intentionally. Howard can't be actually making himself miserable.

This conclusion is not valid. In the new personality theory from which this chapter is drawn, it is shown that the conclusion is fallacious because it is based on Howard's own self-deceiving way of seeing the situation. Howard and Marcia blame others as being causes of their feelings. They are, therefore, deceiving themselves as to the fact that they themselves are producing these feelings as means of accusing Sara and Robert. They are, therefore, not simply pretending to be irritated; being deceived, they are in earnest about it. Their irritability or suffering is something _they actually feel_, in spite of the fact that it is a falsification (neither Sara nor Robert is really causing it).

But if we were to ask Howard if he is being completely honest in his interaction with Sara, the only way as a self-deceiver he could interpret our question would be: "Do you sincerely feel put out, or are you merely pretending?" Since it is obvious to him that he is not pretending, he thinks our question is ridiculous; he wonders why we mistrust him.

> "Howard, we think you are blaming Sara so you can cover up your unwillingness to help her as you should."

> "You think I'm just pretending to be upset so I can watch the game? Is that what you think?"

> "No, you're really upset all right."

> "That's right! So I can't be just pretending, can I?"

> "Well, no."

> "So quit accusing me of being dishonest. Look, I'm so aggravated I haven't even enjoyed the game."

Even if no such confrontation takes place, Howard may succeed in deceiving us as well as himself by his performance. This he does if we accept his self-deceiving viewpoint, which is that either he is sincere, really feels put out, is Sara's victim and is not responsible, or else is only pretending to feel this way, is cynically manipulating and misusing Sara, and is, therefore, responsible.

From Howard's point of view, if he is not being honest it can only mean that he isn't really upset. He cannot be both upset _and_ responsible. So if, like Howard, we let the issue become, "Is he sincere in his feelings or not?" then we also will be _assuming that he cannot be deceiving himself in these feelings_--that he cannot really make himself miserable! We will be rejecting out of hand the kind of theory being discussed in this chapter--not because of any evidence we have, but because we are colluding in, and taken in by, the self-deceptions of self-deceivers.

We cannot stress this point too strongly, for it follows that if Howard _can_ deceive himself, he _can_ make himself miserable, and he _can_ provoke Sara to act irresponsibly so that he will have proof that it is she, and not he, who is responsible for his misery. Similar comments can be made about Marcia. People _can_ turn their families into battlegrounds and simultaneously insist, in earnest, that it is not their fault--indeed, that they are doing everything in their power in spite of the offensive behavior of the others involved.

In our era is has been unfavorable to speak this way. Holding people responsible for their misery seems a callous attitude. Often the most miserable among us come from pathological homes--surely they are not responsible.

But we suggest that it is not the theory we are presenting but the currently accepted ones that tend to be callous. If people are not responsible for their emotional problems, then it is not in their power to correct them. But if they are responsible-- if their unhappiness is the product of the morbid collaboration we are calling "collusion"--then they _can_ change. They can cease to betray themselves. They can come out of self-deception. Correcting family problems is, in general, not something they _do_--it requires no special expertise--but something they _undo_: they stop living a lie.

Howard (entering Sara's room): May I talk with you

551

a minute? (Sara does not answer, but leaves her head buried in her hands.)

Howard: Sara, I'm I, er ... Well, I shouldn't ... Gee, I don't know how to ...

Sara: It's okay, Daddy. I forgive you.

When Howard gives up his self-betrayal his anger dissipates. The feelings he then has for his daughter are non-accusing. He feels love. And even though his confession of the truth is inexpert in the extreme, it is genuine, and she senses how he cares. (This is equally true of Marcia. Her fears and self-pity will vanish as she begins to do precisely as she feels she should.)

That is the conventional situation. But there is another, equally appropriate possibility.

Sara: Daddy, can I talk with you?

Howard: Have you got that homework done?

Sara: Daddy, I've been having bad feelings toward you. Oh, Daddy, I'm sorry. Please forgive me.

Howard (melting): Sara, you shouldn't be asking for forgiveness. I should.

Sara's unhappiness was her own responsibility; she made herself a victim and, by this ploy, accused her father of being a monster, unfeeling, and unfair. The only way out for her too, is to cease to live this lie. And we can say the same of Robert.

Of course, one colluder cannot, by giving up his self-deception, guarantee that others in the collusion will follow suit. But he does, by withdrawing his accusing attitude, give them the best possible encouragement to do so. This is not all; we believe that what people feel when they cease betraying themselves is love and authentic concern for others. It is this newly released set of feelings that can touch the hearts of former colluders and prompt them to respond in kind.

After observing hundreds of cases, we have become convinced that although the solutions to the self-deceiver's personal problems are complicated and

552

difficult from his own perspective, they are actually
as simple as telling oneself, and living by, the truth
--which is that he himself has been collaborating in
the conflict situations that trouble him. It's the
best--the only--way to invite the other family members
to reciprocate. We have witnessed this in cases of
infidelity, depression, alcoholism, teenage rebellion,
intensely recriminatory divorce proceedings, and many
others. The offendedness of each party, the psychic
pain, the feelings of being trapped, the inconsolable
feelings, even the self-deceiving tactics by which the
principals both retaliate and make it appear that the
course of events is beyond their control--all these
tactics can be given up--summarily.

Self-Betrayal and Family Life Education

     Suppose that all we have been saying is true. How
would an educator get someone to see that it is so?
What strategies might he teach by which families could
abandon their tactical devices of hostility, fear,
impatience, and self-pity and leave self-deception
behind? How, in short, would he recommend that people
release the love for one another that is in them?
Recall that it didn't work when Howard was confronted
with the truth; his self-deception meant that he also
deceived himself about the suggestion that he might be
self-deceived.

     In responding to this question, we want to draw on
an implication that our view has for the conduct of
family counselors and therapists as well as educators.
Indeed, we think that it obliterates the distinction
between them. For if it is correct and people come to
understand family conflict in terms of it, that very
understanding requires a letting go of their former
views so they no longer betray themselves; one cannot
freely acknowledge the truth and simultaneously live a
lie. By this means they put themselves in a position
to see what needs to be done to heal the family
relationships and to have the caring attitude necessary
to do it without collusion.

     Let us imagine that we have just finished a
lecture on marital harmony. A student, Tammy, comes up
seeking further understanding. We sense that the
question she asks is not as hypothetical as she wants
it to appear; there is urgency in her voice. She asks
about her friend, Marcia, whom we have already met, and
she describes Marcia's situation.

What will we say to Tammy? We have already
learned that if Tammy suspects Marcia of provoking the
problem in any way--if she tries to see the husband's
side of it, suggesting that Marcia's definition of the
situation is not completely accurate--Marcia can only
understand Tammy as saying that she's insincere. Tammy
may have wanted to explore the possibility that Marcia
might be trapped in a tragic self-deception, but she
can only be heard as accusing her of crassly manipulating both Robert and Tammy! In her very way of seeing
Robert and hearing criticism, Marcia will pervert the
truth into something that is patently false. Marcia
might react in any number of ways, all of which will be
furtherances of the lie she is living.

> "Are you suggesting that our troubles are my
> fault? I thought you were my friend and would
> help me cope with the terrible situation, but
> instead you take his side!"

> Or: "You think I enjoy being hurt, like some kind
> of martyr? You're as insensitive as Robert is.
> I want to be happy, just like other people."

> Or: "Look, I've tried everything I know how to do.
> I start conversations, cook things Robert
> likes, get the children to bed early so we can
> have time together. But he leaves to go out
> with his friends or watches television."

> Or even (abjectly): "I know you're right. It must
> be my fault. I think another woman could have
> made him happy. I'm just not the kind of woman
> who appeals to men."

If the attitude that we lead Tammy to have toward
Marcia provokes Marcia to respond in any of these ways,
Tammy will have "climbed into Marcia's world" with her,
allowing her to define the situation for Tammy, and
will be colluding with Marcia in her lie.

Tammy's advice is very useful to Marcia, because,
by seeing Tammy as either agreeing with her or as
rejecting her, she has evidence that she can't help
what's going on. Marcia's offense-taking is useful to
Tammy also, for she then has proof that Marcia even
mistreats those who are trying to "help" her. Tammy
will be colluding with her in the way Sara colluded
with Howard: she will be validating Marcia's lie.

We see already that teaching is not therapeutically neutral. Attitudes, even of friends, either calm or fuel self-deceptions and either quell or exacerbate family conflict. Family life education is a weightier matter than some sorts of instruction. This becomes more obvious when we realize that Tammy might be Marcia herself. She comes with a disguised plea for help against her husband. If we have the wrong kind of theory, we will collude with her; we will provoke her to pursue even more aggressively than before her evasion of responsibility.

We are no better off if we teach Tammy to regard Marcia's husband as a problem to be dealt with and to think that Marcia needs to learn assertiveness, strategies for coping, or counter-manipulative tactics. If Marcia is provoking or at least utilizing her husband's insensitivity in order to justify her own failure to give herself to the marriage, then by thinking that Marcia must learn any techniques for dealing with him, Tammy will again "climb into her world" as surely as if she opposed her, and reinforce her lie that the problem is how to deal with him. Or, if Marcia is Tammy, we, the teachers, will be the ones to reinforce the lie.

The pitfall for family life professionals of all kinds, including teachers, is the danger of participating either theoretically or personally in the collusive mix of the families they talk about or counsel. When we suppose that people can be victimized by one another --when we accept their contentions that their anger, hostility, offendedness, depression, indifference, self-pity or bitterness can be caused by the other parties involved--we collude. We validate their attempt to shift responsibility to others or to circumstances beyond their control. We give them the message: "Either these people are indeed victims, or else they are phonies, deliberately causing all of this trouble. So I'm going to suggest either that they be indulged, because their problems aren't their fault, or condemned for being cynical manipulators." If this is our position, we will not be able to see the real solution to the problem, for the problem involves them in being neither victims nor phonies. Whatever we suggest will only lead them to deal with counterfeit symptoms and may make matters worse.

Fortunately, we are often guided in our professional roles more by our deep human responsiveness to people than by our theories. As a result, good things frequently happen: some of the individuals we teach discover that the key is simply for people to be honest with themselves, to forgive and forget, to reach out in love toward others. We are more effective than we would be if we always relied on current theories of conflict, but not nearly as effective as we could be if we understood that it is as people rather than as experts and manipulators of lives that we help others.

For several years we and several colleagues have been developing and informally testing an approach to teach people the principles we have discussed in this chapter, believing that for a person simply to understand them is for him to clear away some of the evasion and cover-up by which he avoids the truth. We use case studies. We have the students write cases on their own. Almost always they identify with the cases they hear and write, and in so doing are already telling themselves the truth about past self-betrayals. We have designed learning exercises in which they imaginatively enter a world that is free of offendedness and blame. The imaginative exercises can be as good as actual experience when students see others realistically--with compassion and without accusation. Those who do this are truthful about circumstances that have troubled them. In this, they are true to their own values; we have not imposed values upon them.

The learning experience we have described is not painful; the truth is painful only for those whose private recollections are counterfeit "confessions." For others the experience is liberating. Moreover, the relief and freedom that is enjoyed is the achievement of those who have it; while no one else could have charted the path that would lead them there, they themselves follow it unerringly. Once people have this experience, they own the secret; they are independent of us; they can continue their self-liberation into as many facets of their lives as they will.

In describing all of this so facilely, we do not mean to give the impression that just because this process is simple, it is also easy. It isn't. The process is meticulously designed to avoid collusion between teachers and students--to keep from assisting them in any evasion of responsibility they might attempt in the guise of "getting an intellectual understanding." For this reason, it is more demanding than any other teaching we have tried.

Implications for the Future

We think that besides our own approach, others will be developed, based upon the sort of understanding of family problems that we have sketched in this chapter. Whatever form they take, we suspect they will all imply that the distinctions between educator, counselor, and therapist will tend to fade. They should all teach rather than counsel, guide, manipulate, so that students will more likely act self-reliantly rather than feel provoked to either capitulate or resist.

There will be no room in this broadly conceived educative function of professionals for taking responsibility away from the individuals in the family. By what they teach and the attitude with which they teach, the professional should help individuals take responsibility. If family members refuse to take responsibility, the professional will have done all that could have been done.

For example, there should be little need for the professional to hear histories of family troubles, for it is usually counterproductive. Family members tend to repeat their accusing perception of conflict, helplessness, and suffering, and to ask the professional to reinforce it, either by agreeing or disagreeing with them. In rehearsing his "story," a person can be "honest" in conveying his real feelings, but be as self-deceiving in continuing to have these feelings as he was in having them in the first place.

Diagnosis of specific emotional patterns and prescriptions should be eliminated insomuch as these procedures set the professional up as a "doctor of the soul": if the "doctor" professes to know what is wrong, his pronouncements will tend to be self-deceivingly heard by his "patient" and thereby validate the self-deception. The "patient" is then assisted in evading his responsibility for the problems that beset him. All of this implies that the family life professional can only be effective when his own life is an honest one. Otherwise, he will inevitably use the teaching situation for his own self-justifying purposes. He may, like Howard, see his students as irritants and himself as doing all he can in spite of the difficulty of teaching such people. No expertise will protect him from the effects of this kind of self-deception. If he relies on techniques, he will be manipulative, and his attitude will be that techniques are responsible if

557

good things happen (rather than the honesty of the individuals involved), and he will encourage his students or clients to rely on such techniques themselves, rather than simply tell themselves the truth. People might resist his gem-like utterances or become his devoted disciples, but either way, they will be assisted in their flight from being the independent, whole human beings they are capable of being. Ultimately, the best family life educators will be the persons who teach students what it means to be independent of them.

To our schematic vision of families, their problems, and their hope for wholeness, some might say, "Perhaps so. But then again, perhaps not. What we have read is not an empirical treatment. It might be a fairy tale--a behavioral science fiction." There is an error in this objection. We cannot blithely gather data about the etiology of family problems without incurring the risk that these data are drawn from the self-deceptive worlds of families in collusion. Examples: "Marcia and her husband do not communicate. Her husband either won't or can't. This isolates and wounds Marcia. She withdraws, pouts, and falls into depression." But the truth may be that it is Marcia who helps prevent communication by taking offense in a manner which Robert, also betraying himself, sees as making it impossible to stay home: "She just wants to harangue. I'm getting out of here." Our data may actually be skillful collaborations in the "non-communication" of Marcia and Robert. (For an observer who is not self-deceived, it is clear that Marcia and her husband are sending messages which are being received very well indeed.) Where the possibility exists of the counselor or researcher participating in the self-deceptions of families, then neither diagnosing nor data-gathering can be a straightforward thing.

This means that in the end we cannot abdicate our own humanity in our study of and assistance to families. An authentic, open, caring relationship with them is a precondition of both understanding and helping them. There can be no dispassionate science of family life nor a detached, quasi-medical treatment of its miseries. Here is one region in which the effective professional is first and last a human being, in every respect one with the people he serves, and in which effective service is only partly a matter of art and even less a matter of science, but predominantly a matter of love.

We do have to pay attention to our experiences; social data are not irrelevant. But they are unreliable unless we make our observations with the totality of ourselves, in community with the families we serve. The idea that we can stand apart from this community, scanning it as if it were a cadaver, responding to it with only the "objective" portions of ourselves and suppressing our full range of human, compassionate responses, and obligations--this is a repudiation of our own humanity, which is our only instrument for understanding and helping others. This repudiation may be the most destructive self-deception of all.

NOTES

*Reprinted from Family Relations, Vol. 30 (October, 1981):493-503. Copyrighted 1981 by the National Council on Family Relations. Reprinted by permission.

**C. Terry Warner is Professor of Philosophy and Terrance D. Olson is Professor of Family Sciences at Brigham Young University, Provo, Utah 84602

[1]This theory is set forward in a forthcoming book, by C. Terry Warner, that deals with self-deception, compulsivity, interpersonal conflict, authenticity, freedom, and individual and social cohesiveness. The present article is also based in part upon materials used in the alternative to therapy and counseling that we shall mention later.

[2]So Howard's irritability is not something Sara is provoking; it is not an ingrained love of football; and it is not a residue of day-long pressures at the office. (Indeed the compelling attraction in the game lasts only so long as he needs it, in helping him justify his not leaving it, and his having felt the office pressues all day may well have been the very sort of self-exonerating behavior he is exhibiting with Sara.) The irritability is instead Howard's way of betraying himself and getting away with it-- of defaulting upon his responsibility by making Sara seem responsible for the trouble he is creating.

[3]A substantial part of Howard's self-justifica- tion in his self-betrayal consists in provoking the daughter he blames to betray herself. Her misbehavior serves well to exonerate him. Self-betrayers are troublemakers who can't see that they are. This, then, is the surprising principle concerning human conflict: by his accusing attitude, the self-betrayer provokes those he accuses to do the very kind of thing he accuses them of; he collaborates in produc- ing the problems that make him miserable; he lends his energies to create the very troubles from which he suffers.

CHAPTER 32

COUNSELING WIDOWS

Clifford Alexander*

I. INTRODUCTION

This chapter presents an analysis of widowhood as
it is experienced by Americans today. It examines the
major emotional and psychological aspects of facing
and dealing with widowhood, and will describe the
stages that those who experience the loss of a lifetime
mate normally must go through. Because the majority
of people who lose their mates are approaching later
life, this analysis will also discuss the problems
which face people in aging, and will make clear how
widowhood and aging in combination are a complex of
problems which are being faced by an increasingly
large proportion of the population.

Widowhood (by which is meant, in this chapter,
both males and females who experience the loss of their
spouse) has some very particular problems associated
with it, which can be broken down into special cases.
These include problems of health, being single parents,
economic strains, and facing retirement alone. Each
of these special cases will be examined, and it will
become clear that the single most effective solution
to the problems is a support group system which fills
the unmet needs of those who must go through the trauma
of adjusting to widowhood. The possible private and
governmental programs which might aid in this process
will be discussed in examining this proposed solution.

A large proportion (85%) of those who are widowed
are women. For that reason, more research has been
conducted on the problems which women face in adjusting
to life without their husbands (Strugnell, 1974).

Because of the structure of American society, it
is often the case that the newly widowed woman must
face a world she is unaccustomed to dealing with and
must find the means to support herself, if necessary,
and to make her life meaningful in the absence of the
man who has been husband and partner to her in life.
Many of these women have never worked, and are accustomed to basing their lives around the fulfillment of
the needs and desires of the husband and the children.

Men who face widowhood are less often confronted with this problem, but have, at the same time, a sense of loss which is just as critical emotionally. If the couple had children which are still living at home when the woman who was their mother passes away, the male widow then faces major lifestyle changes similar to the change in role and function that the female widow must confront. In both cases, major adjustments must take place in the lives of the individuals who are left behind if they are to continue to live a life which has the potential for satisfaction and meaningfulness.

II. THE STAGES AFTER WIDOWHOOD

The loss of a lifetime mate is traumatic whether it occurs during middle age or later in life. Younger widows often have a more difficult time in the initial stages of adjustment because the death of the loved one was unexpected. They also have an easier overall adjustment pattern because they are in a position in society which gives them the opportunity to start over, to make new acquaintances, and to work and live a life which still has years of enjoyment and hard work available for them. For those who are elderly (the over-sixty age bracket), there is less sense of unexpected bereavement, but at the same time the long-term adjustment is complicated by the problems incurred with the aging process, particularly in American society.

The Shock Period

The initial phase which the widow must go through has been labeled by Silverman (1974:4-6) as the "shock" period. All people seem to go through some period of time in response to a major loss during which they are relatively "numb" or out of touch with their feelings. The individuals mourning the loss are often described as having a sense of being really lost and of not knowing what to do next. They seem to feel almost suspended from life, are unable to focus on daily activities, cannot concentrate, and in many cases, seem to have very little concern for their own well-being. The fact of the loss has not yet sunk in, because the experience is too painful to bear at first. They have no sense of the reality of the fact of the loss. This is not an abnormal reaction, but a human one. It seems to be nature's way of allowing human beings to endure the initial trauma of significant loss.

For most people, this stage does not last too

long. It is dangerous for anyone to go for any prolonged length of time without attention to their
personal needs, and this is particularly true for the
elderly. In cases where the newly widowed person has
been accustomed to depending primarily on the lost mate
and both were older in years, the family or friends of
the couple will need to look out for the welfare of the
survivor. They might stay in the household, taking
over the housekeeping temporarily, and must make themselves available to the bereaved when moral and
emotional support is needed. The feelings of abandonment which soon surface in normal individuals will need
to be given expression before they are able to function
and to cope with the fact of the loss.

Often, a newly widowed person almost seems to
float through this initial stage of numbness and shock.
Health care professionals are not normally sought out
at this stage primarily because there are most often
many family members and friends who stay in touch with
the widow. However, within a month or so after the
death, most family members and friends will have
returned to their own normal routines and the widow
must now face the prospect of continuing life without
the partner. It is at this point that many seek some
kind of assistance.

Many problems emerge. If a family is eligible for
Social Security, and the total income falls below a
certain established level, the widow will be eligible
for supplemental benefits from public assistance funds
(Silverman, 1974:6). Additionally, there are services
available from family, clergy and other agencies
designed to meet many of the needs of widowed people
during the initial impact period. A major problem
seems to be the fact that many people who are eligible
for such services do not avail themselves of them
(Riley and Foner, 1981). Those who do not seek help
are either diminished in their capacity to determine
their real needs and take the initiative in finding the
right service, or are those who strongly believe in
self-sufficiency as a code for living.

The Period of Mourning

The second stage through which a widow must pass
is the stage where the emotional loss must be directly
experienced and the mourning must be gone through.
There are those who never successfully complete this
stage of the natural process of experiencing a major

and significant loss. At any of these stages, people are known to become fixed and, depending upon the circumstances such as age and state of health, there are some who die as the result of the inability to recognize and work through the stages of grieving.

This second stage is one where many who do not seek some kind of support group or assistance will be unaware or unwilling to deal with the powerful emotions that they feel, and can manifest a continued attempt to deny that the feelings are there.

This second phase, which is not always distinct in its behavioral manifestations from the first stage, can cover a period of time extending from one month to about a year after the death of the loved one has occurred, although it can go on for a much longer time. It is during this time that the widow needs to spend the time necessary to talk about the feelings of loss and to work through the natural anger and anguish which surface in response to the loss. Some widows will find that they are, at some level, actually angry at the lost partner for abandoning them. Although many of the feelings which emerge are irrational, they are at the same time distinctly human and must be dealt with.

Others report that they go through some extended period of time acting exactly as they believe the deceased would have liked them to act, as if trying to recapture the lost one in spirit. A continued need to talk about the deceased or to review the facts of the death over and over again are healthy only to the point that the emotions are acknowledged as grief and anger.

If the need to keep the memory of the loved one alive persists, it is most often the widows' own inability to deal with their own emotions. Ironically, those who cling to the "happy" memories of the deceased are most often those who were and continue to be the angriest at their partners (Sheehy, 1981).

During this stage, the widow will have to experience some acute feelings of loneliness. Even when they are in the company of their families and friends, they will feel pangs of isolation. Many widows report a tendency to withdraw from the couples who were close to him or her as a part of the couple that no longer exists. The women often begin considering some kind of employment, while a man with dependent children will begin seeking some kind of assistance with them.

While the individual may make the adjustments
necessary to continue to function in life, it is
significant that those whose major focus is the past
rather than the future are those who are likeliest to
develop cancer or to experience some other debilitating
illness. Those who have the courage to face this
period of intense emotional stress will sometimes seek
professional help. Many shrink from such activity
because they have not been accustomed to thinking of
themselves as emotionally disturbed persons. They are,
however, experiencing severe emotional disturbance.
One possible solution to this problem is the establishing of emotional support groups of others who have gone
through or are currently going through the grieving
process. More about this lay person support group as
a solution will be discussed later in this chapter.

There are those whose response to this second
phase of grieving is a mature ability to accept their
feelings and to seek avenues for expressing them.
These are people who are well-educated enough or know
enough about themselves to recognize that grieving is
a process that must be gone through. It does seem to
be the case that there are very few special services
available for the widowed that would give them an
opportunity to talk, to mourn, and to find their way
into the future unless professional psychiatric care
is sought.

Even in these cases the widowed person will have
to come to terms with the fact of the loss and will
have to become willing to face the future with renewed
courage and curiosity. This is a valuable growth
stage for those able to confront their own feelings,
and those who emerge from it successfully will feel
prepared to take on new challenges. This success is
somewhat hampered if the widow is approaching or has
reached retirement age, because of the social limitations placed upon the aging in this society.

The Period of Accommodation

The third stage of the grieving process is called
the period of accommodation. This is when true
recovery from the loss begins to manifest itself. If
the widow has been wiling and able to pass through the
difficult emotional disturbance of the second stage,
he or she will find that, while the future still looks
forbidding or uncertain, there is a renewal of enthusiasm and courage, and an ability to find interest

565

in new things and in making new friends. Emotionally, this stage consists of learning how to give up the past and to build a meaningful life as a single person. The widow must learn how to be alone and find resources to fill the needs that the spouse had previously been able to fill. The emotional and social life of the widow, in addition to the new responsibilities that have fallen to her or him because of the loss of the partner, must be shouldered.

This period of adjustment is the most difficult to describe in detail because its various manifestations depend, to a large extent, upon the personality and the background and the skills of the person involved. There are those who periodically sink back into a depression and who have difficulty establishing a continuity to their inner lives. There are others who seemingly uncover interests that had long been dormant and who are more capable and enthusiastic than they have ever before been.

In all of these stages, it must be recognized that the widow is experiencing emotional distress. Distress, if it is understood and effectively dealt with, can lead to a new beginning. Widows are not, properly speaking, suffering from anything other than a natural grieving process which is, to some extent or another, debilitating. The emotional distress which they must deal with can be defined as an inability to cope with a life situation that presents itself. Newly widowed people are all, for some length of time, in a precarious emotional condition. Increasingly, health care professionals have come to recognize this process and have begun to ask what kinds of programs would best serve the widowed.

III. CHARACTERISTICS OF THE WIDOWED

Prior to the discussion of programs which have been created to answer the special problems of the widowed, some discussion will be dedicated to the special cases among the widowed.

Statistically, one out of twenty people in the United States is widowed. Almost 85% of these are women and the majority of these women are fifty-five years of age or older. It is estimated that over one-third of these persons exist at subsistency levels and that they have a continued life expectancy of still another fifteen or twenty years. Progress in medical science in the last half century has meant that the proportion of elderly persons in the United States has increased tremendously (Maddison and Agnes, 1978: 292-306). And while society at large has retreated from the three or four generation household, the population itself contains approximately 15% of the elder generation. People are living longer than they ever have.

Health Care

The first special case to consider in a discussion of widowhood is the problem of continued health care. Since the aged population has increased because of the discoveries and innovations of science, there is an increased burden on society to provide for those whose lives have been lengthened. Serious health problems are known to develop in widows who have not been able to endure the emotional strain of the grieving process, especially if they are elderly. A significant number of people die within two years of the loss of their spouse. However, a much larger group lives on for years and years. The issue of the quality of those years is a large one for this society to face. How do widows adjust to their new lives alone if they are approaching older ages? Are they able to live continued lives with a high quality of living?

Activity Resources

The answer to these questions are related to what social psychologists have called the "activity resources" of elderly people (Green, 1981:29-36). For a widow who is elderly, three important factors may enhance or limit activity: (1) health, (2) financial solvency, and (3) social support systems. With the presence of these three resources, widows are often able to live lives with a relatively high amount of peace. However, activity itself is known to drop off at a certain age. Social psychological theorists have suggested that the reasons for a drop in activity, and a decrease in energy which can lead to health problems may well be the result of the social context in which they must operate. A context is properly understood as the major beliefs about the environment in which a person must operate. From the person's point of view, this context becomes what he or she can expect of himself as a potentially active individual and what others expect of him, respectively. Personal expectations and societal expectations set the boundaries or limitations

out of which people operate. It is this context which
acts as the major influence on an individual's judgment of himself and his behavior and on this sense of
what he can or cannot do.

Once established, individual and social contexts
do not strictly determine the probability of an
individual exhibiting a certain level of satisfaction.
Rather, personal actions being the same, individual
and social contexts influence the life satisfaction of
the individual in particular ways (Green, 1981:29-36).
That is, individual and social contexts operate to
limit an individual's perception of how to cope with
the environment, but the individual remains free, once
he has become able to cope, to select from among the
alternatives presented. Contexts are the perceptual
limits of a person's individual freedom. They are
flexible only when they are recognized as perceptual
phenomena.

The Myth of the Golden Age

The problem confronting widows who are elderly in
relation to their activity level is that they are
expected to lessen it. The American society has perpetuated what some researchers call the "Golden Age"
myth, which envisions the retirement age as one of a
quiet, restful time of life (Gubrium, 1973).

In popular magazines, retirement brochures, newspapers, and in other news and entertainment media under
"human interest information," the myth of the nontur-
bulent later years has created a disjunctive reality
for the elderly widow. This myth is dangerous to the
health of all elderly people and is particularly difficult for widows approaching retirement age. This is
because widows are already dealing with significant
alterations in their lifestyles, and ones that are
assumingly not always welcome. To add to the burden
of loss is the increased difficulty that is obtained
when someone is expected to retire and "enjoy" the
"golden years;" thus this adds burdens that many find
almost impossible to overcome.

The "Golden Years" myth is a popular, conservative and often contradictory set of ideas about several
aspects of the social lives of older people. Expectations about what older people should do with life are
further complicated when they are widowed. Characteristic of public information on the "golden years" is

that it is often glib, complacent and, on the whole,
celebrates old age as a peaceful, free of troubles time
during which people themselves are kind and sweet-
natured.

The general tendency in this society to devalue
the aged and to avoid anything "old", behaviorally
speaking, is in direct contrast with the convenient
general portrayal that everything in old age is simply
lovely. The myth seems to persist in order to allow
the devaluation of old age to continue without feeling
guilty for the underlying attitudes. If the elderly
person is, additionally, a woman whose primary concern
was always the well-being of her family, she must deal
with attitudes in society, a context which tells her
she should be calm and relaxed and happy on the one
hand, and which devalues her for both her age and sex
on the other.

Under these conditions, widowhood can continue to
be traumatic. Only in recent years has it begun to be
recognized by society as a whole that "old age" is a
phenomenon that all will have to reckon with. Particularly in a society which values work and accomplishment
above all else, the "Golden Myth" of retirement is a
dangerous one. Increasingly, the value of continuing
to work is being recognized.

Action vs. Inaction

Instinctively, widows seem to recognize that, in
order to live lives that continue to offer them meaningful activity, they must continue to reach out and to
participate. It is interesting to note that retirement
itself is the event which frequently precipitates life
crisis, illness and even death.

In modern societies, it is most often the simple
fact of achievement coupled with acknowledgment of that
achievement which keeps a person in touch with reality
and, thus, in touch with the living, breathing,
enlivening aspects of life which make it potentially
worthwhile.

Work is, then, a way of life which potentially
makes it worth the living. The problems of widows,
particularly females, become obvious. How do they
experience an ability to make their lives worthwhile?
In the contemporary context of limitations placed on
people because of sex and/or age, it becomes clear that

the emerging issue is a large and difficult one to deal with.

Although we have come some distance since Freud wrote the above, it is still important to note that the single most significant contributor to the health and perceived well-being of the widow is the ability to continue to make some sort of contribution to the lives of those around her or him. If the "activity" factors of health, financial resources or support systems are not present, it is likely that the widow will perceive herself as a burden on others and will experience life as shallow and even despairing. This is a major problem in today's society and one which is only slowly being recognized and dealt with.

Widowed Parents

In addition to the factors of health, finances, and social support (more, later), there is the special case of those widows who are left to care for families without the help of their spouse. Statistically, younger female widows who are still faced with the job of supporting and raising a family are the most likely to seek some form of professional assistance.

A positive note about the continuing examination of parent roles is the fact that fathers who are widowed are discovering the joys of parenting and the trials of single parenthood right along with mothers. And because, among this small population of younger widowed men and women, an increasing number of divorced parents are facing similar problems, more information is available to help them cope with these new roles.

Perhaps not so surprisingly, fathers are discovering the difficulties and the rewards of being a single parent and are discovering along with this a new dimension for their lives. As the role models continue to expand, and as what was once considered appropriate only for mothers to do becomes available for fathers, the problems of the widow with children can be expected to lessen. In large part, this has to do again with the fact that the widowed parent is not alone, that he belongs to a segment of society that is growing in number and is increasingly being validated for its ability to take on the difficulty of raising a family single-handedly (Van Gelder, 1981:47).

An organization called "Parents without Partners"

has developed a support system for all those who find
themselves in the position of raising one or more
dependents and who is single by reason of death,
divorce, separation or never-married. It is the only
known national organization that exists to study the
complex adjustments, ambiguities and emotional conflicts arising out of post-widowhood and post-separa-
tion. Through programs of discussions, professional
speakers, study groups, newsletters and international
publications, real help is provided to the confused and
isolated, to find themselves and to reshape their own
lives to meet the unique and unpredictable conditions
of single-parenthood.

IV. HELP FOR WIDOWS

There are two factors which will now be discussed
which contribute significantly to the ease or difficulty of the problems of widows. The first has to do
with the entire issue of preparedness. The second is
related to the question of how widows can go about
creating and participating in a social support structure which enables them to continue living full and
meaningful lives.

Getting Ready for Death

Preparing for the death of a loved one is a fairly
new concept in the United States. Until recently, there
was an almost complete moratorium on the discussion of
the possibility of death and dying (Sheehy, 1981).

But increasingly, with the rise of medical
science's ability to detect and to predict the course
of life-threatening illnesses such as cancer, the
reality of death is being discussed and faced. In a
climate where death means horror and loss, it is
unlikely that a reasonable discussion will take place.
But, as the inevitability of death is faced and dealt
with in the open more and more, the ability of those
who are left behind to grieve the loss will be enhanced. If the widow has been fortunate enough to have
been engaged in the process of facing and accepting the
inevitable loss of her partner, the grieving process
will have begun prior to the death of the partner.
There is a tremendous growth and love available to
those who are fortunate and brave enough to walk some
part of this difficult and lonely road together.

Preparedness for one's partner's death is

571

confrontative and is particularly difficult because
what is being faced is the inevitability of one's own
mortality. Nevertheless, it is worthwhile to face the
facts of death when they are announced. Preparedness
is an important factor in the ability of the widow to
face and cope with the loss. If the deceased has been
able to face up to his or her own death with dignity,
they will have been able to think about the family
members who will be left behind.

Such issues as financial security and clearing up
old quarrels can be cleared up by those who are willing
to face death. Partners often have a very difficult
time of it when their loved one is close to death.
They will find that their sense of bereavement has
already begun. However, with some balance and maturity,
such preparation has a very high payoff. The partner
who is left behind will recognize the love of the lost
spouse as a true and significant factor in their
ability to go on living. The length of time that it
takes a prepared widow to come to terms with the loss
is often decreased.

To some extent, the possibility of one or the
other partner dying can be dealt with prior to any
indication of the event occurring. Even-headed
partners have discussed the inevitability of one of
them having to endure the loss of the other, and have
agreed upon the issues which will need to be taken care
of in the event of either of them passing on. In
today's world, the education of the population in
general is an important factor in easing the pain and
the isolation of widowhood. Dying is a natural part of
living and the dignity of leaving one's life as a
complete and satisfying journey which one has been
privileged to travel in the company of others lends
both depth and acceptance to the process.

Perhaps the widowed of today will be the last
generation to have been dealt the cruel blow of
bereavement without some kind of preparation for its
occurrence. In any case, those who have carefully
thought about the issue and have realistically planned
for its inevitable occurrence will be further along the
road to recovery from the loss when it does occur. A
clergyman has commented that facing death is discouraged in a mobile society such as America's, and under-
lines the importance of preparedness with this comment:

Facing death, whether you're a mobile person,

or whether you're living in one community all
your life, is something that's very real.
It's not something that one does easily...one
has to start to develop attitudes and a point
of view that allows one to cope with this
from the very outset of life. When we work
with people who are bereaved and have faced
this loss, they are a constant reminder to us
that a death has occurred and we can't run
away from this fact any longer. Thus, they
are stigmatized, if you will (Silverman,
1974:201).

Thus, the problems of widowhood are many. They
include not only the difficult emotional and psychological adjustments required in order to face life alone,
but are made even more awkward by the facts and conditions which surround the widows in this society.
Because the majority of those facing widowhood are
females and are close to retirement age, they must
additionally face the real and perceived problems of
the aging. They are expected, and expect themselves,
to live quiet, "golden age" years of life, and are
given little opportunity to continue to expand their
education, for example, or to work in jobs that allow
them to make a significant contribution to others.
Further, as the quotation above suggests, they are
stigmatized by their close association with the fact of
death.

Many people find it increasingly difficult, as the
months wear on, to deal with friends and relatives
whose reactions contain undercurrents of fear and a
discomfort with the fact of death. As if societal
expectation and personal perceived limitations were not
enough to cope with, the widows who are involved in the
natural process of aging will additionally have to deal
with their diminished energy levels and the threat of
illness and isolation in old age.

In an attempt to find viable solutions to the
increasingly large population of aging widows, both
private and governmental programs have been established
in order to offer assistance. It has been found that
there are still those who are unwilling to accept help
of any kind except from family members, but that the
stigma of widowhood and the isolation of old age have
been factors which motivate some percentage of the
population to join social support groups.

The need for social support in order to successfully process the grief that is a natural part of loss
is well established. It seems that human beings are
not really the independent creatures they often like to
imagine themselves being. In fact, people do not do
well when they are isolated from some kind of community
experience for any length of time. The need for independent action is much more easily filled when it takes
place within a context of group support than when it is
attempted in isolation.

More often than not, those who pridefully withhold
themselves from community support of some kind are less
likely to live full or satisfactory lives. They become
embittered, cynical members of the human race and have
very little to give to others. It is imagined that
their inner lives are shut down, and that they persist
in almost robot-like fashion to their deaths.

V. SUMMARY

Several issues have been discussed in this
chapter. The stages through which anyone will normally
pass who has experienced a traumatic loss have been
discussed in an effort to make clear the psychological
and emotional stress of the widowed. The difficulties
of overcoming the experience of loss are compounded
greatly when the individual is facing the natural
process of aging. Inherent in the United States is the
image of a "Golden Age" retirement which hampers the
aging population in that it is significantly different
from the reality they must face.

The adjustments that must be made to widowhood
after the initial stages of grieving have been endured
include a plethora of problems which are built into the
society. Expectations of the aged contribute to their
inability to deal successfully with creating for themselves a life that has both quality and meaningfulness.
The idea that retirement is restful is being disputed,
and there is an increase in memberships which allow
aging people to participate in society, to gain new
skills or knowledge, and to continue to function as
mature adults. Both cultural agism and cultural sexism
continue to plague the majority of the widowed population.

An awareness of the problems that the aging,
widowed population must face will perhaps be the best
inroad to the possibility of solving some of them.

Preparing for the inevitability of the death of those close to you and for your own death are possibilities that are being increasingly encouraged by health professionals. The need for awareness, preparedness and group support are being recognized as the essentials in helping the widowed live fulfilling and healthy lives.

BIBLIOGRAPHY

ABRAHAMS, Ruby

   1972   "Mutual help for the widowed." <u>Social Work</u>, 17, 54-61.

GREEN, Susan K.

   1981   "Attitudes and perceptions about the elderly: Current and future perspectives." <u>Journal of Aging & Human Development</u>, 13, No. 2, 29-36.

Gubrium, Jaber F.

   1973   <u>The Myth of the Golden Years: A Socio-Environmental Theory of Aging</u>. Springfield, Ill.: Charles C. Thomas, Publisher.

Maddision, D. &
Agnes, Viola

   1978   "The health of widows in the year following bereavement." <u>Journal of Psychosomatic Research</u>, 12, 292-306.

Riley, Matilda White &
Foner, Anne

   1968   <u>Aging and Society</u>. New York: Russell Sage.

Sheehy, Patrick Francis

   1981   <u>On Dying with Dignity</u>. New York: Pinnacle Press.

Silverman, Phyllis, <u>et al</u>. (ed.)

   1974   <u>Helping Each Other in Widowhood</u>. New York: Health Sciences Publishing Corporation.

Strugnell, Cecile

   1974   <u>Adjustment to Widowhood and Some Re-</u>
<u>lated Problems, A Selective and Anno-</u>
<u>tative Bibliography</u>. New York:
Health Sciences Publishing Corporation.

Tibbitts, Clark &
Donahue, Wilma

   1960   <u>Aging in Today's Society</u>. Englewood
Cliffs, New Jersey: Prentice-Hall,
Inc.

Van Gelder, Lindsay

   1981   "Are single mothers the last of the
supermoms?" <u>Ms</u>, IX, No. 10, 47.

*Department of Social Work, University of Nevada,
Las Vegas, Nevada.

CHAPTER 33

BIOFEEDBACK AND FAMILY THERAPY:
AN HOLISTIC INTEGRATION

Erik Peper*
Casi Kushel

This chapter presents an innovative approach
to the integration of self-regulation skills
(biofeedback and autogenic training) and
family therapy. A holistic approach which
includes the individual, the family, the
social network, and the belief system within
which one lives is suggested for the prevention and cure of disease and dysfunction. A
case study of anorexia nervosa illustrates
the utilization of the combined therapies.
The authors describe the thirteen concepts
which merge biofeedback and family therapy into a harmonious and effective unified system.

Traditionally, biofeedback has focused on individuals and their power to self-regulate or self-heal.
Biofeedback has assumed that it is possible to learn to
control physiological functions such as body temperature, heart rate, or muscle tension which were previously thought to be beyond conscious control. Such
control is accomplished through the use of electrical
instruments which detect a body function, amplify it,
and then communicate it (feed it back) through a tone,
light, or meter (Peper, Ancoli, & Quinn, 1979).

Family therapy, or systems work, as it is sometimes called, has focused its attention on the family
unit as a whole and considers the interaction between
family members as the key to change. The goal here
has been to restructure the family and to interrupt
and redirect the flow of dysfunctional communication
and behavior.

Together, biofeedback and family therapy are
part of the movement toward a more holistic health
care approach in which the patients/clients (participants) assume more responsibility for and power over
their own emotional and physical health.

Both approaches are learning experiences which
provide tools for change and therapeutic experiences

which encourage and point the way to self-awareness.

Both approaches, although relatively young in the field of health care, have had successes in relieving pain (either physical or emotional) and in opening the options for life-enhancing, health-giving changes. Much of the most significant learning comes not from these successes, however, but from trying to explain the failures, the cases for which one of the approaches did not work.

In searching for the answer to why certain people did not respond to one of the therapeutic disciplines, we felt that family therapists would benefit from the application of biofeedback in learning to enhance the self-regulation potential of individuals in the family by allowing them to control their own symptoms; and, inversely, that biofeedback practitioners would gain much by becoming aware of and integrating the adjustment of family interactional patterns, especially since most successful biofeedback training programs include home practice. Doing "homework" means the individual will affect his/her own social network.

The bridge to integrate self-regulation skills and family therapy was this use of home practice. Family therapy has also made use of "homework;" self-regulation skills add a new dimension to the potential for developing a sense of competency and a sense of relaxation that is so often missing in the dysfunctional or illness-prone family. Equally hopeful was the fact that all families could benefit from exercises and games designed to increase a sense of peace and closeness in the family and at the same time positively affect their way of interacting. This chapter includes a working definition of biofeedback and family therapy and provides ground rules for holistic combinations of both approaches.

Family Therapy Concept

Family therapy and systems work are defined under one philosophical and functional umbrella. This model emphasizes the importance of the way family members act, speak, and feel about each other. The model assumes that a circular motion of action and interaction exists which can be in some ways either healthy or dysfunctional. Healthy systems produce individuals who are both autonomous and have a sense of belonging or identification with the family and the world around them. These functional families communicate clearly. They encourage independence and provide loving support for their young. They are consistent with discipline and encourage appropriate responsibility. Most importantly, they allow for individual differences and are willing to make appropriate changes in family rules as children grow and circumstances change; i.e., they have no rigid beliefs about how each member should behave. These healthy families are often supported by shared spiritual values or community involvement.

This view is a change from the psychodynamic model which sees sickness and health as a product of the individual's internal mental/emotional process. While family therapy respects the importance of the individual and recognizes that there are large areas where an individual transcends the family system, the emphasis is on joining the family system and effectively altering poorly functioning patterns of interaction. This view of people in context extends to the social networks around families, including schools, churches and work situations. In the beginning years of family therapy, it was common to work with the entire family at once. Early family therapists directed their energy toward restructuring the organization of the whole family, and believed that if the therapist could facilitate changes in the family's interactional patterns, they would change the way in which the family functioned. Those beliefs are still accepted, but it is becoming more common to work with only one or two family members on the theory that it is possible to affect the entire system by shifting the way in which one of its members behaves. This shift is facilitated by altering that one member's self-perception.

Biofeedback Training Concept

Biofeedback is an effective way of facilitating this change of perception. It provides information about something that has just taken place in the body; since body and mind are synchronous, biofeedback also provides information that something took place in the mind. By paying attention to feedback about internal states, most people can learn control over functions previously thought to be beyond conscious control. These automatic or autonomic functions may include body temperature, heart rate, muscle tension and brain waves. Biofeedback consists of displaying normally unnoticed physiological information about an organism back to itself. With such a psychophysiological

581

mirror, people may become more self aware and be able
to change their own psychophysiology. The information
displayed plays the role of an unbiased observer--the
information is neutral. How a person uses this information depends on the set and the setting.

The basic steps in feedback learning are:

1. Monitoring the physiological system to feedback
   changes in that system, since information only
   exists if there is change.

2. Becoming aware of the feedback and objectively or
   subjectively linking it to some internal or
   external sensation. In some cases a person needs to
   become aware that, for instance, each time the
   telephone rings, he frowns.

3. Controlling the physiological system with the help
   of the feedback signal.

4. Maintaining the psychophysiological control without
   feedback which means that the person has to
   internalize the learning process.

As a tool of self-regulation, biofeedback can be
useful for self-healing. Its clinical applications
have included treatment of headaches, Raynaud's
disease, cardiac arrhythmia, epilepsy, essential hyper-
tension, migraines, and backaches, as well as many
other stress-related diseases (Peper, Ancoli, Quinn,
1979). Clinical success is highly related to the
amount of home practice done. The more the participant
integrates the learned skills into daily life, the more
likely is clinical success.

Although biofeedback offers a promise for health,
in many cases clinical success does not occur if
autonomic self-regulation is done outside a holistic
context. For example, we worked with a participant who
had Raynaud's disease, a vasoconstrictive disorder.
Although she had learned how to warm her hands (an
increase in vasodilation), we did not account for the
fact that she would not practice at home in the
presence of her husband. This led to the diminuation
of the benefits of the biofeedback. In this sense, we
had to say that "the operation was a success and the
patient died." We had not considered teaching assertiveness skills or other tools with which she could
change her family pattern. This omission was corrected
when we merged biofeedback with family therapy and is

illustrated in our work with a 17-year-old female anorexic patient.

The Integration of Biofeedback and Family Therapy: Anorexia Nervosa as a Case Example

Anorexia nervosa, a syndrome of self-starvation, is a disease defined by both physical and psychological criteria. The physical symptoms include a loss of over 25% of the body weight and one or more of the following conditions: amenorrhea, hyperactivity, hypothermia. The psychological symptoms include a pursuit of thinness, fear of gaining weight, denial of hunger, distorted body image, sense of ineffectiveness, and struggle for control (Minuchin, Rossman & Baker, 1978).

Originally, anorexia nervosa was treated medically with little success. As psychiatry advanced, anorexics were treated individually over long periods of time, with some success. Unfortunately, the "disease" would often recur in the same family, and treatment would have to begin all over again. Most recently, anorexia has been acknowledged as a family disease, and family therapy has been used with superior results (Minuchin et al., 1978). However, this treatment plan involves hospitalization for the anorexic, which, although sometimes necessary, should be avoided.

Our method generally incorporates the family approach of Minuchin et. al. (1978) and adds several interventions derived from the holistic model. To alter the psychological symptom of feelings of ineffectiveness and need for control, we introduced biofeedback and self-regulation skills for the anorexic. In the process of learning these skills, the participant's gastro-intestinal cramping and involuntary vomiting decreased as she practiced pro-homeostatic physiological exercises, e.g., gentle abdominal breathing during which her thorax stayed relaxed while her abdomen moved gently in and out. With the successful acquisition of physiological control, a change in self-concept began to occur. Unconscious thoughts and beliefs associated with her anorexic syndrome began to be verbalized in family sessions. The family's extreme enmeshment is shown by the participant's admission that, "If I get better, my mother will have nothing to do and she'll go crazy." Later during the same session the mother was able to acknowledge that, "If she were just thin enough, everything would be perfect." As we worked with the family, it became clear that what each member thought or felt was commented on in such a way that anxiety was increased in other family members.

In the family work, we emphasized communication techniques that would discourage the enmeshed process of the family. We taught family members to speak for themselves, avoid "you feel" statements, and own their own feelings with "I feel" statements. What made this difficult was that there had never been room in this family for individuals to express themselves. Their efforts had always gone to guessing what everyone else might be feeling. An elaborate system of assuming what each person felt and responding to that feeling by trying to behave appropriately had evolved. This process further included an unshakable faith that each person knew what the others felt better than the person who was supposed to be feeling. Biofeedback enabled the anorexic to disengage from the family process by authenticating her own feelings for herself. Relaxation and autogenic training was introduced to the rest of the family members to offer them an opportunity to focus on their own physical and emotional feelings.

The case example illustrates the integration of biofeedback and family therapy. It also helped develop a broader set of ground rules for holistic therapy from which to build other case interventions. In developing these ground rules, we looked to an experimental study which had explored a variety of holistic techniques for somatic disorders. This study by Peper, Robinson, Craig, and Jampolsky in 1979 used group interaction, biofeedback, visualization, and other tools of self-healing with nineteen participants who had open-angle glaucoma (average age--53.6 years; mean years of disease--12.1). At the end of the ten-week training period, the recorded eye pressures dropped significantly for 10 of the participants. Their eye pressure continued to remain low after a 1.6 year follow-up, as is shown in Figure 1. For many of the participants, this holistic program has changed their lives (Peper, Pelletier & Tandy, 1979).

This study demonstrated that a chronic degenerative disease could be reversed when treated not with medication but with an interdisciplinary combination of physiological, interactional and psychological interventions in an holistic approach. By analyzing this study and our integration of biofeedback and family therapy, we observed a number of common concepts which underlay the successful holistic approach. The

584

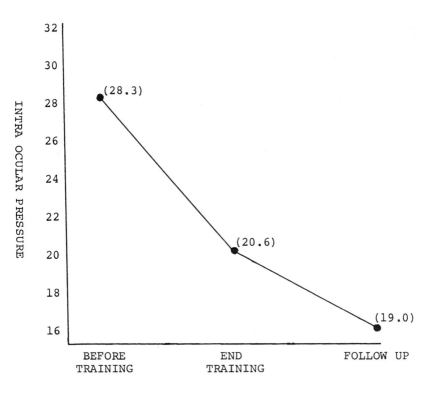

FIGURE 1: The average intra-ocular pressure (IOP) of the 10 successful trainees (out of the 19 who partici-pated). Success was defined as a significant decrease in IOP or medication during and following the 10-week holistic training program. Average followup was 1.6 years.

following thirteen rules are recommended as appropriate for holistic practitioners using any variety of techniques within a system/holistic framework.

1. <u>What is communicated by word, act, attitude and setting will affect the potential for change</u>. Everything, from the choice of words to the type of room in which one practices, communicates something. There is no way to avoid communicating. Silence is an important message as well. When a friend passes without looking or speaking to us, we assume she is angry with us. When a doctor avoids answering a question about our health, we assume the worst. When we walk into a bright yellow room filled with sunshine, our spirits rise. If the practitioner who greets us shakes our hands and leads us into a comfortable room saying, "What have you all come to learn today?," we will feel that we are about to learn something. As we look around our own house and office, what does it say to someone who visits? Be aware of what our message is. Negative messages have consequences. Consciously choose a congruent message of positive change.

2. <u>What we believe is important</u>. Of all the many things we communicate, the most essential is belief. What we believe affects our self-image. It affects our actions. It affects our health and our capacity for self-healing. For example, Schweiger and Parducci (1978) reported that two thirds of the subjects studied reported mild headaches when they were told that the experiment, which involved passing an electrical current through their heads, might cause a headache. In fact, no electricity was used.

Again and again we observed that if the practitioner believed that the participant could change the temperature of his/her hand and conveyed that by choice of words, tone, and attitude, the participant was much more likely to succeed than if any negativity was present. Further, when someone does raise his/her own hand temperature and the equipment feeds back that information, belief in the ability to change successfully is heightened.

3. <u>Perceive ourselves and our client as a whole</u>. When working with a participant, always perceive the person as a whole and not as a pathology. Perceive the cancer patient as a person who has cancer, and not as a cancer with a person attached to it. By perceiving the person as a whole, we encourage growth of the whole

person. By focusing on the pathology, we encourage the unhealthy parts of a person. If we do not perceive the participant as a whole, we can never do justice to his/ her growth because we have set arbitrary limits on what can be achieved. Being labeled without the wholeness feels demeaning and reduces individuality.

4. The practitioner needs to be self-experienced. When a practitioner is teaching or sharing skills and concepts based upon self-experience, there is a strong congruence between belief and action. The self- experience is the basis of the verbal and nonverbal cues by which the practitioner knowingly or uncon- sciously communicates to the participant that what is being taught and shared has meaning. By having had the self-experience there is no doubt that what is being taught is possible to be achieved. If the prac- titioner can achieve it, anyone can. The data ob- served in biofeedback training demonstrates that practitioners who can themselves warm their hands or have other control over their autonomic body functions have a higher success rate in teaching others this skill than those who cannot themselves change the physiology (Peper, Ancoli & Quinn, 1979). The prac- titioner must be an example in action of his teachings.

5. Every part is connected to every other part; every part in the system affects every other part. The participant, family, and therapist are all part of the system. In a network, they are all inter- connected and have an effect on each other. There is no such thing as an independent observer. The moment one observes, one affects the system. The therapist's viewpoint affects what they can see. This is analogous to the paradox in physics where light behaves either as a particle or as a wave; what one sees depends upon what tools one looks with. In addition, physics also describes the observer-affecting-the-observed pheno- menon.

6. Teaching competence is the basis of change. This means teaching the skills in such a manner that the participant cannot fail. The experience of a success affects the person's belief and will affect future progress, so that the feeling of learned compe- tence translates into other aspects of life. For ex- ample, when a person observes she/he can warm his/her hands 6°F, the possibility of success shifts to an experience of success. One of our participants with migraine illustrated this in her report of how she

warmed her hands:

> I imagine my hands warming. I feel them
> warming. I imagine hot soup going down my
> arm. (The biofeedback equipment would
> indicate that she was successful.) I am
> proud of myself because I have warmed my
> hands (Peper & Grossman, 1979).

7. Develop and support a positive self-image. To
change it is helpful; to be able to accept and like
one's self-image is the basis of health. Often someone
who has suffered a stroke feels angry and dislikes the
limb that is "crippled." He is disgusted with that
part of himself. "My arm is dead," might be what he is
telling himself. To perceive of oneself as whole, to
own the limb again and accept it with love is the
beginning of recovery.

An exercise we found useful with this participant
was to have the woman gently massage her arm, attending
to all the sensations, while maintaining an image of
herself as whole and the arm a part of that wholeness.

8. Encourage learning without judgment. To
develop the self-awareness necessary for change, it is
beneficial to allow all learning experiences to occur
without judgment. For the participant with a stroke,
this means feeling the tingling sensations in the arm
without labeling those feelings as signs of illness.
This "attending to the process" encourages accepting an
experience without measuring it or anticipating the
outcome. This allowed her to feel sensation in her arm
without negating it by saying, "but I still can't move
it like I used to." In a system view, this could mean
learning about your mate's dreams and wishes without
deciding whether they were "acceptable" or "silly," but
simply listening to your partner to know him/her
better.

9. Acknowledge all changes, however slight. Every
change leads to the possibility of another change.
Each change should be appreciated as progress.

10. Reframe experience positively. Thus, "the
glass is half full instead of half empty" attitude
allows one to use illness as a learning experience, an
opportunity to grow. A family fight can be translated
as an opportunity to learn new ways to handle anger and
learn conflict resolution. Pain is a signal and is the

body's way of saying that it needs attention. Emotional pain is a similar signal for attention.

Our internal language and thoughts are changeable. When we change our internal dialogue, we often change our experience. For example, one of our depressed participants looked with trepidation, fear and worry about noise. He was to move next to a railroad track, and was worried with the fear that he could not go to sleep. When he learned to reframe his internal dialogue from, "I hate this noise," to "I look forward to the noise as it will remind me to practice the relaxation exercise," he no longer noticed the noise.

11. <u>New skills must be practiced at home</u>. Learning is an on-going process and should not be limited to the practitioner's office. Skills should be integrated into all areas of life. A family learning to improve its communication skills can practice making statements which begin with "I feel" or "I think" as a way of taking home the learning that "owning" one's statements helps eliminate blaming from family interaction. The participant with a stroke may do twenty minutes of exercises every night. Further, it is necessary to be aware that the same participant may do those exercises and then "forget" them until the next practice session. Although it may be difficult to use the affected limb, for example, while opening a door or while eating, this facilitates both learning the necessary dexterity and the attitude of "I can do it." Practicing at home also implies the involvement of the whole family. Their support (not sympathy or interference) becomes crucial. They become part of the participant's support network by not opening that door or offering to feed her.

12. <u>Fear of failure leads to failure</u>. Often fears are prophecies. Negative anticipation creates tension and increases the potential for failure. A participant with a stroke who is faced with relearning to walk often fears falling. Then she tenses his/her muscles, pulls up his/her knee slightly, and is unable to maintain balance. She falls. A young mother believes that if she asks her husband to help with the baby, he will become angry and refuse. She waits until she is tired and resentful and then blurts out that he never helps and she doesn't need him anyway. He doesn't offer to help.

Failures are not necessary. Participants can be taught how to fall without injury and learn that

falling is part of the road to successful walking. The
wife can learn to ask in a positive and assertive way
which assumes that her husband will share in the baby's
care.

    13. Be present-oriented. Consciously stay in the
present. Experience and be aware of what is happening
now. There is much to learn from the past, but change
takes place in the present. The family that constantly
rehashes old grudges is less likely to feel the
potential for or even recognize new behavior in the
present.

    It is a totality of experience which affects well-
ness. To treat and prevent disease and dysfunction,
one must continue to explore models which integrate
physiology, interaction, psychology, attitudes, and
environments. The integration of biofeedback and
family therapy and the adoption of holistic rules are
the beginning of developing a holistic approach.

B I B L I O G R A P H Y

Minuchin, S., Rossman, B. L., &
Baker, L.

1978   Psychosomatic families. Cambridge:
            Harvard University Press.

Peper, E., Ancoli, S., &
Quinn, M. (Eds.)

1979   Mind/body integration: Essential read-
            ings in biofeedback. New York: Plenum.

Peper, E., &
Grossman, E.

1979   "Thermal, biofeedback training in
            children with headache." In E. Peper
            et al. (Eds.), Mind/body integration:
            Essential readings in biofeedback.
            New York: Plenum.

Peper, E., Pelletier, K., &
Tandy, B.

1979   "Biofeedback training: Holistic and
            transpersonal frontiers." In E. Peper
            et al. (Eds.), Mind/body integration:
            Essential readings in biofeedback.
            New York: Plenum, 161.

Schweiger, A., &
Parducci, A.

1978   "Placebo in reverse." Brain/Mind
            Bulletin, 3(23), 1.

*Erik Peper, Ph.D; Center for Interdisciplinary
Science, San Francisco State University; Director,
Biofeedback and Family Therapy Institute, Berkeley;
co-author, Mind/Body Integration: Essential Readings
in Biofeedback; past-president, Biofeedback Society
of America; 2236 Derby Street, Berkeley, CA 94705.

591

Casi Kushel, M.F.C.C., Co-Director, Biofeedback and
Family Therapy Institute, Berkeley; private practice,
Berkeley; faculty, California Graduate School of
Marital and Family Therapy; formerly associate staff,
University of California (San Francisco) Human
Sexuality Program.